SUPERMAN

THE MAN OF STEEL

VOLUME THREE

Dan DiDio VP-Editorial Andrew Helfer Editor-original series Robert Greenberger Senior Editor-collected edition Robbin Brosterman Senior Art Director
Paul Levitz President & Publisher Georg Brewer VP-Design & Retail Product Development Richard Bruning Senior VP-Creative Director
Patrick Caldon Senior VP-Finance & Operations Chris Caramalis VP-Finance Terri Cunningham VP-Managing Editor Alison Gill VP-Manufacturing
Rich Johnson VP-Book Trade Sales Hank Kanalz VP-General Manager, WildStorm Lillian Laserson Senior VP & General Counsel
Jim Lee Editorial Director-WildStorm David McKillips VP-Advertising & Custom Publishing John Nee VP-Business Development Gregory Noveck Senior VP-Creative Affairs
Cheryl Rubin Senior VP-Brand Management Bob Wayne VP-Sales & Marketing

SUPERMAN: THE MAN OF STEEL VOL. 3
Published by DC Comics. Cover, introduction and compilation copyright © 2004 DC Comics. All Rights Reserved.
Originally published in single magazine form in SUPERMAN 4-6, ACTION COMICS 587-589,
THE ADVENTURES OF SUPERMAN 427-429. Copyright © 1987 DC Comics. All Rights Reserved.
All characters, their distinctive likenesses and related elements featured in this publication are trademarks of DC Comics.
The stories, characters and incidents featured in this publication are entirely fictional.
DC Comics does not read or accept unsolicited submissions of ideas, stories or artwork.
DC Comics, 1700 Broadway, New York, NY 10019. A Warner Bros. Entertainment Company
Printed in Canada. First Printing. ISBN: 1-4012-0246-2. Cover illustration by Jerry Ordway. Cover color by Tanya & Richard Horie.

ERMAN

John Byrne Marv Wolfman
Writers

John Byrne Jerry Ordway
Pencillers

Dick Giordano Karl Kesel Jerry Ordway
Inkers

John Costanza Albert T. DeGuzman
Letterers

Tom Ziuko
Colorist

John Byrne & Jerry Ordway Original Series Covers

OF STEEL

V O L U M E   T H R E E

SUPERMAN Created by
JERRY SIEGEL &
JOE SHUSTER

Introduction

By JERRY ORDWAY

The brainchild of writer Jerry Siegel and artist Joe Shuster, Superman is one of the most recognized icons of the modern world. Recently, while reading the newspaper, I happened upon a story about the former chairman of the New York Stock Exchange. The photo next to the headline showed the former chairman in his office, standing in front of a framed illustration of Superman.

"Truth, Justice, and the American Way" inspires us all.

As a child, my first exposure to Superman came from a grocery bag full of well-read early 1960s DC comics given to us by a family friend. Later on, I noticed something called The Adventures of Superman on TV – old reruns, sandwiched between cartoons on Saturday mornings. Cool character, but it didn't change my life. If anything, Superman primed me for liking other super-heroes, such as Batman. Upon discovering the "Marvelous" competition by age nine, I instantly relegated DC to the status of "kid stuff." As a devout "Marvelmaniac" I didn't give Superman comics much notice, the notable exception being Jack Kirby's issues of SUPERMAN'S PAL, JIMMY OLSEN. Stan Lee's approach to super-hero angst was my cup of tea.

In late 1978, I saw the Richard Donner directed Superman: The Movie and that did it. The incredible life and emotion given to the mythos opened my eyes to the concept. Oddly enough, the Superman in the comics didn't reflect what I'd seen in the movie.

I started my comics career with DC Comics in 1980, and in those days, you had to prove yourself before being assigned to one of their top titles. I spent six years doing that, but the offer to be part of the Superman relaunch was still intimidating. In the comic shops, sales had fallen, and more than one fan opined, "Superman is boring." I knew John Byrne could deliver an audience, and that DC would put a lot of marketing effort into selling it, but I wasn't sure I was the right guy to draw one of the titles, as my strongest inspiration came from the first movie and not the comics themselves. I guess I was kind of relieved to hear that my lack of Superman comics lore would not be a hindrance, as they were starting everything over from the ground up, according to editor Andy Helfer. John Byrne was resetting the continuity via his MAN OF STEEL miniseries, to be followed by the three monthly Superman titles. I was teaming up with Marv Wolfman, the architect of the "Lex Luthor as Charles Foster Kane" angle, and our book would have a slightly darker edge than either ACTION COMICS or the main SUPER-MAN comic. I was really getting jazzed now.

Early on, I lobbied hard to incorporate Jack Kirby's Jimmy Olsen/Fourth World concepts into our book, such as the Cadmus Project, the Guardian, Morgan Edge, etc., but was told no go. "Too early," said Andy.

Mike Machlan, Al Vey and I shared a studio in Milwaukee at that time, and Machlan was to be my inker on ADVENTURES, so he and I often batted story ideas around. Taking our cue from what Marv and Andy had said about darker-edged stories, Mike and I put a lot of thought into how the Guardian could be a good counterpoint character to Superman, handling low-level street crime in Suicide Slum, while Superman fought the super-villains. Eventually, many of those ideas were implemented by revising and renaming the character Gangbuster.

Al Vey, Mike and I "studio-plotted" the ADVENTURES OF SUPERMAN chapter of the "Superman on Apokolips" story-line (see volume two) when Marv was unavailable. That became my first official co-plot-ting credit, although the plot was reworked by John Byrne before I put pencil to paper.

Studio-mates often pitched in to help each other out of deadline troubles. For instance, while Machlan moved on to other inking assignments after ADVENTURES OF SUPERMAN #424, he helped out by doing uncredited layouts for pages 10-14, 17-18 on issue #427. And sometimes, local artists like John Statema came through, by doing layouts for pages 16-22 on issue #429, as I was slowly drowning under the weight of deadlines.

I wasn't able to both pencil and ink a monthly comic in less than five weeks. I was a young guy, trying to prove myself worthy of being a Superman artist of the caliber of Curt Swan, who held the assignment for over thirty years. I was also competing with fellow artist John Byrne, who seemed to get all the fan press while writing and drawing SUPERMAN and ACTION COMICS. I'm sure it was harder for Marv, who had already earned a high standing in the industry, to find himself working on "that other Superman book."

The key element of the "rebooted" Superman was that Clark Kent would be the real persona, and Superman the disguise he adopts to use his powers. Fans and pros still argue that that bit undermines the concept, but I disagree. Clark lives his life as an adopted child, and the Kents truly become his parents, imparting all the life lessons and values of a normal small-town kid. The knowledge that Clark is from Krypton does nothing to undo the life experiences that made him a Kent. That humanity is what makes this Superman meaningful to me. He's not like us, but in his heart he thinks he is. Again, the great warmth of Superman, the Movie is the bond that exists for Clark, with the people he loves and the world that adopted him. That's the Superman I wanted to be part of.

The stories by Marv and me in this volume stand apart from the more classic approach

" The brainchild of writer Jerry Siegel and artist Joe Shuster, Superman is one of the most recognized icons of the modern world. "

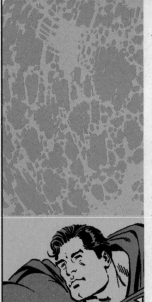

" Truth, Justice, and the American Way inspires us all."

that John Byrne was using, and show how hard we worked to give ADVENTURES OF SUPER-MAN its own personality. While our first story in this volume had Superman destroying a Middle Eastern despot's weapons of mass destruction, still relevant to today's world, the following two tales evoked the best elements of the George Reeves Superman TV show, and the magic of Christopher Reeve's perform-ance as Clark Kent.

"Personal Best" puts Perry White's journalistic integrity on the line and shows the reader a Superman willing to intimidate bad guys in a way not seen since the early Siegel and Shuster stories. It was also packed with enough content to fill three issues of most current comics, but we did things like that then, as the three Superman books were not yet linked in a read-along fashion. In his plot, Marv called for a "big, tough guy" in the bar scene, and I modeled this guy on a great old man I knew as a kid – a dockworker who was a regular at our family's tavern – a guy who looked every bit like a live action Popeye to me as a kid. I called him Jo-jo. Mike Carlin, who had just joined on as Andy's colleague but hadn't quite taken the reins yet, renamed him "Bibbo" after a bit character in an old Jackie Gleason Honeymooners episode. As with Professor Emil Hamilton, we later took these bit players and developed them into regulars when I began

co-plotting the series with Byrne.

In "Old Ties" Marv supplied an interesting backstory for Cat Grant, and we got Clark Kent out of his suit and tie and into ski gear, on a romantic get-away with Cat Grant. Cat was now being modeled after inker John Beatty's sister Jane with her full blessing and photo-reference. That helped make her more "real" to the reader, I think. Marv had introduced Cat into the Superman mythos to shake up the Lois Lane-Superman romantic angle. Cat was interested in Clark Kent, and not Superman. It gave us the opportunity to soften Lois Lane's hard edge by giving her twinges of jealousy.

It wouldn't be right to end this without focusing a bit on the other contributions to this volume. As a fan, I thought it was pretty cool at the time to see John Byrne tackle charac-ters like the Green Lantern Corps and the Demon. His dynamic storytelling gave these established DC heroes a contemporary edge. ACTION COMICS was my favorite for that reason. Dick Giordano brought a gritty approach to those inks, which suited the subject matter well. Inker Karl Kesel brought a smooth, polished look, well suited to the flagship title. Letterers John Costanza and Albert DeGuzman, along with colorist Tom Ziuko, contributed their talents as well. What a terrific time it was to work on Superman from the ground up!

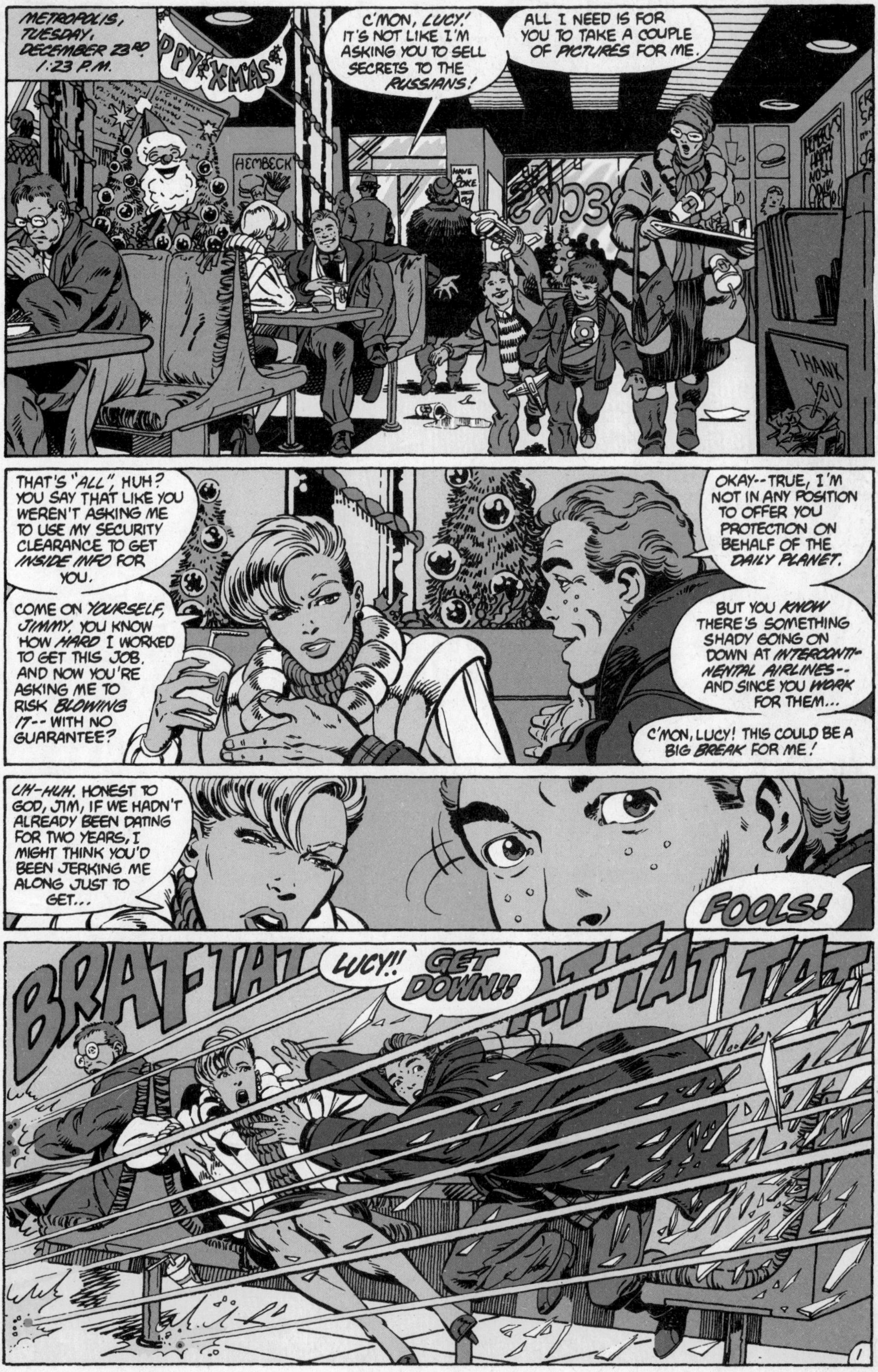
METROPOLIS, TUESDAY, DECEMBER 23RD 1:23 P.M.
PPY X-MAS
C'MON, LUCY! IT'S NOT LIKE I'M ASKING YOU TO SELL SECRETS TO THE RUSSIANS!
ALL I NEED IS FOR YOU TO TAKE A COUPLE OF PICTURES FOR ME.
HEMBECK
THANK YOU
THAT'S "ALL", HUH? YOU SAY THAT LIKE YOU WEREN'T ASKING ME TO USE MY SECURITY CLEARANCE TO GET INSIDE INFO FOR YOU.
COME ON YOURSELF, JIMMY. YOU KNOW HOW HARD I WORKED TO GET THIS JOB. AND NOW YOU'RE ASKING ME TO RISK BLOWING IT-- WITH NO GUARANTEE?
OKAY--TRUE, I'M NOT IN ANY POSITION TO OFFER YOU PROTECTION ON BEHALF OF THE DAILY PLANET.
BUT YOU KNOW THERE'S SOMETHING SHADY GOING ON DOWN AT INTERCONTINENTAL AIRLINES-- AND SINCE YOU WORK FOR THEM...
C'MON, LUCY! THIS COULD BE A BIG BREAK FOR ME!
UH-HUH. HONEST TO GOD, JIM, IF WE HADN'T ALREADY BEEN DATING FOR TWO YEARS, I MIGHT THINK YOU'D BEEN JERKING ME ALONG JUST TO GET...
FOOLS!
BRAT-TAT
LUCY!! GET DOWN!!
TAT-TAT TAT
1

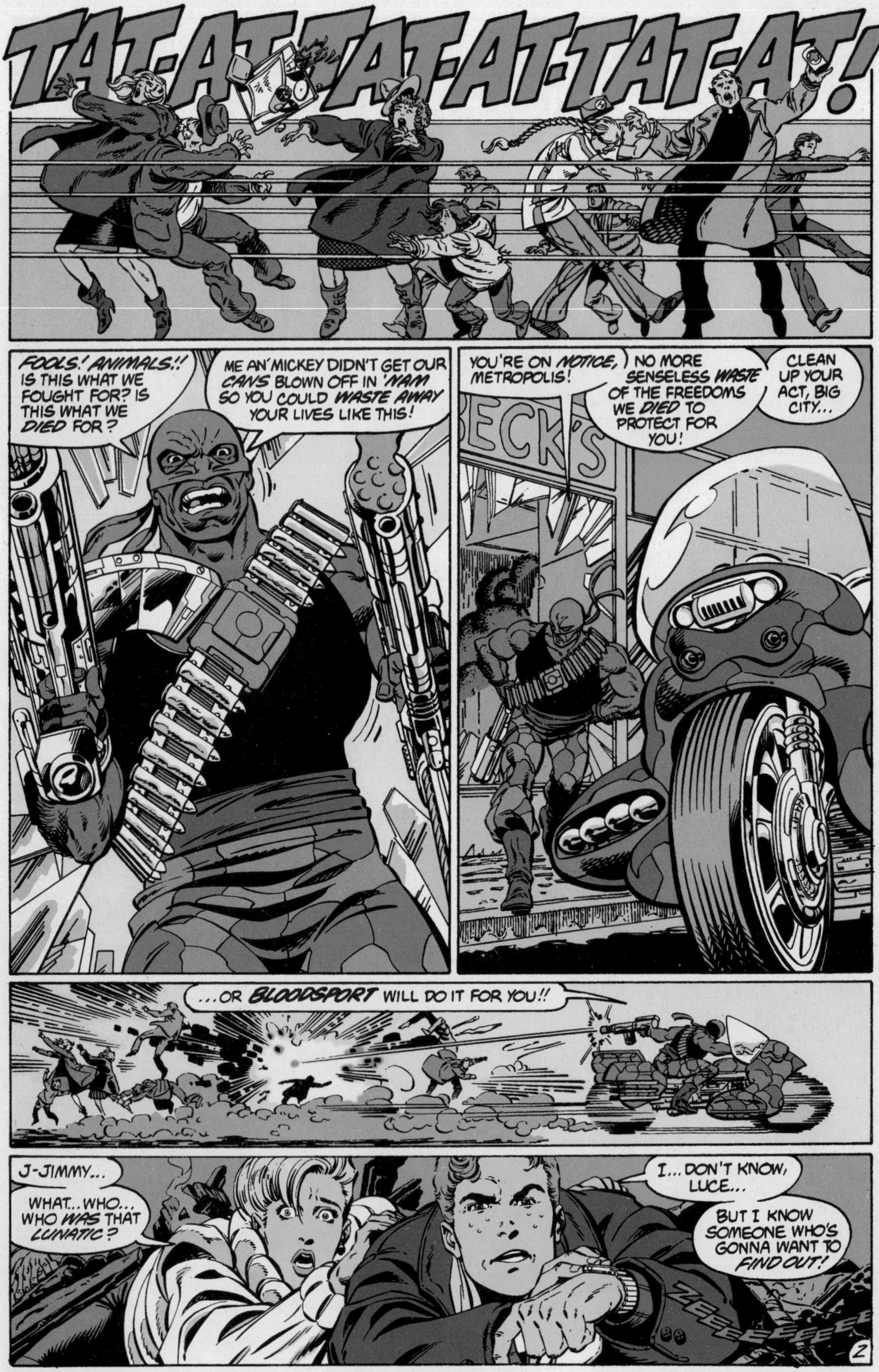
TAT-AT-TAT-AT-TAT-AT!
FOOLS! ANIMALS!! IS THIS WHAT WE FOUGHT FOR? IS THIS WHAT WE DIED FOR?
ME AN' MICKEY DIDN'T GET OUR CANS BLOWN OFF IN 'NAM SO YOU COULD WASTE AWAY YOUR LIVES LIKE THIS!
YOU'RE ON NOTICE, METROPOLIS!
NO MORE SENSELESS WASTE OF THE FREEDOMS WE DIED TO PROTECT FOR YOU!
CLEAN UP YOUR ACT, BIG CITY...
BECK'S
...OR BLOODSPORT WILL DO IT FOR YOU!!
J-JIMMY...
WHAT... WHO... WHO WAS THAT LUNATIC?
I... DON'T KNOW, LUCE...
BUT I KNOW SOMEONE WHO'S GONNA WANT TO FIND OUT!
ZEEEEEEEEE
2

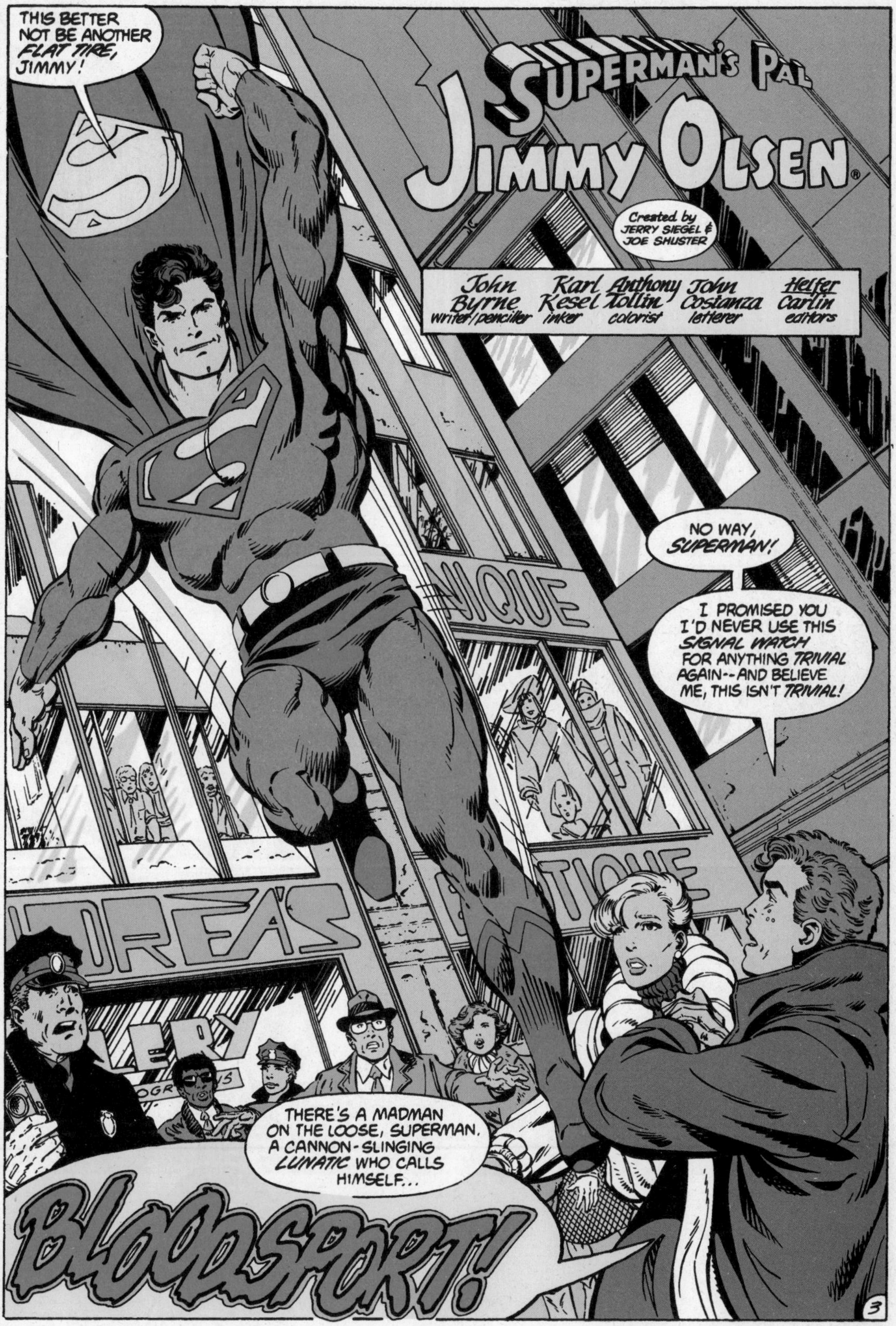

THIS BETTER NOT BE ANOTHER FLAT TIRE, JIMMY!
SUPERMAN'S PAL JIMMY OLSEN®
Created by JERRY SIEGEL & JOE SHUSTER
John Byrne writer/penciller Karl Kesel inker Anthony Tollin colorist John Costanza letterer Helfer Carlin editors
NO WAY, SUPERMAN!
I PROMISED YOU I'D NEVER USE THIS SIGNAL WATCH FOR ANYTHING TRIVIAL AGAIN--AND BELIEVE ME, THIS ISN'T TRIVIAL!
THERE'S A MADMAN ON THE LOOSE, SUPERMAN. A CANNON-SLINGING LUNATIC WHO CALLS HIMSELF...
BLOODSPORT!
3

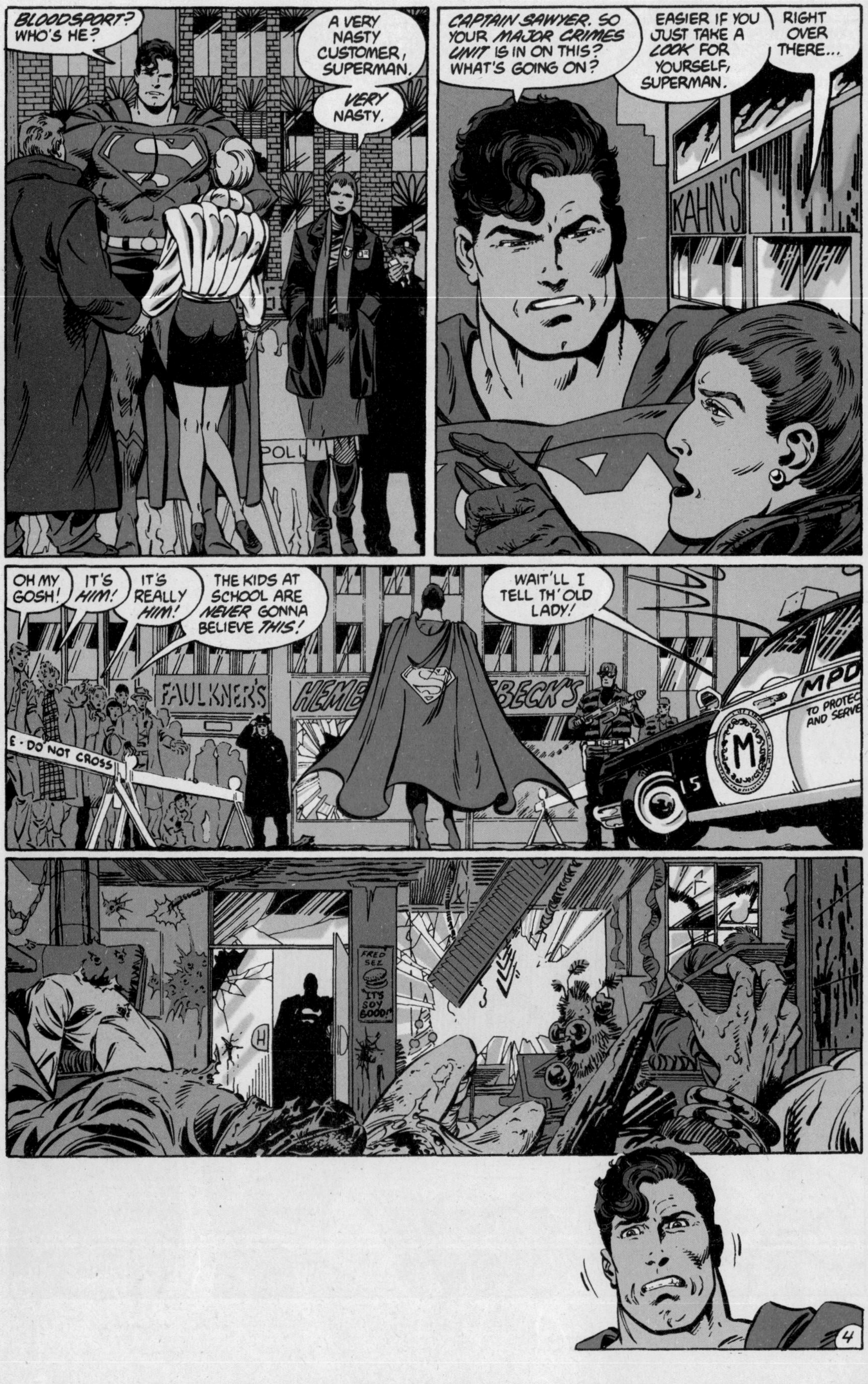
BLOODSPORT? WHO'S HE?
A VERY NASTY CUSTOMER, SUPERMAN.
VERY NASTY.
POLI
CAPTAIN SAWYER. SO YOUR MAJOR CRIMES UNIT IS IN ON THIS? WHAT'S GOING ON?
EASIER IF YOU JUST TAKE A LOOK FOR YOURSELF, SUPERMAN.
RIGHT OVER THERE...
KAHN'S
OH MY GOSH!
IT'S HIM!
IT'S REALLY HIM!
THE KIDS AT SCHOOL ARE NEVER GONNA BELIEVE THIS!
WAIT'LL I TELL TH' OLD LADY!
FAULKNER'S
BECK'S
E · DO NOT CROSS
MPD
TO PROTEC
AND SERVE
M
15
FRED SEZ
IT'S SOY GOOD!
4

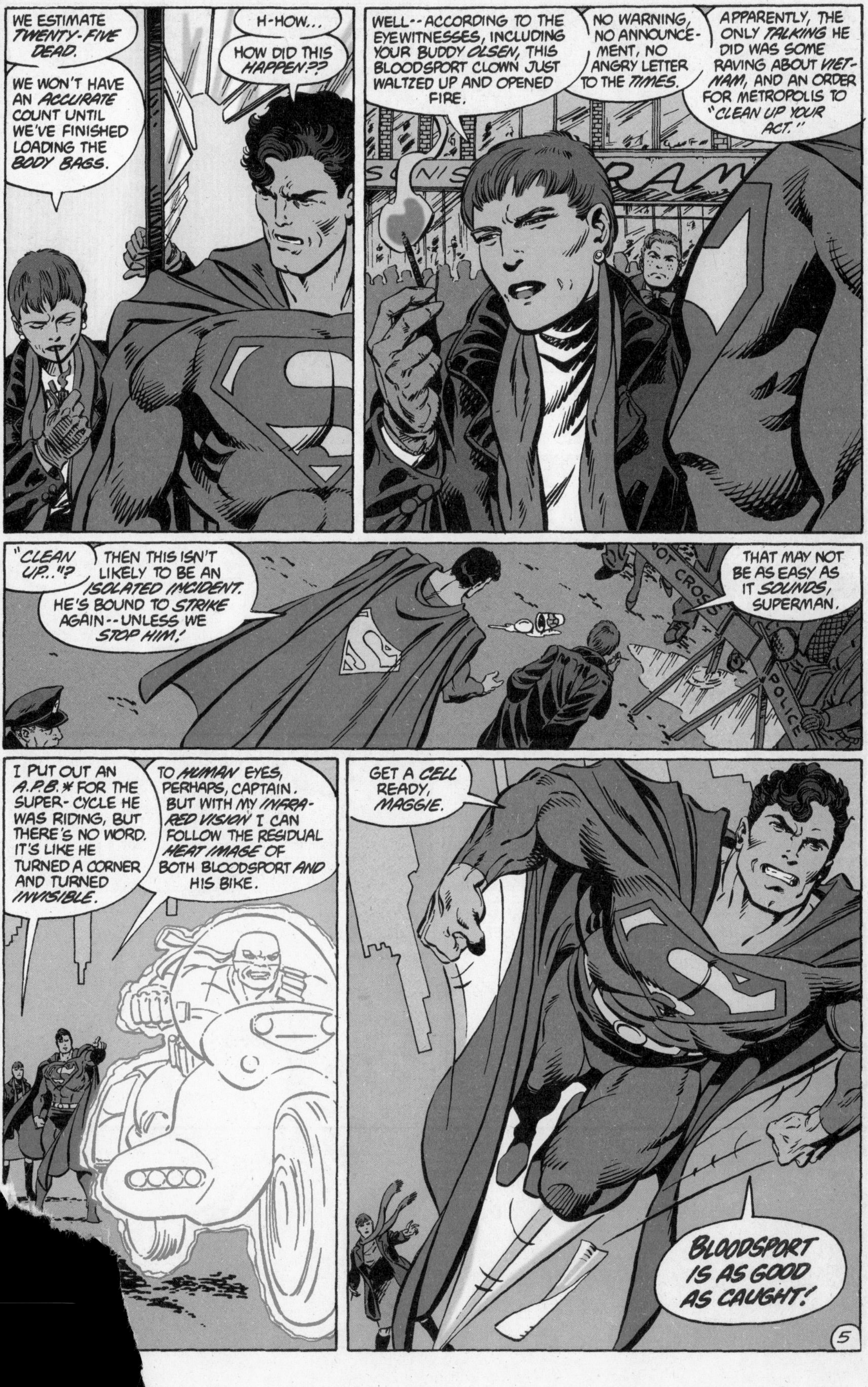
WE ESTIMATE TWENTY-FIVE DEAD.
WE WON'T HAVE AN ACCURATE COUNT UNTIL WE'VE FINISHED LOADING THE BODY BAGS.
H-HOW...
HOW DID THIS HAPPEN??
WELL--ACCORDING TO THE EYEWITNESSES, INCLUDING YOUR BUDDY OLSEN, THIS BLOODSPORT CLOWN JUST WALTZED UP AND OPENED FIRE.
NO WARNING, NO ANNOUNCEMENT, NO ANGRY LETTER TO THE TIMES.
APPARENTLY, THE ONLY TALKING HE DID WAS SOME RAVING ABOUT VIETNAM, AND AN ORDER FOR METROPOLIS TO "CLEAN UP YOUR ACT."
"CLEAN UP..."?
THEN THIS ISN'T LIKELY TO BE AN ISOLATED INCIDENT. HE'S BOUND TO STRIKE AGAIN--UNLESS WE STOP HIM!
THAT MAY NOT BE AS EASY AS IT SOUNDS, SUPERMAN.
POLICE
I PUT OUT AN A.P.B.* FOR THE SUPER-CYCLE HE WAS RIDING, BUT THERE'S NO WORD. IT'S LIKE HE TURNED A CORNER AND TURNED INVISIBLE.
TO HUMAN EYES, PERHAPS, CAPTAIN. BUT WITH MY INFRA-RED VISION I CAN FOLLOW THE RESIDUAL HEAT IMAGE OF BOTH BLOODSPORT AND HIS BIKE.
GET A CELL READY, MAGGIE.
BLOODSPORT IS AS GOOD AS CAUGHT!
5

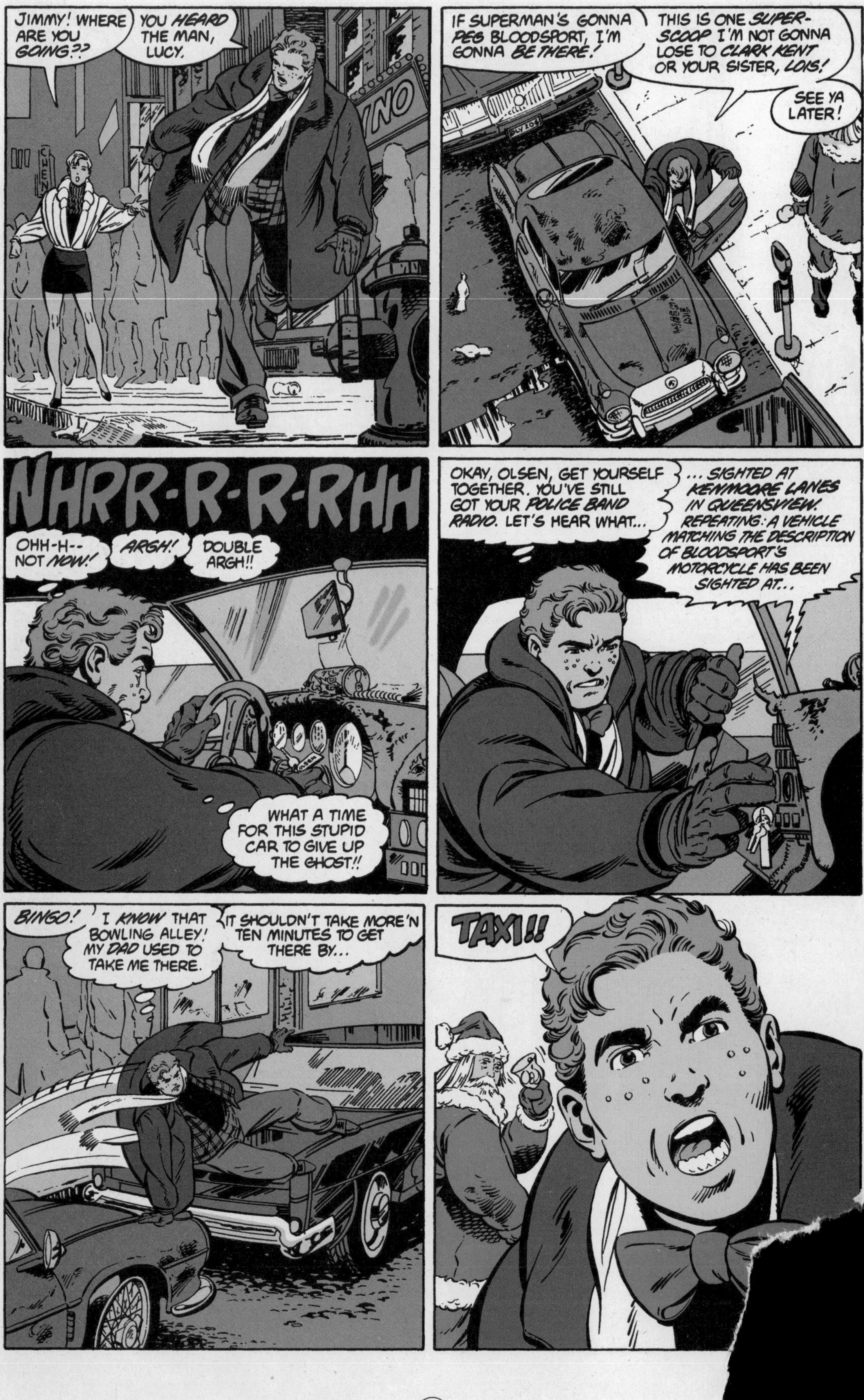
JIMMY! WHERE ARE YOU GOING??
YOU HEARD THE MAN, LUCY.
IF SUPERMAN'S GONNA PEG BLOODSPORT, I'M GONNA BE THERE!
THIS IS ONE SUPER-SCOOP I'M NOT GONNA LOSE TO CLARK KENT OR YOUR SISTER, LOIS!
SEE YA LATER!
NHRR-R-R-RHH
OHH-H-- NOT NOW!
ARGH!
DOUBLE ARGH!!
WHAT A TIME FOR THIS STUPID CAR TO GIVE UP THE GHOST!!
OKAY, OLSEN, GET YOURSELF TOGETHER. YOU'VE STILL GOT YOUR POLICE BAND RADIO. LET'S HEAR WHAT...
... SIGHTED AT KENMOORE LANES IN QUEENSVIEW. REPEATING: A VEHICLE MATCHING THE DESCRIPTION OF BLOODSPORT'S MOTORCYCLE HAS BEEN SIGHTED AT...
BINGO!
I KNOW THAT BOWLING ALLEY! MY DAD USED TO TAKE ME THERE.
IT SHOULDN'T TAKE MORE'N TEN MINUTES TO GET THERE BY...
TAXI!!

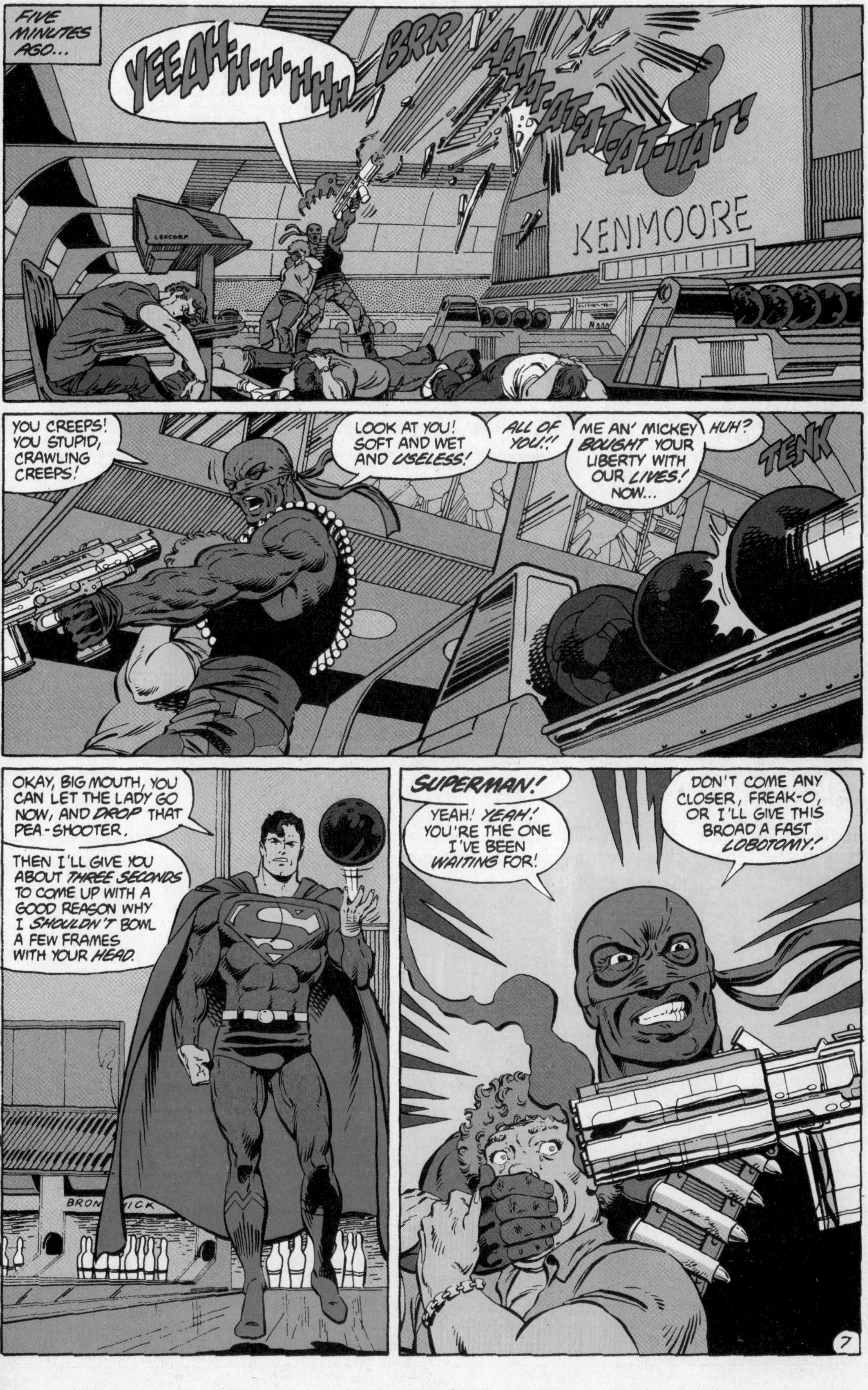
FIVE MINUTES AGO...
YEEAAH-H-H-HHH
BRR AAAAT-AT-AT-AT-TAT!
LEXCORP
KENMOORE
YOU CREEPS! YOU STUPID, CRAWLING CREEPS!
LOOK AT YOU! SOFT AND WET AND USELESS!
ALL OF YOU!!
ME AN' MICKEY BOUGHT YOUR LIBERTY WITH OUR LIVES! NOW...
HUH?
TENK
OKAY, BIG MOUTH, YOU CAN LET THE LADY GO NOW, AND DROP THAT PEA-SHOOTER.
THEN I'LL GIVE YOU ABOUT THREE SECONDS TO COME UP WITH A GOOD REASON WHY I SHOULDN'T BOWL A FEW FRAMES WITH YOUR HEAD.
SUPERMAN!
YEAH! YEAH! YOU'RE THE ONE I'VE BEEN WAITING FOR!
DON'T COME ANY CLOSER, FREAK-O, OR I'LL GIVE THIS BROAD A FAST LOBOTOMY!
7

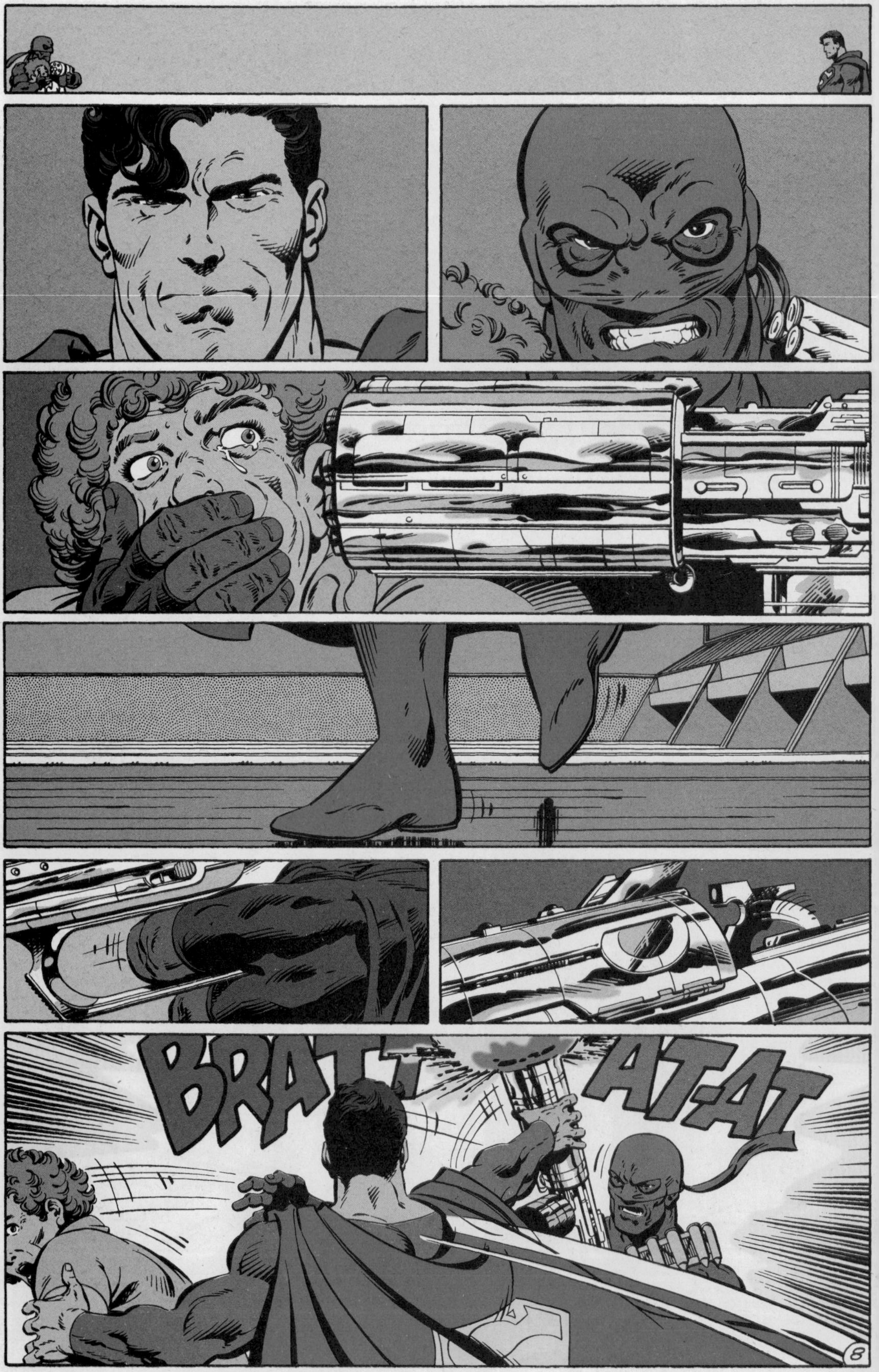
BRATT
AT-AT

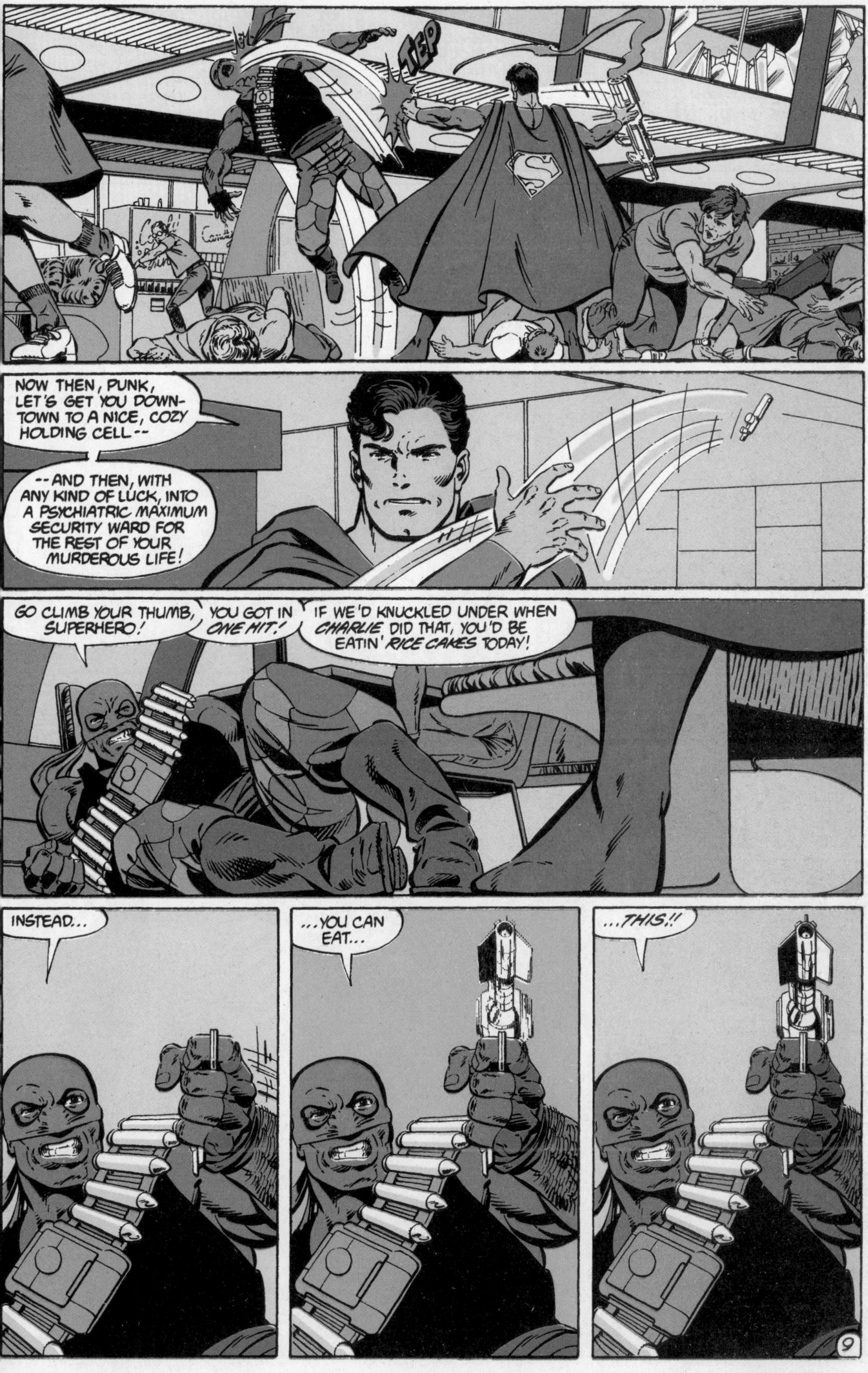
STEP
NOW THEN, PUNK, LET'S GET YOU DOWN-TOWN TO A NICE, COZY HOLDING CELL--
--AND THEN, WITH ANY KIND OF LUCK, INTO A PSYCHIATRIC MAXIMUM SECURITY WARD FOR THE REST OF YOUR MURDEROUS LIFE!
GO CLIMB YOUR THUMB, SUPERHERO!
YOU GOT IN ONE HIT!
IF WE'D KNUCKLED UNDER WHEN CHARLIE DID THAT, YOU'D BE EATIN' RICE CAKES TODAY!
INSTEAD...
...YOU CAN EAT...
...THIS!!
9

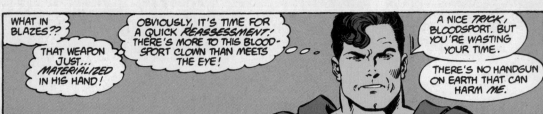

WHAT IN BLAZES??

THAT WEAPON JUST... *MATERIALIZED* IN HIS HAND!

OBVIOUSLY, IT'S TIME FOR A QUICK *REASSESSMENT!* THERE'S MORE TO THIS BLOOD-SPORT CLOWN THAN MEETS THE EYE!

A NICE *TRICK*, BLOODSPORT. BUT YOU'RE WASTING YOUR TIME.

THERE'S NO HANDGUN ON EARTH THAT CAN HARM *ME*.

MAYBE THAT'S HOW IT *USED TO BE*, SUPERMAN... BUT THIS WEAPON WAS DESIGNED AND BUILT SPECIFICALLY WITH *YOU* IN MIND.

AND IT CAN *KILL YOU!!*

AHGH!!

PHFFFT!

HA HA HA HA!

NOT SO *SMUG* NOW, EH, SUPES-BABY? NOT SO HIGH AND MIGHTY AFTER ALL!

KRYPTONITE! THAT THING FIRES NEEDLES OF *KRYPTONITE!*

THAT'S RIGHT, PAL. LITTLE *SLIVERS* OF ROCK FROM THE ALIEN PLANET YOU CAME FROM!

RADIOACTIVE ROCK, THAT KNOCKS OUT YOUR POWERS AND MAKES YOU JUST AS *VULNER-ABLE* AS ANYBODY ELSE.

SAY "GOODNIGHT, GRACIE..."

HOLD IT, CREEP!!

10

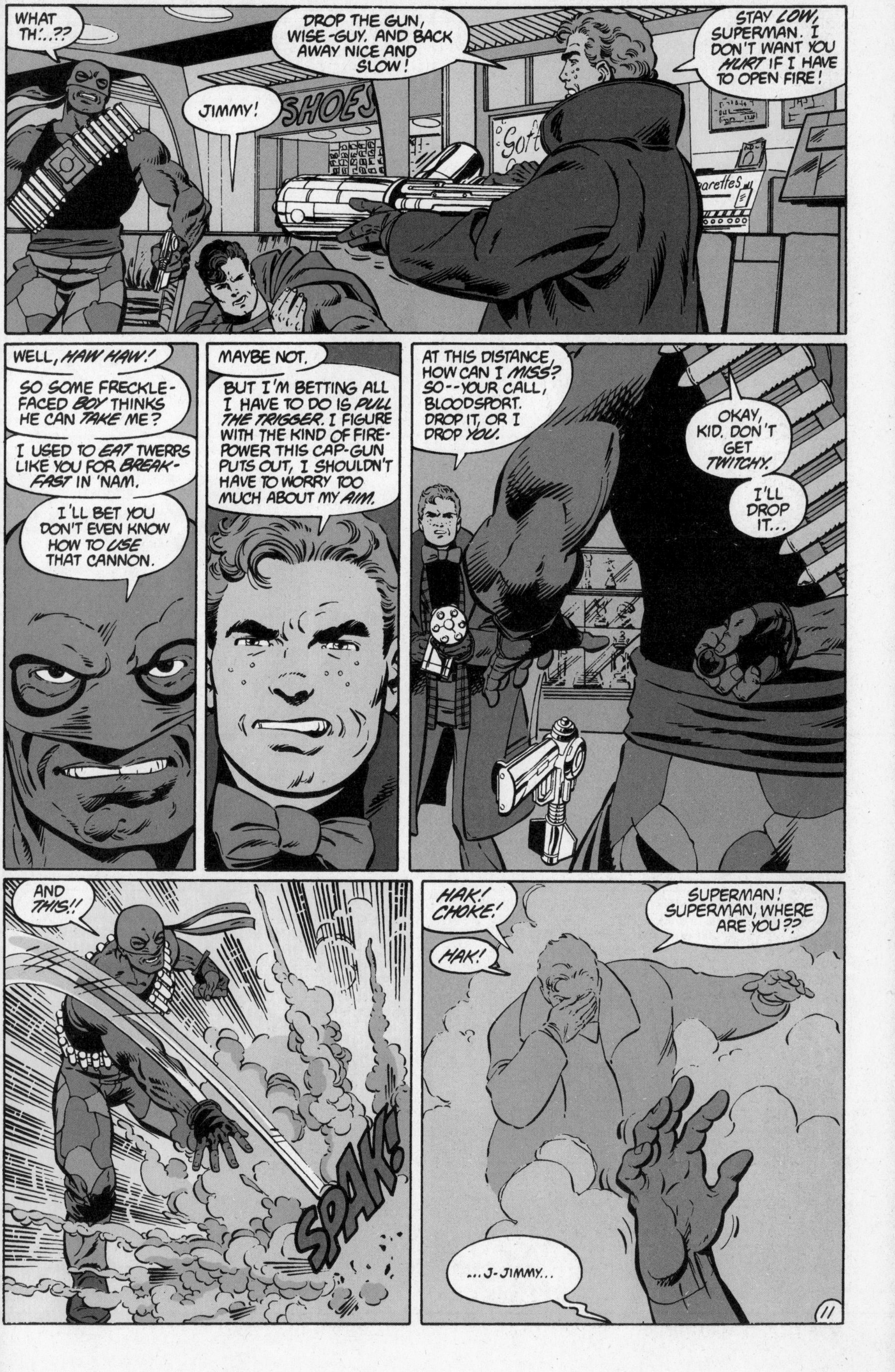
WHAT TH'...??
DROP THE GUN, WISE-GUY. AND BACK AWAY NICE AND SLOW!
STAY LOW, SUPERMAN. I DON'T WANT YOU HURT IF I HAVE TO OPEN FIRE!
JIMMY!
SHOES
Soft
garettes
WELL, HAW HAW!
SO SOME FRECKLE-FACED BOY THINKS HE CAN TAKE ME?
I USED TO EAT TWERPS LIKE YOU FOR BREAKFAST IN 'NAM.
I'LL BET YOU DON'T EVEN KNOW HOW TO USE THAT CANNON.
MAYBE NOT.
BUT I'M BETTING ALL I HAVE TO DO IS PULL THE TRIGGER. I FIGURE WITH THE KIND OF FIRE-POWER THIS CAP-GUN PUTS OUT, I SHOULDN'T HAVE TO WORRY TOO MUCH ABOUT MY AIM.
AT THIS DISTANCE, HOW CAN I MISS? SO--YOUR CALL, BLOODSPORT. DROP IT, OR I DROP YOU.
OKAY, KID. DON'T GET TWITCHY.
I'LL DROP IT...
AND THIS!!
SPAK!
HAK! CHOKE!
HAK!
SUPERMAN! SUPERMAN, WHERE ARE YOU??
...J-JIMMY...
11

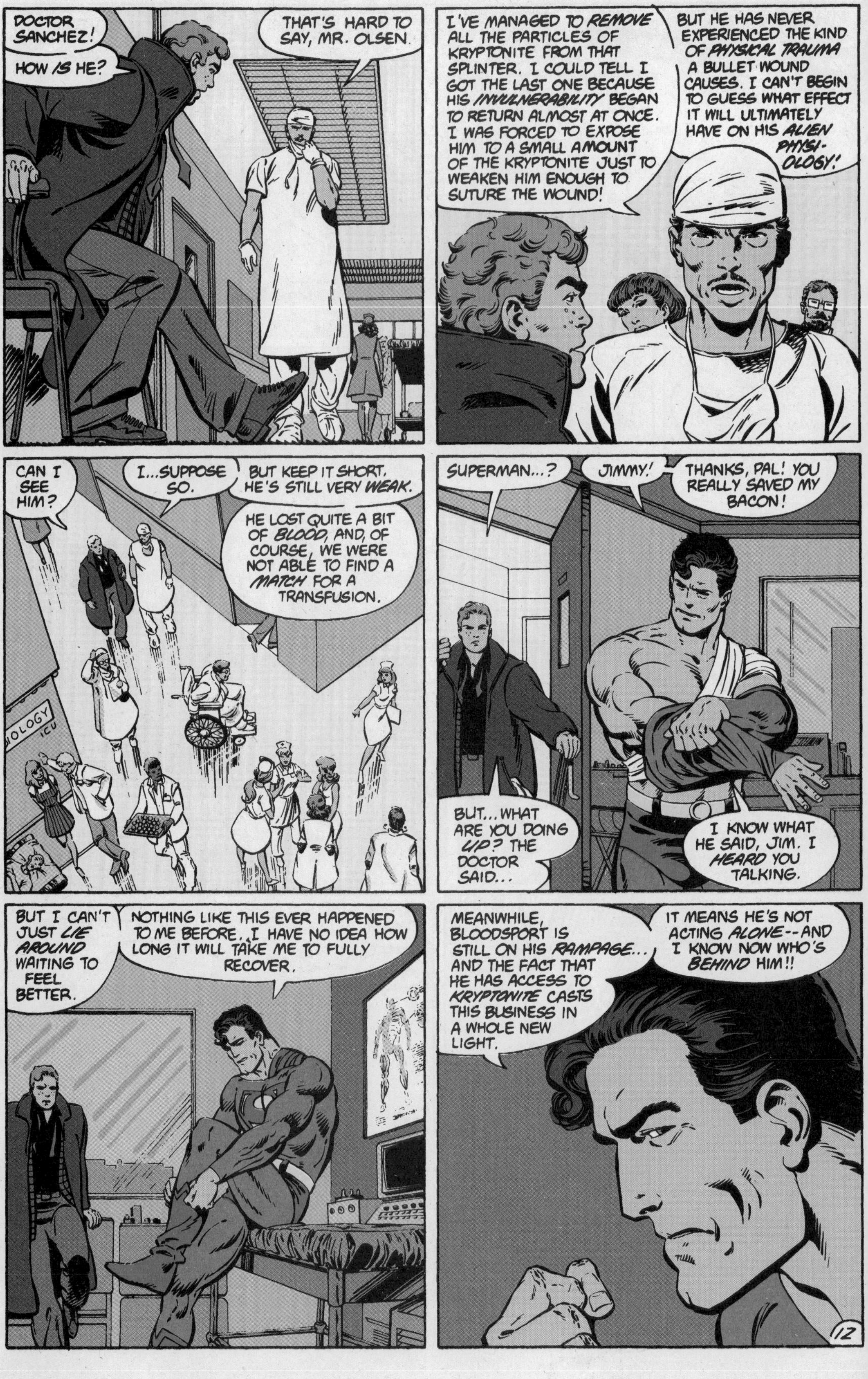
DOCTOR SANCHEZ!
HOW IS HE?
THAT'S HARD TO SAY, MR. OLSEN.
I'VE MANAGED TO REMOVE ALL THE PARTICLES OF KRYPTONITE FROM THAT SPLINTER. I COULD TELL I GOT THE LAST ONE BECAUSE HIS INVULNERABILITY BEGAN TO RETURN ALMOST AT ONCE. I WAS FORCED TO EXPOSE HIM TO A SMALL AMOUNT OF THE KRYPTONITE JUST TO WEAKEN HIM ENOUGH TO SUTURE THE WOUND!
BUT HE HAS NEVER EXPERIENCED THE KIND OF PHYSICAL TRAUMA A BULLET WOUND CAUSES. I CAN'T BEGIN TO GUESS WHAT EFFECT IT WILL ULTIMATELY HAVE ON HIS ALIEN PHYSIOLOGY!
CAN I SEE HIM?
I...SUPPOSE SO.
BUT KEEP IT SHORT. HE'S STILL VERY WEAK.
HE LOST QUITE A BIT OF BLOOD, AND, OF COURSE, WE WERE NOT ABLE TO FIND A MATCH FOR A TRANSFUSION.
IOLOGY ICU
SUPERMAN...?
JIMMY!
THANKS, PAL! YOU REALLY SAVED MY BACON!
BUT...WHAT ARE YOU DOING UP? THE DOCTOR SAID...
I KNOW WHAT HE SAID, JIM. I HEARD YOU TALKING.
BUT I CAN'T JUST LIE AROUND WAITING TO FEEL BETTER.
NOTHING LIKE THIS EVER HAPPENED TO ME BEFORE. I HAVE NO IDEA HOW LONG IT WILL TAKE ME TO FULLY RECOVER.
MEANWHILE, BLOODSPORT IS STILL ON HIS RAMPAGE... AND THE FACT THAT HE HAS ACCESS TO KRYPTONITE CASTS THIS BUSINESS IN A WHOLE NEW LIGHT.
IT MEANS HE'S NOT ACTING ALONE--AND I KNOW NOW WHO'S BEHIND HIM!!
12

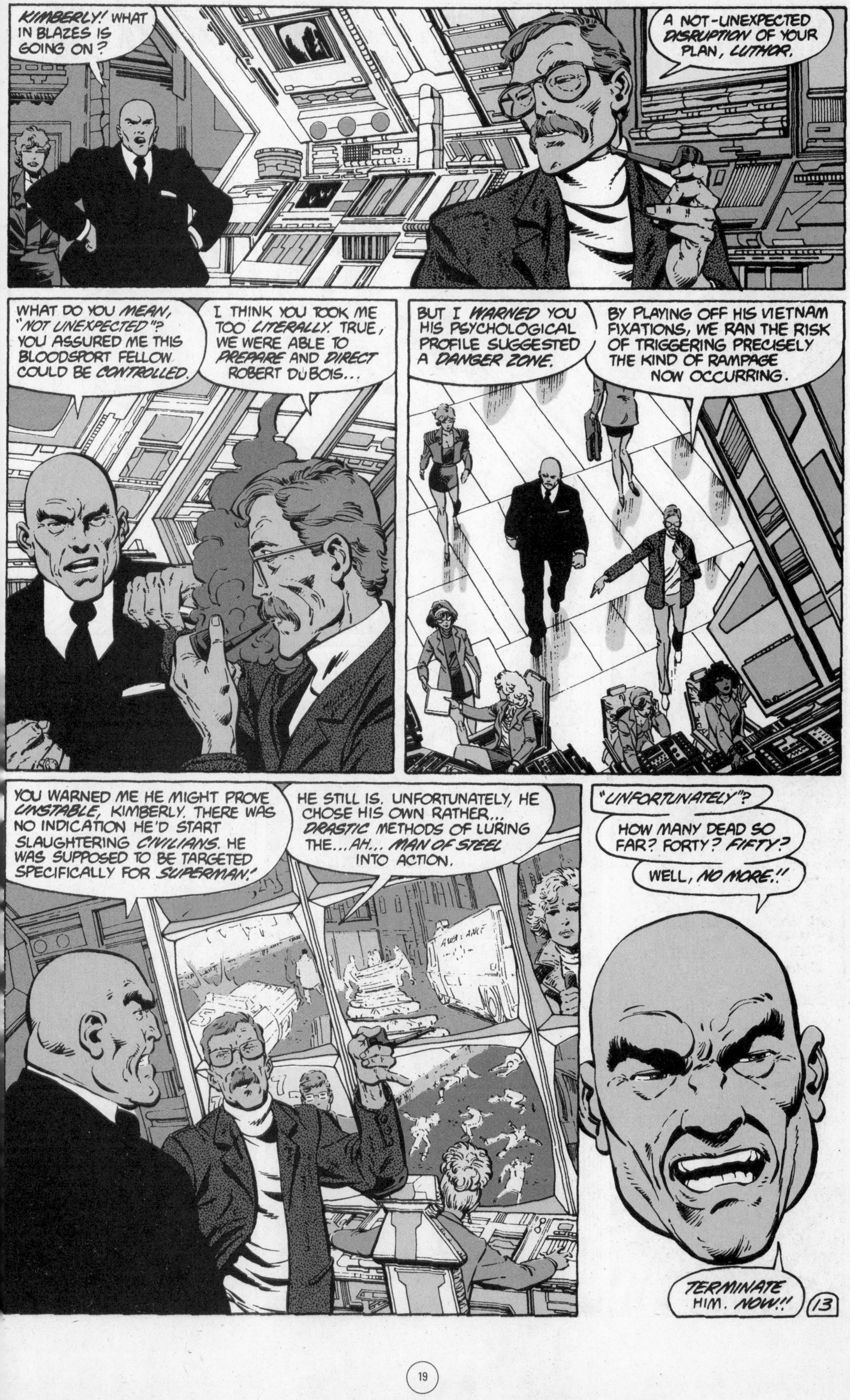
KIMBERLY! WHAT IN BLAZES IS GOING ON?
A NOT-UNEXPECTED DISRUPTION OF YOUR PLAN, LUTHOR.
WHAT DO YOU MEAN, "NOT UNEXPECTED"? YOU ASSURED ME THIS BLOODSPORT FELLOW COULD BE CONTROLLED.
I THINK YOU TOOK ME TOO LITERALLY. TRUE, WE WERE ABLE TO PREPARE AND DIRECT ROBERT DuBOIS...
BUT I WARNED YOU HIS PSYCHOLOGICAL PROFILE SUGGESTED A DANGER ZONE.
BY PLAYING OFF HIS VIETNAM FIXATIONS, WE RAN THE RISK OF TRIGGERING PRECISELY THE KIND OF RAMPAGE NOW OCCURRING.
YOU WARNED ME HE MIGHT PROVE UNSTABLE, KIMBERLY. THERE WAS NO INDICATION HE'D START SLAUGHTERING CIVILIANS. HE WAS SUPPOSED TO BE TARGETED SPECIFICALLY FOR SUPERMAN!
HE STILL IS. UNFORTUNATELY, HE CHOSE HIS OWN RATHER... DRASTIC METHODS OF LURING THE...AH... MAN OF STEEL INTO ACTION.
"UNFORTUNATELY"?
HOW MANY DEAD SO FAR? FORTY? FIFTY?
WELL, NO MORE!!
TERMINATE HIM. NOW!!
13

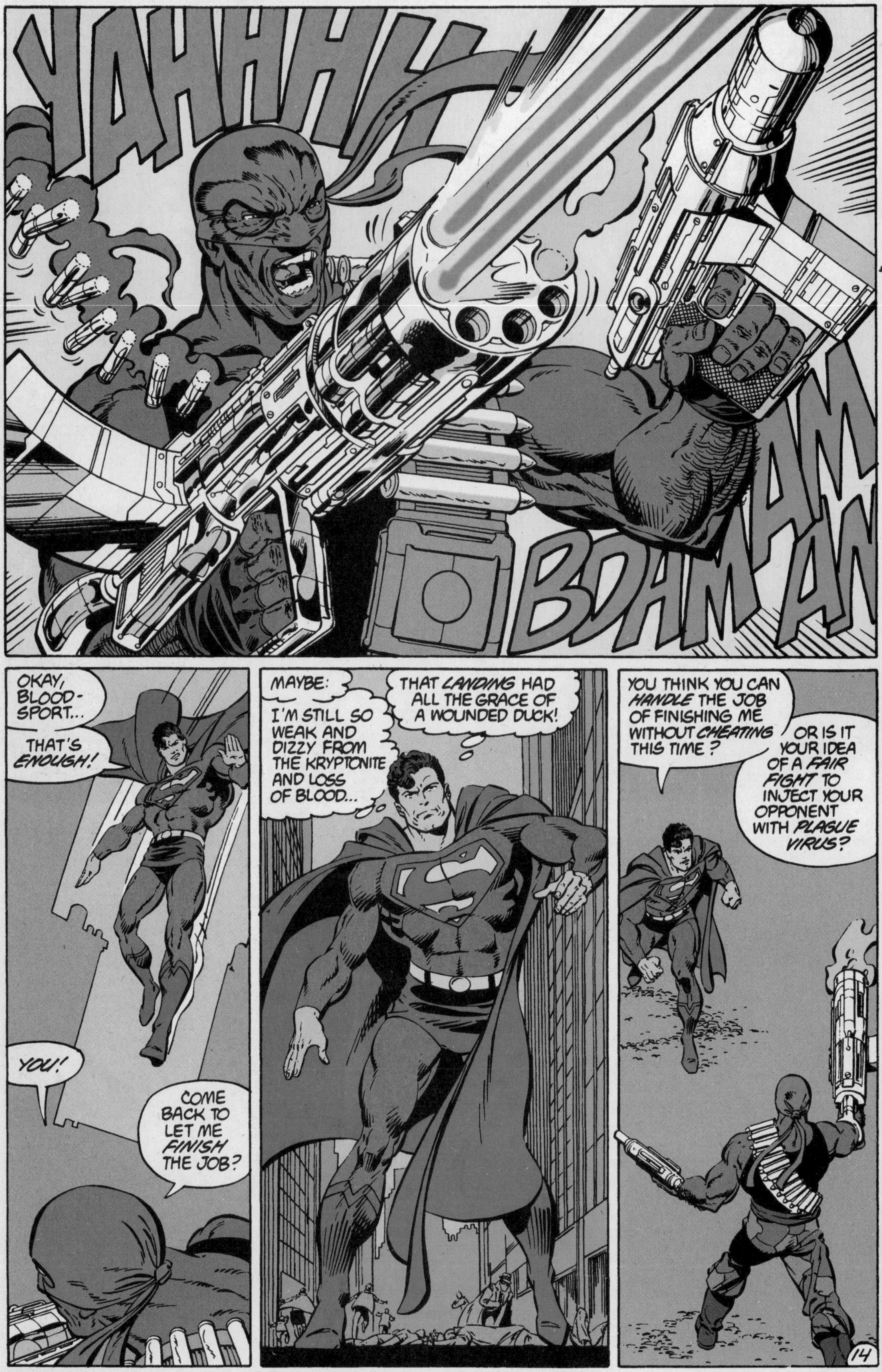

YAHHHH
BDAM AM
BDAM AN
OKAY, BLOOD-SPORT...
THAT'S ENOUGH!
YOU!
COME BACK TO LET ME FINISH THE JOB?
MAYBE:
THAT LANDING HAD ALL THE GRACE OF A WOUNDED DUCK!
I'M STILL SO WEAK AND DIZZY FROM THE KRYPTONITE AND LOSS OF BLOOD...
YOU THINK YOU CAN HANDLE THE JOB OF FINISHING ME WITHOUT CHEATING THIS TIME?
OR IS IT YOUR IDEA OF A FAIR FIGHT TO INJECT YOUR OPPONENT WITH PLAGUE VIRUS?
14

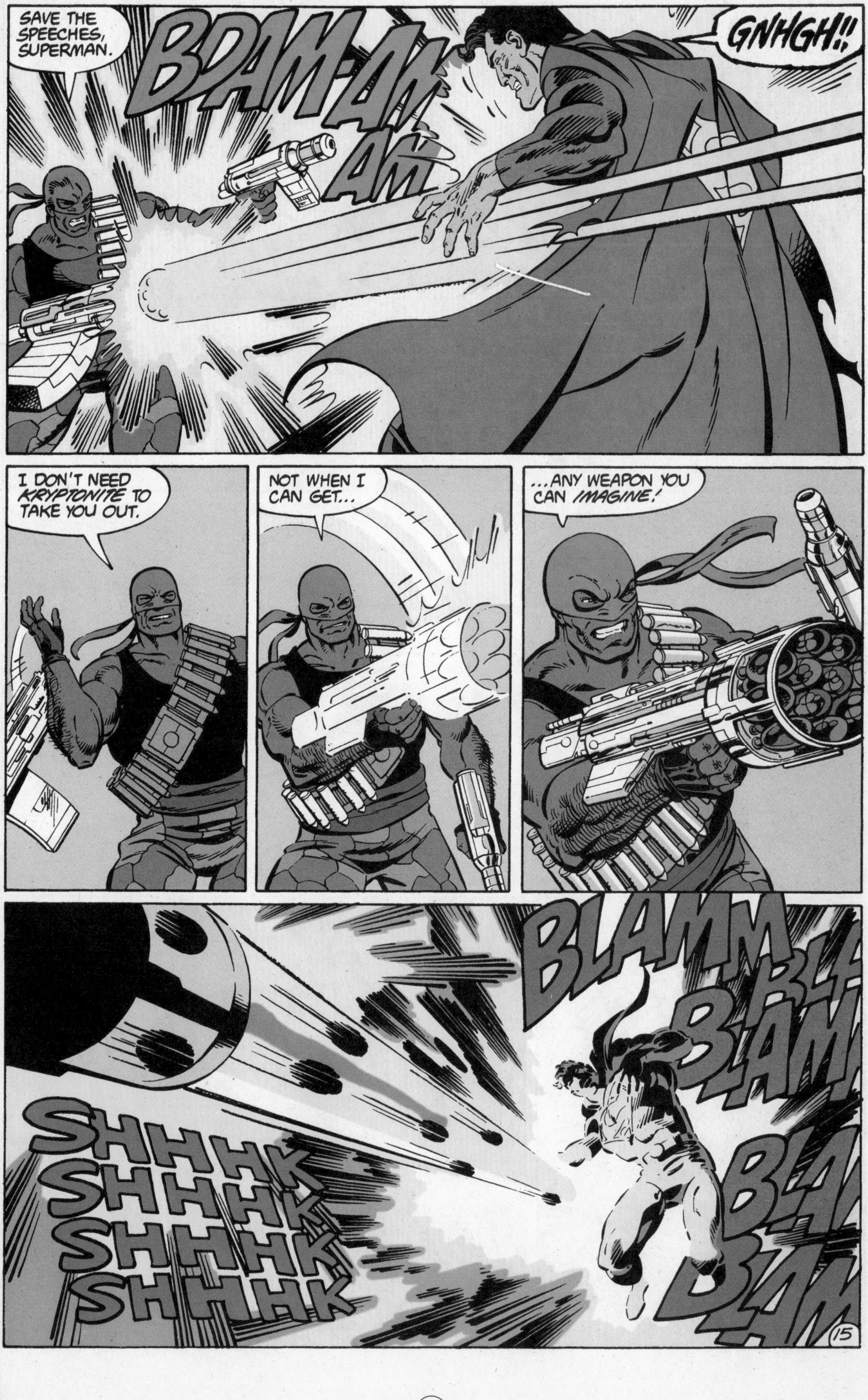

SAVE THE SPEECHES, SUPERMAN.
BDAM-AM-AM
GNHGH!!
I DON'T NEED *KRYPTONITE* TO TAKE YOU OUT.
NOT WHEN I CAN GET...
...ANY WEAPON YOU CAN *IMAGINE!*
BLAMM
BLAM
SHHHK SHHHK SHHHK SHHHK
BLAM
BLAM
15

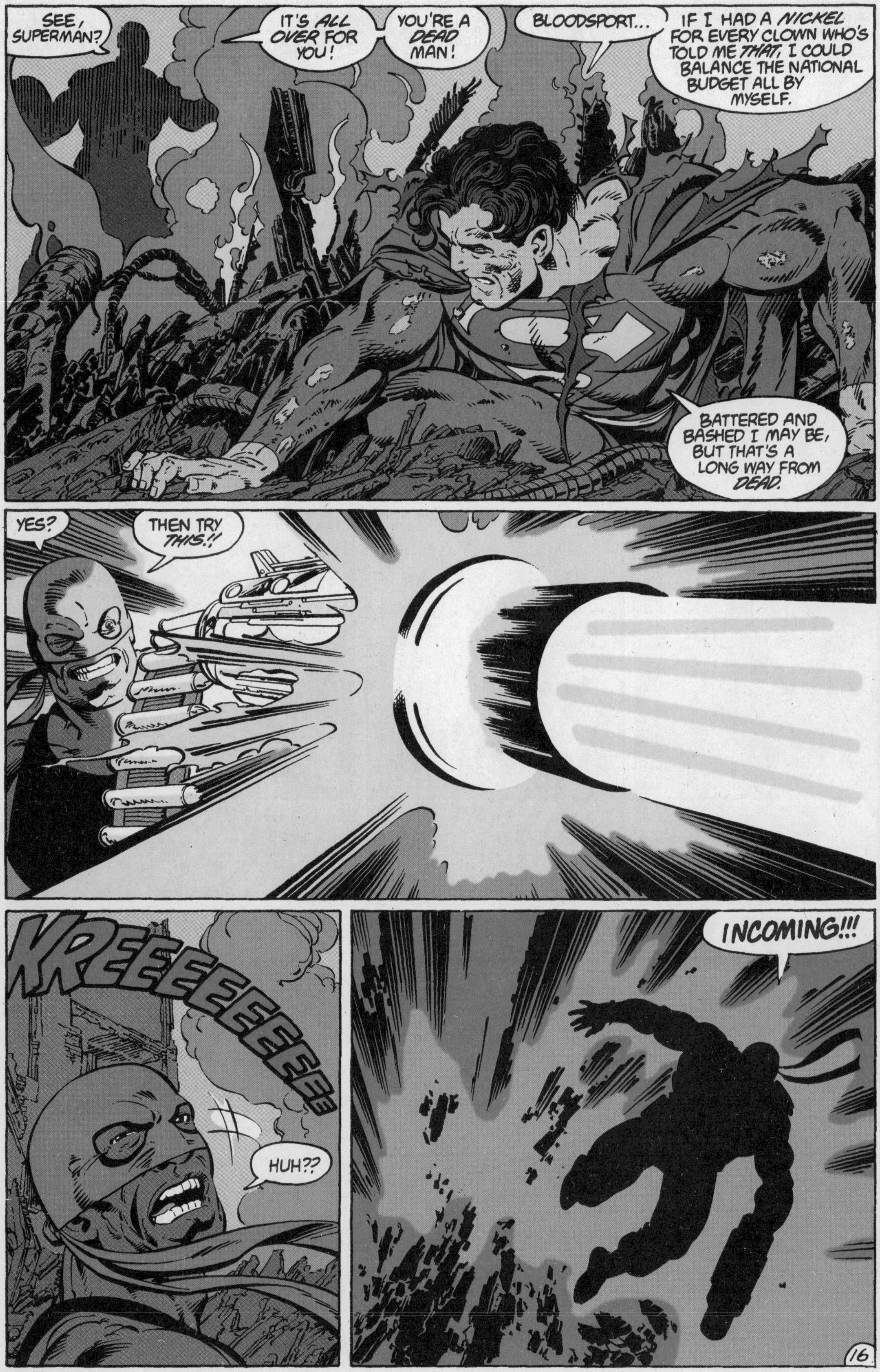
SEE, SUPERMAN?
IT'S ALL OVER FOR YOU!
YOU'RE A DEAD MAN!
BLOODSPORT...
IF I HAD A NICKEL FOR EVERY CLOWN WHO'S TOLD ME THAT, I COULD BALANCE THE NATIONAL BUDGET ALL BY MYSELF.
BATTERED AND BASHED I MAY BE, BUT THAT'S A LONG WAY FROM DEAD.
YES?
THEN TRY THIS!!
KREEEEEEEEEEEE
HUH??
INCOMING!!!
16

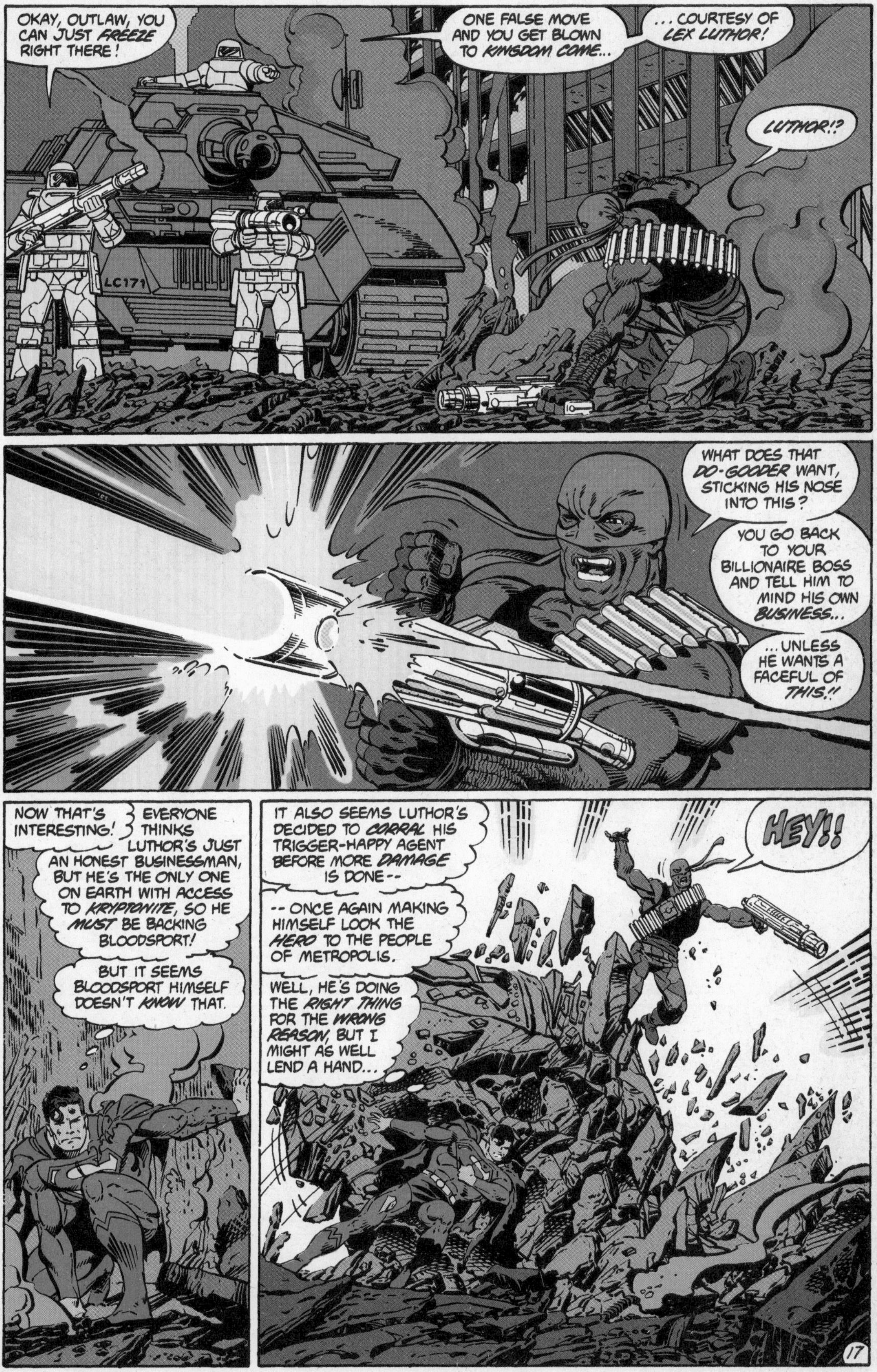
OKAY, OUTLAW, YOU CAN JUST FREEZE RIGHT THERE!
ONE FALSE MOVE AND YOU GET BLOWN TO KINGDOM COME...
...COURTESY OF LEX LUTHOR!
LUTHOR!?
LC171
WHAT DOES THAT DO-GOODER WANT, STICKING HIS NOSE INTO THIS?
YOU GO BACK TO YOUR BILLIONAIRE BOSS AND TELL HIM TO MIND HIS OWN BUSINESS...
...UNLESS HE WANTS A FACEFUL OF THIS!!
NOW THAT'S INTERESTING! EVERYONE THINKS LUTHOR'S JUST AN HONEST BUSINESSMAN, BUT HE'S THE ONLY ONE ON EARTH WITH ACCESS TO KRYPTONITE, SO HE MUST BE BACKING BLOODSPORT!
BUT IT SEEMS BLOODSPORT HIMSELF DOESN'T KNOW THAT.
IT ALSO SEEMS LUTHOR'S DECIDED TO CORRAL HIS TRIGGER-HAPPY AGENT BEFORE MORE DAMAGE IS DONE--
--ONCE AGAIN MAKING HIMSELF LOOK THE HERO TO THE PEOPLE OF METROPOLIS.
WELL, HE'S DOING THE RIGHT THING FOR THE WRONG REASON, BUT I MIGHT AS WELL LEND A HAND...
HEY!!
17

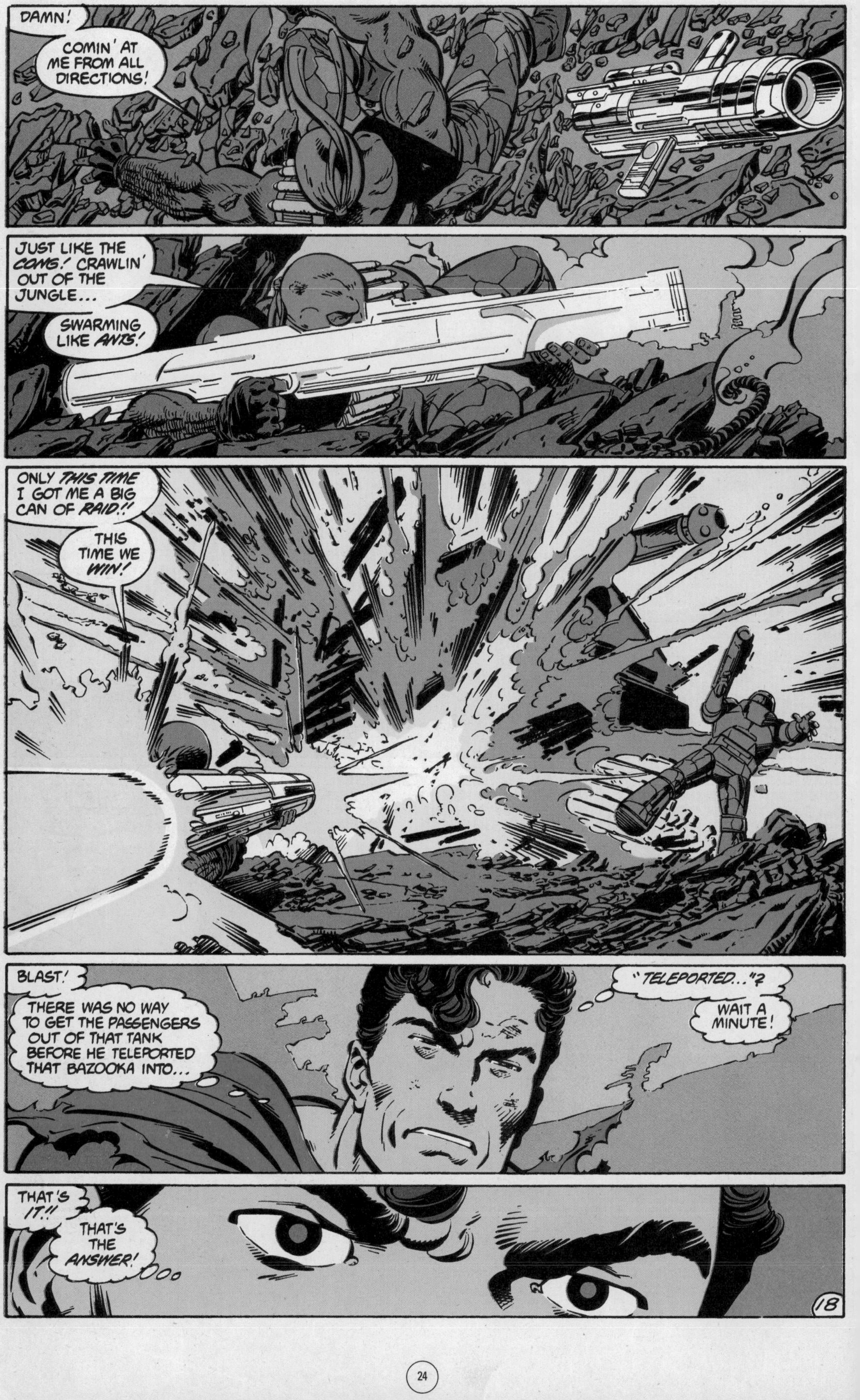
DAMN!
COMIN' AT ME FROM ALL DIRECTIONS!
JUST LIKE THE *CONG!* CRAWLIN' OUT OF THE JUNGLE...
SWARMING LIKE *ANTS!*
ONLY *THIS TIME* I GOT ME A BIG CAN OF *RAID!!*
THIS TIME WE *WIN!*
BLAST!
THERE WAS NO WAY TO GET THE PASSENGERS OUT OF THAT TANK BEFORE HE TELEPORTED THAT BAZOOKA INTO...
"*TELEPORTED...*"?
WAIT A MINUTE!
THAT'S *IT!!*
THAT'S THE *ANSWER!*
18

HUH? WHAT'S GOING...

...ON...

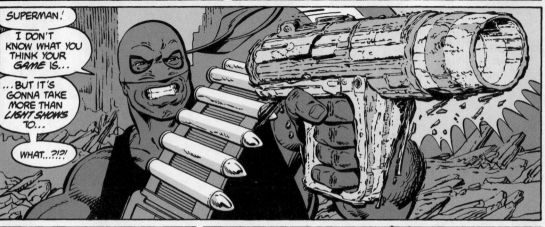

SUPERMAN! I DON'T KNOW WHAT YOU THINK YOUR *GAME* IS...

...BUT IT'S GONNA TAKE MORE THAN *LIGHT SHOWS* TO...

WHAT...?!?!

M-MY WEAPONS?!?

WHAT'S HAPPENED TO MY WEAPONS??

I HAPPENED, BLOODSPORT. I REALIZED YOU WEREN'T *CREATING* THOSE WEAPONS, AS I FIRST THOUGHT.

YOU WERE *TELEPORTING THEM* FROM ANOTHER LOCATION.

SO I USED MY *HEAT VISION* TO *IONIZE* THE AIR AROUND YOU!

AND THAT *SCRAMBLED* YOUR TELEPORTATION GIZMO!

THAP!

N-NOO!!!

19

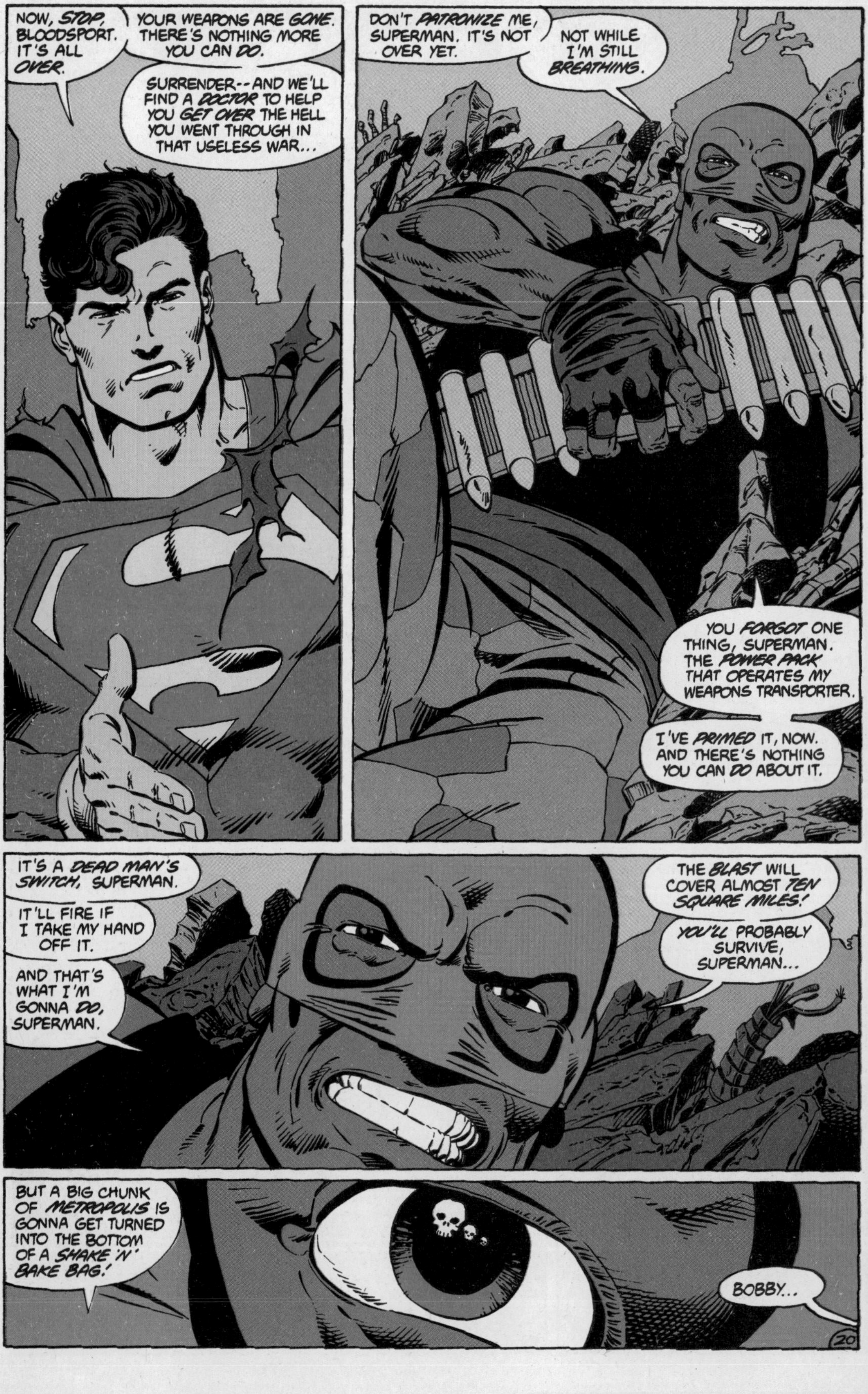
NOW, STOP, BLOODSPORT. IT'S ALL OVER.
YOUR WEAPONS ARE GONE. THERE'S NOTHING MORE YOU CAN DO.
SURRENDER--AND WE'LL FIND A DOCTOR TO HELP YOU GET OVER THE HELL YOU WENT THROUGH IN THAT USELESS WAR...
DON'T PATRONIZE ME, SUPERMAN. IT'S NOT OVER YET.
NOT WHILE I'M STILL BREATHING.
YOU FORGOT ONE THING, SUPERMAN. THE POWER PACK THAT OPERATES MY WEAPONS TRANSPORTER.
I'VE PRIMED IT, NOW. AND THERE'S NOTHING YOU CAN DO ABOUT IT.
IT'S A DEAD MAN'S SWITCH, SUPERMAN.
IT'LL FIRE IF I TAKE MY HAND OFF IT.
AND THAT'S WHAT I'M GONNA DO, SUPERMAN.
THE BLAST WILL COVER ALMOST TEN SQUARE MILES!
YOU'LL PROBABLY SURVIVE, SUPERMAN...
BUT A BIG CHUNK OF METROPOLIS IS GONNA GET TURNED INTO THE BOTTOM OF A SHAKE 'N' BAKE BAG!
BOBBY...
20

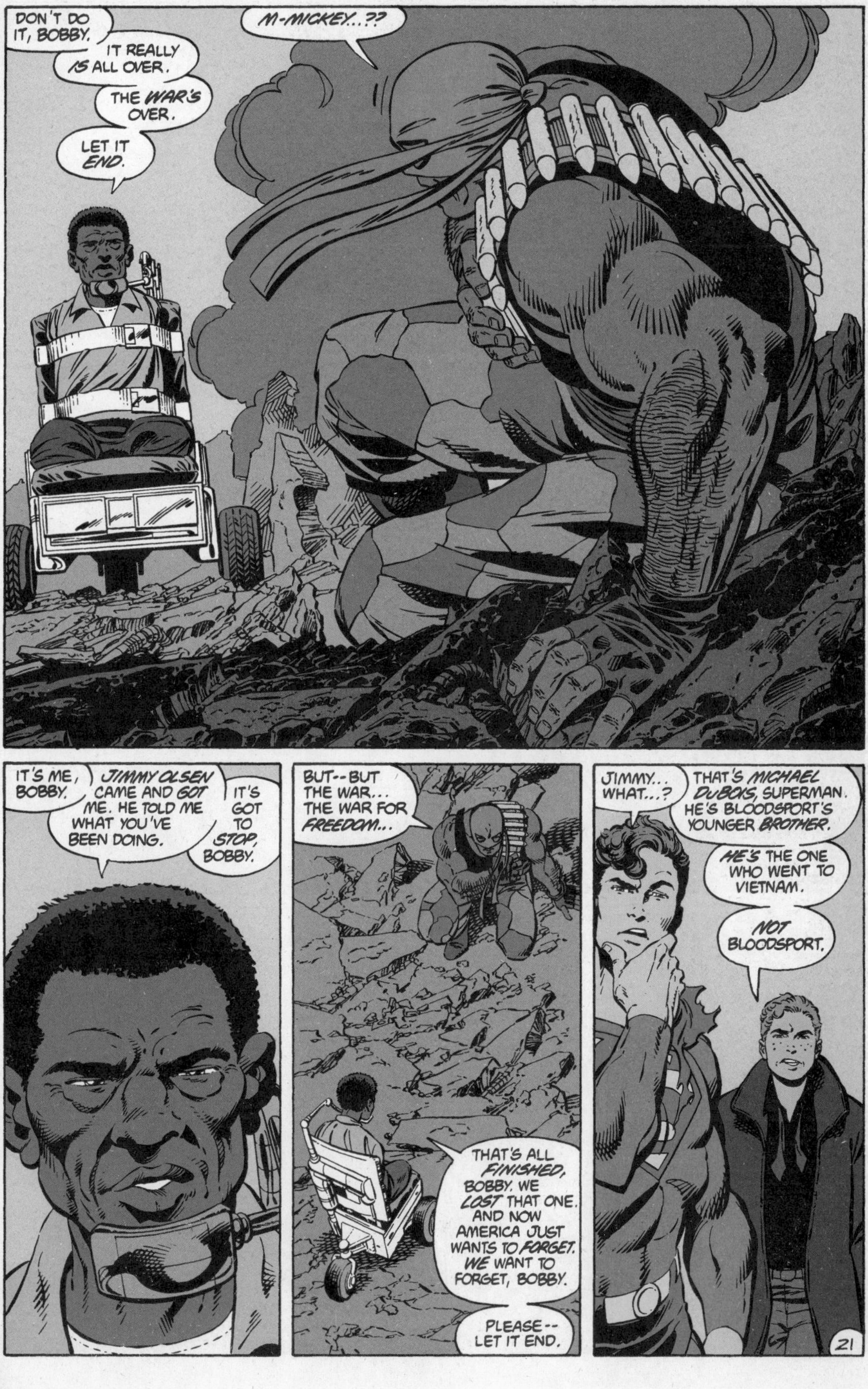
DON'T DO IT, BOBBY.
IT REALLY IS ALL OVER.
THE WAR'S OVER.
LET IT END.
M-MICKEY...??
IT'S ME, BOBBY.
JIMMY OLSEN CAME AND GOT ME. HE TOLD ME WHAT YOU'VE BEEN DOING.
IT'S GOT TO STOP, BOBBY.
BUT--BUT THE WAR... THE WAR FOR FREEDOM...
THAT'S ALL FINISHED, BOBBY. WE LOST THAT ONE. AND NOW AMERICA JUST WANTS TO FORGET. WE WANT TO FORGET, BOBBY.
PLEASE-- LET IT END.
JIMMY... WHAT...?
THAT'S MICHAEL DuBOIS, SUPERMAN. HE'S BLOODSPORT'S YOUNGER BROTHER.
HE'S THE ONE WHO WENT TO VIETNAM.
NOT BLOODSPORT.
21

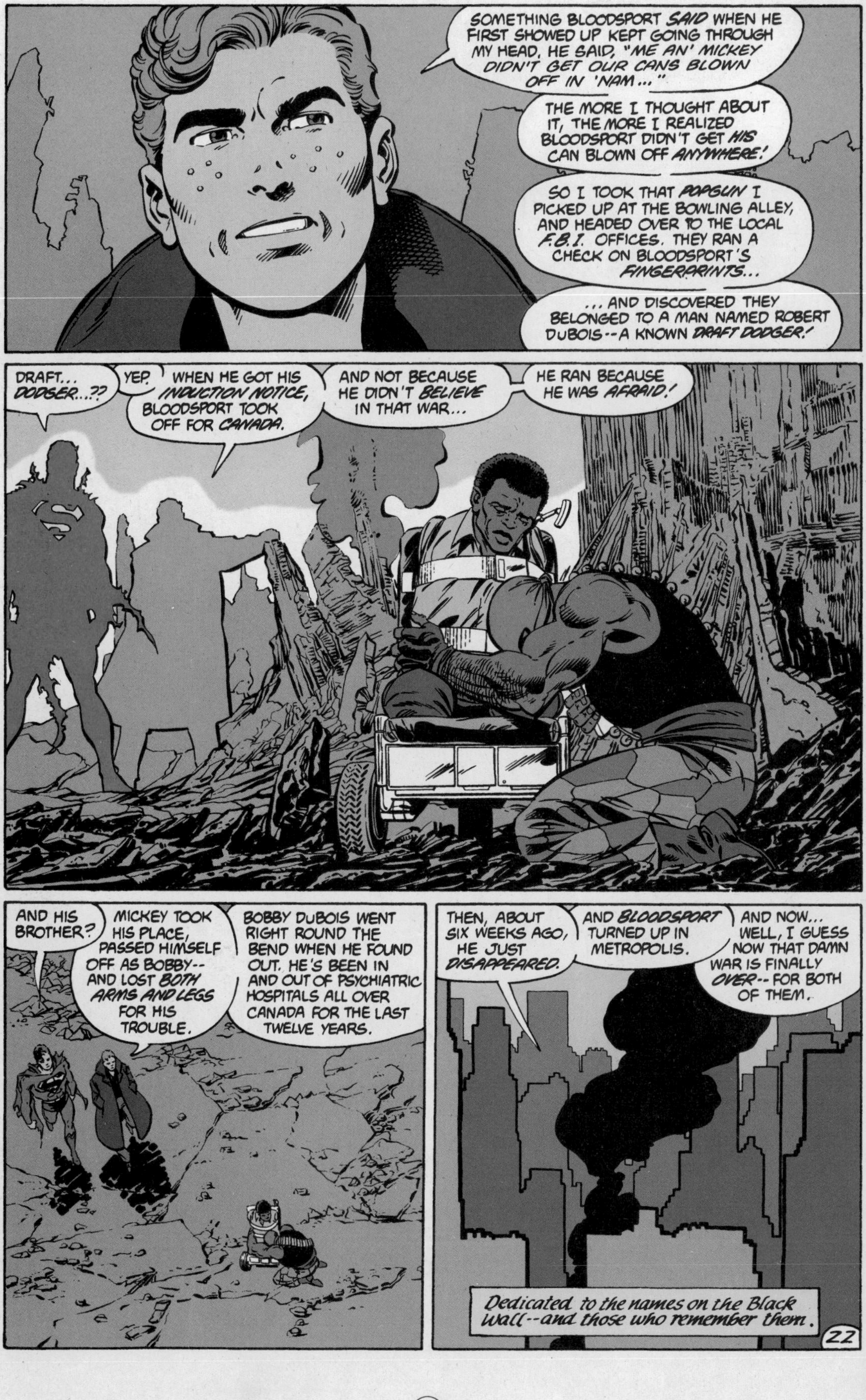

SOMETHING BLOODSPORT SAID WHEN HE FIRST SHOWED UP KEPT GOING THROUGH MY HEAD. HE SAID, "ME AN' MICKEY DIDN'T GET OUR CANS BLOWN OFF IN 'NAM..."
THE MORE I THOUGHT ABOUT IT, THE MORE I REALIZED BLOODSPORT DIDN'T GET HIS CAN BLOWN OFF ANYWHERE!
SO I TOOK THAT POPGUN I PICKED UP AT THE BOWLING ALLEY, AND HEADED OVER TO THE LOCAL F.B.I. OFFICES. THEY RAN A CHECK ON BLOODSPORT'S FINGERPRINTS...
...AND DISCOVERED THEY BELONGED TO A MAN NAMED ROBERT DUBOIS--A KNOWN DRAFT DODGER!
DRAFT... DODGER...??
YEP. WHEN HE GOT HIS INDUCTION NOTICE, BLOODSPORT TOOK OFF FOR CANADA.
AND NOT BECAUSE HE DIDN'T BELIEVE IN THAT WAR...
HE RAN BECAUSE HE WAS AFRAID!
AND HIS BROTHER?
MICKEY TOOK HIS PLACE, PASSED HIMSELF OFF AS BOBBY--AND LOST BOTH ARMS AND LEGS FOR HIS TROUBLE.
BOBBY DUBOIS WENT RIGHT ROUND THE BEND WHEN HE FOUND OUT. HE'S BEEN IN AND OUT OF PSYCHIATRIC HOSPITALS ALL OVER CANADA FOR THE LAST TWELVE YEARS.
THEN, ABOUT SIX WEEKS AGO, HE JUST DISAPPEARED.
AND BLOODSPORT TURNED UP IN METROPOLIS.
AND NOW... WELL, I GUESS NOW THAT DAMN WAR IS FINALLY OVER--FOR BOTH OF THEM.
Dedicated to the names on the Black Wall--and those who remember them.
22

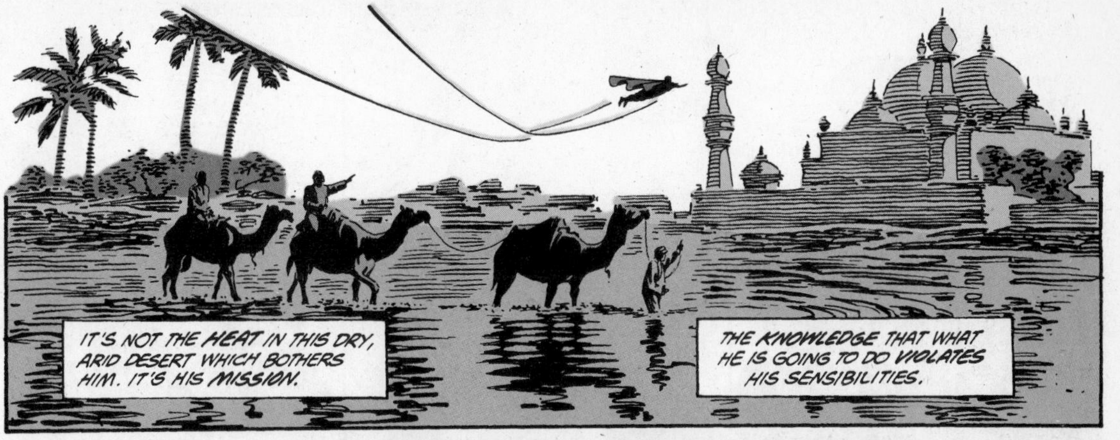
IT'S NOT THE HEAT IN THIS DRY, ARID DESERT WHICH BOTHERS HIM. IT'S HIS MISSION.
THE KNOWLEDGE THAT WHAT HE IS GOING TO DO VIOLATES HIS SENSIBILITIES.

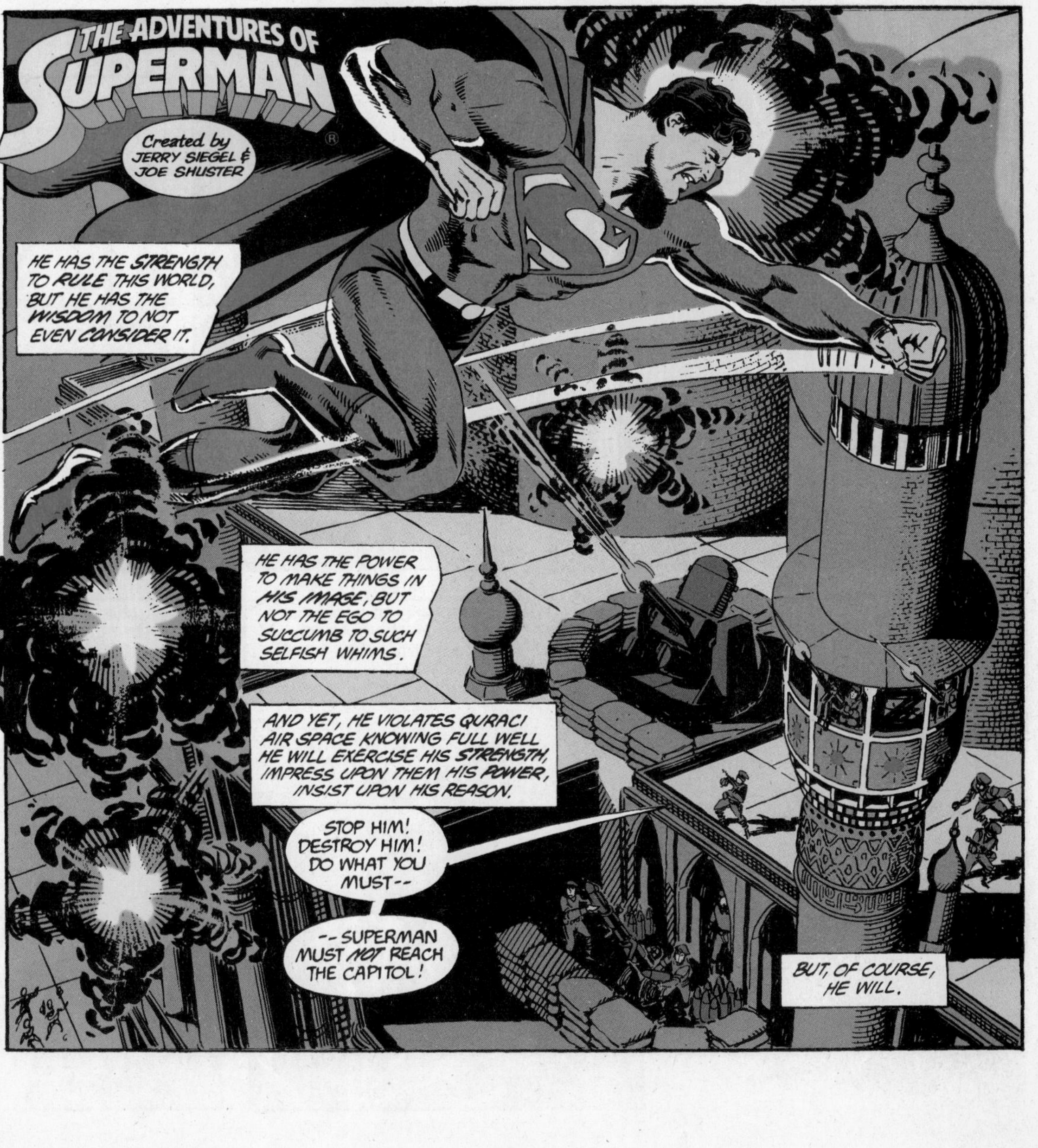
THE ADVENTURES OF SUPERMAN
Created by JERRY SIEGEL & JOE SHUSTER
HE HAS THE STRENGTH TO RULE THIS WORLD, BUT HE HAS THE WISDOM TO NOT EVEN CONSIDER IT.
HE HAS THE POWER TO MAKE THINGS IN HIS IMAGE, BUT NOT THE EGO TO SUCCUMB TO SUCH SELFISH WHIMS.
AND YET, HE VIOLATES QURACI AIR SPACE KNOWING FULL WELL HE WILL EXERCISE HIS STRENGTH, IMPRESS UPON THEM HIS POWER, INSIST UPON HIS REASON.
STOP HIM! DESTROY HIM! DO WHAT YOU MUST--
--SUPERMAN MUST NOT REACH THE CAPITOL!
BUT, OF COURSE, HE WILL.

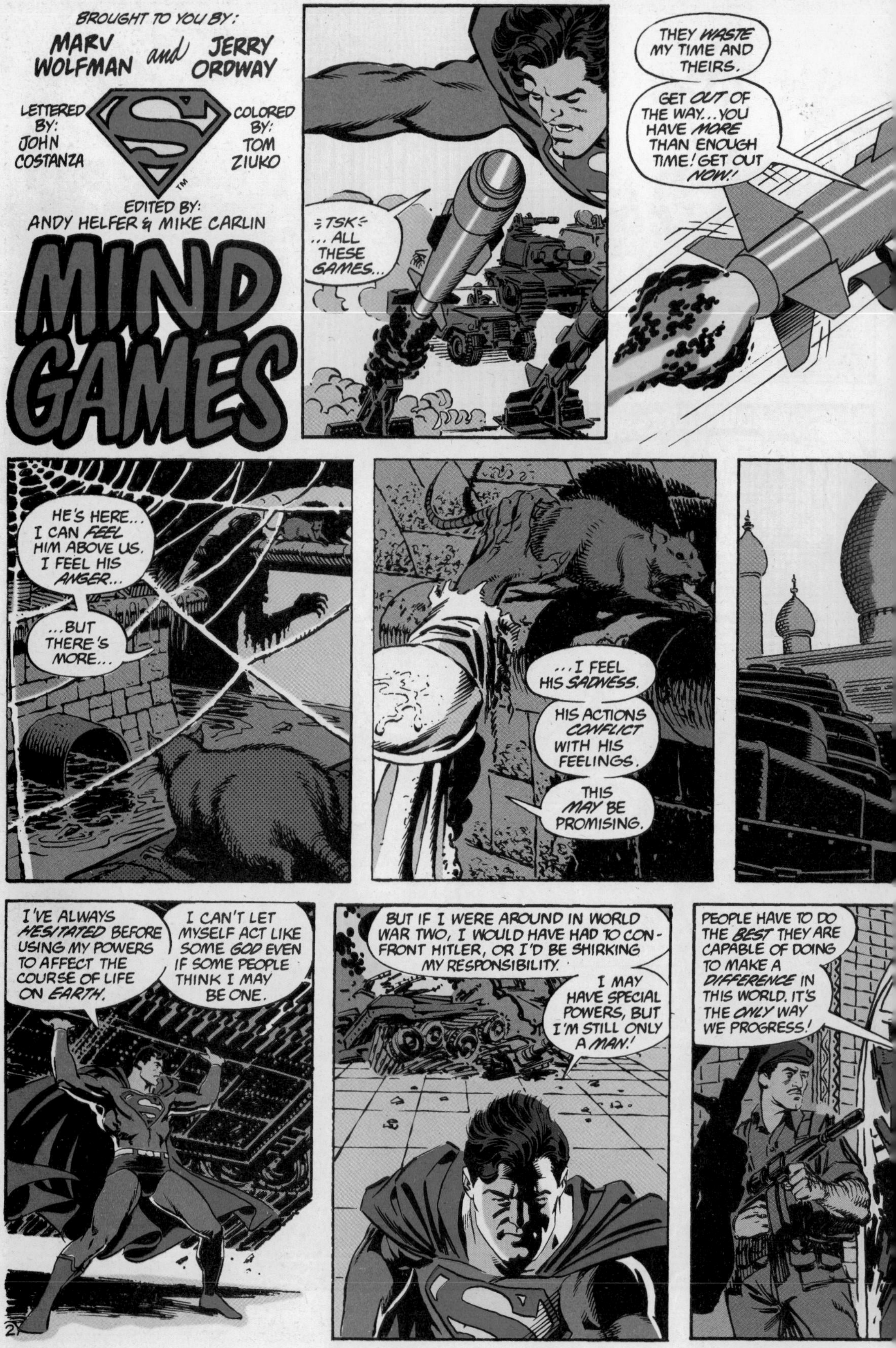

BROUGHT TO YOU BY:
MARV WOLFMAN and JERRY ORDWAY
LETTERED BY: JOHN COSTANZA
COLORED BY: TOM ZIUKO
EDITED BY: ANDY HELFER & MIKE CARLIN
MIND GAMES
TSK ... ALL THESE GAMES...
THEY WASTE MY TIME AND THEIRS.
GET OUT OF THE WAY... YOU HAVE MORE THAN ENOUGH TIME! GET OUT NOW!
HE'S HERE... I CAN FEEL HIM ABOVE US. I FEEL HIS ANGER...
...BUT THERE'S MORE...
...I FEEL HIS SADNESS.
HIS ACTIONS CONFLICT WITH HIS FEELINGS.
THIS MAY BE PROMISING.
I'VE ALWAYS HESITATED BEFORE USING MY POWERS TO AFFECT THE COURSE OF LIFE ON EARTH.
I CAN'T LET MYSELF ACT LIKE SOME GOD EVEN IF SOME PEOPLE THINK I MAY BE ONE.
BUT IF I WERE AROUND IN WORLD WAR TWO, I WOULD HAVE HAD TO CONFRONT HITLER, OR I'D BE SHIRKING MY RESPONSIBILITY.
I MAY HAVE SPECIAL POWERS, BUT I'M STILL ONLY A MAN!
PEOPLE HAVE TO DO THE BEST THEY ARE CAPABLE OF DOING TO MAKE A DIFFERENCE IN THIS WORLD. IT'S THE ONLY WAY WE PROGRESS!
2

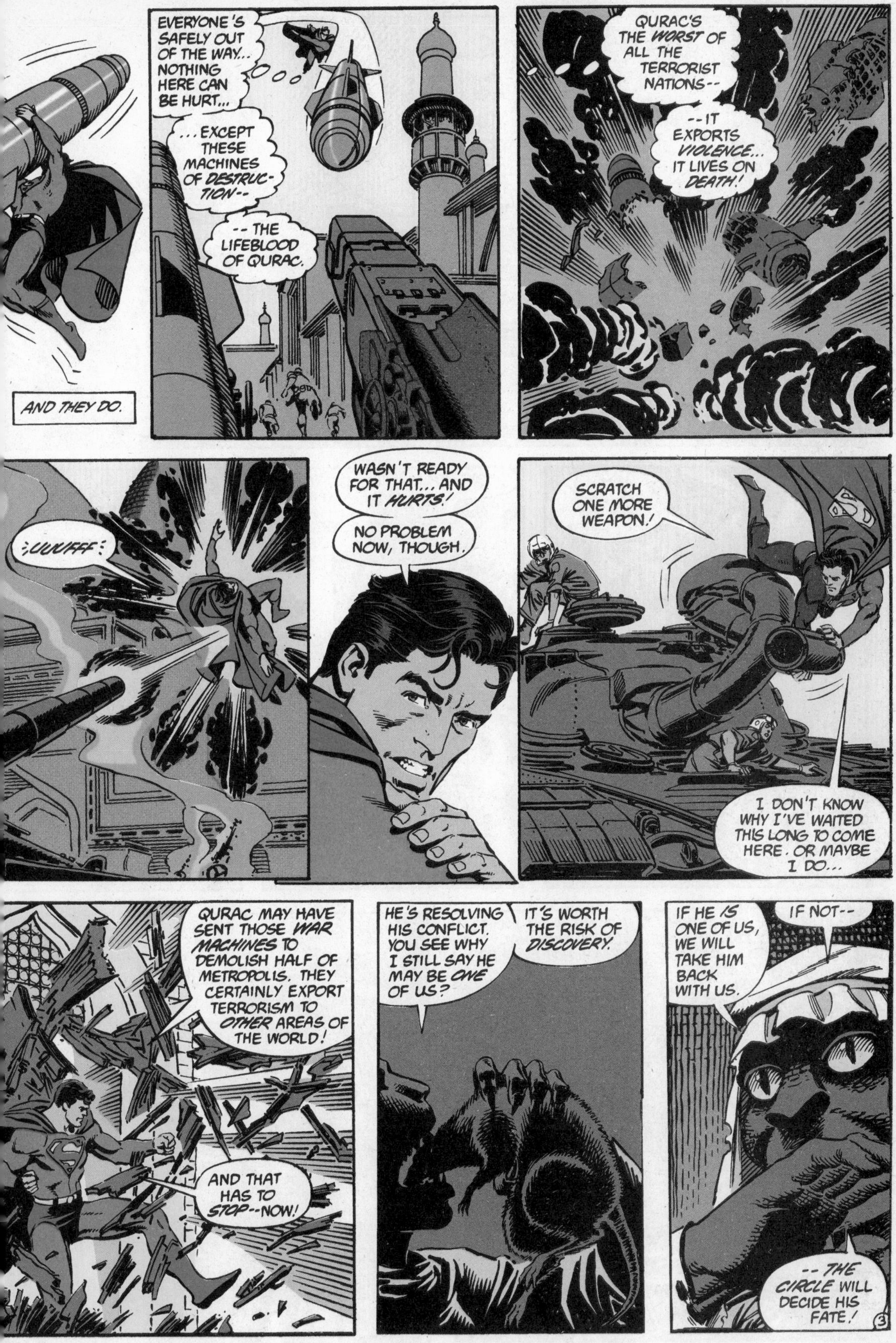
AND THEY DO.
EVERYONE'S SAFELY OUT OF THE WAY... NOTHING HERE CAN BE HURT...
...EXCEPT THESE MACHINES OF DESTRUCTION--
--THE LIFEBLOOD OF QURAC.
QURAC'S THE WORST OF ALL THE TERRORIST NATIONS--
--IT EXPORTS VIOLENCE... IT LIVES ON DEATH!
UUUFFF
WASN'T READY FOR THAT... AND IT HURTS!
NO PROBLEM NOW, THOUGH.
SCRATCH ONE MORE WEAPON!
I DON'T KNOW WHY I'VE WAITED THIS LONG TO COME HERE. OR MAYBE I DO...
QURAC MAY HAVE SENT THOSE WAR MACHINES TO DEMOLISH HALF OF METROPOLIS. THEY CERTAINLY EXPORT TERRORISM TO OTHER AREAS OF THE WORLD!
AND THAT HAS TO STOP--NOW!
HE'S RESOLVING HIS CONFLICT. YOU SEE WHY I STILL SAY HE MAY BE ONE OF US?
IT'S WORTH THE RISK OF DISCOVERY.
IF HE IS ONE OF US, WE WILL TAKE HIM BACK WITH US.
IF NOT--
--THE CIRCLE WILL DECIDE HIS FATE!
3

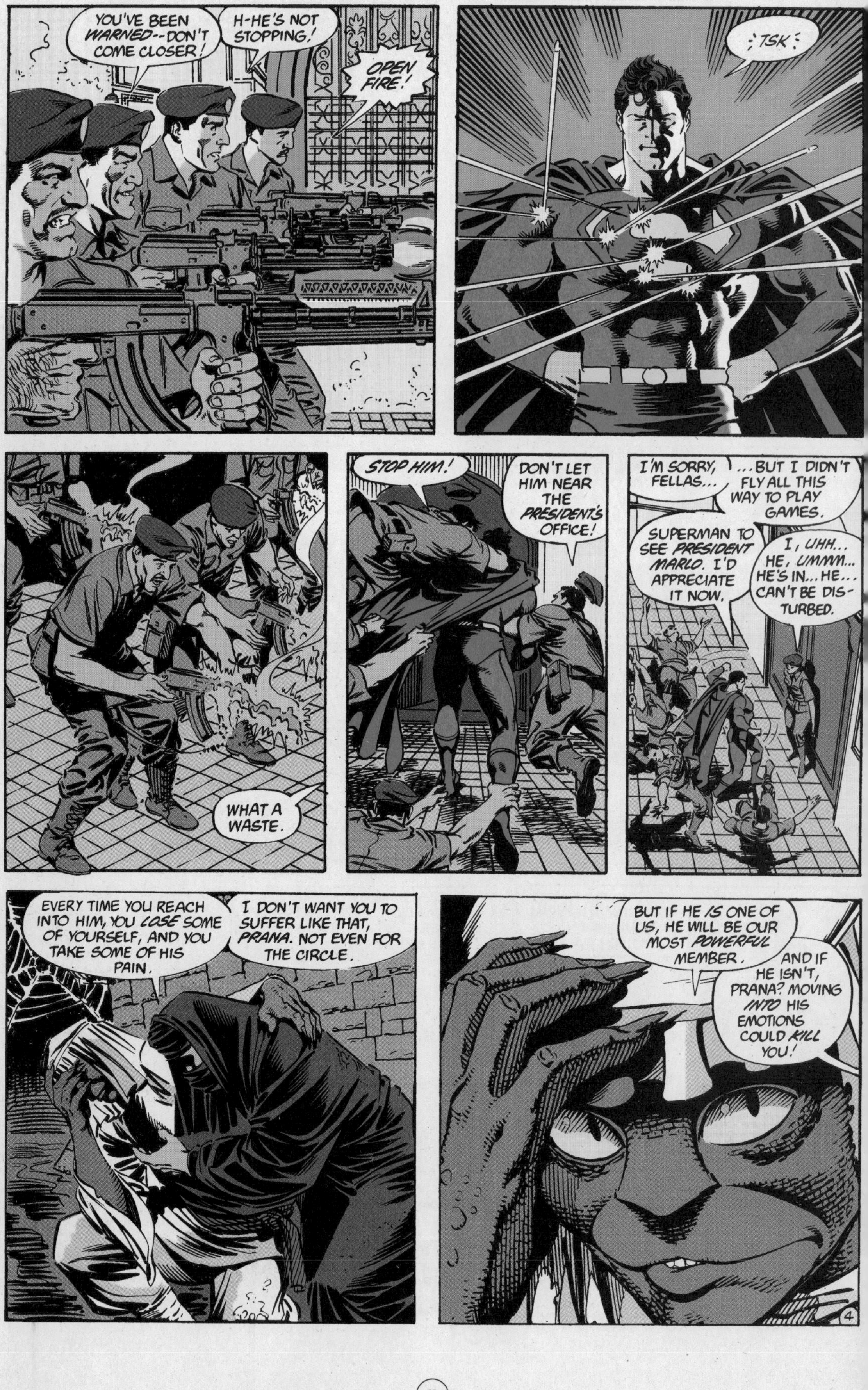
YOU'VE BEEN WARNED--DON'T COME CLOSER!
H-HE'S NOT STOPPING!
OPEN FIRE!
TSK
WHAT A WASTE.
STOP HIM!
DON'T LET HIM NEAR THE PRESIDENT'S OFFICE!
I'M SORRY, FELLAS...
...BUT I DIDN'T FLY ALL THIS WAY TO PLAY GAMES.
SUPERMAN TO SEE PRESIDENT MARLO. I'D APPRECIATE IT NOW.
I, UHH... HE, UMMM... HE'S IN... HE... CAN'T BE DISTURBED.
EVERY TIME YOU REACH INTO HIM, YOU LOSE SOME OF YOURSELF, AND YOU TAKE SOME OF HIS PAIN.
I DON'T WANT YOU TO SUFFER LIKE THAT, PRANA. NOT EVEN FOR THE CIRCLE.
BUT IF HE IS ONE OF US, HE WILL BE OUR MOST POWERFUL MEMBER.
AND IF HE ISN'T, PRANA? MOVING INTO HIS EMOTIONS COULD KILL YOU!
4

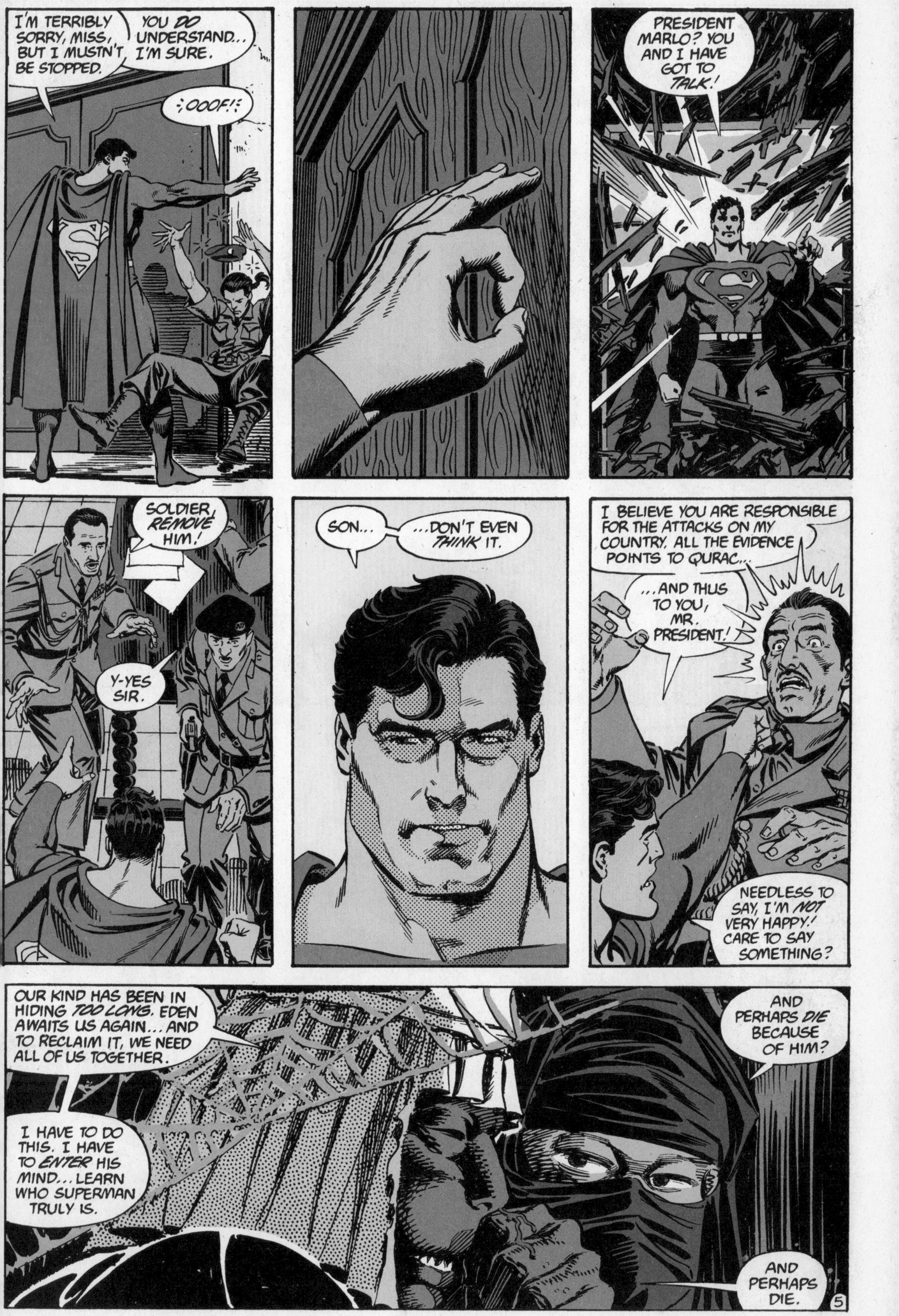
I'M TERRIBLY SORRY, MISS, BUT I MUSTN'T BE STOPPED.
YOU DO UNDERSTAND... I'M SURE.
OOOF!
PRESIDENT MARLO? YOU AND I HAVE GOT TO TALK!
SOLDIER, REMOVE HIM!
Y-YES SIR.
SON...
...DON'T EVEN THINK IT.
I BELIEVE YOU ARE RESPONSIBLE FOR THE ATTACKS ON MY COUNTRY. ALL THE EVIDENCE POINTS TO QURAC...
...AND THUS TO YOU, MR. PRESIDENT!
NEEDLESS TO SAY, I'M NOT VERY HAPPY! CARE TO SAY SOMETHING?
OUR KIND HAS BEEN IN HIDING TOO LONG. EDEN AWAITS US AGAIN... AND TO RECLAIM IT, WE NEED ALL OF US TOGETHER.
AND PERHAPS DIE BECAUSE OF HIM?
I HAVE TO DO THIS. I HAVE TO ENTER HIS MIND... LEARN WHO SUPERMAN TRULY IS.
AND PERHAPS DIE.
5

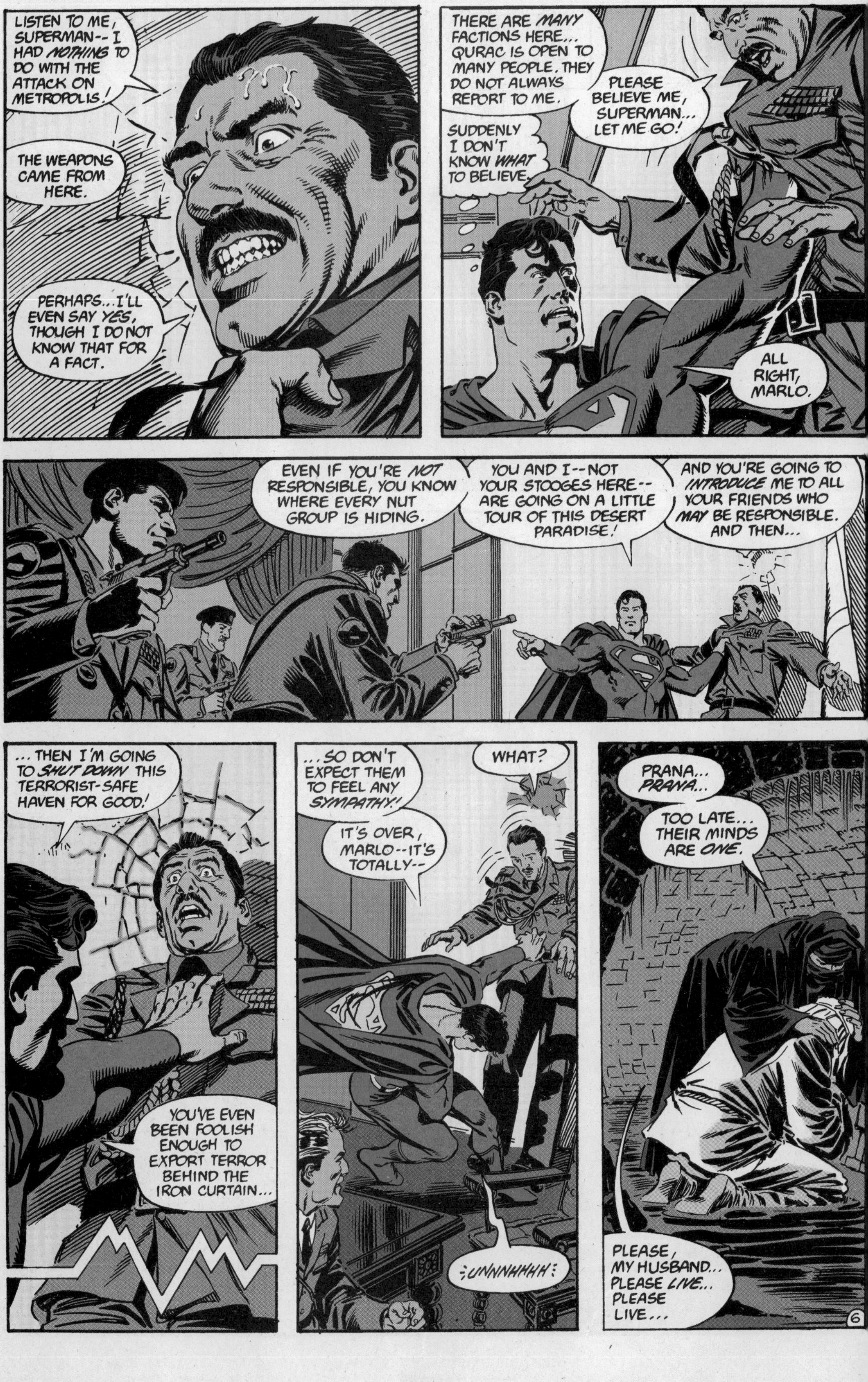
LISTEN TO ME, SUPERMAN-- I HAD NOTHING TO DO WITH THE ATTACK ON METROPOLIS!
THE WEAPONS CAME FROM HERE.
PERHAPS...I'LL EVEN SAY YES, THOUGH I DO NOT KNOW THAT FOR A FACT.
THERE ARE MANY FACTIONS HERE... QURAC IS OPEN TO MANY PEOPLE. THEY DO NOT ALWAYS REPORT TO ME.
PLEASE BELIEVE ME, SUPERMAN... LET ME GO!
SUDDENLY I DON'T KNOW WHAT TO BELIEVE.
ALL RIGHT, MARLO.
EVEN IF YOU'RE NOT RESPONSIBLE, YOU KNOW WHERE EVERY NUT GROUP IS HIDING.
YOU AND I--NOT YOUR STOOGES HERE--ARE GOING ON A LITTLE TOUR OF THIS DESERT PARADISE!
AND YOU'RE GOING TO INTRODUCE ME TO ALL YOUR FRIENDS WHO MAY BE RESPONSIBLE. AND THEN...
...THEN I'M GOING TO SHUT DOWN THIS TERRORIST-SAFE HAVEN FOR GOOD!
YOU'VE EVEN BEEN FOOLISH ENOUGH TO EXPORT TERROR BEHIND THE IRON CURTAIN...
...SO DON'T EXPECT THEM TO FEEL ANY SYMPATHY!
WHAT?
IT'S OVER, MARLO--IT'S TOTALLY--
UNNNHHHH
PRANA... PRANA...
TOO LATE... THEIR MINDS ARE ONE.
PLEASE, MY HUSBAND... PLEASE LIVE... PLEASE LIVE...
6

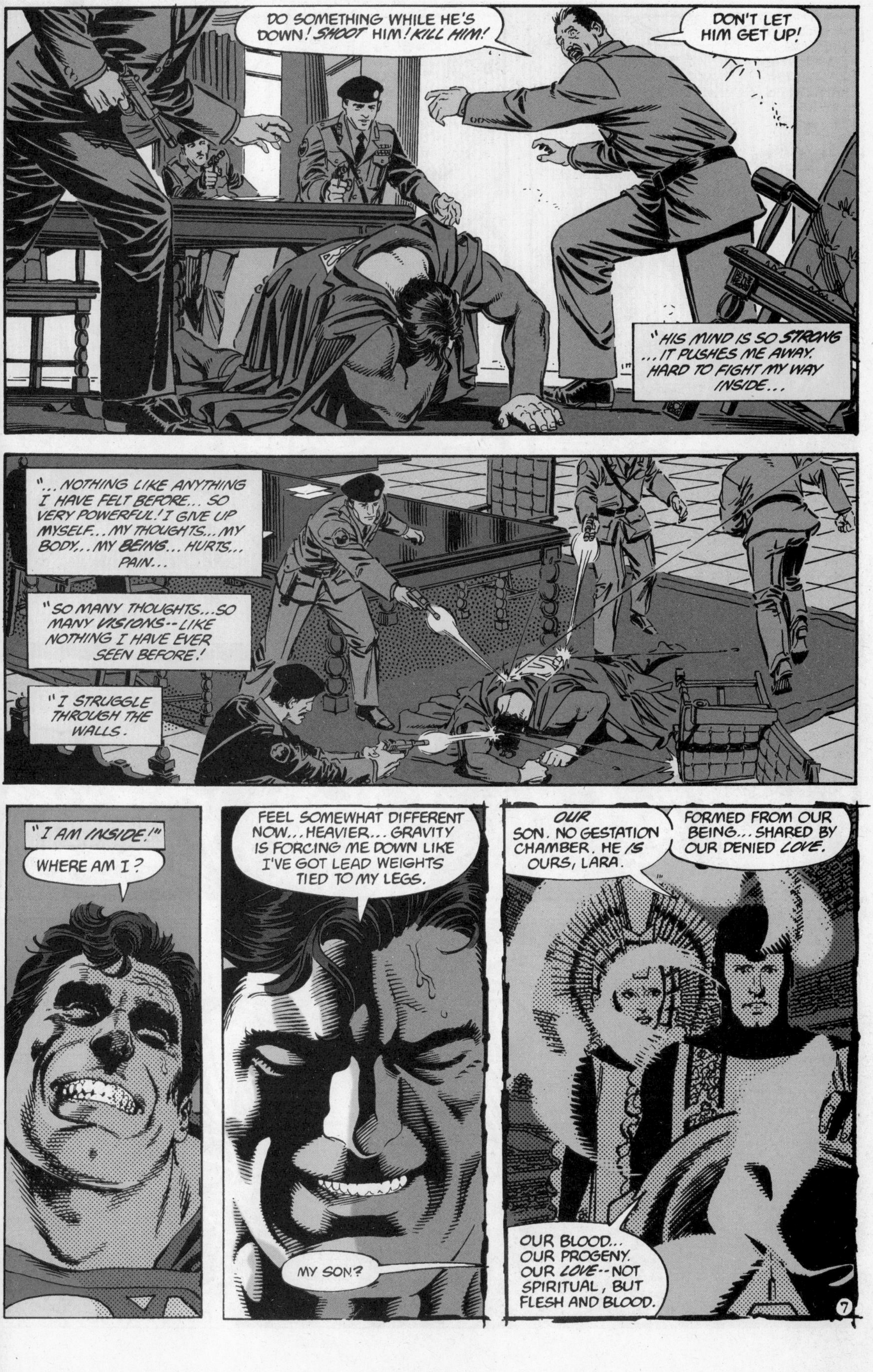
DO SOMETHING WHILE HE'S DOWN! SHOOT HIM! KILL HIM!
DON'T LET HIM GET UP!
"HIS MIND IS SO STRONG ...IT PUSHES ME AWAY. HARD TO FIGHT MY WAY INSIDE...
"...NOTHING LIKE ANYTHING I HAVE FELT BEFORE... SO VERY POWERFUL! I GIVE UP MYSELF... MY THOUGHTS... MY BODY... MY BEING... HURTS... PAIN...
"SO MANY THOUGHTS... SO MANY VISIONS--LIKE NOTHING I HAVE EVER SEEN BEFORE!
"I STRUGGLE THROUGH THE WALLS.
"I AM INSIDE!"
WHERE AM I?
FEEL SOMEWHAT DIFFERENT NOW... HEAVIER... GRAVITY IS FORCING ME DOWN LIKE I'VE GOT LEAD WEIGHTS TIED TO MY LEGS.
MY SON?
OUR SON. NO GESTATION CHAMBER. HE IS OURS, LARA.
FORMED FROM OUR BEING... SHARED BY OUR DENIED LOVE.
OUR BLOOD... OUR PROGENY. OUR LOVE--NOT SPIRITUAL, BUT FLESH AND BLOOD.
7

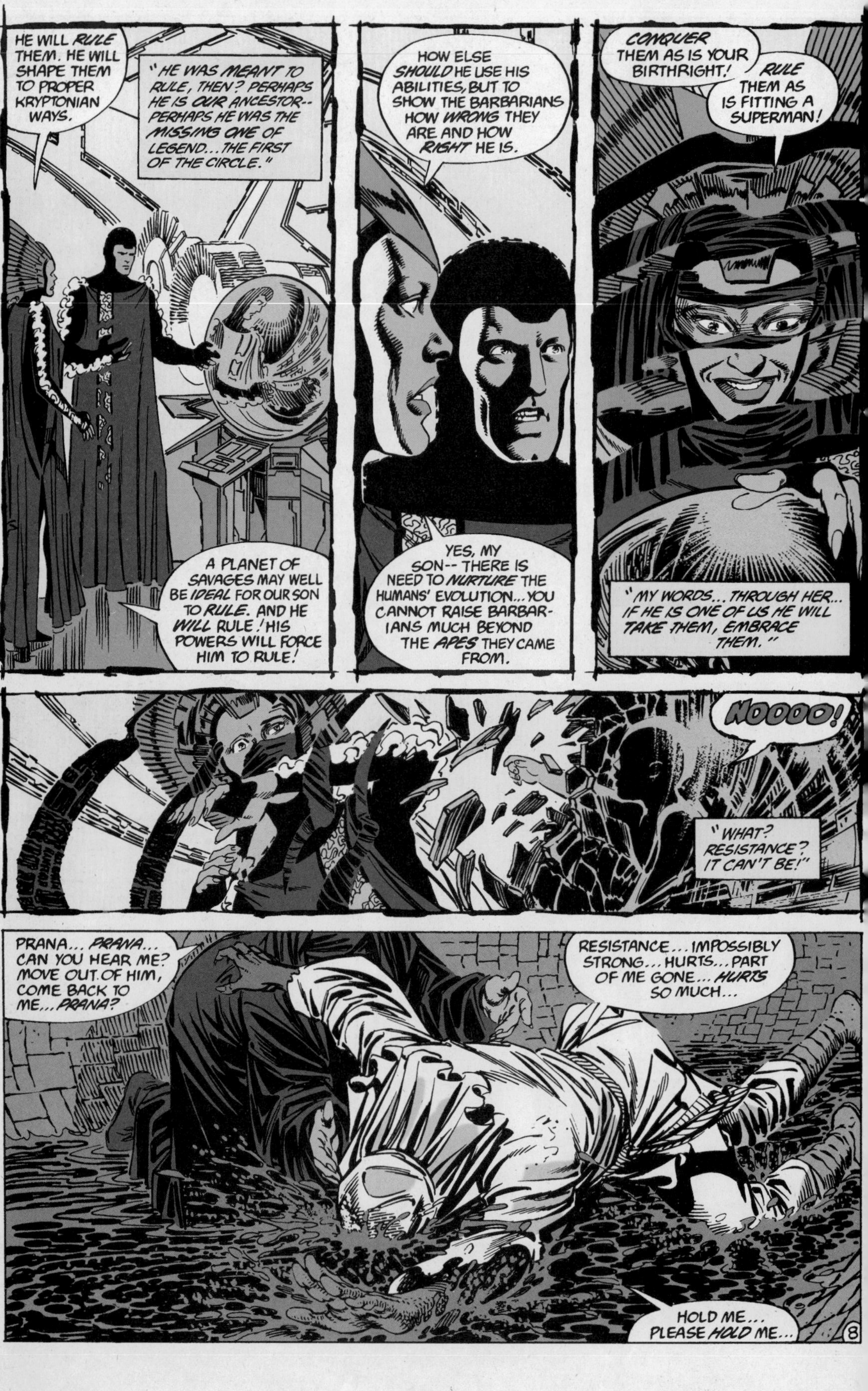
HE WILL RULE THEM. HE WILL SHAPE THEM TO PROPER KRYPTONIAN WAYS.
"HE WAS MEANT TO RULE, THEN? PERHAPS HE IS OUR ANCESTOR-- PERHAPS HE WAS THE MISSING ONE OF LEGEND... THE FIRST OF THE CIRCLE."
A PLANET OF SAVAGES MAY WELL BE IDEAL FOR OUR SON TO RULE. AND HE WILL RULE! HIS POWERS WILL FORCE HIM TO RULE!
HOW ELSE SHOULD HE USE HIS ABILITIES, BUT TO SHOW THE BARBARIANS HOW WRONG THEY ARE AND HOW RIGHT HE IS.
YES, MY SON-- THERE IS NEED TO NURTURE THE HUMANS' EVOLUTION... YOU CANNOT RAISE BARBAR-IANS MUCH BEYOND THE APES THEY CAME FROM.
CONQUER THEM AS IS YOUR BIRTHRIGHT!
RULE THEM AS IS FITTING A SUPERMAN!
"MY WORDS... THROUGH HER... IF HE IS ONE OF US HE WILL TAKE THEM, EMBRACE THEM."
NOOOO!
"WHAT? RESISTANCE? IT CAN'T BE!"
PRANA... PRANA... CAN YOU HEAR ME? MOVE OUT OF HIM, COME BACK TO ME... PRANA?
RESISTANCE... IMPOSSIBLY STRONG... HURTS... PART OF ME GONE... HURTS SO MUCH...
HOLD ME... PLEASE HOLD ME...
8

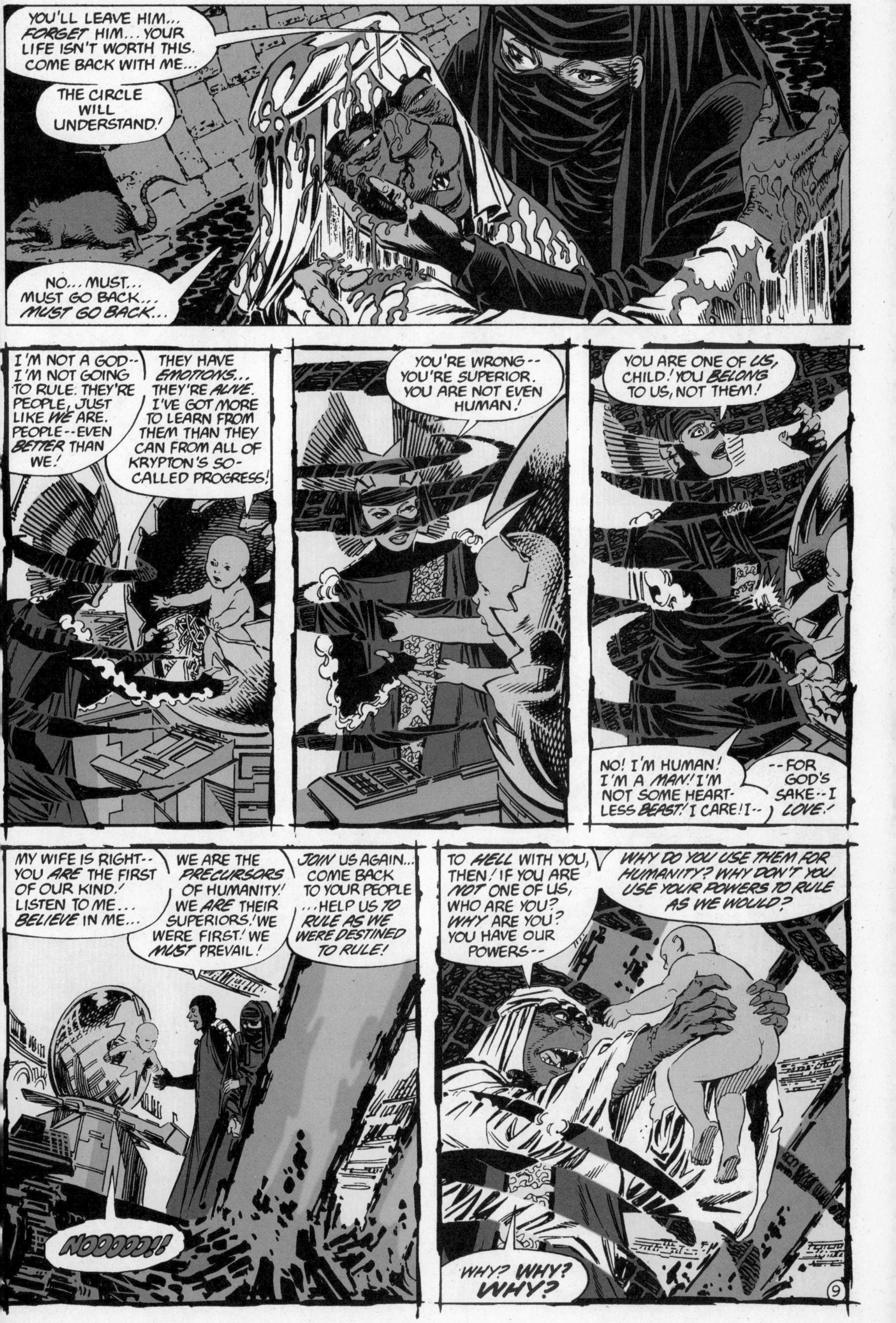

YOU'LL LEAVE HIM... FORGET HIM... YOUR LIFE ISN'T WORTH THIS. COME BACK WITH ME...
THE CIRCLE WILL UNDERSTAND!
NO... MUST... MUST GO BACK... MUST GO BACK...
I'M NOT A GOD-- I'M NOT GOING TO RULE. THEY'RE PEOPLE, JUST LIKE WE ARE. PEOPLE--EVEN BETTER THAN WE!
THEY HAVE EMOTIONS... THEY'RE ALIVE. I'VE GOT MORE TO LEARN FROM THEM THAN THEY CAN FROM ALL OF KRYPTON'S SO-CALLED PROGRESS!
YOU'RE WRONG-- YOU'RE SUPERIOR. YOU ARE NOT EVEN HUMAN!
YOU ARE ONE OF US, CHILD! YOU BELONG TO US, NOT THEM!
NO! I'M HUMAN! I'M A MAN! I'M NOT SOME HEART-LESS BEAST! I CARE! I--
--FOR GOD'S SAKE--I LOVE!
MY WIFE IS RIGHT-- YOU ARE THE FIRST OF OUR KIND! LISTEN TO ME... BELIEVE IN ME...
WE ARE THE PRECURSORS OF HUMANITY! WE ARE THEIR SUPERIORS! WE WERE FIRST! WE MUST PREVAIL!
JOIN US AGAIN... COME BACK TO YOUR PEOPLE ...HELP US TO RULE AS WE WERE DESTINED TO RULE!
NOOOOOO!
TO HELL WITH YOU, THEN! IF YOU ARE NOT ONE OF US, WHO ARE YOU? WHY ARE YOU? YOU HAVE OUR POWERS--
WHY DO YOU USE THEM FOR HUMANITY? WHY DON'T YOU USE YOUR POWERS TO RULE AS WE WOULD?
WHY? WHY? WHY?
9

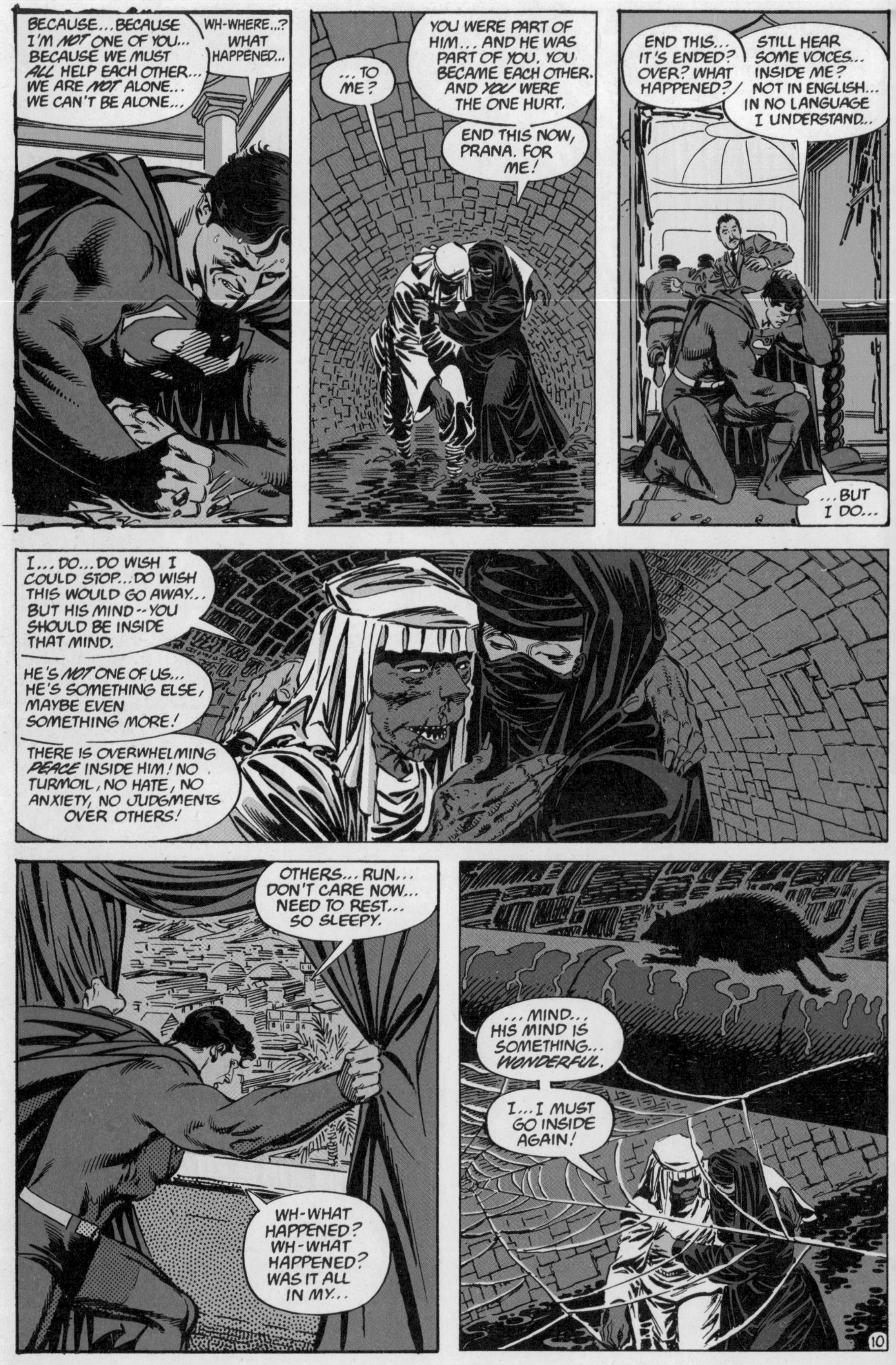

BECAUSE... BECAUSE I'M NOT ONE OF YOU... BECAUSE WE MUST ALL HELP EACH OTHER... WE ARE NOT ALONE... WE CAN'T BE ALONE...
WH-WHERE...? WHAT HAPPENED...
...TO ME?
YOU WERE PART OF HIM... AND HE WAS PART OF YOU. YOU BECAME EACH OTHER. AND YOU WERE THE ONE HURT.
END THIS NOW, PRANA. FOR ME!
END THIS... IT'S ENDED? OVER? WHAT HAPPENED?
STILL HEAR SOME VOICES... INSIDE ME? NOT IN ENGLISH... IN NO LANGUAGE I UNDERSTAND...
...BUT I DO...
I... DO... DO WISH I COULD STOP... DO WISH THIS WOULD GO AWAY... BUT HIS MIND--YOU SHOULD BE INSIDE THAT MIND.
HE'S NOT ONE OF US... HE'S SOMETHING ELSE, MAYBE EVEN SOMETHING MORE!
THERE IS OVERWHELMING PEACE INSIDE HIM! NO TURMOIL, NO HATE, NO ANXIETY, NO JUDGMENTS OVER OTHERS!
OTHERS... RUN... DON'T CARE NOW... NEED TO REST... SO SLEEPY.
WH-WHAT HAPPENED? WH-WHAT HAPPENED? WAS IT ALL IN MY...
...MIND... HIS MIND IS SOMETHING... WONDERFUL.
I...I MUST GO INSIDE AGAIN!
10

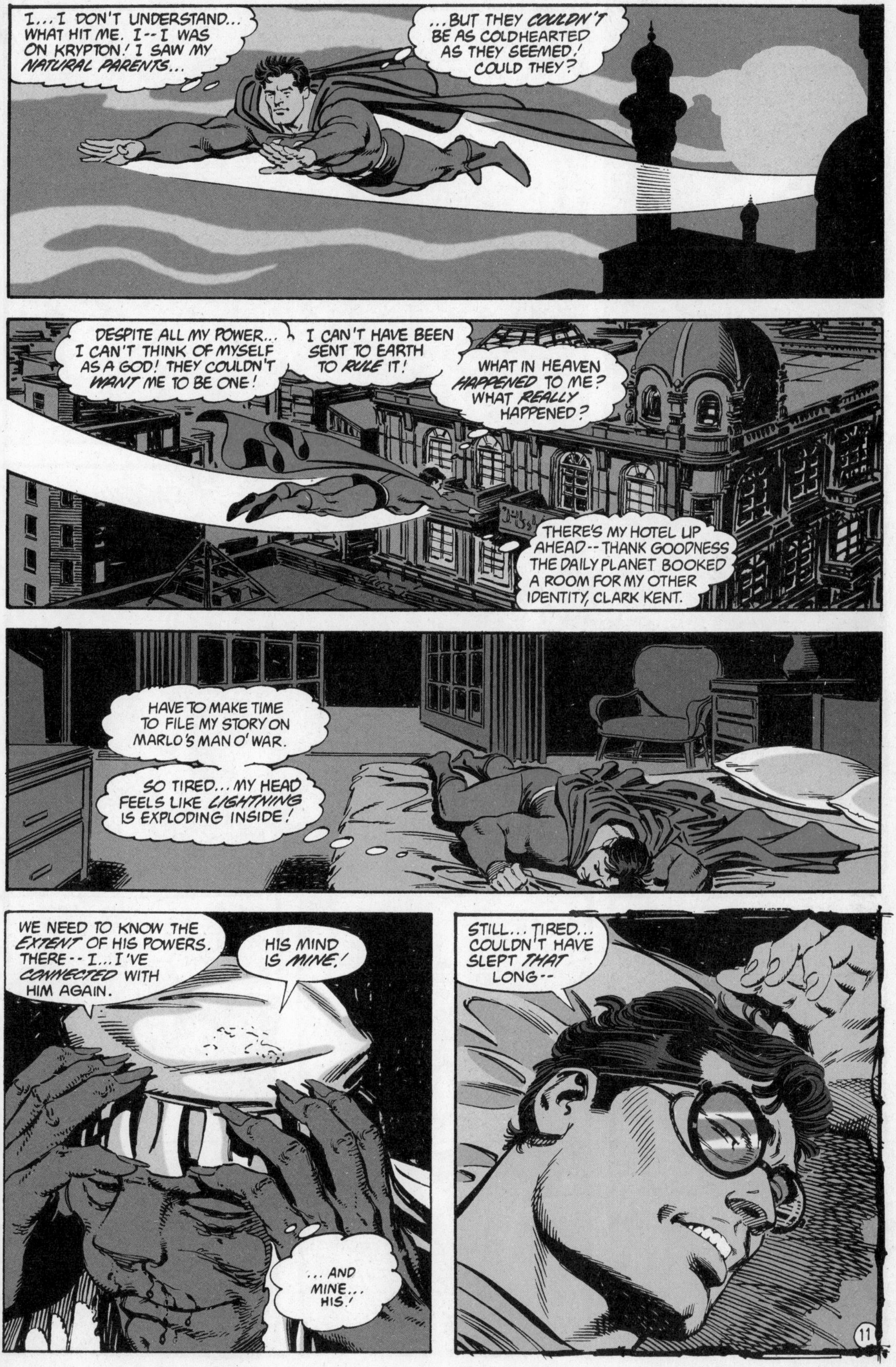
I... I DON'T UNDERSTAND... WHAT HIT ME. I-- I WAS ON KRYPTON! I SAW MY NATURAL PARENTS...
...BUT THEY COULDN'T BE AS COLDHEARTED AS THEY SEEMED! COULD THEY?
DESPITE ALL MY POWER... I CAN'T THINK OF MYSELF AS A GOD! THEY COULDN'T WANT ME TO BE ONE!
I CAN'T HAVE BEEN SENT TO EARTH TO RULE IT!
WHAT IN HEAVEN HAPPENED TO ME? WHAT REALLY HAPPENED?
THERE'S MY HOTEL UP AHEAD -- THANK GOODNESS THE DAILY PLANET BOOKED A ROOM FOR MY OTHER IDENTITY, CLARK KENT.
HAVE TO MAKE TIME TO FILE MY STORY ON MARLO'S MAN O' WAR.
SO TIRED... MY HEAD FEELS LIKE LIGHTNING IS EXPLODING INSIDE!
WE NEED TO KNOW THE EXTENT OF HIS POWERS. THERE -- I... I'VE CONNECTED WITH HIM AGAIN.
HIS MIND IS MINE!
...AND MINE... HIS!
STILL... TIRED... COULDN'T HAVE SLEPT THAT LONG --
11

SUPERMAN...

WE'RE HERE FOR YOU!

UHNNH?

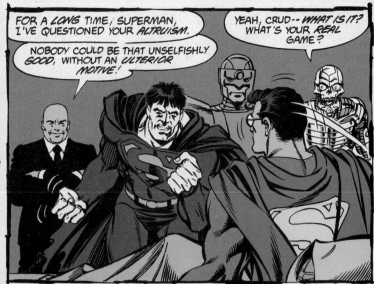

FOR A *LONG* TIME, SUPERMAN, I'VE QUESTIONED YOUR *ALTRUISM.*

NOBODY COULD BE THAT UNSELFISHLY *GOOD,* WITHOUT AN *ULTERIOR MOTIVE!*

YEAH, CRUD-- *WHAT IS IT?* WHAT'S YOUR *REAL* GAME?

RAGGHHHHHHH!!

WE WANT *ANSWERS,* SUPERMAN! AND SYNAPSE IS PREPARED TO GET THEM!

WHAT ARE YOU *REALLY* UP TO, SUPERMAN? YOU'RE SETTING EVERYONE UP, AREN'T YOU? MAKING THEM *DEPENDENT* ON YOU!

THEN YOU INTEND TO *TAKE OVER,* DON'T YOU?

ADMIT IT, SUPERMAN, YOU'RE JUST LIKE US-- YOU WANT TO *CONTROL* THE FOOLS OUT THERE!

ADMIT IT!

I'LL *BURN* THE TRUTH OUT OF YOU, SUPERMAN. *ADMIT* IT!

N-NO...*NO!* I...I DON'T WANT ANYTHING...ANYTHING BUT TO *HELP.*

THAT'S ALL I'M DOING!

12

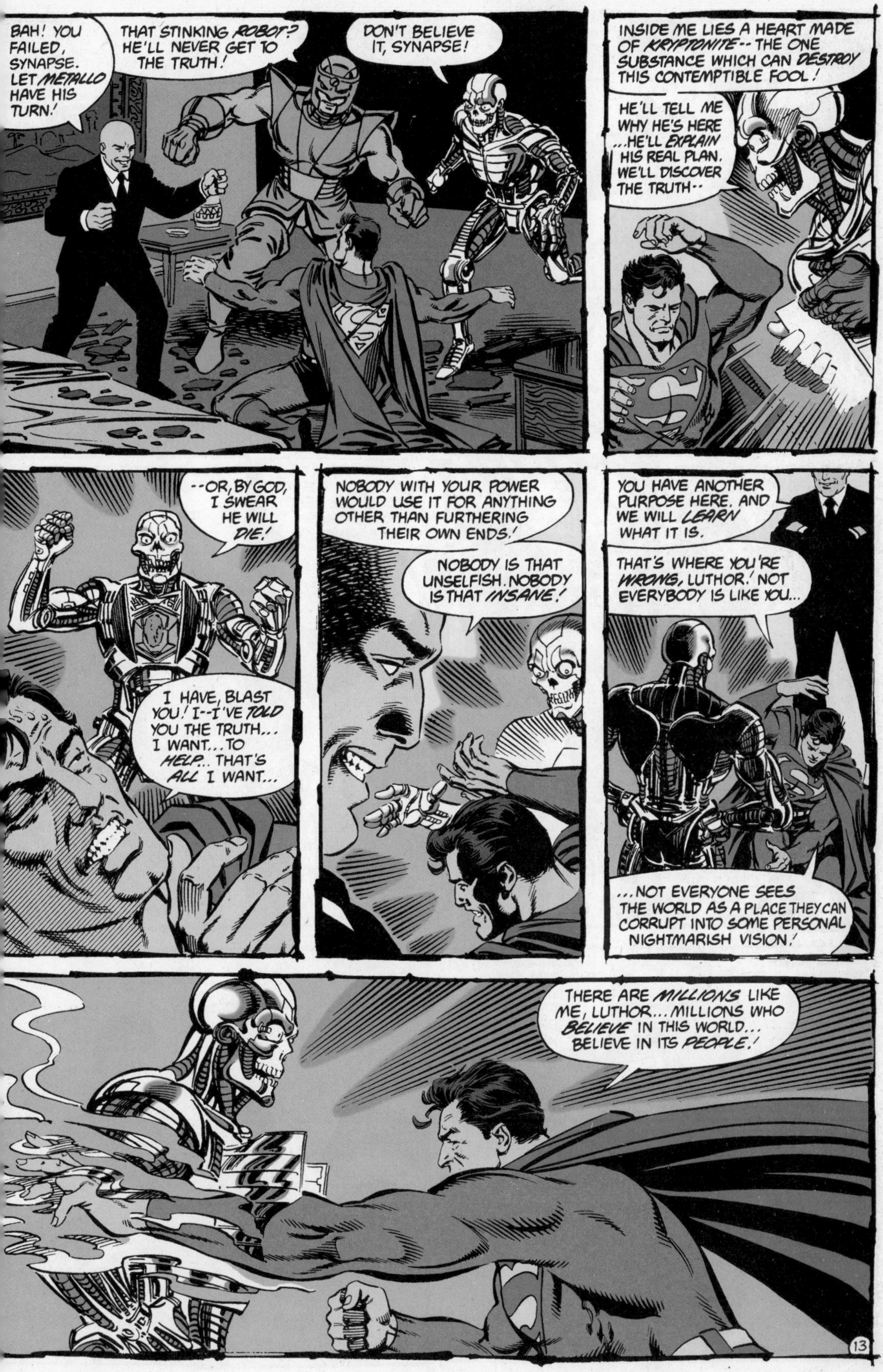
BAH! YOU FAILED, SYNAPSE. LET METALLO HAVE HIS TURN!
THAT STINKING ROBOT? HE'LL NEVER GET TO THE TRUTH!
DON'T BELIEVE IT, SYNAPSE!
INSIDE ME LIES A HEART MADE OF KRYPTONITE-- THE ONE SUBSTANCE WHICH CAN DESTROY THIS CONTEMPTIBLE FOOL!
HE'LL TELL ME WHY HE'S HERE ...HE'LL EXPLAIN HIS REAL PLAN. WE'LL DISCOVER THE TRUTH--
--OR, BY GOD, I SWEAR HE WILL DIE!
I HAVE, BLAST YOU! I--I'VE TOLD YOU THE TRUTH... I WANT... TO HELP.. THAT'S ALL I WANT...
NOBODY WITH YOUR POWER WOULD USE IT FOR ANYTHING OTHER THAN FURTHERING THEIR OWN ENDS!
NOBODY IS THAT UNSELFISH. NOBODY IS THAT INSANE!
YOU HAVE ANOTHER PURPOSE HERE. AND WE WILL LEARN WHAT IT IS.
THAT'S WHERE YOU'RE WRONG, LUTHOR! NOT EVERYBODY IS LIKE YOU...
...NOT EVERYONE SEES THE WORLD AS A PLACE THEY CAN CORRUPT INTO SOME PERSONAL NIGHTMARISH VISION!
THERE ARE MILLIONS LIKE ME, LUTHOR... MILLIONS WHO BELIEVE IN THIS WORLD... BELIEVE IN ITS PEOPLE!
13

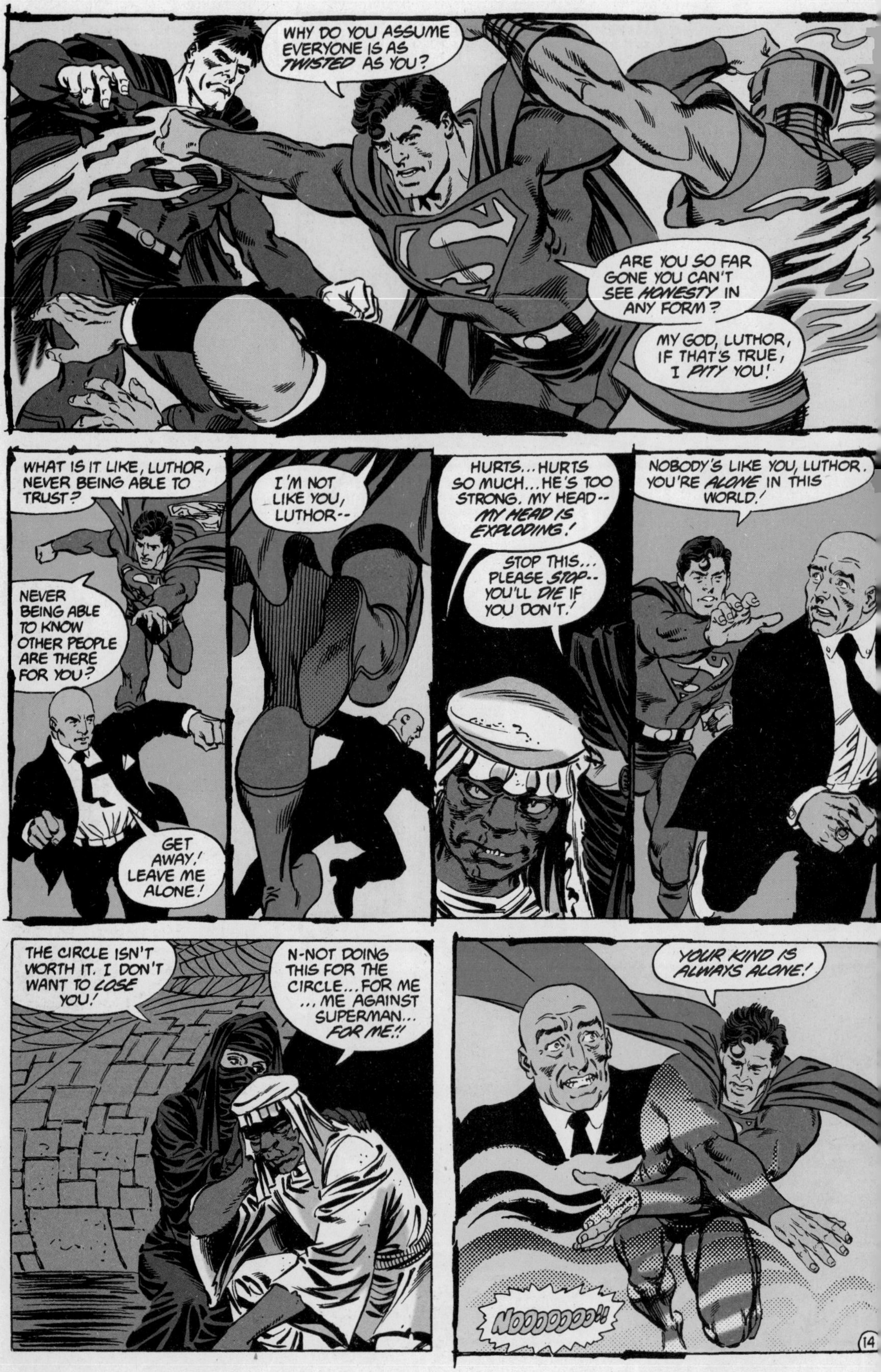
WHY DO YOU ASSUME EVERYONE IS AS *TWISTED* AS YOU?
ARE YOU SO FAR GONE YOU CAN'T SEE *HONESTY* IN ANY FORM?
MY GOD, LUTHOR, IF THAT'S TRUE, I *PITY* YOU!
WHAT IS IT LIKE, LUTHOR, NEVER BEING ABLE TO TRUST?
NEVER BEING ABLE TO KNOW OTHER PEOPLE ARE THERE FOR YOU?
GET AWAY! LEAVE ME ALONE!
I'M NOT LIKE YOU, LUTHOR--
HURTS... HURTS SO MUCH... HE'S TOO STRONG. MY HEAD-- *MY HEAD IS EXPLODING!*
STOP THIS... PLEASE *STOP*-- YOU'LL *DIE* IF YOU DON'T!
NOBODY'S LIKE YOU, LUTHOR. YOU'RE *ALONE* IN THIS WORLD!
THE CIRCLE ISN'T WORTH IT. I DON'T WANT TO *LOSE* YOU!
N-NOT DOING THIS FOR THE CIRCLE... FOR ME ...ME AGAINST SUPERMAN... *FOR ME!!*
YOUR KIND IS ALWAYS ALONE!
NOOOOOOO!!
14

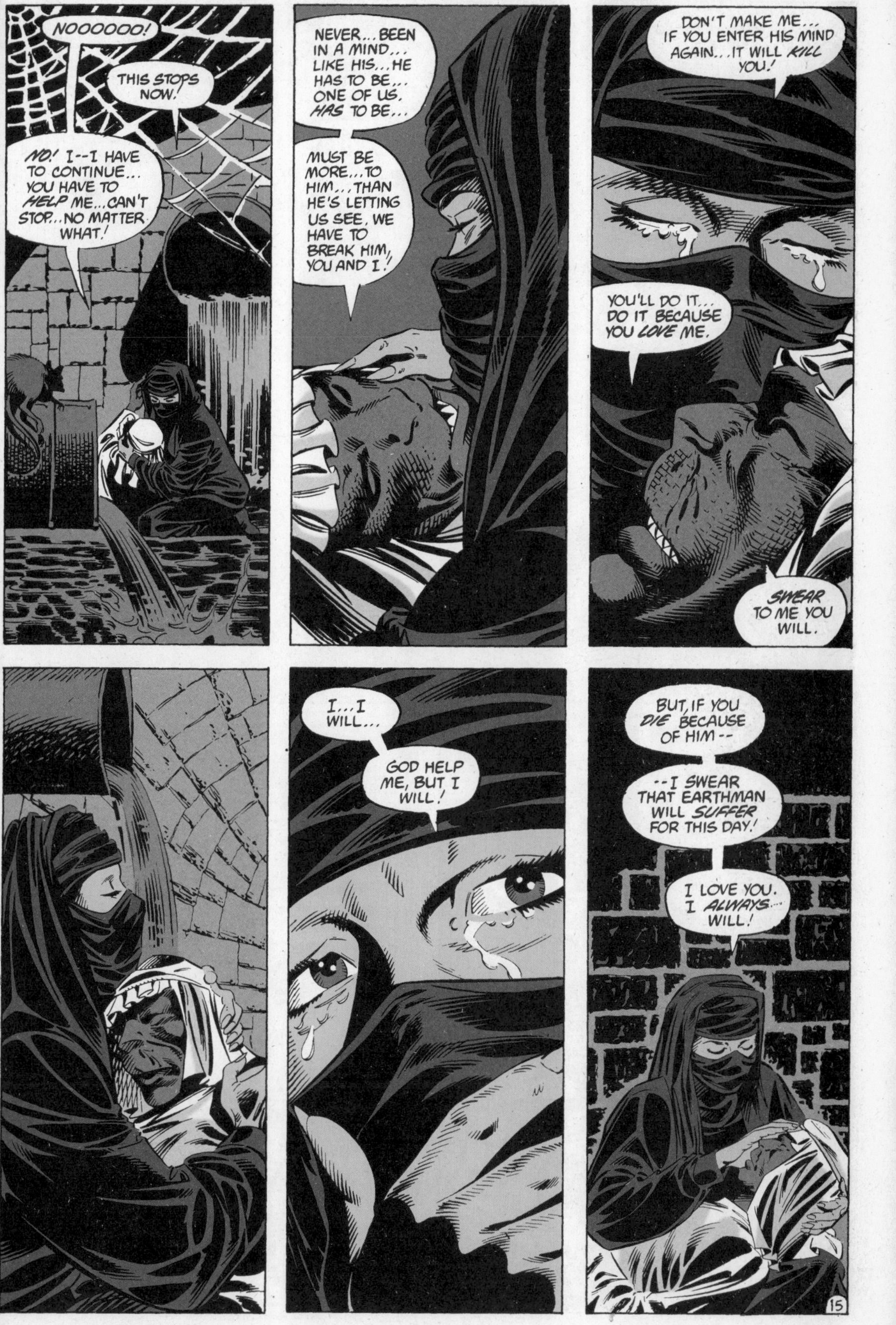
NOOOOOO!
THIS STOPS NOW.
NO! I--I HAVE TO CONTINUE... YOU HAVE TO HELP ME...CAN'T STOP...NO MATTER WHAT!
NEVER...BEEN IN A MIND... LIKE HIS...HE HAS TO BE... ONE OF US. HAS TO BE...
MUST BE MORE...TO HIM...THAN HE'S LETTING US SEE, WE HAVE TO BREAK HIM, YOU AND I.!
DON'T MAKE ME... IF YOU ENTER HIS MIND AGAIN...IT WILL KILL YOU.!
YOU'LL DO IT... DO IT BECAUSE YOU LOVE ME.
SWEAR TO ME YOU WILL.
I...I WILL...
GOD HELP ME, BUT I WILL!
BUT, IF YOU DIE BECAUSE OF HIM--
--I SWEAR THAT EARTHMAN WILL SUFFER FOR THIS DAY!
I LOVE YOU. I ALWAYS... WILL!
15

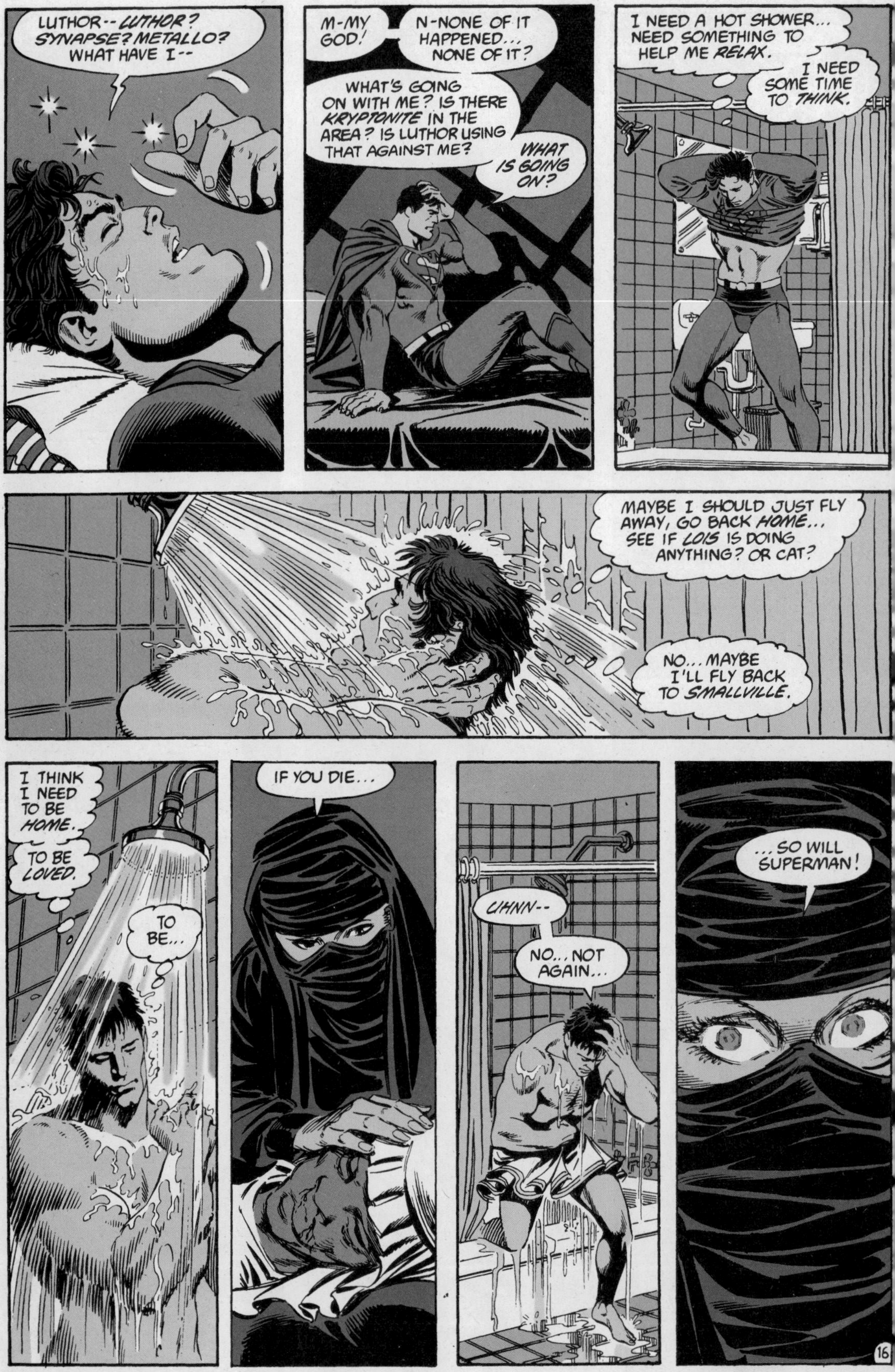
LUTHOR -- LUTHOR? SYNAPSE? METALLO? WHAT HAVE I --
M-MY GOD!
N-NONE OF IT HAPPENED... NONE OF IT?
WHAT'S GOING ON WITH ME? IS THERE KRYPTONITE IN THE AREA? IS LUTHOR USING THAT AGAINST ME?
WHAT IS GOING ON?
I NEED A HOT SHOWER... NEED SOMETHING TO HELP ME RELAX.
I NEED SOME TIME TO THINK.
MAYBE I SHOULD JUST FLY AWAY, GO BACK HOME... SEE IF LOIS IS DOING ANYTHING? OR CAT?
NO... MAYBE I'LL FLY BACK TO SMALLVILLE.
I THINK I NEED TO BE HOME.
TO BE LOVED.
TO BE...
IF YOU DIE...
UHNN--
NO... NOT AGAIN...
...SO WILL SUPERMAN!
16

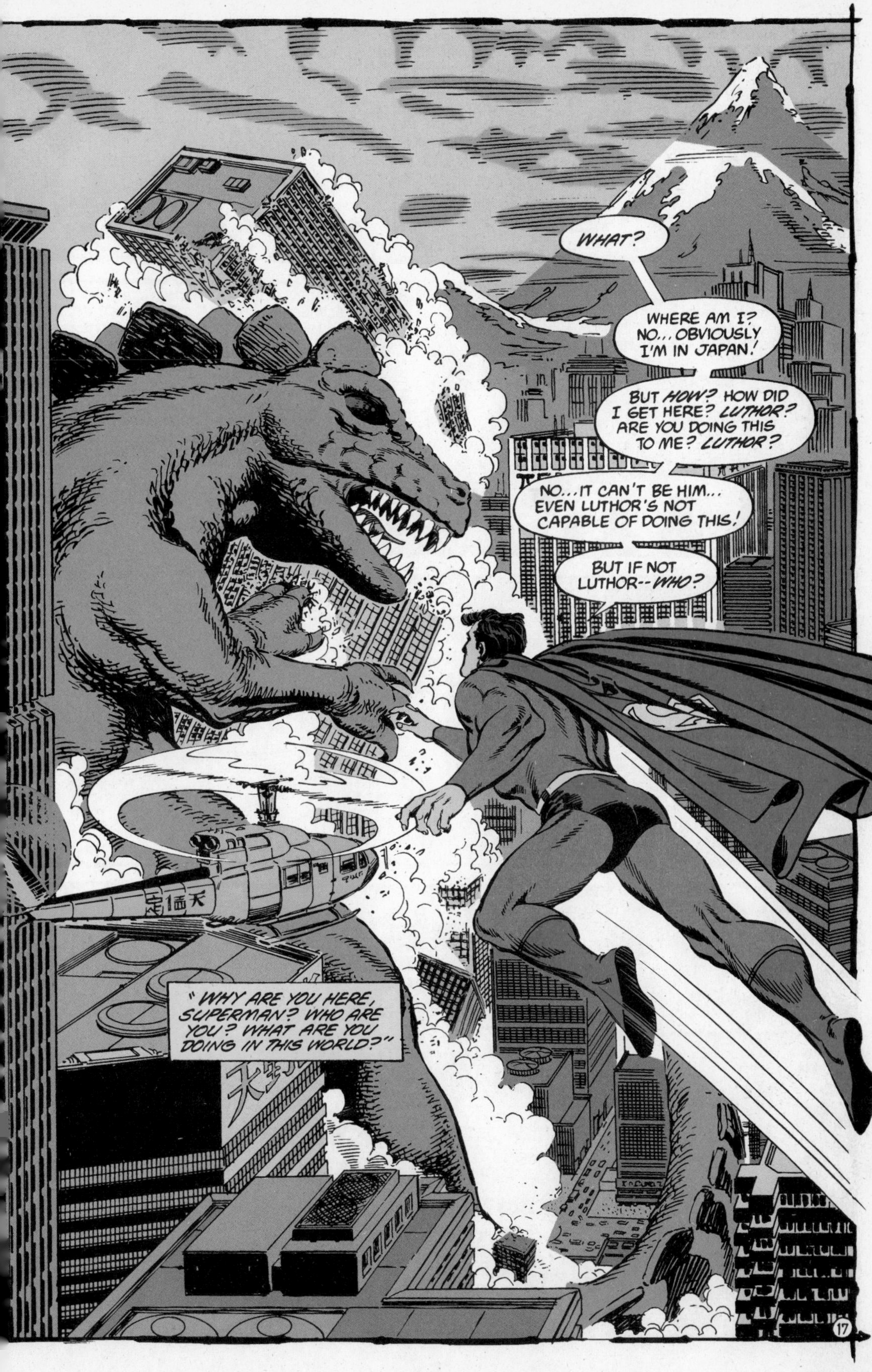
WHAT?
WHERE AM I? NO... OBVIOUSLY I'M IN JAPAN!
BUT HOW? HOW DID I GET HERE? LUTHOR? ARE YOU DOING THIS TO ME? LUTHOR?
NO... IT CAN'T BE HIM... EVEN LUTHOR'S NOT CAPABLE OF DOING THIS!
BUT IF NOT LUTHOR--WHO?
"WHY ARE YOU HERE, SUPERMAN? WHO ARE YOU? WHAT ARE YOU DOING IN THIS WORLD?"
17

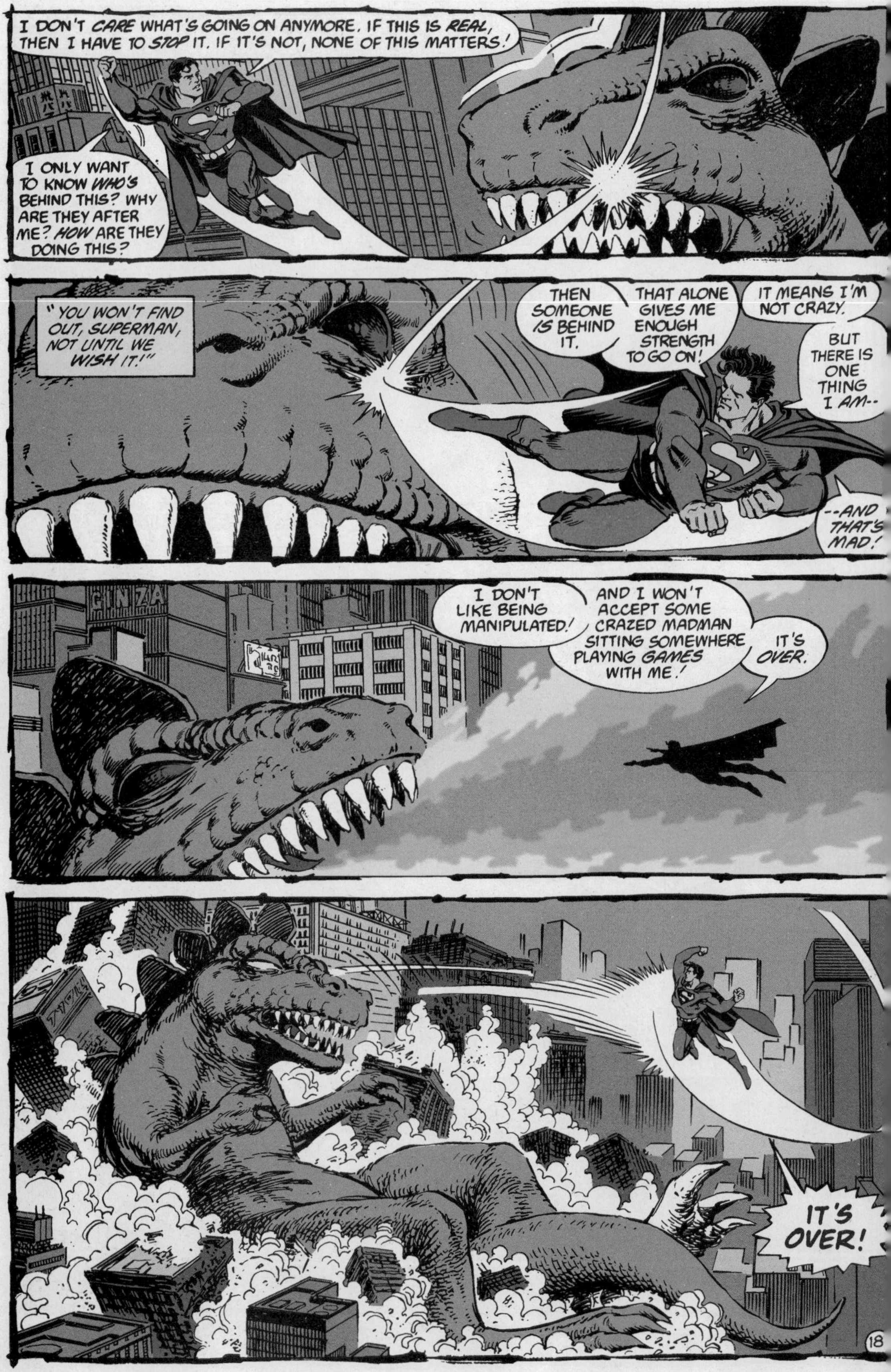

I DON'T CARE WHAT'S GOING ON ANYMORE. IF THIS IS REAL, THEN I HAVE TO STOP IT. IF IT'S NOT, NONE OF THIS MATTERS!
I ONLY WANT TO KNOW WHO'S BEHIND THIS? WHY ARE THEY AFTER ME? HOW ARE THEY DOING THIS?
"YOU WON'T FIND OUT, SUPERMAN, NOT UNTIL WE WISH IT!"
THEN SOMEONE IS BEHIND IT.
THAT ALONE GIVES ME ENOUGH STRENGTH TO GO ON!
IT MEANS I'M NOT CRAZY.
BUT THERE IS ONE THING I AM--
--AND THAT'S MAD!
GINZA
I DON'T LIKE BEING MANIPULATED!
AND I WON'T ACCEPT SOME CRAZED MADMAN SITTING SOMEWHERE PLAYING GAMES WITH ME!
IT'S OVER.
IT'S OVER!
18

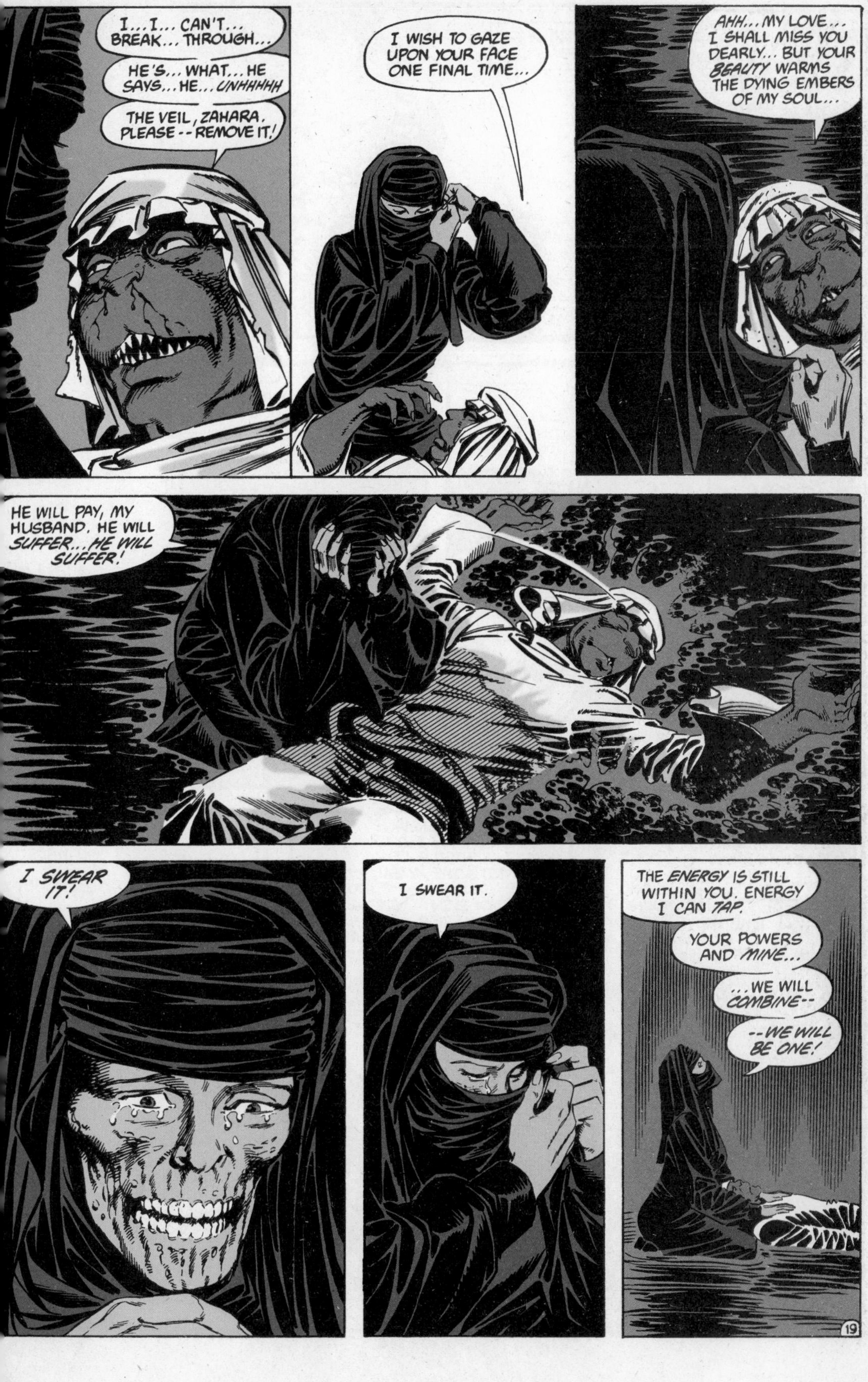

I... I... CAN'T... BREAK... THROUGH...
HE'S... WHAT... HE SAYS... HE... UNHHHHH
THE VEIL, ZAHARA. PLEASE -- REMOVE IT!
I WISH TO GAZE UPON YOUR FACE ONE FINAL TIME...
AHH... MY LOVE... I SHALL MISS YOU DEARLY... BUT YOUR BEAUTY WARMS THE DYING EMBERS OF MY SOUL...
HE WILL PAY, MY HUSBAND. HE WILL SUFFER... HE WILL SUFFER!
I SWEAR IT!
I SWEAR IT.
THE ENERGY IS STILL WITHIN YOU. ENERGY I CAN TAP.
YOUR POWERS AND MINE...
...WE WILL COMBINE--
--WE WILL BE ONE!
19

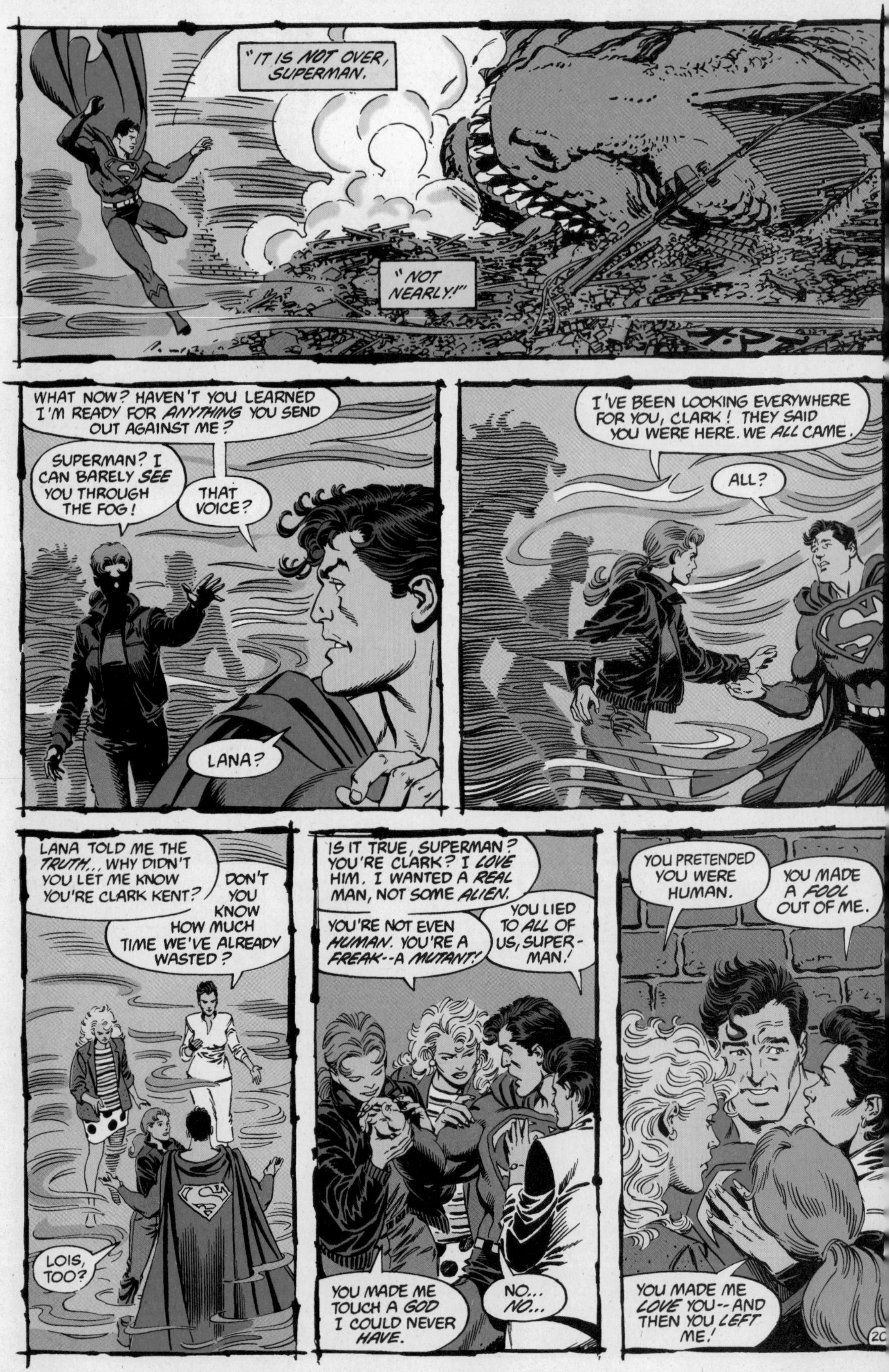

"IT IS NOT OVER, SUPERMAN.
"NOT NEARLY!"
WHAT NOW? HAVEN'T YOU LEARNED I'M READY FOR ANYTHING YOU SEND OUT AGAINST ME?
SUPERMAN? I CAN BARELY SEE YOU THROUGH THE FOG!
THAT VOICE?
LANA?
I'VE BEEN LOOKING EVERYWHERE FOR YOU, CLARK! THEY SAID YOU WERE HERE. WE ALL CAME.
ALL?
LANA TOLD ME THE TRUTH... WHY DIDN'T YOU LET ME KNOW YOU'RE CLARK KENT?
DON'T YOU KNOW HOW MUCH TIME WE'VE ALREADY WASTED?
LOIS, TOO?
IS IT TRUE, SUPERMAN? YOU'RE CLARK? I LOVE HIM. I WANTED A REAL MAN, NOT SOME ALIEN.
YOU'RE NOT EVEN HUMAN. YOU'RE A FREAK--A MUTANT!
YOU LIED TO ALL OF US, SUPER-MAN!
YOU MADE ME TOUCH A GOD I COULD NEVER HAVE.
NO... NO...
YOU PRETENDED YOU WERE HUMAN.
YOU MADE A FOOL OUT OF ME.
YOU MADE ME LOVE YOU--AND THEN YOU LEFT ME!
20

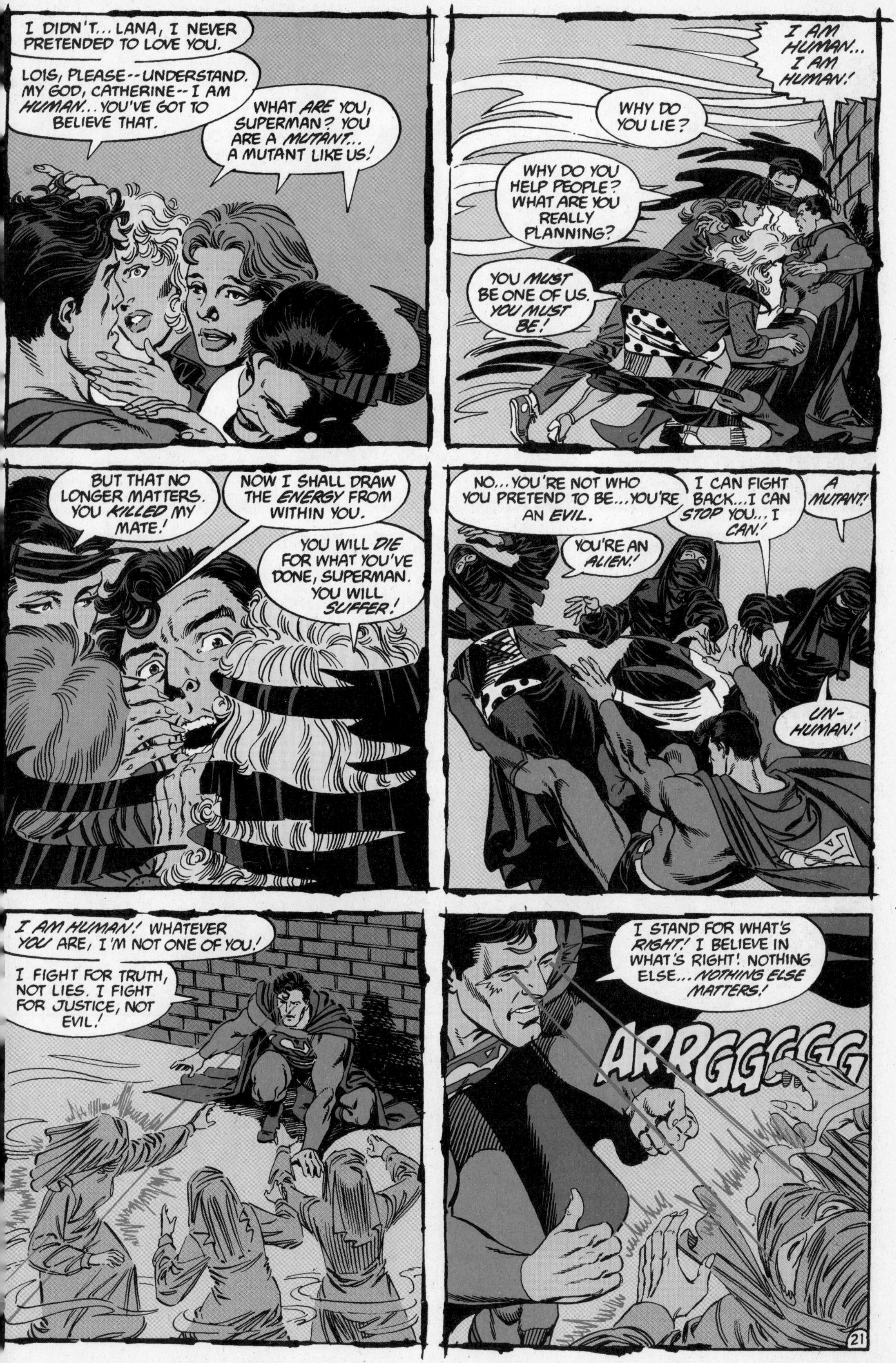

I DIDN'T... LANA, I NEVER PRETENDED TO LOVE YOU.
LOIS, PLEASE--UNDERSTAND. MY GOD, CATHERINE--I AM HUMAN... YOU'VE GOT TO BELIEVE THAT.
WHAT ARE YOU, SUPERMAN? YOU ARE A MUTANT... A MUTANT LIKE US!
I AM HUMAN... I AM HUMAN!
WHY DO YOU LIE?
WHY DO YOU HELP PEOPLE? WHAT ARE YOU REALLY PLANNING?
YOU MUST BE ONE OF US. YOU MUST BE!
BUT THAT NO LONGER MATTERS. YOU KILLED MY MATE!
NOW I SHALL DRAW THE ENERGY FROM WITHIN YOU.
YOU WILL DIE FOR WHAT YOU'VE DONE, SUPERMAN. YOU WILL SUFFER!
NO... YOU'RE NOT WHO YOU PRETEND TO BE... YOU'RE AN EVIL.
I CAN FIGHT BACK... I CAN STOP YOU... I CAN!
A MUTANT!
YOU'RE AN ALIEN!
UN-HUMAN!
I AM HUMAN! WHATEVER YOU ARE, I'M NOT ONE OF YOU!
I FIGHT FOR TRUTH, NOT LIES. I FIGHT FOR JUSTICE, NOT EVIL!
I STAND FOR WHAT'S RIGHT! I BELIEVE IN WHAT'S RIGHT! NOTHING ELSE... NOTHING ELSE MATTERS!
ARRGGGGG
21

THERE SHE IS!

PRANA'S DEAD. SHE STILL LIVES.

AND SHE *FAILED*, AND HE *FAILED*!

WITHOUT AN ANSWER-- IS SUPERMAN ONE OF US?

STILL TO BE DETERMINED!

LET'S RETURN TO THE OTHERS!

YES--WE MUST PREPARE FOR OUR DEPARTURE-- QURAC IS NO LONGER A *SAFE HAVEN* FOR US...

MARLO IS NO LONGER DEPEND- ABLE. LOOK HOW HE USED THE *MACHINES* WE SUPPLIED HIM. HE WAS *WARNED*!

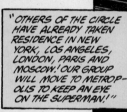

"OTHERS OF THE CIRCLE HAVE ALREADY TAKEN RESIDENCE IN NEW YORK, LOS ANGELES, LONDON, PARIS AND MOSCOW! OUR GROUP WILL MOVE TO METROP- OLIS TO KEEP AN EYE ON THE SUPERMAN!"

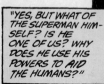

"YES, BUT WHAT OF THE SUPERMAN HIM- SELF? IS HE ONE OF US? WHY DOES HE USE HIS POWERS TO AID THE HUMANS?"

"WE WILL LEARN THE TRUTH SOON ENOUGH. IF HE IS ONE OF US, HE WILL BE FORCED TO REJOIN THE CIRCLE. AND IF HE ISN'T..."

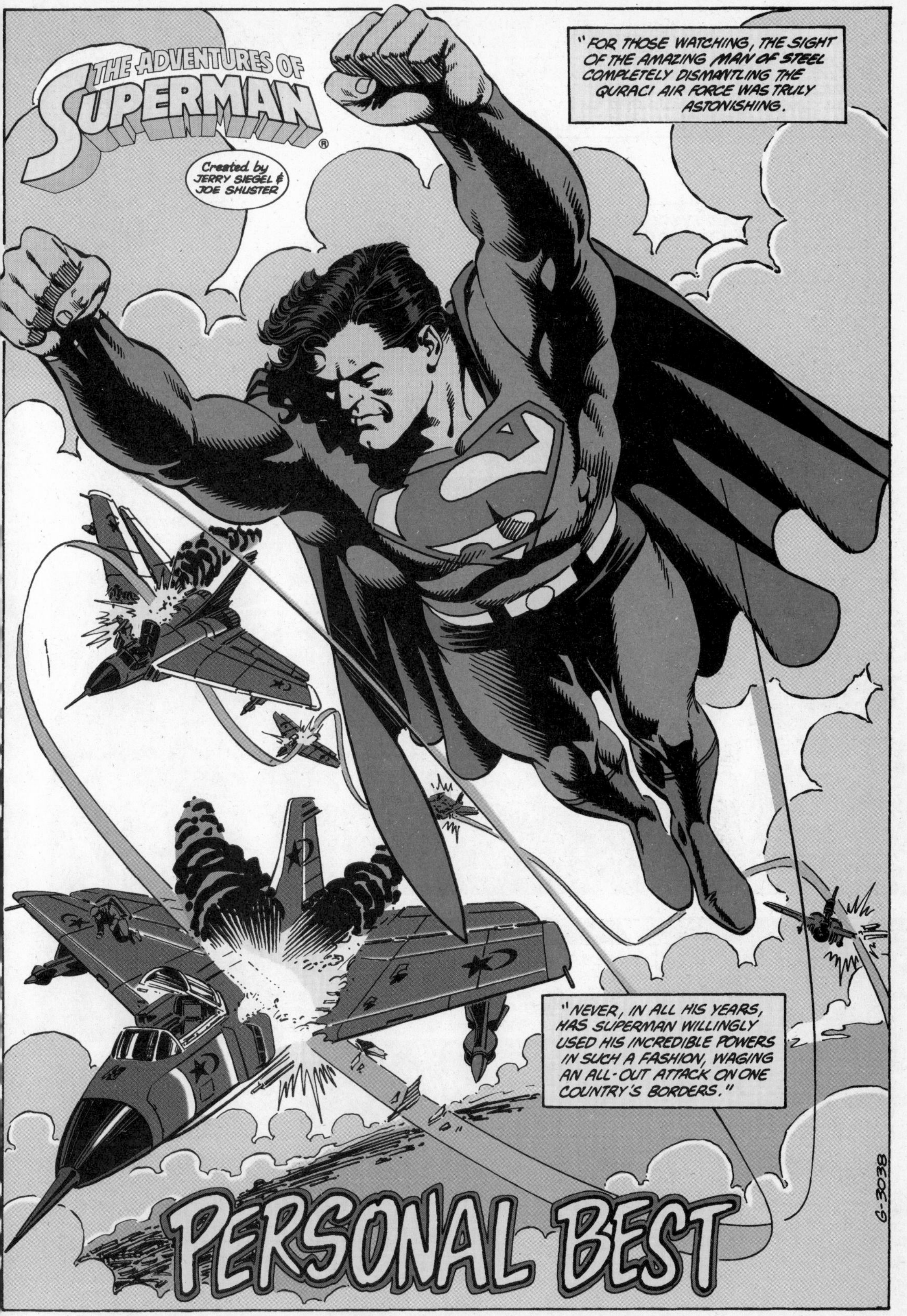
THE ADVENTURES OF SUPERMAN
Created by JERRY SIEGEL & JOE SHUSTER
"FOR THOSE WATCHING, THE SIGHT OF THE AMAZING MAN OF STEEL COMPLETELY DISMANTLING THE QURACI AIR FORCE WAS TRULY ASTONISHING.
"NEVER, IN ALL HIS YEARS, HAS SUPERMAN WILLINGLY USED HIS INCREDIBLE POWERS IN SUCH A FASHION, WAGING AN ALL-OUT ATTACK ON ONE COUNTRY'S BORDERS."
G-3038
PERSONAL BEST

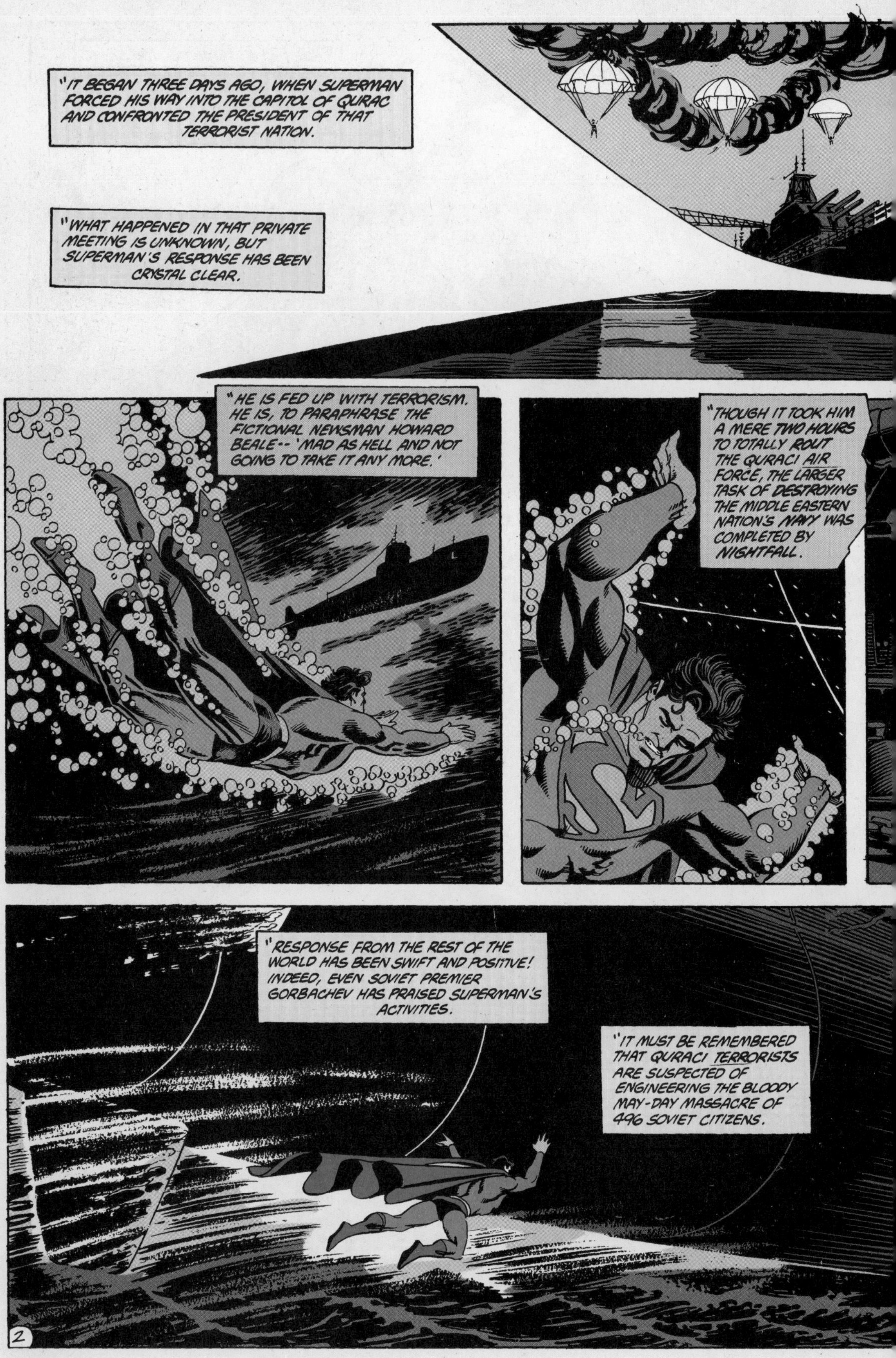
"IT BEGAN THREE DAYS AGO, WHEN SUPERMAN FORCED HIS WAY INTO THE CAPITOL OF QURAC AND CONFRONTED THE PRESIDENT OF THAT TERRORIST NATION.
"WHAT HAPPENED IN THAT PRIVATE MEETING IS UNKNOWN, BUT SUPERMAN'S RESPONSE HAS BEEN CRYSTAL CLEAR.
"HE IS FED UP WITH TERRORISM. HE IS, TO PARAPHRASE THE FICTIONAL NEWSMAN HOWARD BEALE-- 'MAD AS HELL AND NOT GOING TO TAKE IT ANY MORE.'
"THOUGH IT TOOK HIM A MERE TWO HOURS TO TOTALLY ROUT THE QURACI AIR FORCE, THE LARGER TASK OF DESTROYING THE MIDDLE EASTERN NATION'S NAVY WAS COMPLETED BY NIGHTFALL.
"RESPONSE FROM THE REST OF THE WORLD HAS BEEN SWIFT AND POSITIVE! INDEED, EVEN SOVIET PREMIER GORBACHEV HAS PRAISED SUPERMAN'S ACTIVITIES.
"IT MUST BE REMEMBERED THAT QURACI TERRORISTS ARE SUSPECTED OF ENGINEERING THE BLOODY MAY-DAY MASSACRE OF 496 SOVIET CITIZENS.
2

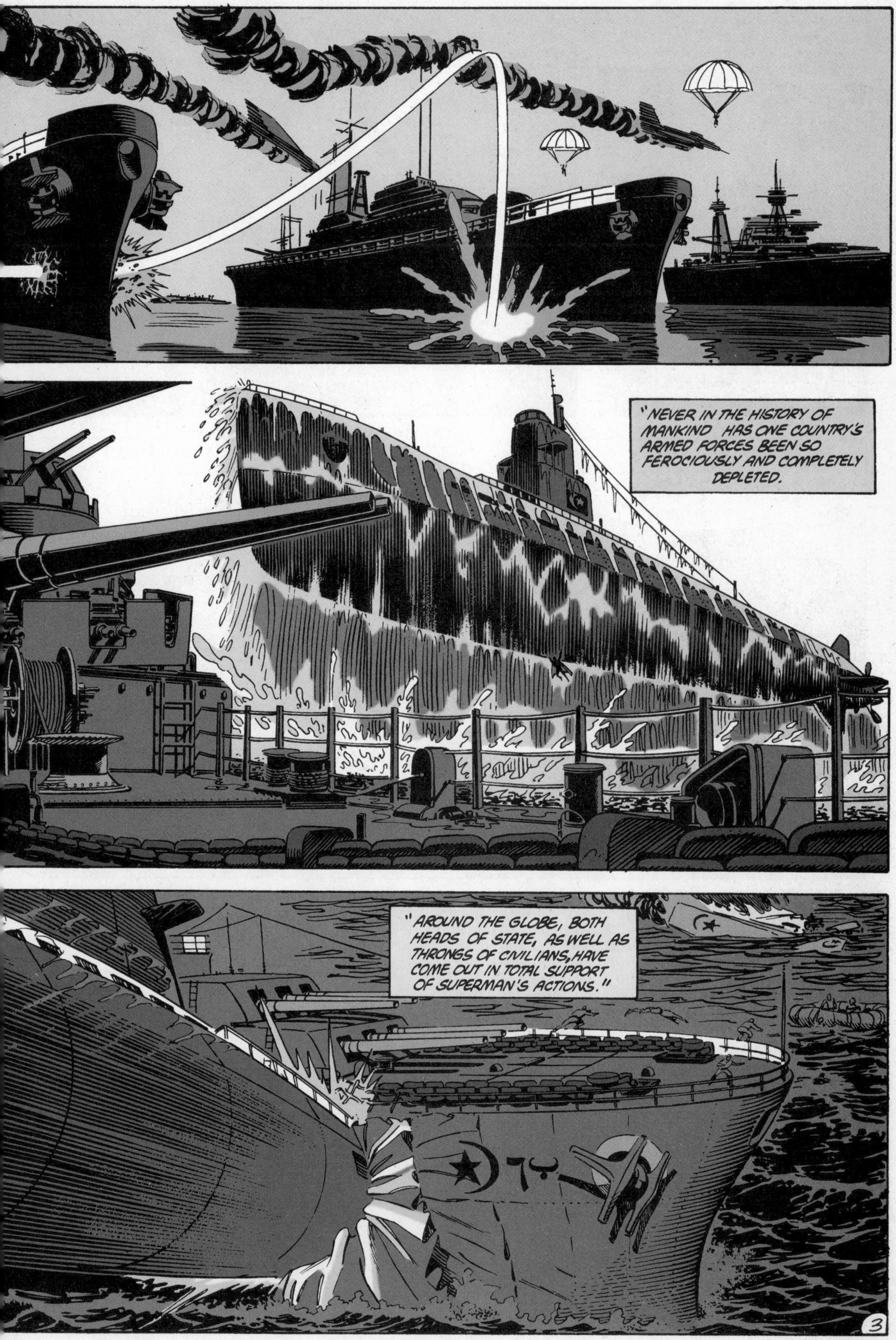
"NEVER IN THE HISTORY OF MANKIND HAS ONE COUNTRY'S ARMED FORCES BEEN SO FEROCIOUSLY AND COMPLETELY DEPLETED.
"AROUND THE GLOBE, BOTH HEADS OF STATE, AS WELL AS THRONGS OF CIVILIANS, HAVE COME OUT IN TOTAL SUPPORT OF SUPERMAN'S ACTIONS."
3

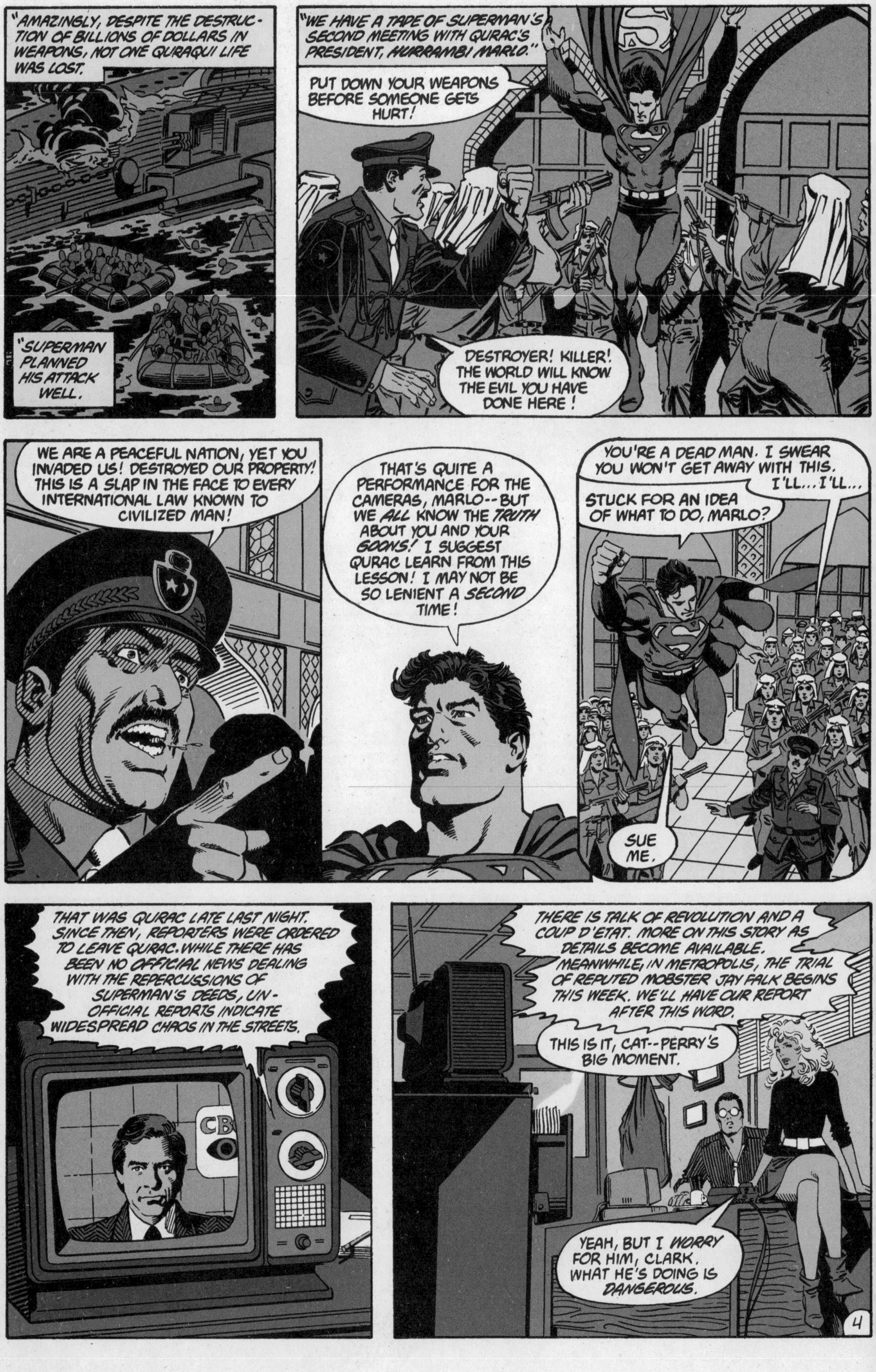
"AMAZINGLY, DESPITE THE DESTRUCTION OF BILLIONS OF DOLLARS IN WEAPONS, NOT ONE QURAQUI LIFE WAS LOST.
"SUPERMAN PLANNED HIS ATTACK WELL.
"WE HAVE A TAPE OF SUPERMAN'S SECOND MEETING WITH QURAC'S PRESIDENT, HURRAMBI MARLO."
PUT DOWN YOUR WEAPONS BEFORE SOMEONE GETS HURT!
DESTROYER! KILLER! THE WORLD WILL KNOW THE EVIL YOU HAVE DONE HERE!
WE ARE A PEACEFUL NATION, YET YOU INVADED US! DESTROYED OUR PROPERTY! THIS IS A SLAP IN THE FACE TO EVERY INTERNATIONAL LAW KNOWN TO CIVILIZED MAN!
THAT'S QUITE A PERFORMANCE FOR THE CAMERAS, MARLO--BUT WE ALL KNOW THE TRUTH ABOUT YOU AND YOUR GOONS! I SUGGEST QURAC LEARN FROM THIS LESSON! I MAY NOT BE SO LENIENT A SECOND TIME!
YOU'RE A DEAD MAN. I SWEAR YOU WON'T GET AWAY WITH THIS. I'LL... I'LL...
STUCK FOR AN IDEA OF WHAT TO DO, MARLO?
SUE ME.
THAT WAS QURAC LATE LAST NIGHT. SINCE THEN, REPORTERS WERE ORDERED TO LEAVE QURAC. WHILE THERE HAS BEEN NO OFFICIAL NEWS DEALING WITH THE REPERCUSSIONS OF SUPERMAN'S DEEDS, UNOFFICIAL REPORTS INDICATE WIDESPREAD CHAOS IN THE STREETS.
THERE IS TALK OF REVOLUTION AND A COUP D'ETAT. MORE ON THIS STORY AS DETAILS BECOME AVAILABLE. MEANWHILE, IN METROPOLIS, THE TRIAL OF REPUTED MOBSTER JAY FALK BEGINS THIS WEEK. WE'LL HAVE OUR REPORT AFTER THIS WORD.
THIS IS IT, CAT--PERRY'S BIG MOMENT.
YEAH, BUT I WORRY FOR HIM, CLARK. WHAT HE'S DOING IS DANGEROUS.
4

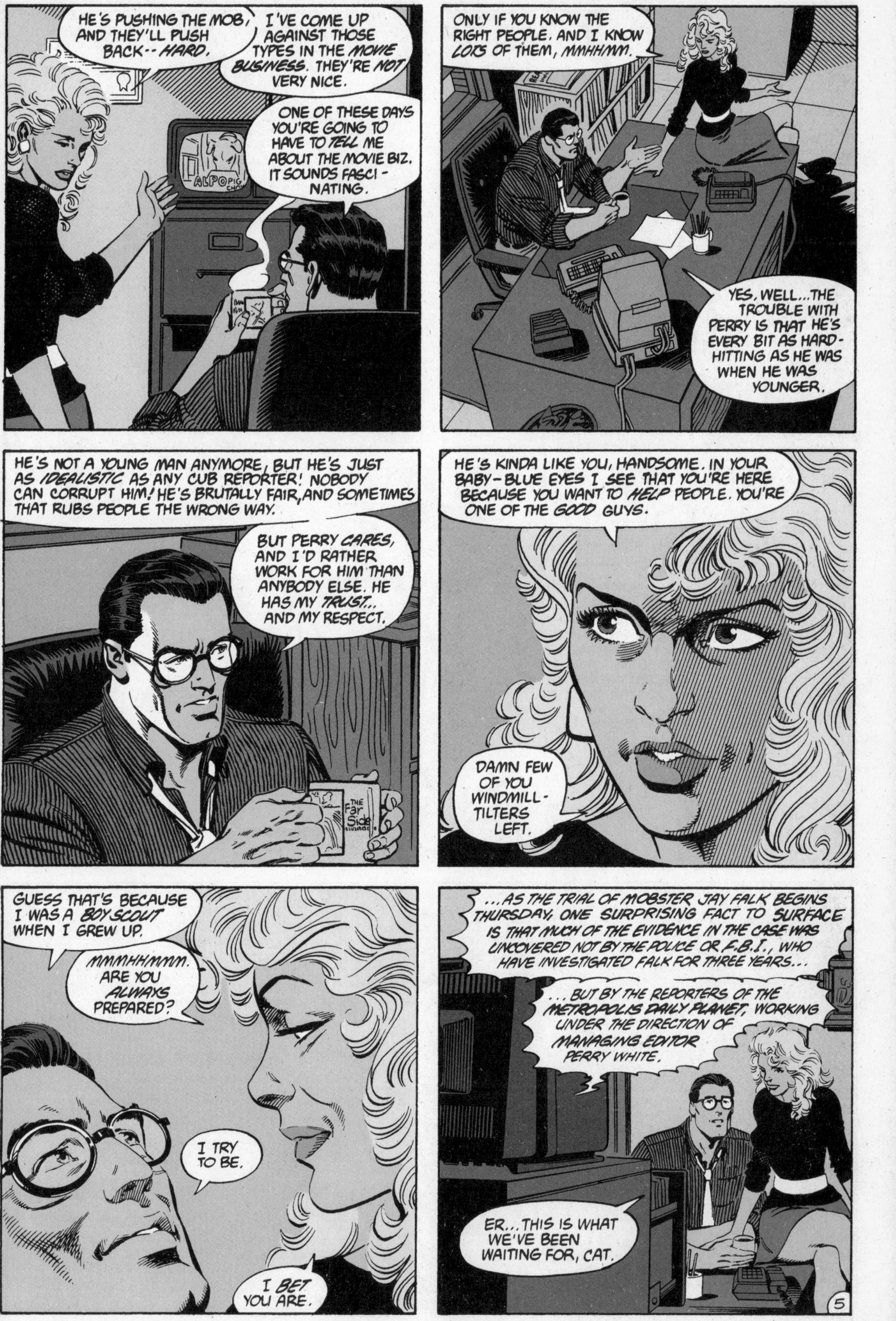
HE'S PUSHING THE MOB, AND THEY'LL PUSH BACK--HARD.
I'VE COME UP AGAINST THOSE TYPES IN THE MOVIE BUSINESS. THEY'RE NOT VERY NICE.
ONE OF THESE DAYS YOU'RE GOING TO HAVE TO TELL ME ABOUT THE MOVIE BIZ. IT SOUNDS FASCI-NATING.
ALPO
ONLY IF YOU KNOW THE RIGHT PEOPLE. AND I KNOW LOTS OF THEM, MMHHMM.
YES, WELL...THE TROUBLE WITH PERRY IS THAT HE'S EVERY BIT AS HARD-HITTING AS HE WAS WHEN HE WAS YOUNGER.
HE'S NOT A YOUNG MAN ANYMORE, BUT HE'S JUST AS IDEALISTIC AS ANY CUB REPORTER! NOBODY CAN CORRUPT HIM! HE'S BRUTALLY FAIR, AND SOMETIMES THAT RUBS PEOPLE THE WRONG WAY.
BUT PERRY CARES, AND I'D RATHER WORK FOR HIM THAN ANYBODY ELSE. HE HAS MY TRUST... AND MY RESPECT.
THE Far Side
HE'S KINDA LIKE YOU, HANDSOME. IN YOUR BABY-BLUE EYES I SEE THAT YOU'RE HERE BECAUSE YOU WANT TO HELP PEOPLE. YOU'RE ONE OF THE GOOD GUYS.
DAMN FEW OF YOU WINDMILL-TILTERS LEFT.
GUESS THAT'S BECAUSE I WAS A BOY SCOUT WHEN I GREW UP.
MMMHHMMM. ARE YOU ALWAYS PREPARED?
I TRY TO BE.
I BET YOU ARE.
...AS THE TRIAL OF MOBSTER JAY FALK BEGINS THURSDAY, ONE SURPRISING FACT TO SURFACE IS THAT MUCH OF THE EVIDENCE IN THE CASE WAS UNCOVERED NOT BY THE POLICE OR F.B.I., WHO HAVE INVESTIGATED FALK FOR THREE YEARS...
...BUT BY THE REPORTERS OF THE METROPOLIS DAILY PLANET, WORKING UNDER THE DIRECTION OF MANAGING EDITOR PERRY WHITE.
ER...THIS IS WHAT WE'VE BEEN WAITING FOR, CAT.
5

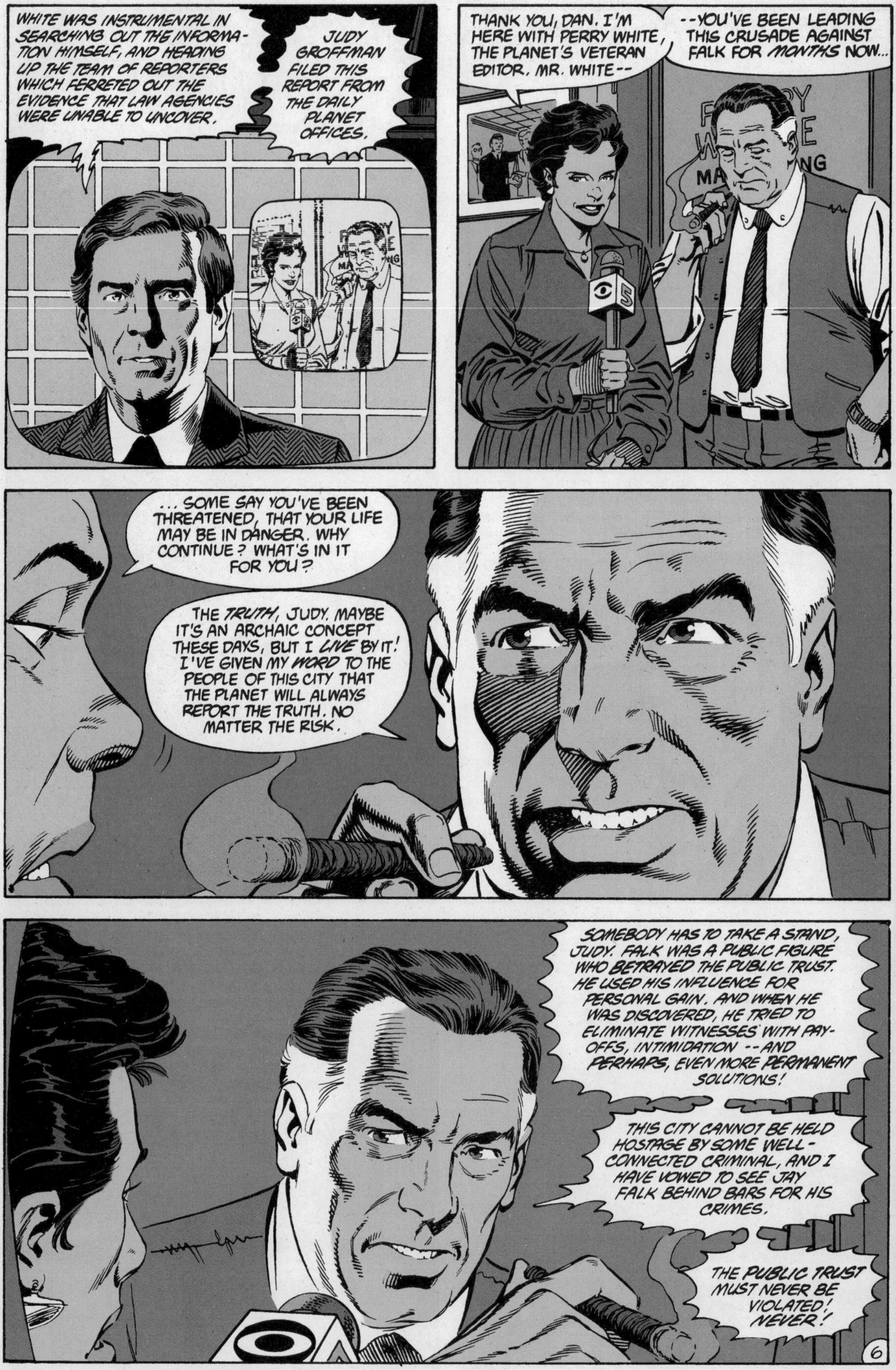
WHITE WAS INSTRUMENTAL IN SEARCHING OUT THE INFORMATION HIMSELF, AND HEADING UP THE TEAM OF REPORTERS WHICH FERRETED OUT THE EVIDENCE THAT LAW AGENCIES WERE UNABLE TO UNCOVER.
JUDY GROFFMAN FILED THIS REPORT FROM THE DAILY PLANET OFFICES.
THANK YOU, DAN. I'M HERE WITH PERRY WHITE, THE PLANET'S VETERAN EDITOR. MR. WHITE--
--YOU'VE BEEN LEADING THIS CRUSADE AGAINST FALK FOR MONTHS NOW...
... SOME SAY YOU'VE BEEN THREATENED, THAT YOUR LIFE MAY BE IN DANGER. WHY CONTINUE? WHAT'S IN IT FOR YOU?
THE TRUTH, JUDY. MAYBE IT'S AN ARCHAIC CONCEPT THESE DAYS, BUT I LIVE BY IT! I'VE GIVEN MY WORD TO THE PEOPLE OF THIS CITY THAT THE PLANET WILL ALWAYS REPORT THE TRUTH. NO MATTER THE RISK.
SOMEBODY HAS TO TAKE A STAND, JUDY. FALK WAS A PUBLIC FIGURE WHO BETRAYED THE PUBLIC TRUST. HE USED HIS INFLUENCE FOR PERSONAL GAIN. AND WHEN HE WAS DISCOVERED, HE TRIED TO ELIMINATE WITNESSES WITH PAY-OFFS, INTIMIDATION --AND PERHAPS, EVEN MORE PERMANENT SOLUTIONS!
THIS CITY CANNOT BE HELD HOSTAGE BY SOME WELL-CONNECTED CRIMINAL, AND I HAVE VOWED TO SEE JAY FALK BEHIND BARS FOR HIS CRIMES.
THE PUBLIC TRUST MUST NEVER BE VIOLATED! NEVER!
6

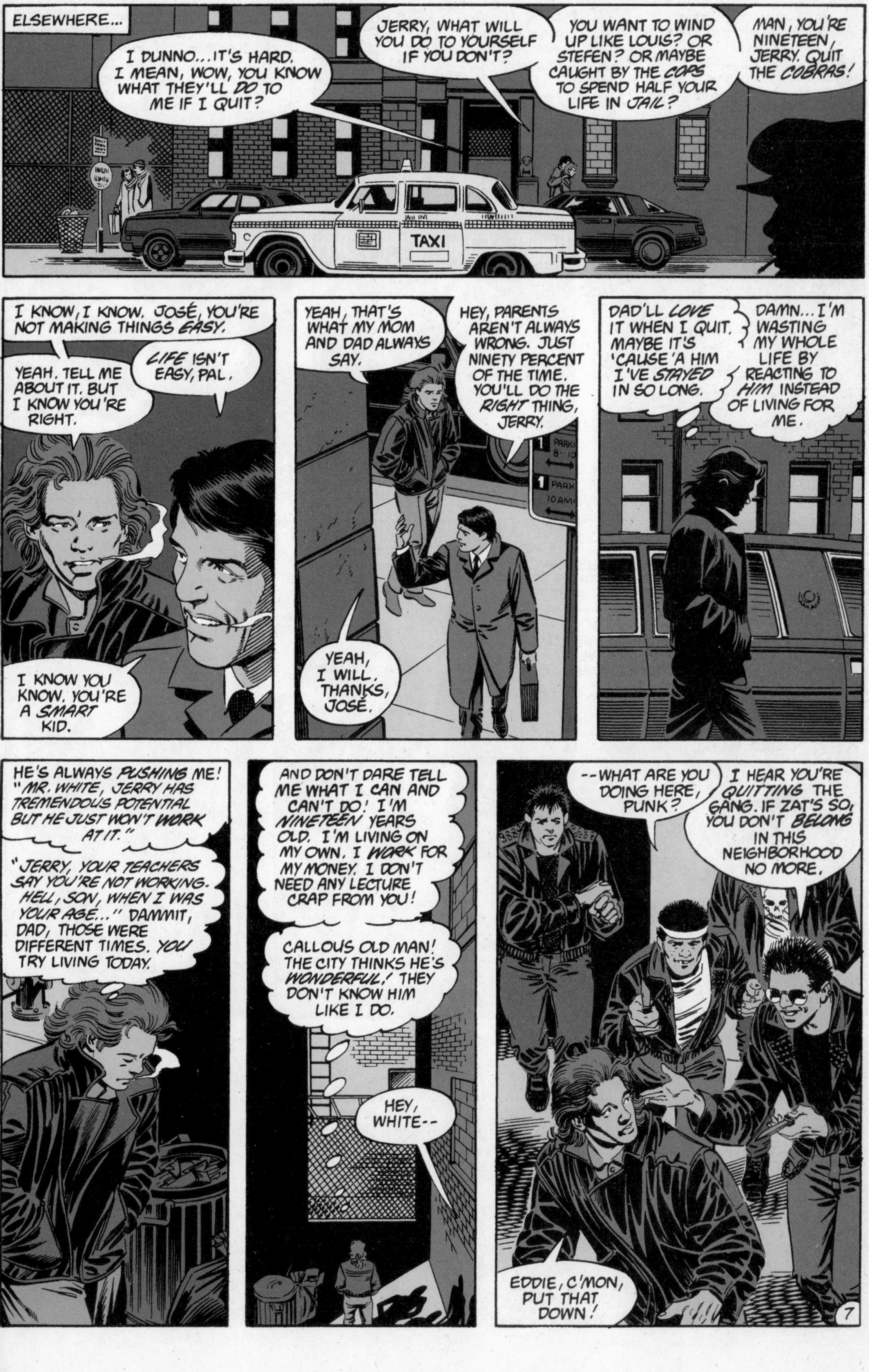
ELSEWHERE...
I DUNNO...IT'S HARD. I MEAN, WOW, YOU KNOW WHAT THEY'LL DO TO ME IF I QUIT?
JERRY, WHAT WILL YOU DO TO YOURSELF IF YOU DON'T?
YOU WANT TO WIND UP LIKE LOUIS? OR STEFEN? OR MAYBE CAUGHT BY THE COPS TO SPEND HALF YOUR LIFE IN JAIL?
MAN, YOU'RE NINETEEN, JERRY. QUIT THE COBRAS!
TAXI
I KNOW, I KNOW. JOSÉ, YOU'RE NOT MAKING THINGS EASY.
LIFE ISN'T EASY, PAL.
YEAH. TELL ME ABOUT IT. BUT I KNOW YOU'RE RIGHT.
I KNOW YOU KNOW. YOU'RE A SMART KID.
YEAH, THAT'S WHAT MY MOM AND DAD ALWAYS SAY.
HEY, PARENTS AREN'T ALWAYS WRONG. JUST NINETY PERCENT OF THE TIME. YOU'LL DO THE RIGHT THING, JERRY.
YEAH, I WILL. THANKS, JOSÉ.
DAD'LL LOVE IT WHEN I QUIT. MAYBE IT'S 'CAUSE 'A HIM I'VE STAYED IN SO LONG.
DAMN... I'M WASTING MY WHOLE LIFE BY REACTING TO HIM INSTEAD OF LIVING FOR ME.
HE'S ALWAYS PUSHING ME! "MR. WHITE, JERRY HAS TREMENDOUS POTENTIAL BUT HE JUST WON'T WORK AT IT."
"JERRY, YOUR TEACHERS SAY YOU'RE NOT WORKING. HELL, SON, WHEN I WAS YOUR AGE..." DAMMIT, DAD, THOSE WERE DIFFERENT TIMES. YOU TRY LIVING TODAY.
AND DON'T DARE TELL ME WHAT I CAN AND CAN'T DO! I'M NINETEEN YEARS OLD. I'M LIVING ON MY OWN. I WORK FOR MY MONEY. I DON'T NEED ANY LECTURE CRAP FROM YOU!
CALLOUS OLD MAN! THE CITY THINKS HE'S WONDERFUL! THEY DON'T KNOW HIM LIKE I DO.
HEY, WHITE--
--WHAT ARE YOU DOING HERE, PUNK?
I HEAR YOU'RE QUITTING THE GANG. IF ZAT'S SO, YOU DON'T BELONG IN THIS NEIGHBORHOOD NO MORE.
EDDIE, C'MON, PUT THAT DOWN!
7

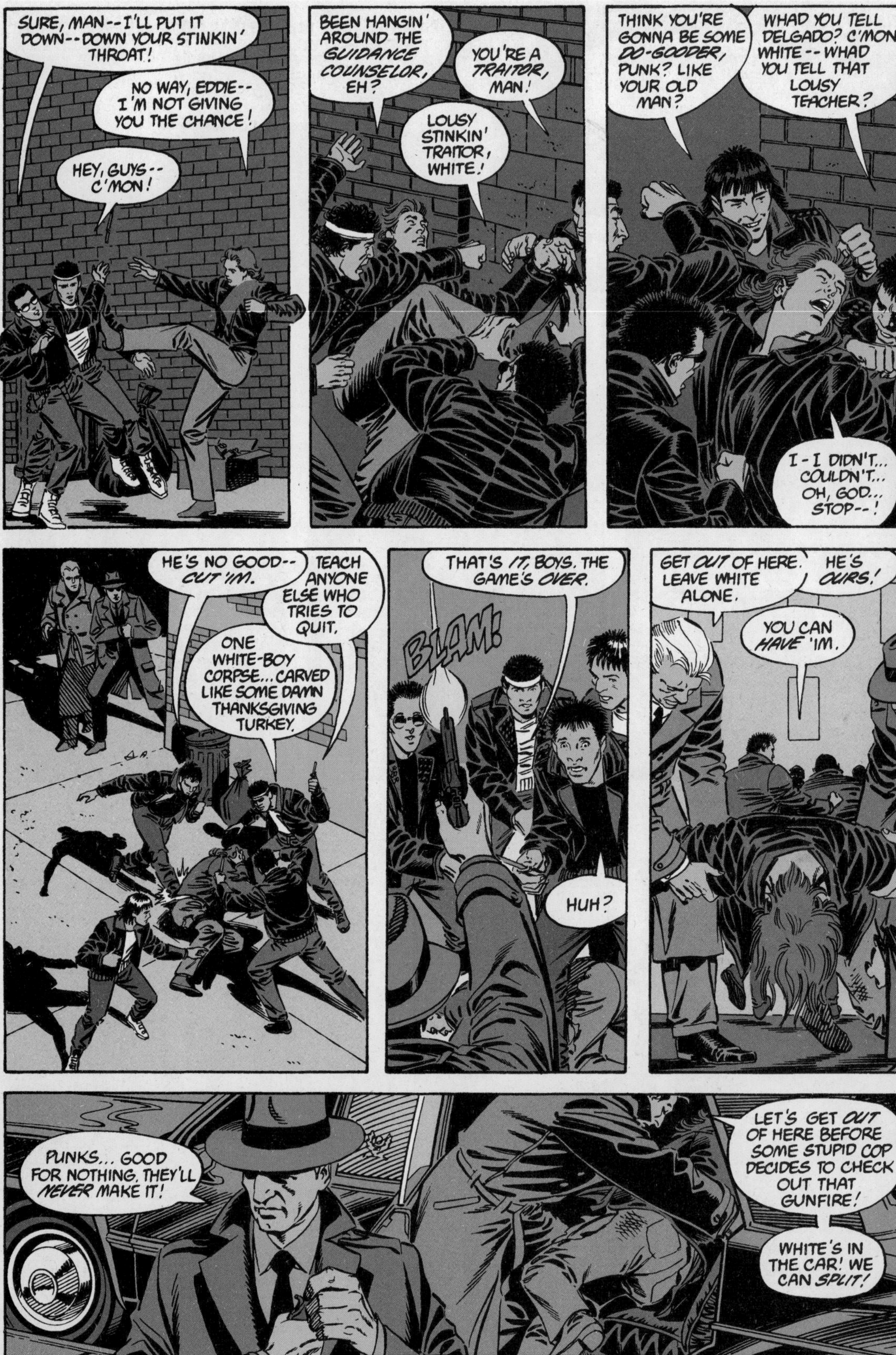
SURE, MAN--I'LL PUT IT DOWN--DOWN YOUR STINKIN' THROAT!
NO WAY, EDDIE--I'M NOT GIVING YOU THE CHANCE!
HEY, GUYS--C'MON!
BEEN HANGIN' AROUND THE GUIDANCE COUNSELOR, EH?
YOU'RE A TRAITOR, MAN!
LOUSY STINKIN' TRAITOR, WHITE!
THINK YOU'RE GONNA BE SOME DO-GOODER, PUNK? LIKE YOUR OLD MAN?
WHAD YOU TELL DELGADO? C'MON, WHITE--WHAD YOU TELL THAT LOUSY TEACHER?
I-I DIDN'T... COULDN'T... OH, GOD... STOP--!
HE'S NO GOOD--CUT 'IM.
TEACH ANYONE ELSE WHO TRIES TO QUIT.
ONE WHITE-BOY CORPSE... CARVED LIKE SOME DAMN THANKSGIVING TURKEY.
THAT'S IT, BOYS. THE GAME'S OVER.
BLAM!
HUH?
GET OUT OF HERE. LEAVE WHITE ALONE.
HE'S OURS!
YOU CAN HAVE 'IM.
PUNKS... GOOD FOR NOTHING. THEY'LL NEVER MAKE IT!
LET'S GET OUT OF HERE BEFORE SOME STUPID COP DECIDES TO CHECK OUT THAT GUNFIRE!
WHITE'S IN THE CAR! WE CAN SPLIT!
8

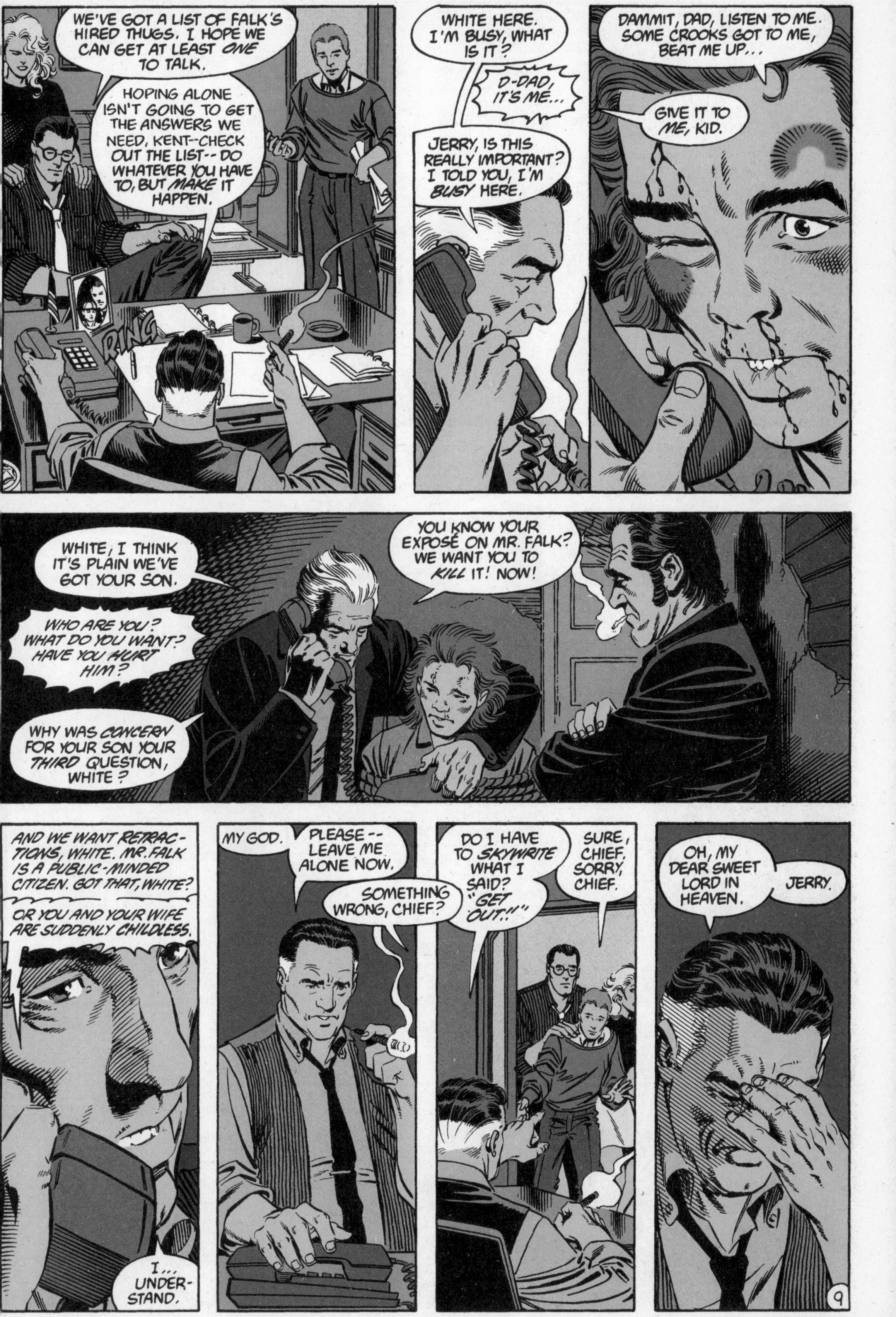
WE'VE GOT A LIST OF FALK'S HIRED THUGS. I HOPE WE CAN GET AT LEAST ONE TO TALK.
HOPING ALONE ISN'T GOING TO GET THE ANSWERS WE NEED, KENT--CHECK OUT THE LIST-- DO WHATEVER YOU HAVE TO, BUT MAKE IT HAPPEN.
RING
WHITE HERE. I'M BUSY, WHAT IS IT?
D-DAD, IT'S ME...
JERRY, IS THIS REALLY IMPORTANT? I TOLD YOU, I'M BUSY HERE.
DAMMIT, DAD, LISTEN TO ME. SOME CROOKS GOT TO ME, BEAT ME UP...
GIVE IT TO ME, KID.
WHITE, I THINK IT'S PLAIN WE'VE GOT YOUR SON.
YOU KNOW YOUR EXPOSÉ ON MR. FALK? WE WANT YOU TO KILL IT! NOW!
WHO ARE YOU? WHAT DO YOU WANT? HAVE YOU HURT HIM?
WHY WAS CONCERN FOR YOUR SON YOUR THIRD QUESTION, WHITE?
AND WE WANT RETRACTIONS, WHITE. MR. FALK IS A PUBLIC-MINDED CITIZEN. GOT THAT, WHITE?
OR YOU AND YOUR WIFE ARE SUDDENLY CHILDLESS.
I... UNDERSTAND.
MY GOD.
PLEASE-- LEAVE ME ALONE NOW.
SOMETHING WRONG, CHIEF?
DO I HAVE TO SKYWRITE WHAT I SAID? "GET OUT!!"
SURE, CHIEF. SORRY, CHIEF.
OH, MY DEAR SWEET LORD IN HEAVEN.
JERRY.
9

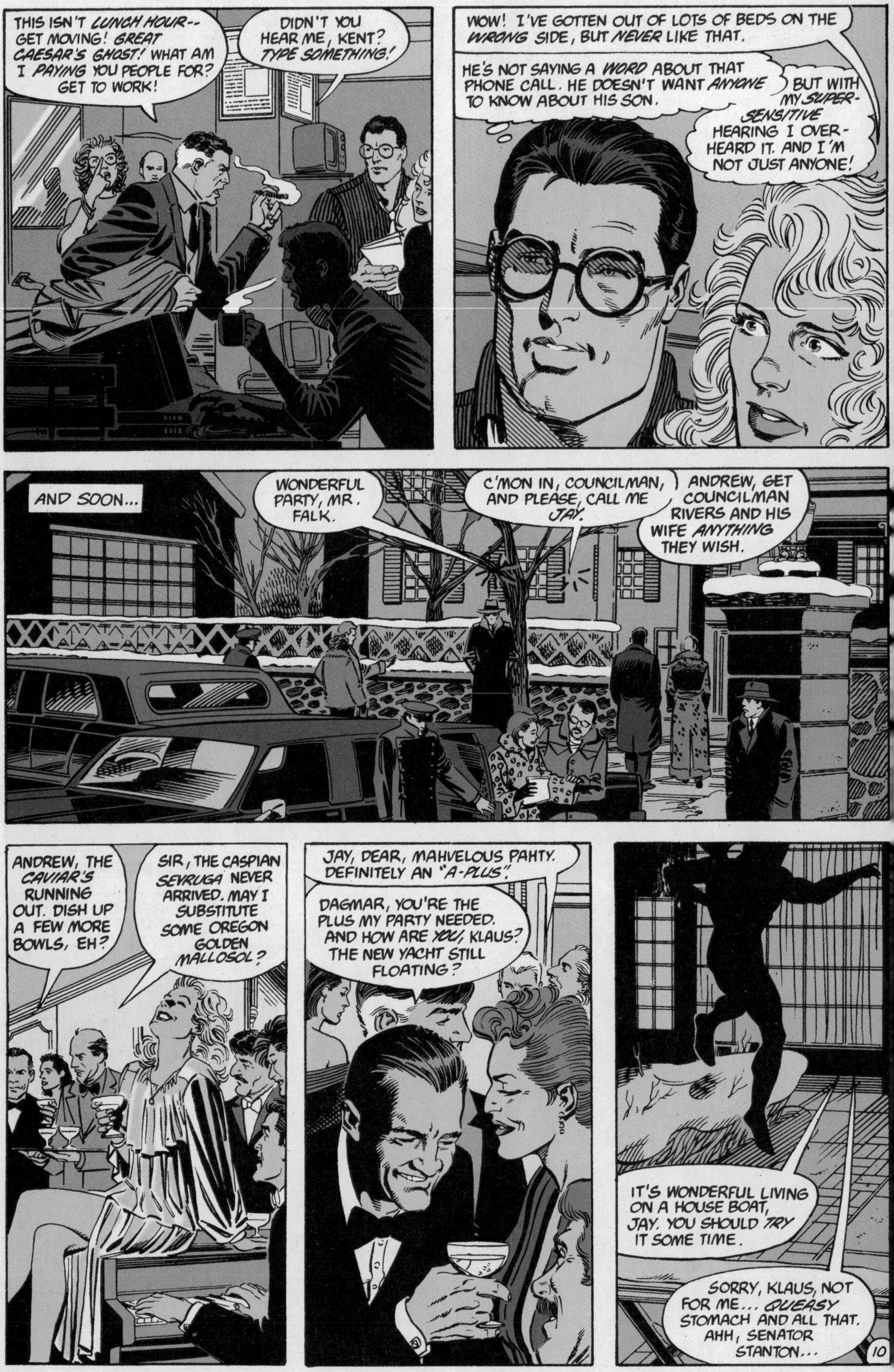

THIS ISN'T LUNCH HOUR-- GET MOVING! GREAT CAESAR'S GHOST! WHAT AM I PAYING YOU PEOPLE FOR? GET TO WORK!
DIDN'T YOU HEAR ME, KENT? TYPE SOMETHING!
WOW! I'VE GOTTEN OUT OF LOTS OF BEDS ON THE WRONG SIDE, BUT NEVER LIKE THAT.
HE'S NOT SAYING A WORD ABOUT THAT PHONE CALL. HE DOESN'T WANT ANYONE TO KNOW ABOUT HIS SON.
BUT WITH MY SUPER-SENSITIVE HEARING I OVERHEARD IT. AND I'M NOT JUST ANYONE!
AND SOON...
WONDERFUL PARTY, MR. FALK.
C'MON IN, COUNCILMAN, AND PLEASE, CALL ME JAY.
ANDREW, GET COUNCILMAN RIVERS AND HIS WIFE ANYTHING THEY WISH.
ANDREW, THE CAVIAR'S RUNNING OUT. DISH UP A FEW MORE BOWLS, EH?
SIR, THE CASPIAN SEVRUGA NEVER ARRIVED. MAY I SUBSTITUTE SOME OREGON GOLDEN MALLOSOL?
JAY, DEAR, MAHVELOUS PAHTY. DEFINITELY AN "A-PLUS".
DAGMAR, YOU'RE THE PLUS MY PARTY NEEDED. AND HOW ARE YOU, KLAUS? THE NEW YACHT STILL FLOATING?
IT'S WONDERFUL LIVING ON A HOUSE BOAT, JAY. YOU SHOULD TRY IT SOME TIME.
SORRY, KLAUS, NOT FOR ME... QUEASY STOMACH AND ALL THAT. AHH, SENATOR STANTON...
10

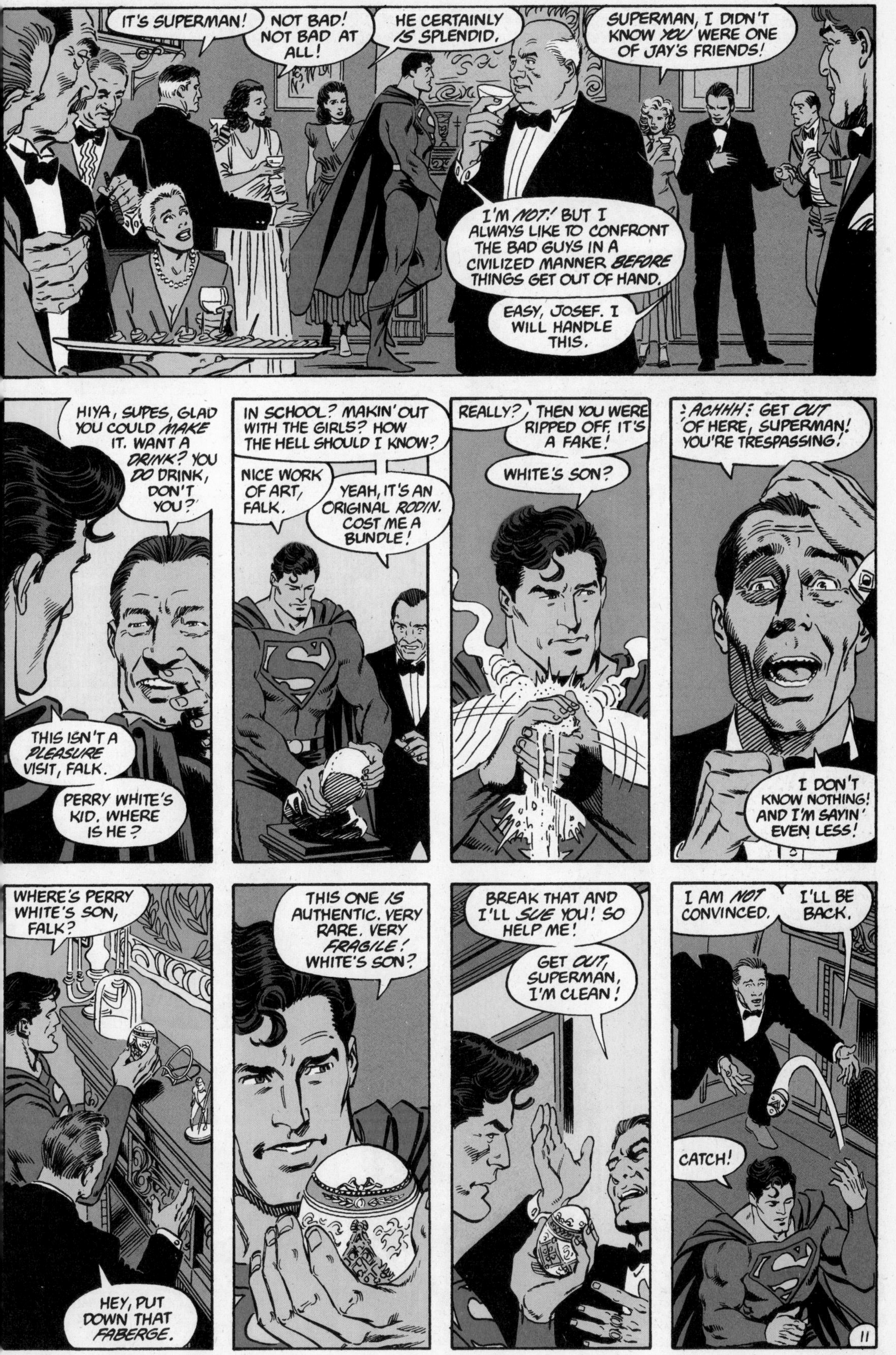
IT'S SUPERMAN!
NOT BAD! NOT BAD AT ALL!
HE CERTAINLY IS SPLENDID.
SUPERMAN, I DIDN'T KNOW YOU WERE ONE OF JAY'S FRIENDS!
I'M NOT! BUT I ALWAYS LIKE TO CONFRONT THE BAD GUYS IN A CIVILIZED MANNER BEFORE THINGS GET OUT OF HAND.
EASY, JOSEF. I WILL HANDLE THIS.
HIYA, SUPES, GLAD YOU COULD MAKE IT. WANT A DRINK? YOU DO DRINK, DON'T YOU?
THIS ISN'T A PLEASURE VISIT, FALK.
PERRY WHITE'S KID. WHERE IS HE?
IN SCHOOL? MAKIN' OUT WITH THE GIRLS? HOW THE HELL SHOULD I KNOW?
NICE WORK OF ART, FALK.
YEAH, IT'S AN ORIGINAL RODIN. COST ME A BUNDLE!
REALLY?
THEN YOU WERE RIPPED OFF. IT'S A FAKE!
WHITE'S SON?
ACHHH! GET OUT OF HERE, SUPERMAN! YOU'RE TRESPASSING!
I DON'T KNOW NOTHING! AND I'M SAYIN' EVEN LESS!
WHERE'S PERRY WHITE'S SON, FALK?
HEY, PUT DOWN THAT FABERGE.
THIS ONE IS AUTHENTIC. VERY RARE. VERY FRAGILE! WHITE'S SON?
BREAK THAT AND I'LL SUE YOU! SO HELP ME!
GET OUT, SUPERMAN, I'M CLEAN!
I AM NOT CONVINCED.
I'LL BE BACK.
CATCH!
11

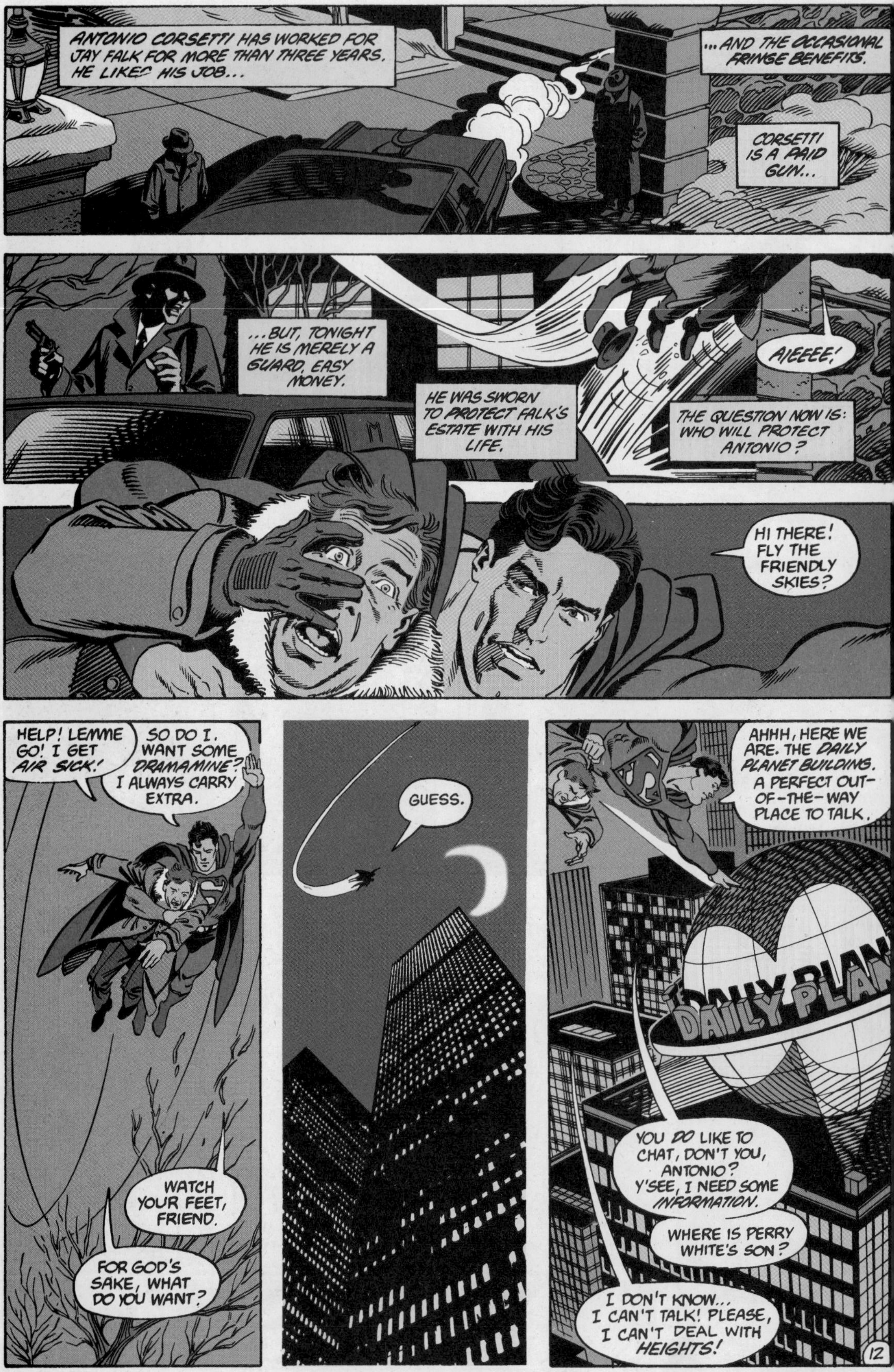

ANTONIO CORSETTI HAS WORKED FOR JAY FALK FOR MORE THAN THREE YEARS. HE LIKES HIS JOB...
...AND THE OCCASIONAL FRINGE BENEFITS.
CORSETTI IS A PAID GUN...
...BUT, TONIGHT HE IS MERELY A GUARD. EASY MONEY.
HE WAS SWORN TO PROTECT FALK'S ESTATE WITH HIS LIFE.
AIEEEE!
THE QUESTION NOW IS: WHO WILL PROTECT ANTONIO?
HI THERE! FLY THE FRIENDLY SKIES?
HELP! LEMME GO! I GET AIR SICK!
SO DO I. WANT SOME DRAMAMINE? I ALWAYS CARRY EXTRA.
WATCH YOUR FEET, FRIEND.
FOR GOD'S SAKE, WHAT DO YOU WANT?
GUESS.
AHHH, HERE WE ARE. THE DAILY PLANET BUILDING. A PERFECT OUT-OF-THE-WAY PLACE TO TALK.
DAILY PLANET
YOU DO LIKE TO CHAT, DON'T YOU, ANTONIO? Y'SEE, I NEED SOME INFORMATION.
WHERE IS PERRY WHITE'S SON?
I DON'T KNOW... I CAN'T TALK! PLEASE, I CAN'T DEAL WITH HEIGHTS!
12

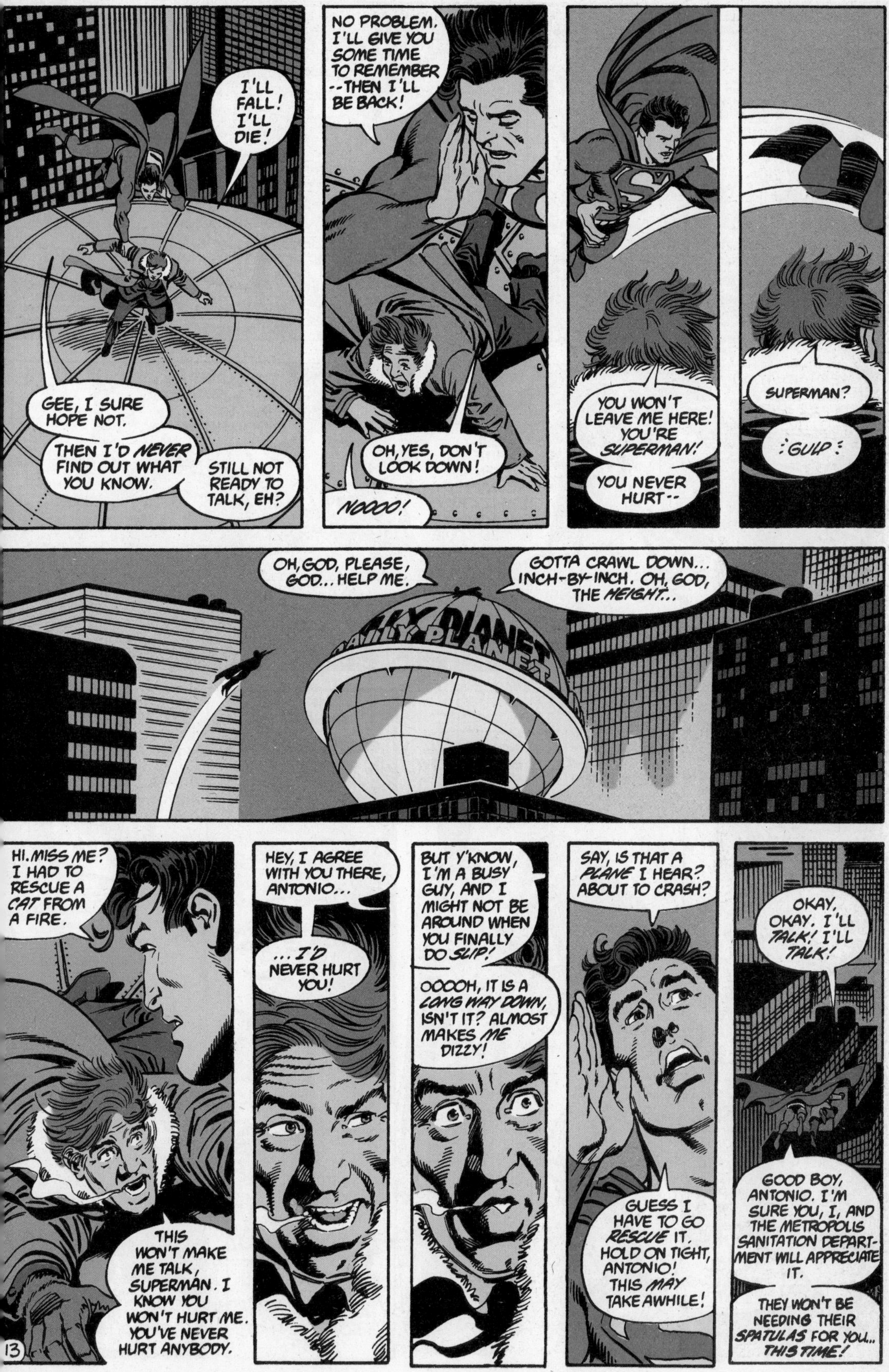
I'LL FALL! I'LL DIE!
GEE, I SURE HOPE NOT.
THEN I'D NEVER FIND OUT WHAT YOU KNOW.
STILL NOT READY TO TALK, EH?
NO PROBLEM. I'LL GIVE YOU SOME TIME TO REMEMBER --THEN I'LL BE BACK!
OH, YES, DON'T LOOK DOWN!
NOOOO!
YOU WON'T LEAVE ME HERE! YOU'RE SUPERMAN!
YOU NEVER HURT--
SUPERMAN?
:GULP:
OH, GOD, PLEASE, GOD... HELP ME.
GOTTA CRAWL DOWN... INCH-BY-INCH. OH, GOD, THE HEIGHT...
DAILY PLANET
HI. MISS ME? I HAD TO RESCUE A CAT FROM A FIRE.
THIS WON'T MAKE ME TALK, SUPERMAN. I KNOW YOU WON'T HURT ME. YOU'VE NEVER HURT ANYBODY.
13
HEY, I AGREE WITH YOU THERE, ANTONIO...
...I'D NEVER HURT YOU!
BUT Y'KNOW, I'M A BUSY GUY, AND I MIGHT NOT BE AROUND WHEN YOU FINALLY DO SLIP!
OOOOH, IT IS A LONG WAY DOWN, ISN'T IT? ALMOST MAKES ME DIZZY!
SAY, IS THAT A PLANE I HEAR? ABOUT TO CRASH?
GUESS I HAVE TO GO RESCUE IT. HOLD ON TIGHT, ANTONIO! THIS MAY TAKE AWHILE!
OKAY. OKAY. I'LL TALK! I'LL TALK!
GOOD BOY, ANTONIO. I'M SURE YOU, I, AND THE METROPOLIS SANITATION DEPARTMENT WILL APPRECIATE IT.
THEY WON'T BE NEEDING THEIR SPATULAS FOR YOU... THIS TIME!

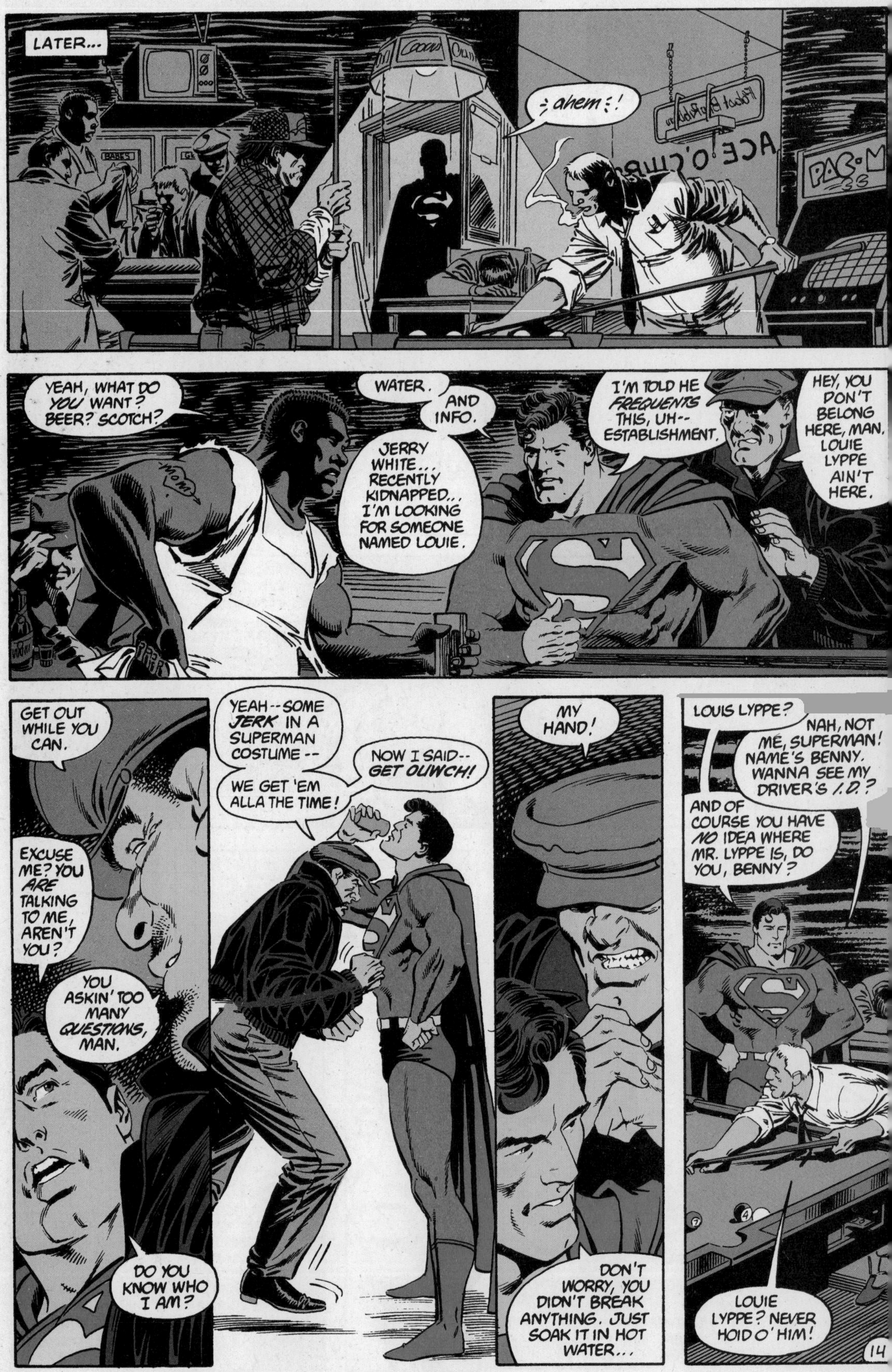

LATER...
:ahem:!
ACE O'CLUB
PAC-M
YEAH, WHAT DO YOU WANT? BEER? SCOTCH?
WATER.
AND INFO.
JERRY WHITE... RECENTLY KIDNAPPED... I'M LOOKING FOR SOMEONE NAMED LOUIE.
I'M TOLD HE FREQUENTS THIS, UH-- ESTABLISHMENT.
HEY, YOU DON'T BELONG HERE, MAN. LOUIE LYPPE AIN'T HERE.
GET OUT WHILE YOU CAN.
EXCUSE ME? YOU ARE TALKING TO ME, AREN'T YOU?
YOU ASKIN' TOO MANY QUESTIONS, MAN.
DO YOU KNOW WHO I AM?
YEAH--SOME JERK IN A SUPERMAN COSTUME --
WE GET 'EM ALLA THE TIME!
NOW I SAID-- GET OUWCH!
MY HAND!
DON'T WORRY, YOU DIDN'T BREAK ANYTHING. JUST SOAK IT IN HOT WATER...
LOUIS LYPPE?
NAH, NOT ME, SUPERMAN! NAME'S BENNY. WANNA SEE MY DRIVER'S I.D.?
AND OF COURSE YOU HAVE NO IDEA WHERE MR. LYPPE IS, DO YOU, BENNY?
LOUIE LYPPE? NEVER HOID O' HIM!
14

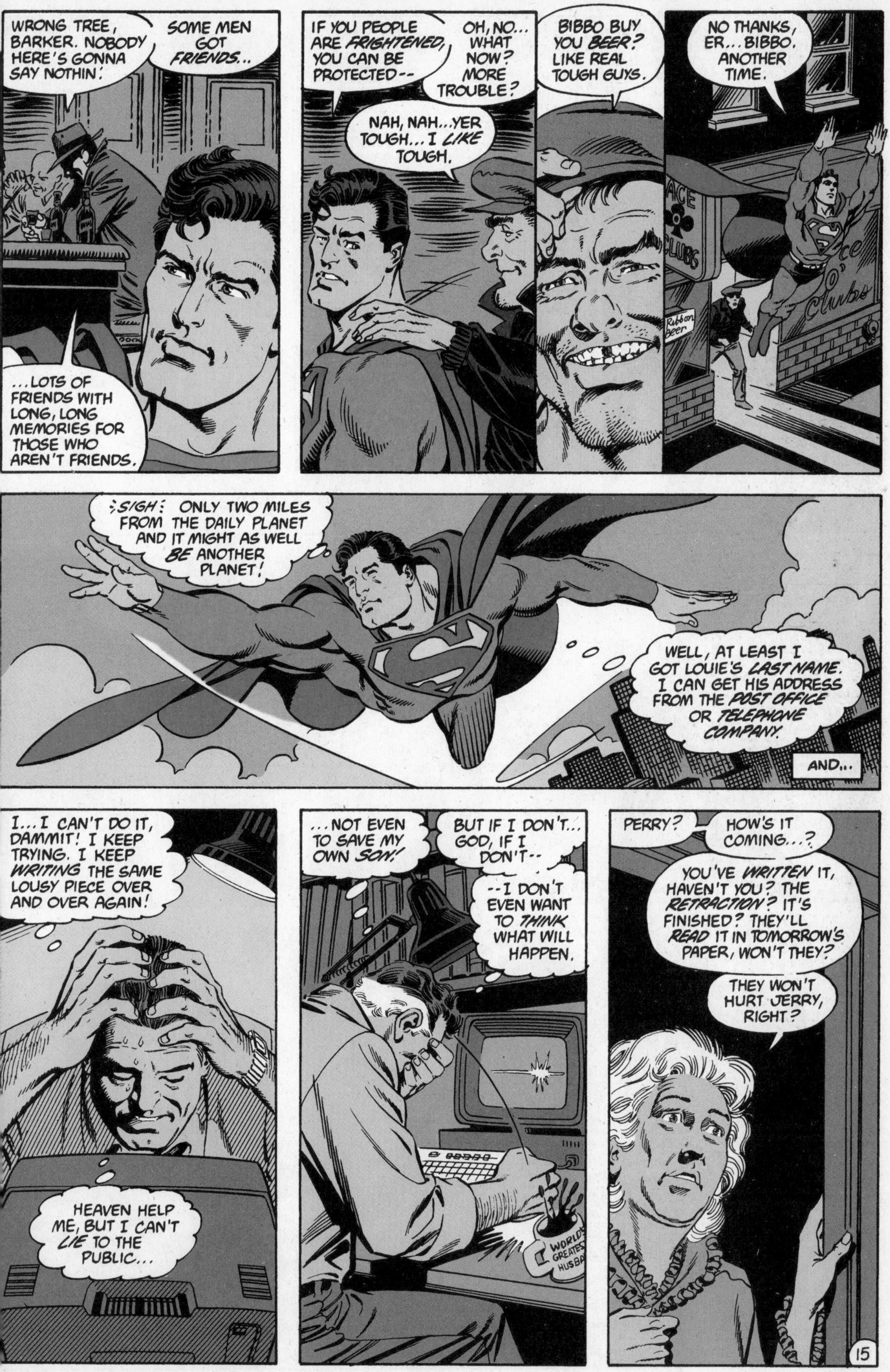

WRONG TREE, BARKER. NOBODY HERE'S GONNA SAY NOTHIN'.
SOME MEN GOT FRIENDS...
...LOTS OF FRIENDS WITH LONG, LONG MEMORIES FOR THOSE WHO AREN'T FRIENDS.
IF YOU PEOPLE ARE FRIGHTENED, YOU CAN BE PROTECTED--
OH, NO... WHAT NOW? MORE TROUBLE?
NAH, NAH... YER TOUGH... I LIKE TOUGH.
BIBBO BUY YOU BEER? LIKE REAL TOUGH GUYS.
NO THANKS, ER... BIBBO. ANOTHER TIME.
Ribbon Beer
:SIGH: ONLY TWO MILES FROM THE DAILY PLANET AND IT MIGHT AS WELL BE ANOTHER PLANET!
WELL, AT LEAST I GOT LOUIE'S LAST NAME. I CAN GET HIS ADDRESS FROM THE POST OFFICE OR TELEPHONE COMPANY.
AND...
I... I CAN'T DO IT, DAMMIT! I KEEP TRYING. I KEEP WRITING THE SAME LOUSY PIECE OVER AND OVER AGAIN!
HEAVEN HELP ME, BUT I CAN'T LIE TO THE PUBLIC...
...NOT EVEN TO SAVE MY OWN SON!
BUT IF I DON'T... GOD, IF I DON'T--
--I DON'T EVEN WANT TO THINK WHAT WILL HAPPEN.
WORLD'S GREATEST HUSBA
PERRY?
HOW'S IT COMING...?
YOU'VE WRITTEN IT, HAVEN'T YOU? THE RETRACTION? IT'S FINISHED? THEY'LL READ IT IN TOMORROW'S PAPER, WON'T THEY?
THEY WON'T HURT JERRY, RIGHT?
15

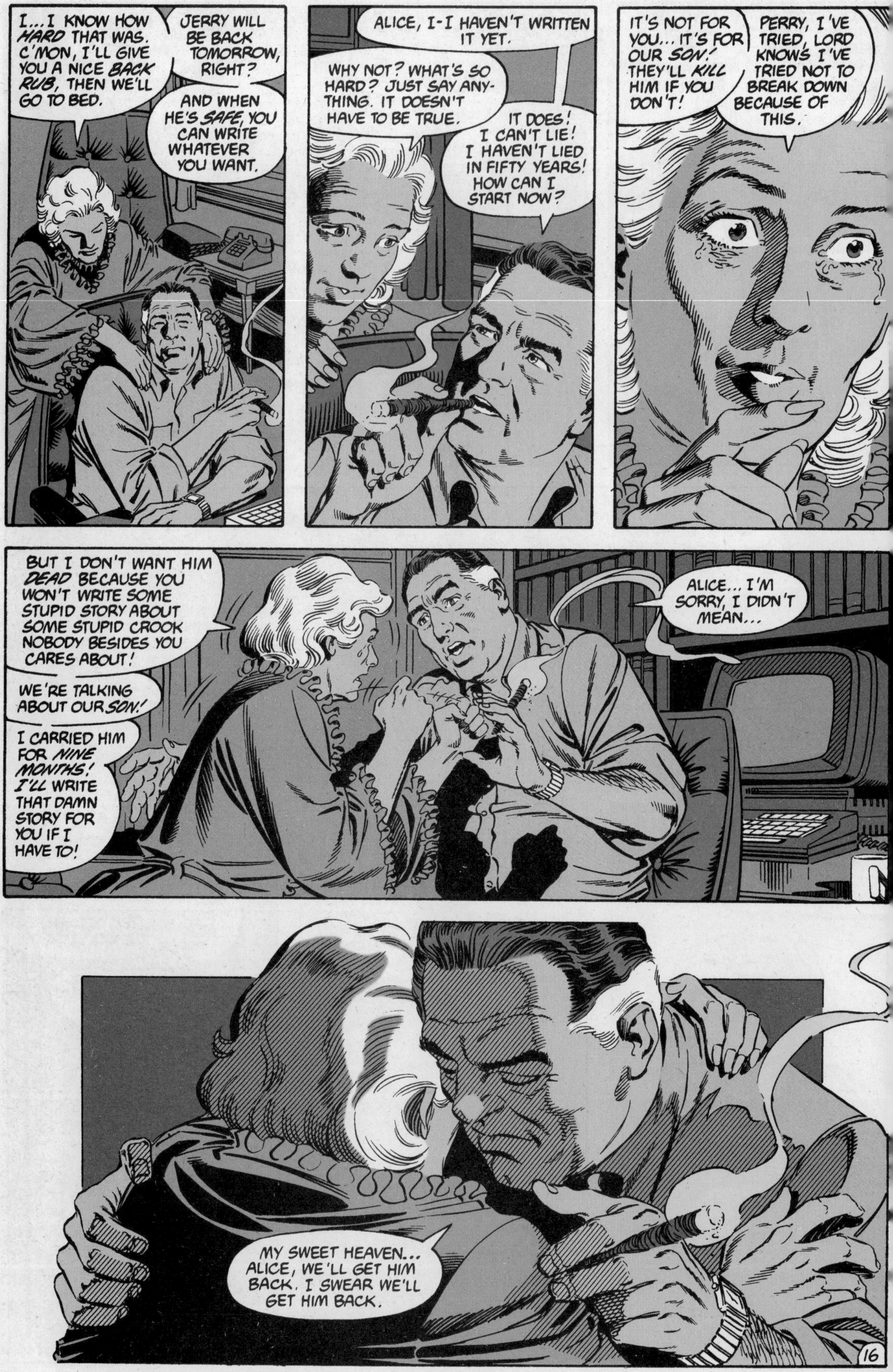
I... I KNOW HOW HARD THAT WAS. C'MON, I'LL GIVE YOU A NICE BACK RUB, THEN WE'LL GO TO BED.
JERRY WILL BE BACK TOMORROW, RIGHT?
AND WHEN HE'S SAFE, YOU CAN WRITE WHATEVER YOU WANT.
ALICE, I-I HAVEN'T WRITTEN IT YET.
WHY NOT? WHAT'S SO HARD? JUST SAY ANY-THING. IT DOESN'T HAVE TO BE TRUE.
IT DOES! I CAN'T LIE! I HAVEN'T LIED IN FIFTY YEARS! HOW CAN I START NOW?
IT'S NOT FOR YOU... IT'S FOR OUR SON! THEY'LL KILL HIM IF YOU DON'T!
PERRY, I'VE TRIED, LORD KNOWS I'VE TRIED NOT TO BREAK DOWN BECAUSE OF THIS.
BUT I DON'T WANT HIM DEAD BECAUSE YOU WON'T WRITE SOME STUPID STORY ABOUT SOME STUPID CROOK NOBODY BESIDES YOU CARES ABOUT!
WE'RE TALKING ABOUT OUR SON!
I CARRIED HIM FOR NINE MONTHS! I'LL WRITE THAT DAMN STORY FOR YOU IF I HAVE TO!
ALICE... I'M SORRY, I DIDN'T MEAN...
MY SWEET HEAVEN... ALICE, WE'LL GET HIM BACK. I SWEAR WE'LL GET HIM BACK.
16

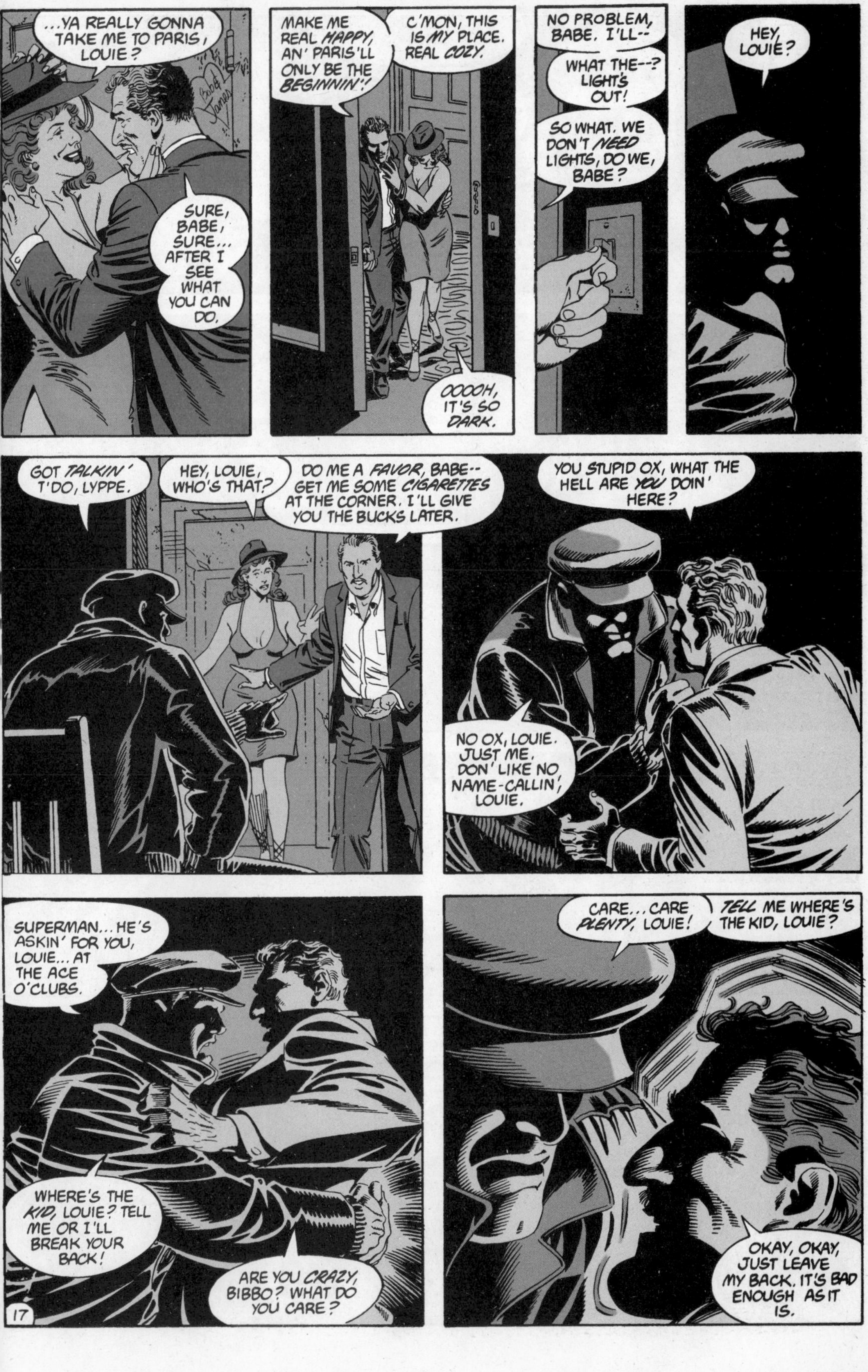
...YA REALLY GONNA TAKE ME TO PARIS, LOUIE?
SURE, BABE, SURE... AFTER I SEE WHAT YOU CAN DO.
MAKE ME REAL HAPPY, AN' PARIS'LL ONLY BE THE BEGINNIN'!
C'MON, THIS IS MY PLACE. REAL COZY.
OOOOH, IT'S SO DARK.
NO PROBLEM, BABE. I'LL--
WHAT THE--? LIGHT'S OUT!
SO WHAT. WE DON'T NEED LIGHTS, DO WE, BABE?
HEY, LOUIE?
GOT TALKIN' T'DO, LYPPE.
HEY, LOUIE, WHO'S THAT?
DO ME A FAVOR, BABE-- GET ME SOME CIGARETTES AT THE CORNER. I'LL GIVE YOU THE BUCKS LATER.
YOU STUPID OX, WHAT THE HELL ARE YOU DOIN' HERE?
NO OX, LOUIE. JUST ME. DON' LIKE NO NAME-CALLIN', LOUIE.
SUPERMAN... HE'S ASKIN' FOR YOU, LOUIE... AT THE ACE O'CLUBS.
WHERE'S THE KID, LOUIE? TELL ME OR I'LL BREAK YOUR BACK!
ARE YOU CRAZY, BIBBO? WHAT DO YOU CARE?
17
CARE... CARE PLENTY, LOUIE!
TELL ME WHERE'S THE KID, LOUIE?
OKAY, OKAY, JUST LEAVE MY BACK. IT'S BAD ENOUGH AS IT IS.

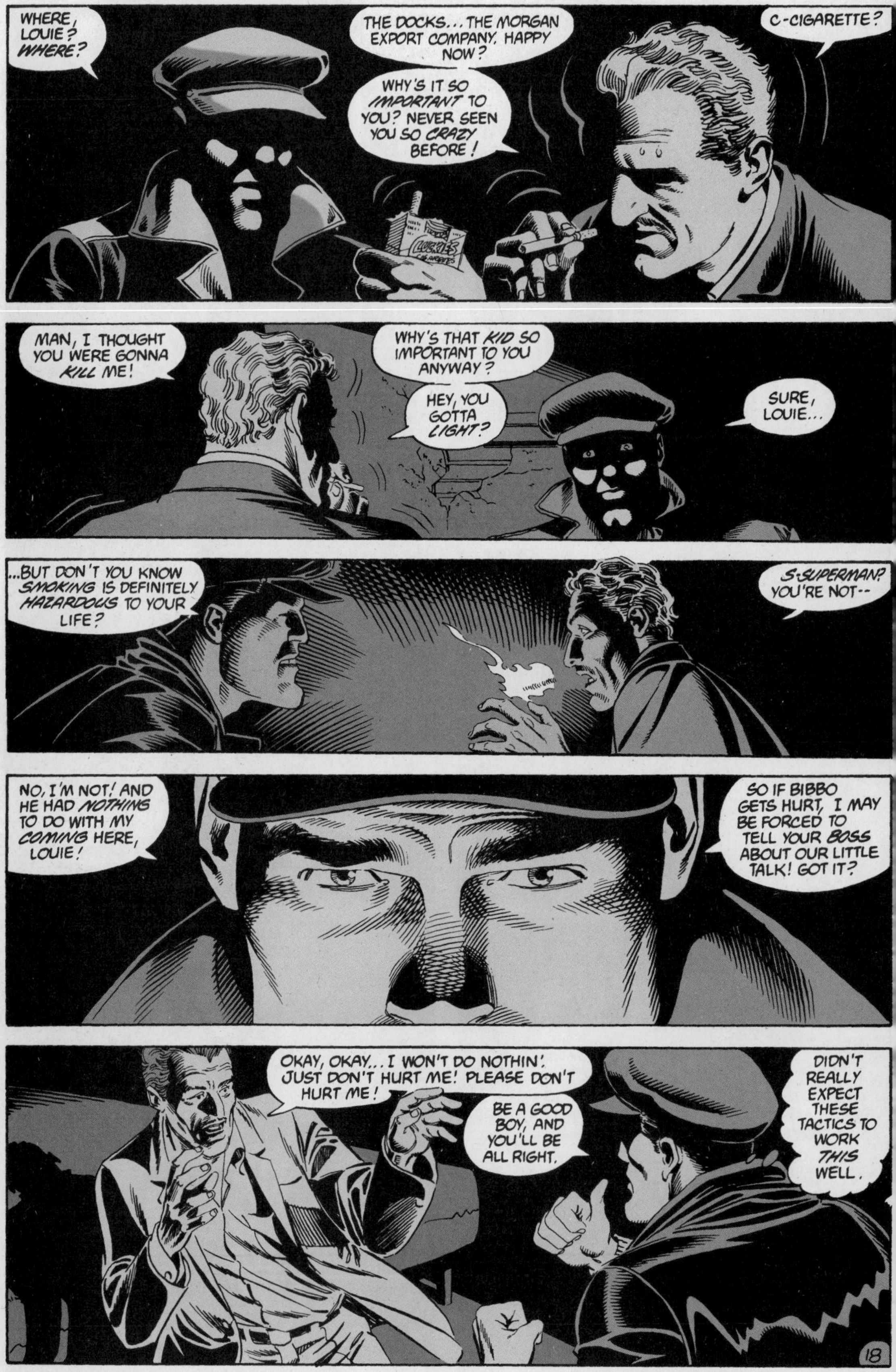
WHERE, LOUIE? WHERE?
THE DOCKS... THE MORGAN EXPORT COMPANY. HAPPY NOW?
WHY'S IT SO IMPORTANT TO YOU? NEVER SEEN YOU SO CRAZY BEFORE!
C-CIGARETTE?
MAN, I THOUGHT YOU WERE GONNA KILL ME!
WHY'S THAT KID SO IMPORTANT TO YOU ANYWAY?
HEY, YOU GOTTA LIGHT?
SURE, LOUIE...
...BUT DON'T YOU KNOW SMOKING IS DEFINITELY HAZARDOUS TO YOUR LIFE?
S-SUPERMAN? YOU'RE NOT--
NO, I'M NOT! AND HE HAD NOTHING TO DO WITH MY COMING HERE, LOUIE!
SO IF BIBBO GETS HURT, I MAY BE FORCED TO TELL YOUR BOSS ABOUT OUR LITTLE TALK! GOT IT?
OKAY, OKAY... I WON'T DO NOTHIN'. JUST DON'T HURT ME! PLEASE DON'T HURT ME!
BE A GOOD BOY, AND YOU'LL BE ALL RIGHT.
DIDN'T REALLY EXPECT THESE TACTICS TO WORK THIS WELL.
18

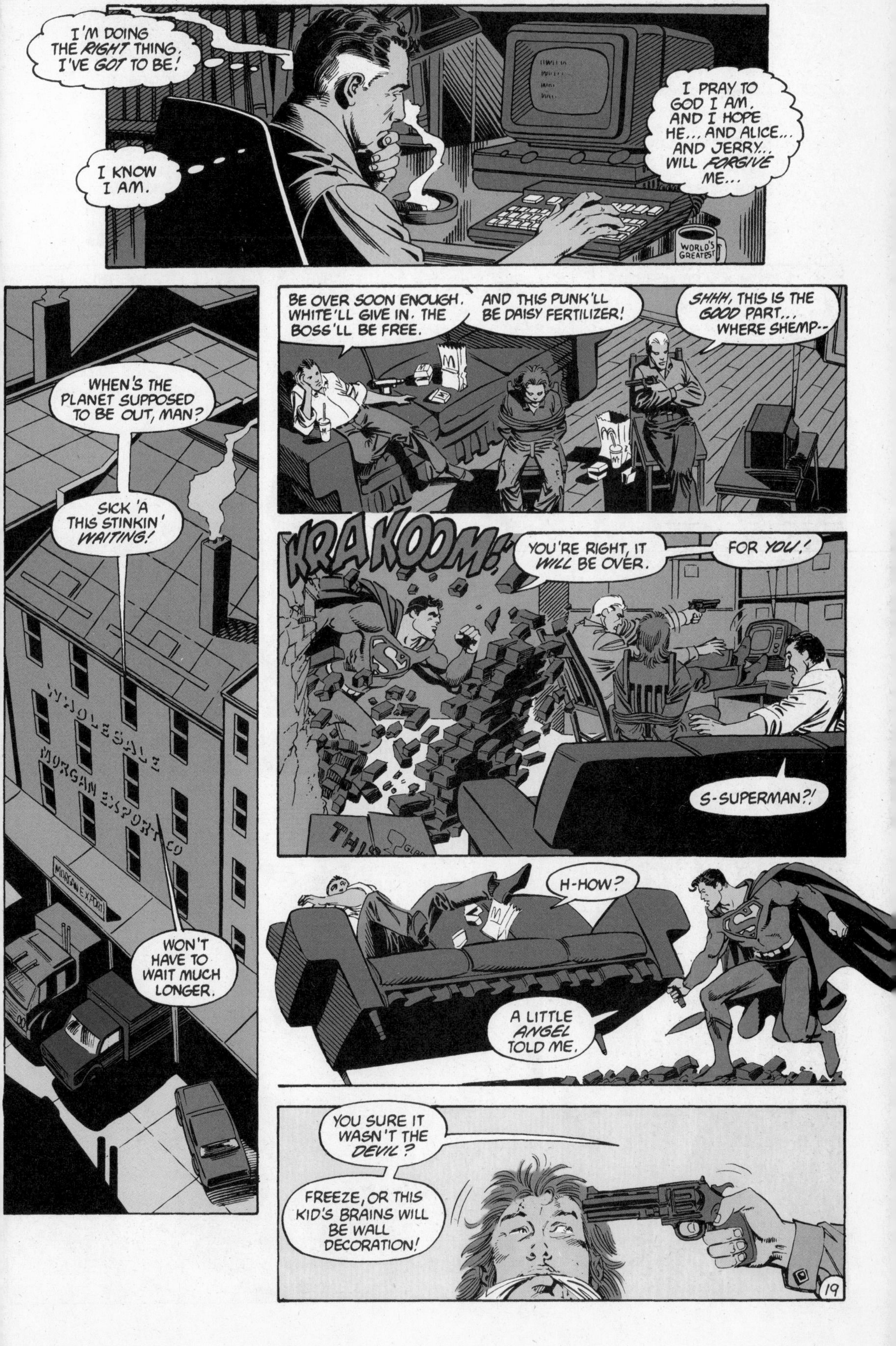
I'M DOING THE RIGHT THING. I'VE GOT TO BE!
I KNOW I AM.
I PRAY TO GOD I AM. AND I HOPE HE... AND ALICE... AND JERRY... WILL FORGIVE ME...
WORLD'S GREATEST
WHEN'S THE PLANET SUPPOSED TO BE OUT, MAN?
SICK 'A THIS STINKIN' WAITING!
WHOLESALE
MORGAN EXPORT CO
MORGAN EXPORT
WON'T HAVE TO WAIT MUCH LONGER.
BE OVER SOON ENOUGH. WHITE'LL GIVE IN. THE BOSS'LL BE FREE.
AND THIS PUNK'LL BE DAISY FERTILIZER!
SHHH, THIS IS THE GOOD PART... WHERE SHEMP--
KRAKOOM!
YOU'RE RIGHT, IT WILL BE OVER.
FOR YOU!
S-SUPERMAN?!
H-HOW?
A LITTLE ANGEL TOLD ME.
YOU SURE IT WASN'T THE DEVIL?
FREEZE, OR THIS KID'S BRAINS WILL BE WALL DECORATION!
19

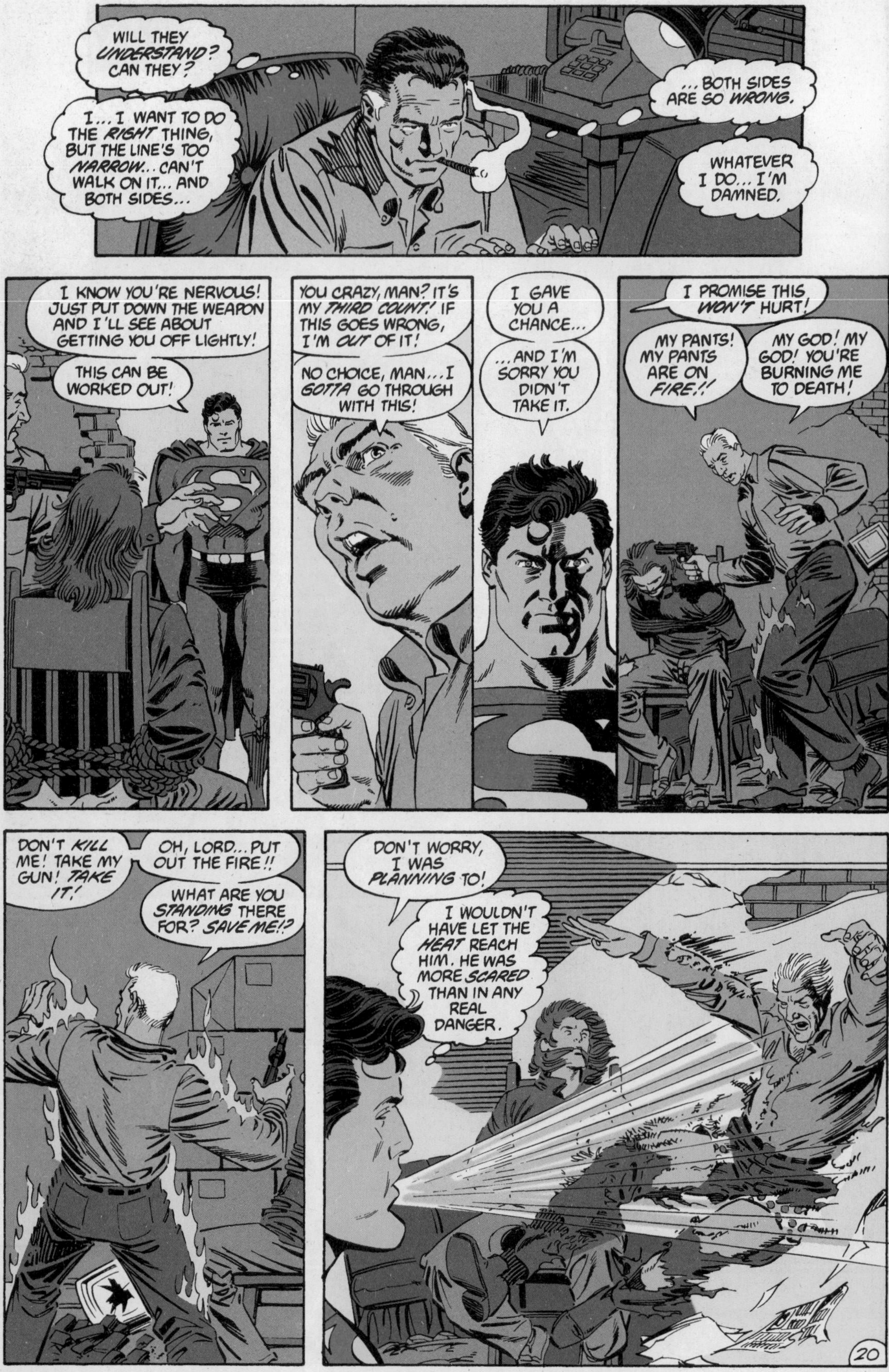
WILL THEY UNDERSTAND? CAN THEY?
I... I WANT TO DO THE RIGHT THING, BUT THE LINE'S TOO NARROW... CAN'T WALK ON IT... AND BOTH SIDES...
...BOTH SIDES ARE SO WRONG.
WHATEVER I DO... I'M DAMNED.
I KNOW YOU'RE NERVOUS! JUST PUT DOWN THE WEAPON AND I'LL SEE ABOUT GETTING YOU OFF LIGHTLY!
THIS CAN BE WORKED OUT!
YOU CRAZY, MAN? IT'S MY THIRD COUNT! IF THIS GOES WRONG, I'M OUT OF IT!
NO CHOICE, MAN... I GOTTA GO THROUGH WITH THIS!
I GAVE YOU A CHANCE...
...AND I'M SORRY YOU DIDN'T TAKE IT.
I PROMISE THIS WON'T HURT!
MY PANTS! MY PANTS ARE ON FIRE!!
MY GOD! MY GOD! YOU'RE BURNING ME TO DEATH!
DON'T KILL ME! TAKE MY GUN! TAKE IT!
OH, LORD... PUT OUT THE FIRE!!
WHAT ARE YOU STANDING THERE FOR? SAVE ME!?
DON'T WORRY, I WAS PLANNING TO!
I WOULDN'T HAVE LET THE HEAT REACH HIM. HE WAS MORE SCARED THAN IN ANY REAL DANGER.
20

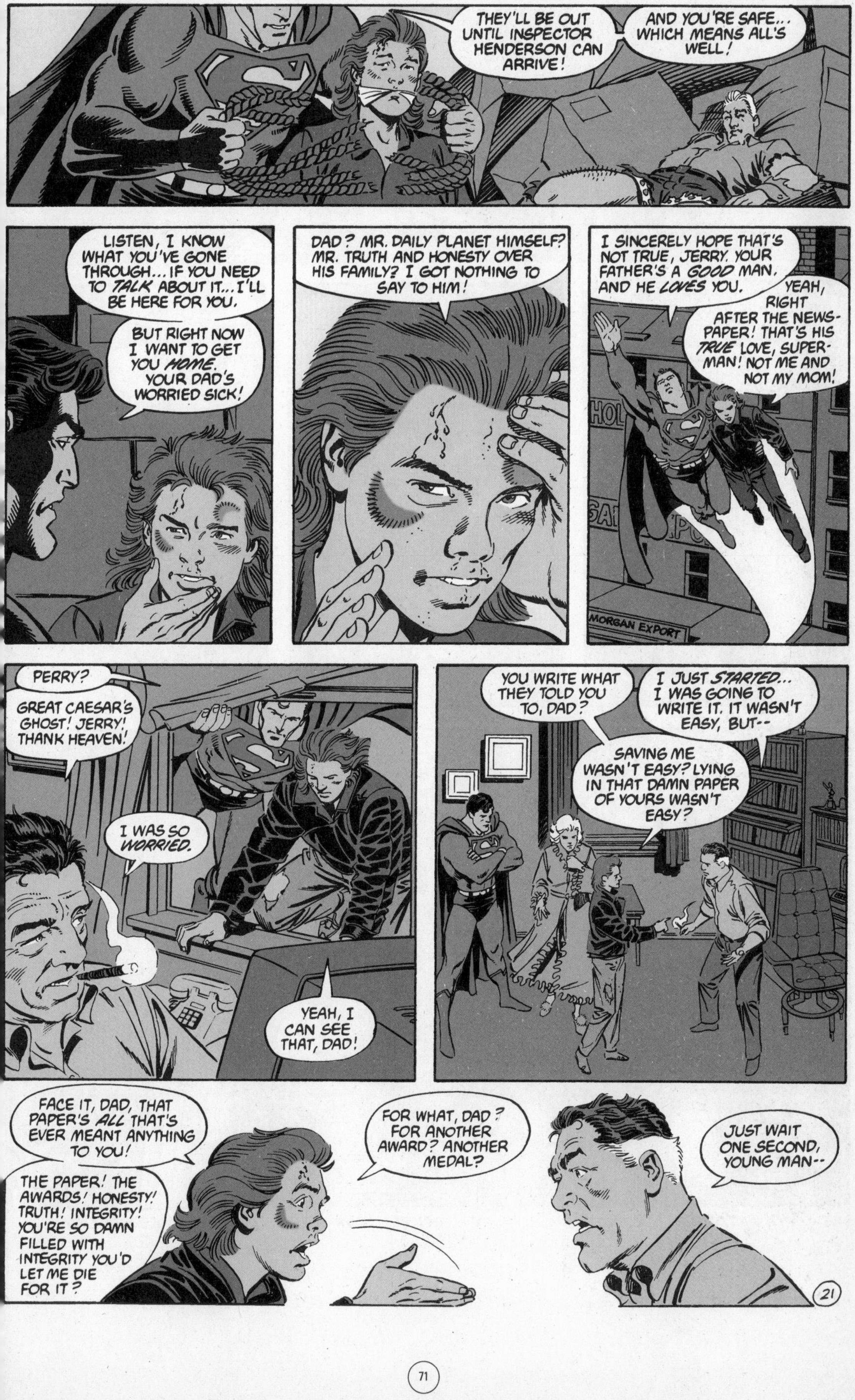

THEY'LL BE OUT UNTIL INSPECTOR HENDERSON CAN ARRIVE!
AND YOU'RE SAFE... WHICH MEANS ALL'S WELL!
LISTEN, I KNOW WHAT YOU'VE GONE THROUGH... IF YOU NEED TO TALK ABOUT IT... I'LL BE HERE FOR YOU.
BUT RIGHT NOW I WANT TO GET YOU HOME. YOUR DAD'S WORRIED SICK!
DAD? MR. DAILY PLANET HIMSELF? MR. TRUTH AND HONESTY OVER HIS FAMILY? I GOT NOTHING TO SAY TO HIM!
I SINCERELY HOPE THAT'S NOT TRUE, JERRY. YOUR FATHER'S A GOOD MAN. AND HE LOVES YOU.
YEAH, RIGHT AFTER THE NEWSPAPER! THAT'S HIS TRUE LOVE, SUPERMAN! NOT ME AND NOT MY MOM!
MORGAN EXPORT
PERRY?
GREAT CAESAR'S GHOST! JERRY! THANK HEAVEN!
I WAS SO WORRIED.
YEAH, I CAN SEE THAT, DAD!
YOU WRITE WHAT THEY TOLD YOU TO, DAD?
I JUST STARTED... I WAS GOING TO WRITE IT. IT WASN'T EASY, BUT--
SAVING ME WASN'T EASY? LYING IN THAT DAMN PAPER OF YOURS WASN'T EASY?
FACE IT, DAD, THAT PAPER'S ALL THAT'S EVER MEANT ANYTHING TO YOU!
THE PAPER! THE AWARDS! HONESTY! TRUTH! INTEGRITY! YOU'RE SO DAMN FILLED WITH INTEGRITY YOU'D LET ME DIE FOR IT?
FOR WHAT, DAD? FOR ANOTHER AWARD? ANOTHER MEDAL?
JUST WAIT ONE SECOND, YOUNG MAN--
21

NO, *YOU* WAIT! I'VE *HAD* IT! YOU WEREN'T THERE TIED UP WITH THOSE MADMEN! YOU DIDN'T HEAR THEM *CHUCKLING* OVER WHAT THEY'D DO TO ME!

I WAS GOING TO SAVE YOU!

YOU DON'T UNDERSTAND WHAT I HAD TO DO! YOU DON'T UNDERSTAND THE *SACRIFICE* I WAS GOING TO MAKE!

OH, DAD, I UNDERSTAND ALL ABOUT SACRIFICE.

THIS YOUR LITTLE ARTICLE OF LIES, DAD? TOO LITTLE, POPS!

AND FAR, FAR TOO LATE!

JERRY--

NO, MA, LEAVE ME BE, OKAY?

IF IT WERE UP TO DAD, HE'D'VE LET ME *DIE* RATHER THAN WRITE SOME LIE IN THAT GREAT BIG PAPER OF HIS!

I...I GOTTA GET OUTTA HERE!

I GOTTA GO THINK!

AND MAYBE, DAD, MAYBE-- YOU SHOULD DO SOME THINKING, TOO.

Marv Wolfman *writer*   **Jerry Ordway** *artist*   **John Costanza** *letterer*   **Tom Ziuko** *colorist*   **Andy Helfer & Mike Carlin** *editors*

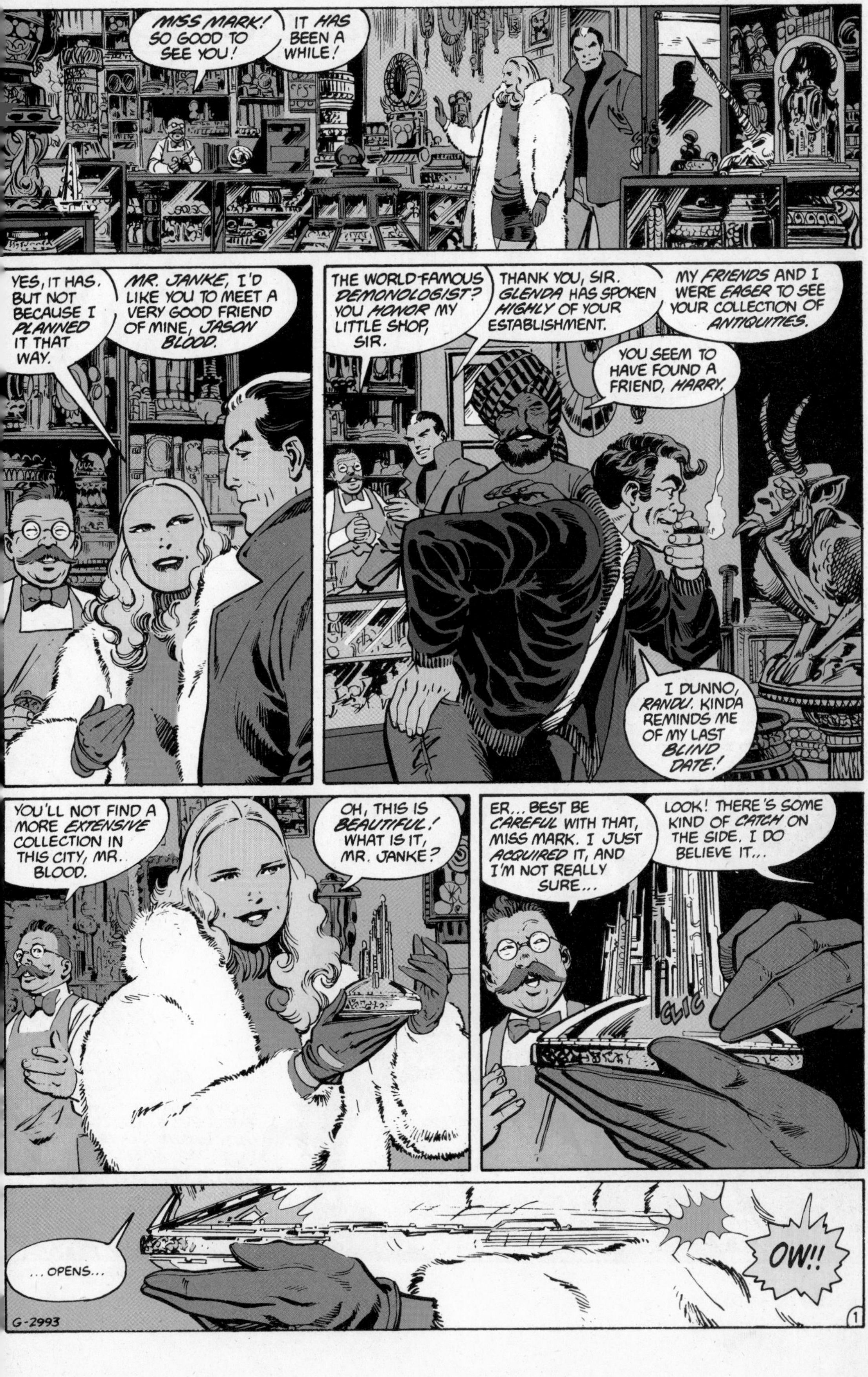

MISS MARK! SO GOOD TO SEE YOU!
IT HAS BEEN A WHILE!
YES, IT HAS. BUT NOT BECAUSE I PLANNED IT THAT WAY.
MR. JANKE, I'D LIKE YOU TO MEET A VERY GOOD FRIEND OF MINE, JASON BLOOD.
THE WORLD-FAMOUS DEMONOLOGIST? YOU HONOR MY LITTLE SHOP, SIR.
THANK YOU, SIR. GLENDA HAS SPOKEN HIGHLY OF YOUR ESTABLISHMENT.
MY FRIENDS AND I WERE EAGER TO SEE YOUR COLLECTION OF ANTIQUITIES.
YOU SEEM TO HAVE FOUND A FRIEND, HARRY.
I DUNNO, RANDU. KINDA REMINDS ME OF MY LAST BLIND DATE!
YOU'LL NOT FIND A MORE EXTENSIVE COLLECTION IN THIS CITY, MR. BLOOD.
OH, THIS IS BEAUTIFUL! WHAT IS IT, MR. JANKE?
ER... BEST BE CAREFUL WITH THAT, MISS MARK. I JUST ACQUIRED IT, AND I'M NOT REALLY SURE...
LOOK! THERE'S SOME KIND OF CATCH ON THE SIDE. I DO BELIEVE IT...
CLIC
...OPENS...
OW!!
G-2993
1

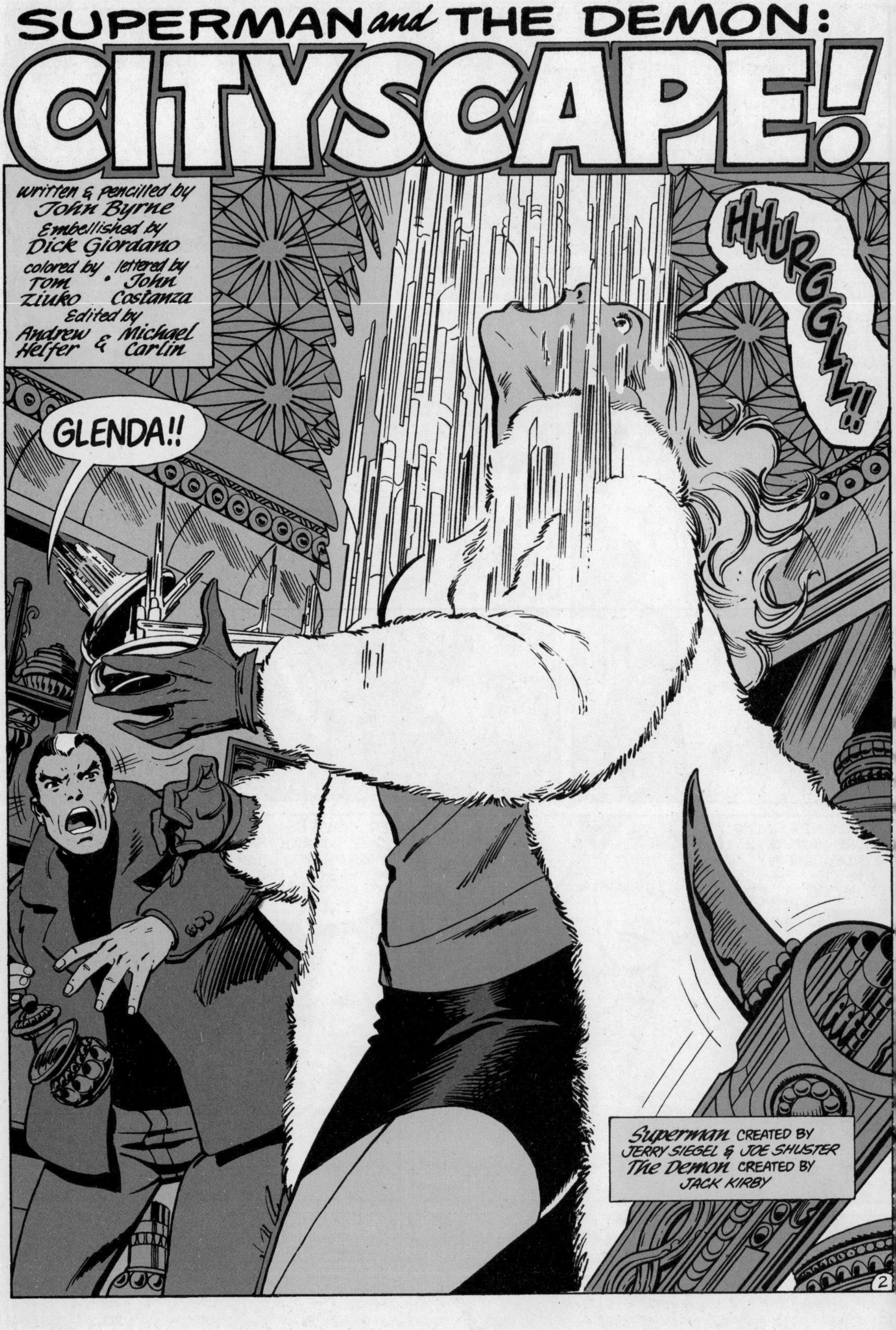
SUPERMAN and THE DEMON:
CITYSCAPE!
written & pencilled by John Byrne
Embellished by Dick Giordano
colored by Tom Ziuko • lettered by John Costanza
Edited by Andrew Helfer & Michael Carlin
HHURGGLL!!
GLENDA!!
Superman CREATED BY JERRY SIEGEL & JOE SHUSTER
The Demon CREATED BY JACK KIRBY
2

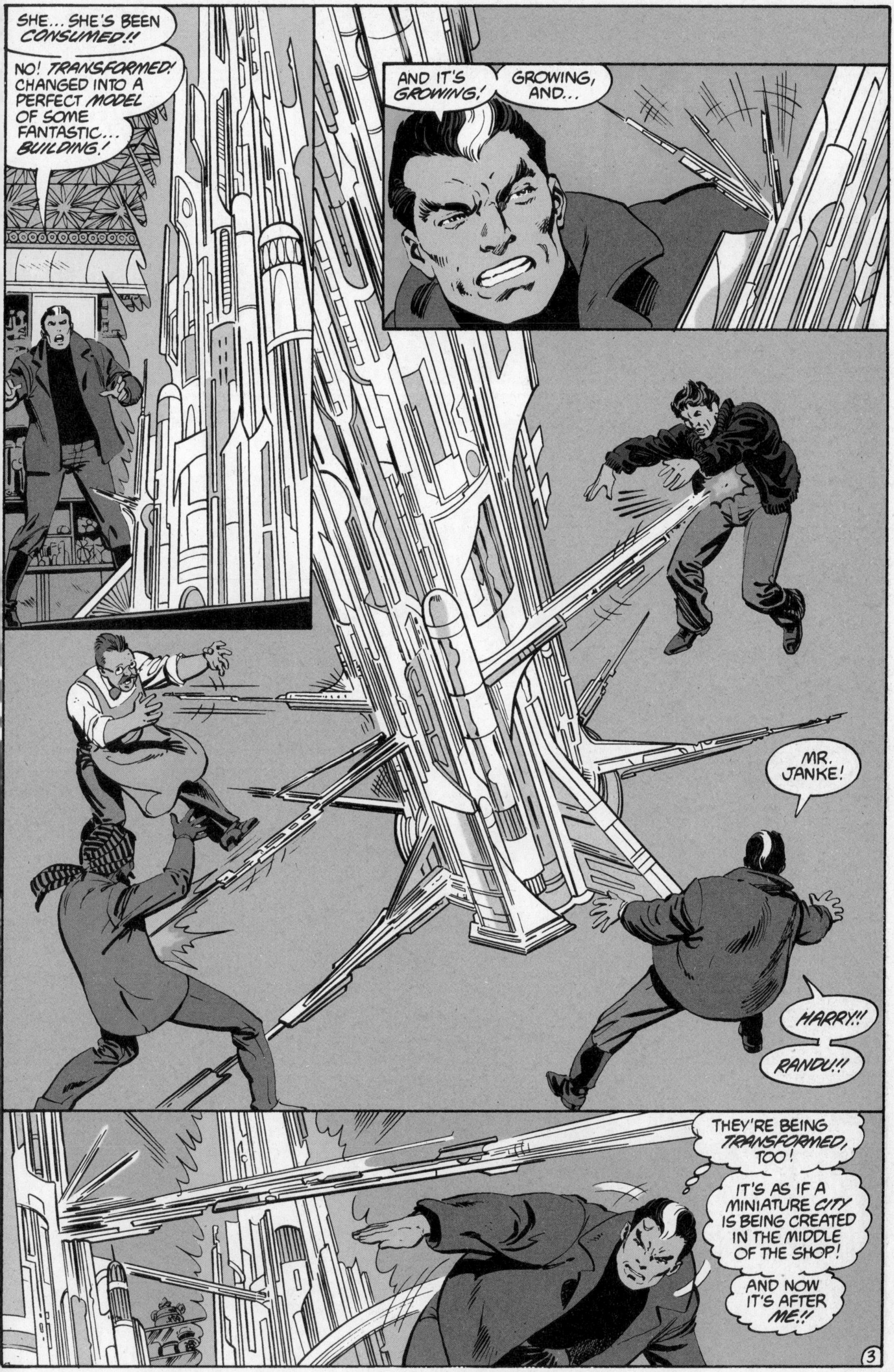
SHE... SHE'S BEEN CONSUMED!!
NO! TRANSFORMED! CHANGED INTO A PERFECT MODEL OF SOME FANTASTIC... BUILDING!
AND IT'S GROWING!
GROWING, AND...
MR. JANKE!
HARRY!!
RANDU!!
THEY'RE BEING TRANSFORMED, TOO!
IT'S AS IF A MINIATURE CITY IS BEING CREATED IN THE MIDDLE OF THE SHOP!
AND NOW IT'S AFTER ME!!
3

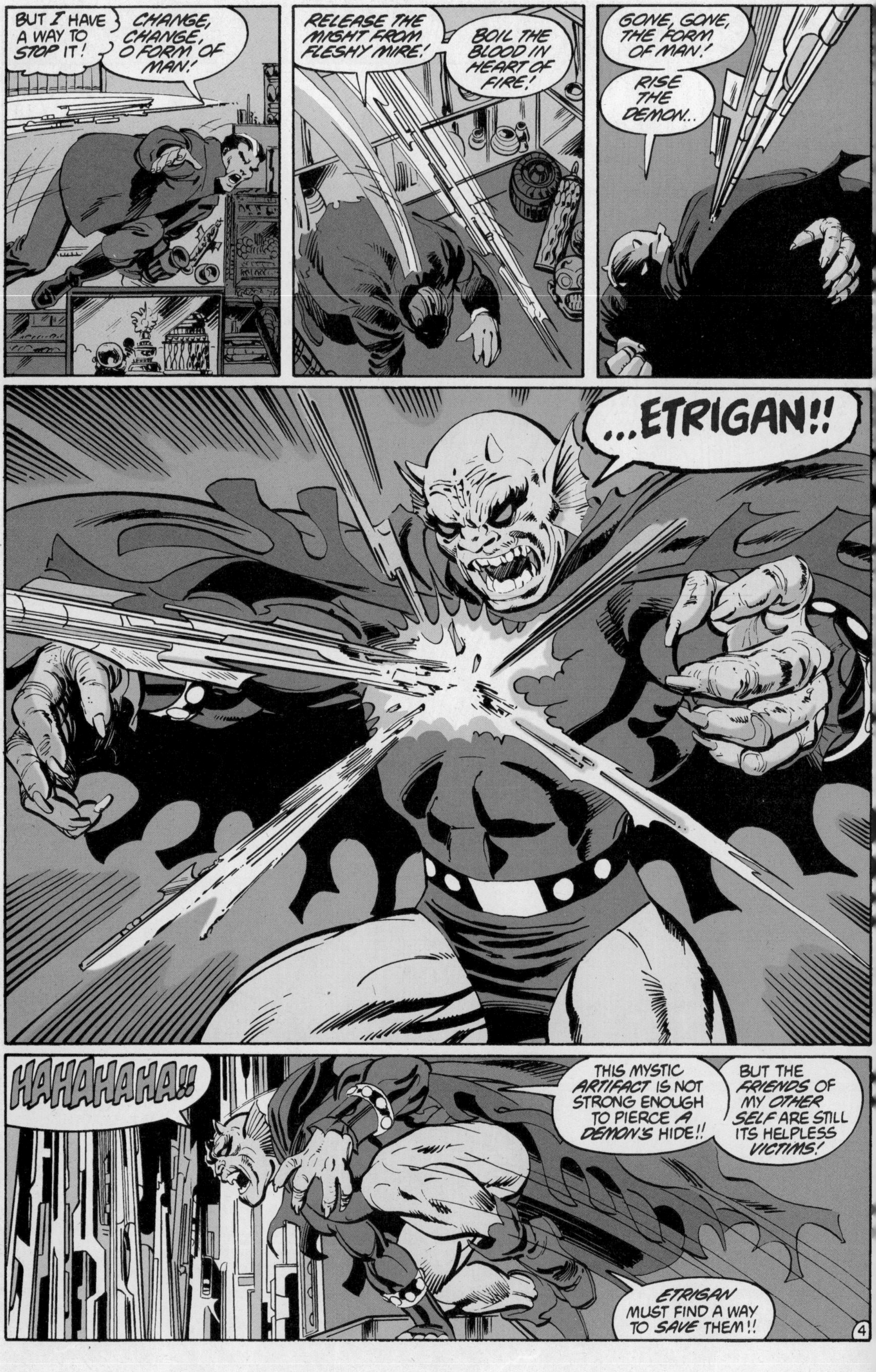
BUT I HAVE A WAY TO STOP IT!
CHANGE, CHANGE, O FORM OF MAN!
RELEASE THE MIGHT FROM FLESHY MIRE!
BOIL THE BLOOD IN HEART OF FIRE!
GONE, GONE, THE FORM OF MAN!
RISE THE DEMON...
...ETRIGAN!!
HAHAHAHA!!
THIS MYSTIC ARTIFACT IS NOT STRONG ENOUGH TO PIERCE A DEMON'S HIDE!!
BUT THE FRIENDS OF MY OTHER SELF ARE STILL ITS HELPLESS VICTIMS!
ETRIGAN MUST FIND A WAY TO SAVE THEM!!
4

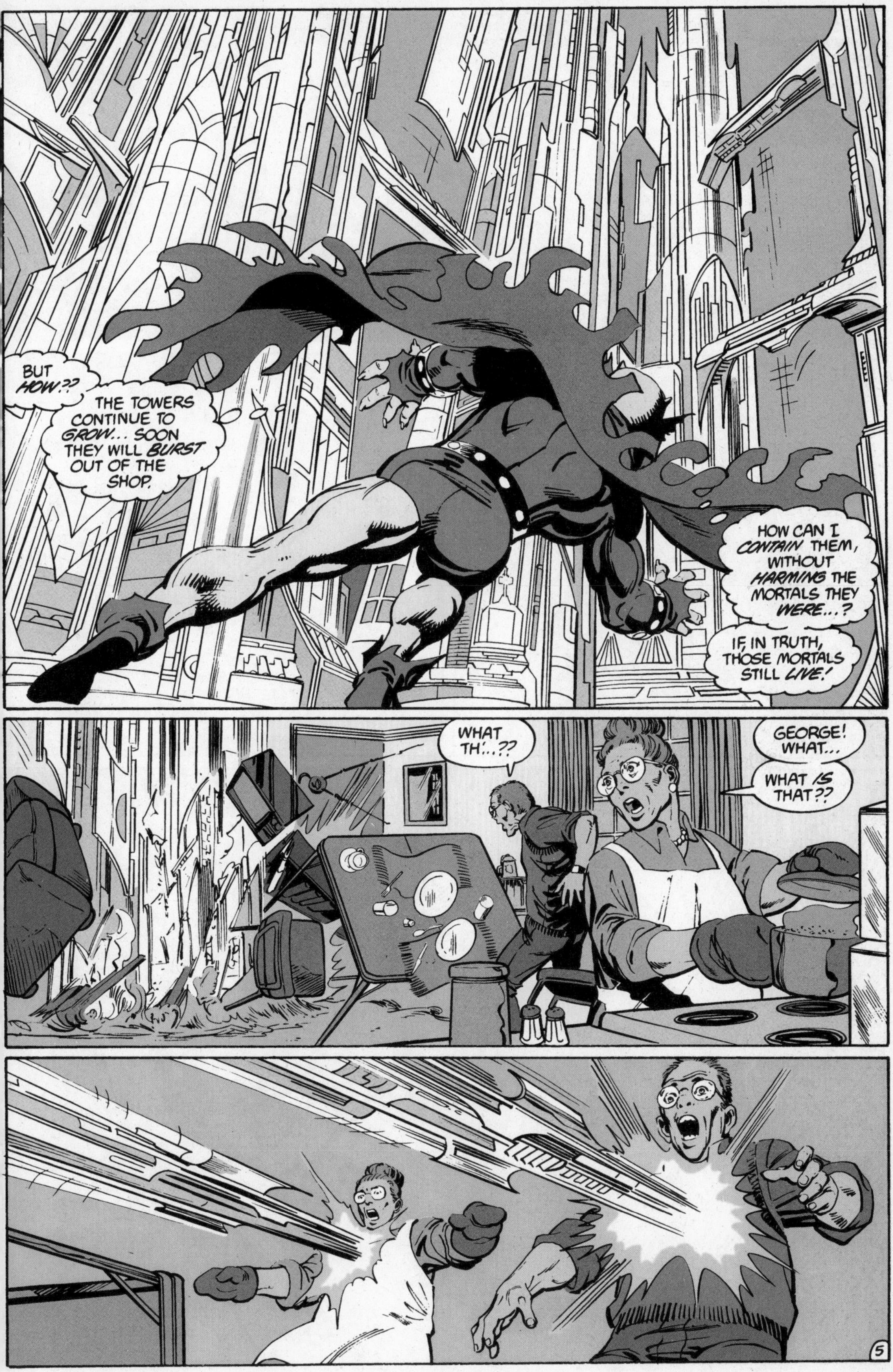
BUT HOW??
THE TOWERS CONTINUE TO GROW... SOON THEY WILL BURST OUT OF THE SHOP.
HOW CAN I CONTAIN THEM, WITHOUT HARMING THE MORTALS THEY WERE...?
IF, IN TRUTH, THOSE MORTALS STILL LIVE!
WHAT TH'...??
GEORGE! WHAT...
WHAT IS THAT??
5

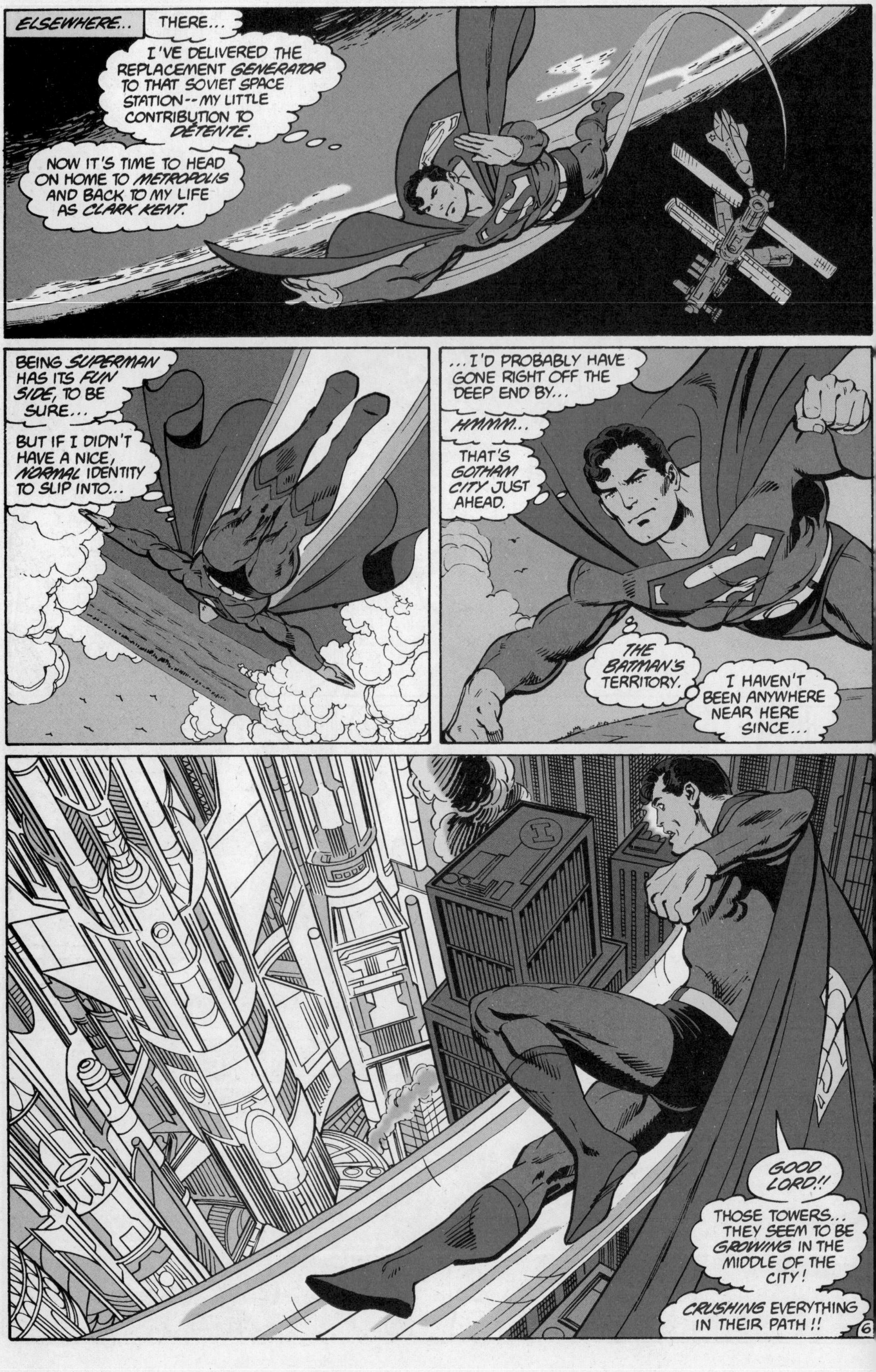
ELSEWHERE...
THERE...
I'VE DELIVERED THE REPLACEMENT GENERATOR TO THAT SOVIET SPACE STATION-- MY LITTLE CONTRIBUTION TO DÉTENTE.
NOW IT'S TIME TO HEAD ON HOME TO METROPOLIS AND BACK TO MY LIFE AS CLARK KENT.
BEING SUPERMAN HAS ITS FUN SIDE, TO BE SURE...
BUT IF I DIDN'T HAVE A NICE, NORMAL IDENTITY TO SLIP INTO...
...I'D PROBABLY HAVE GONE RIGHT OFF THE DEEP END BY...
HMMM...
THAT'S GOTHAM CITY JUST AHEAD.
THE BATMAN'S TERRITORY.
I HAVEN'T BEEN ANYWHERE NEAR HERE SINCE...
GOOD LORD!!
THOSE TOWERS... THEY SEEM TO BE GROWING IN THE MIDDLE OF THE CITY!
CRUSHING EVERYTHING IN THEIR PATH!!
6

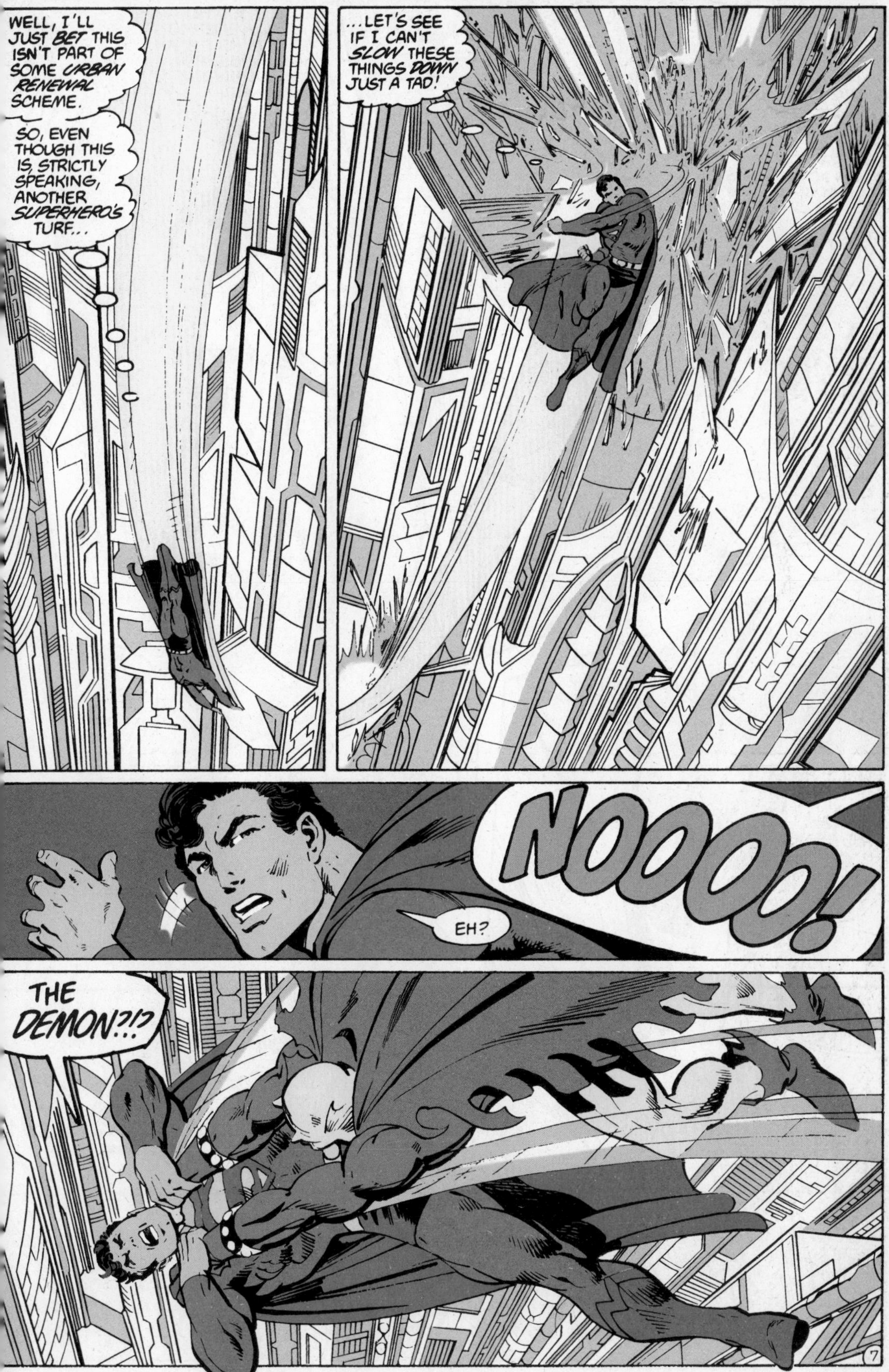
WELL, I'LL JUST BET THIS ISN'T PART OF SOME URBAN RENEWAL SCHEME.
SO, EVEN THOUGH THIS IS, STRICTLY SPEAKING, ANOTHER SUPERHERO'S TURF...
...LET'S SEE IF I CAN'T SLOW THESE THINGS DOWN JUST A TAD!
NOOOOO!
EH?
THE DEMON?!?
7

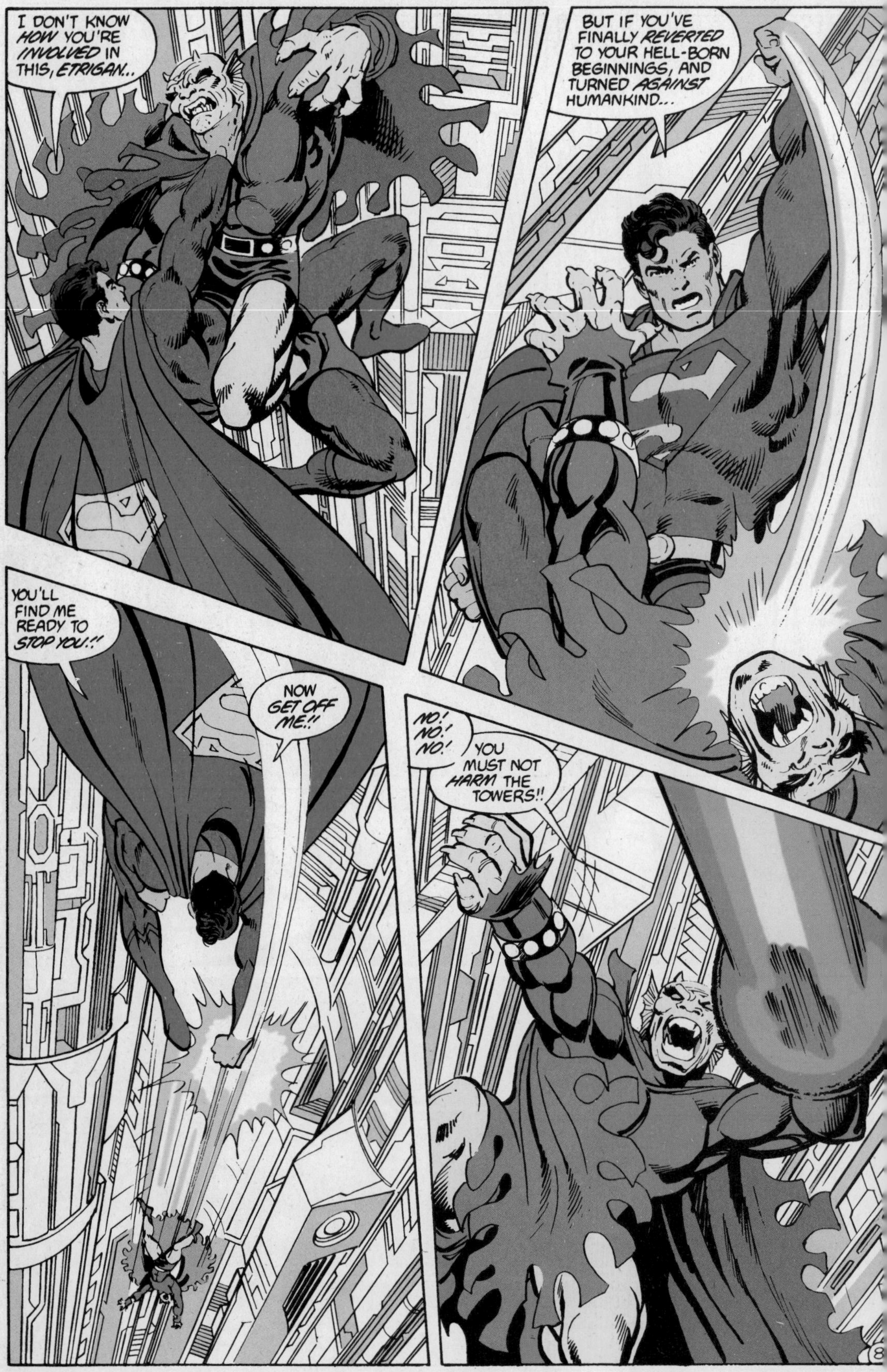

I DON'T KNOW *HOW* YOU'RE *INVOLVED* IN THIS, *ETRIGAN*...
BUT IF YOU'VE FINALLY *REVERTED* TO YOUR HELL-BORN BEGINNINGS, AND TURNED *AGAINST* HUMANKIND...
YOU'LL FIND ME READY TO *STOP YOU!!*
NOW *GET OFF ME!!*
NO! NO! NO!
YOU MUST NOT *HARM* THE TOWERS!!
8

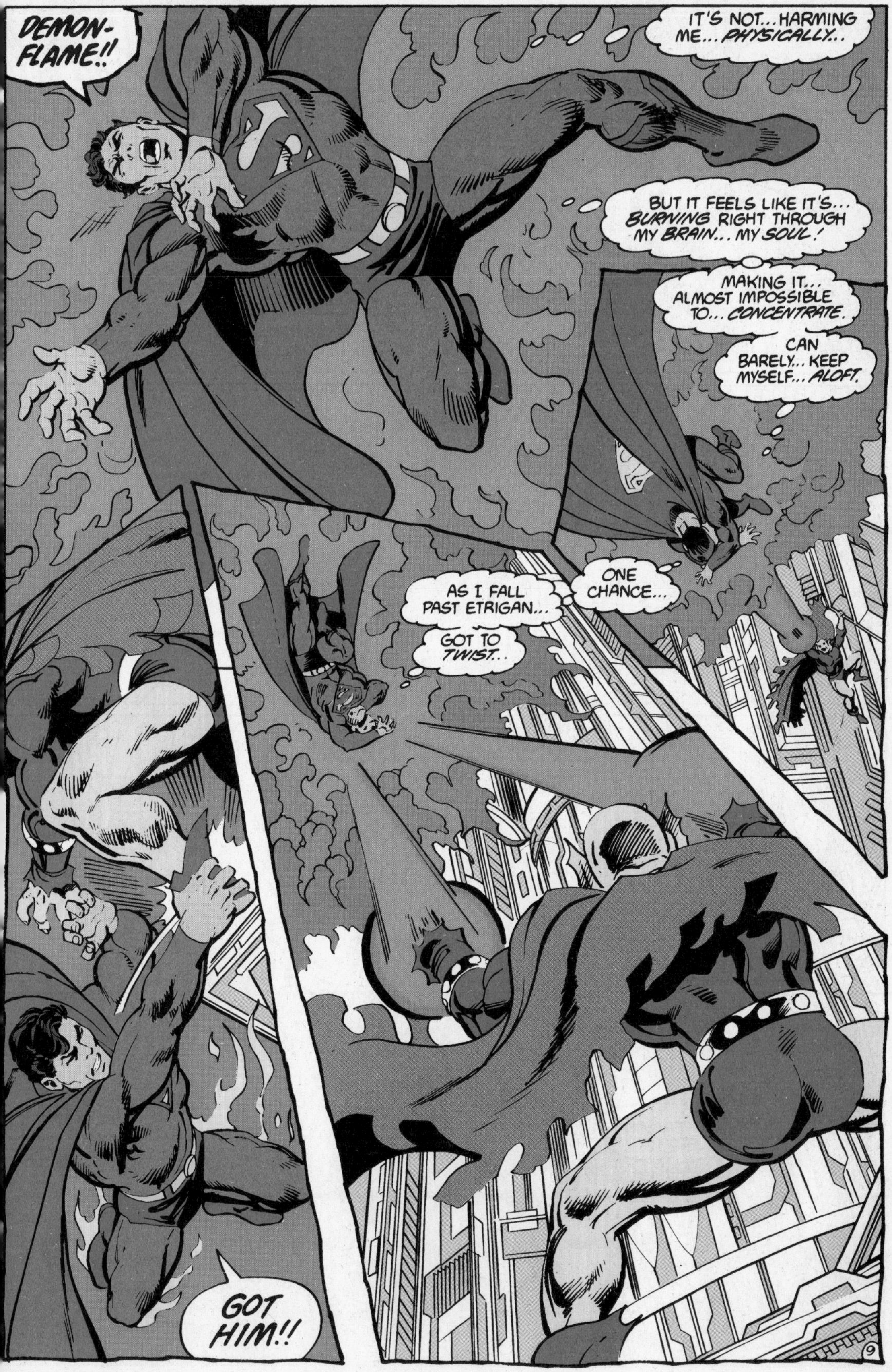

DEMON-FLAME!!
IT'S NOT... HARMING ME... PHYSICALLY...
BUT IT FEELS LIKE IT'S... BURNING RIGHT THROUGH MY BRAIN... MY SOUL!
MAKING IT... ALMOST IMPOSSIBLE TO... CONCENTRATE.
CAN BARELY... KEEP MYSELF... ALOFT.
ONE CHANCE...
AS I FALL PAST ETRIGAN...
GOT TO TWIST...
GOT HIM!!
9

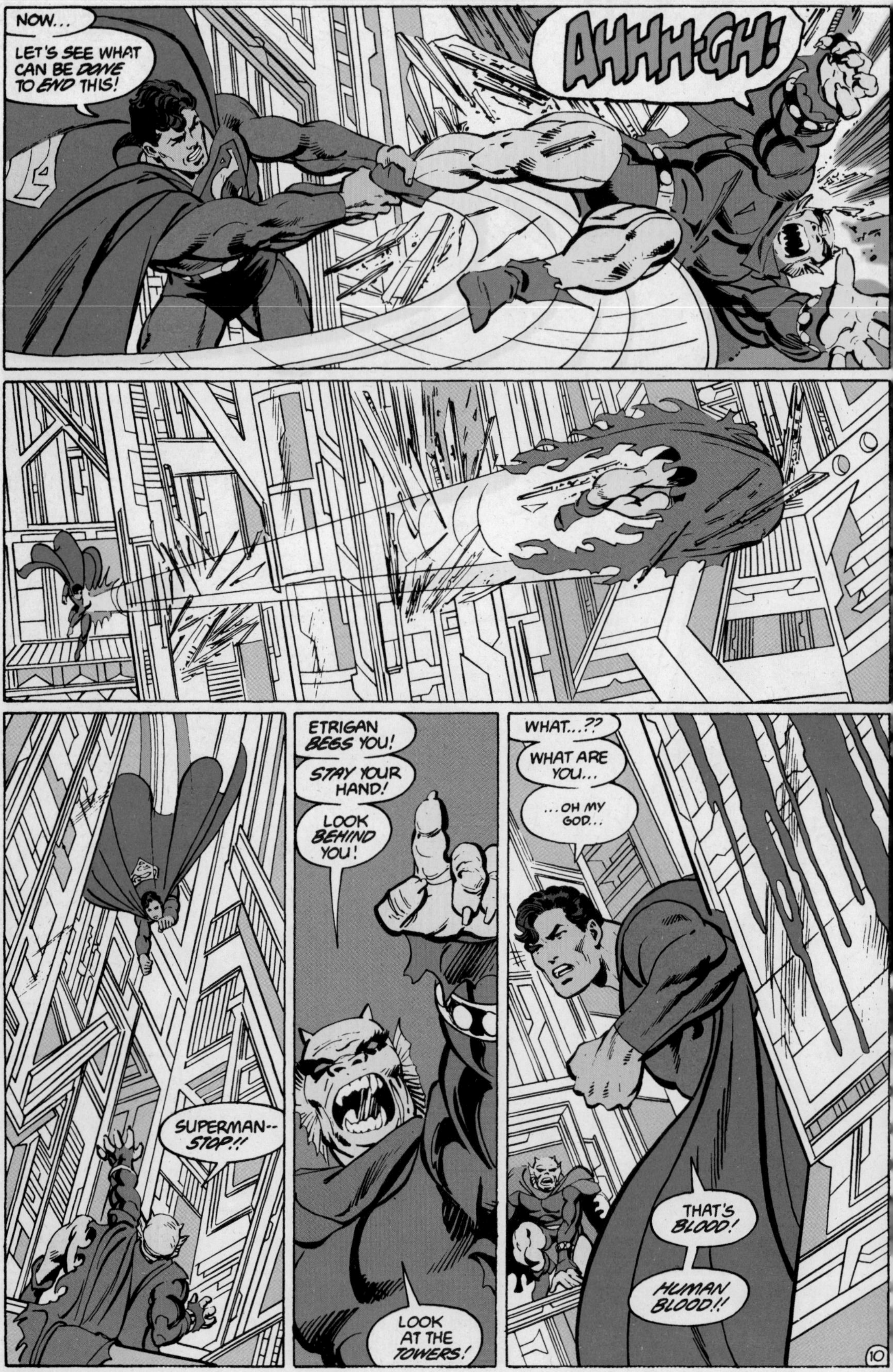
NOW...
LET'S SEE WHAT CAN BE DONE TO END THIS!
AHHH-GH!
ETRIGAN BEGS YOU!
STAY YOUR HAND!
LOOK BEHIND YOU!
SUPERMAN-- STOP!!
LOOK AT THE TOWERS!
WHAT...??
WHAT ARE YOU...
...OH MY GOD...
THAT'S BLOOD!
HUMAN BLOOD!!
10

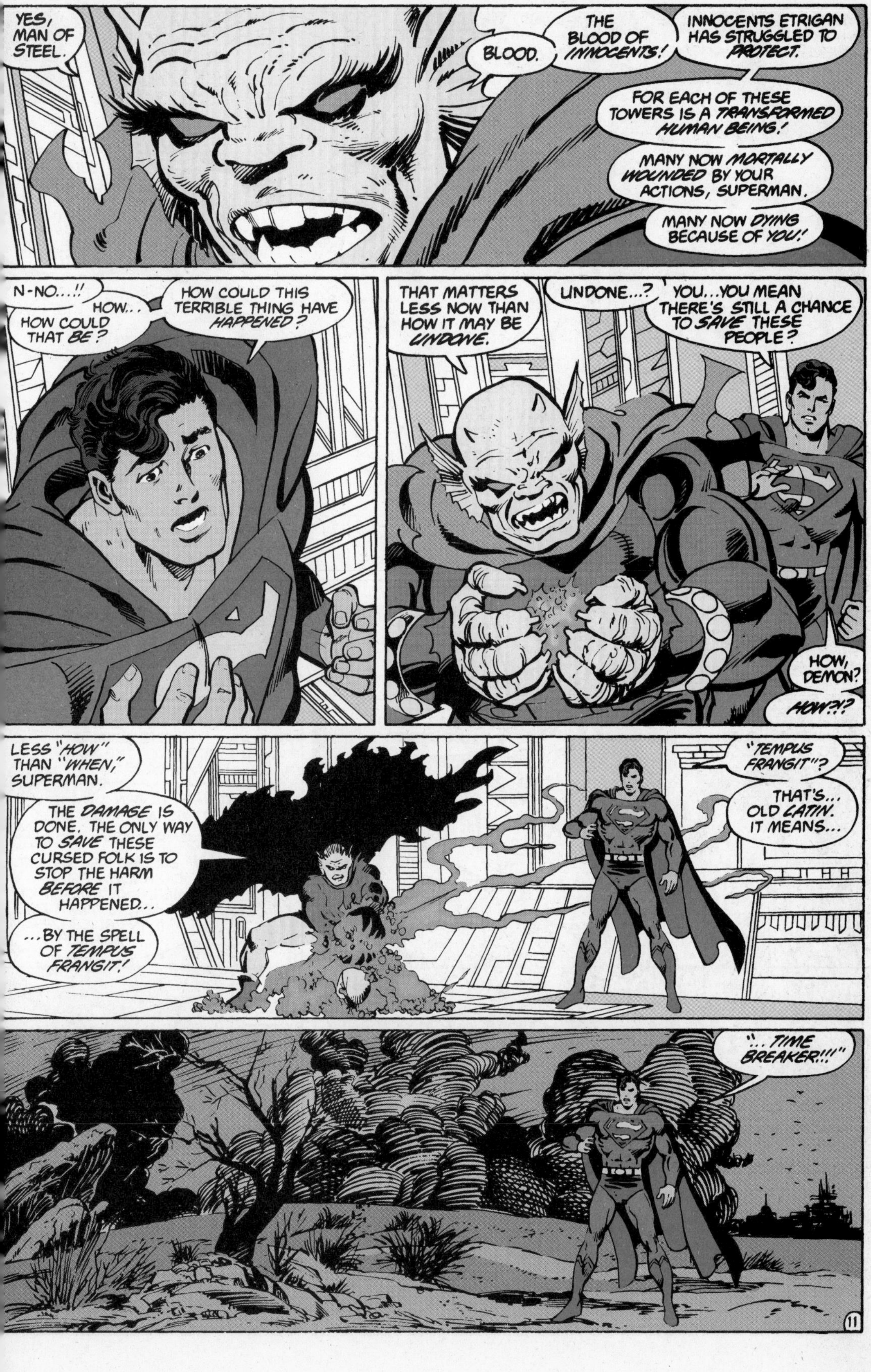

YES, MAN OF STEEL.
BLOOD.
THE BLOOD OF INNOCENTS!
INNOCENTS ETRIGAN HAS STRUGGLED TO PROTECT.
FOR EACH OF THESE TOWERS IS A TRANSFORMED HUMAN BEING!
MANY NOW MORTALLY WOUNDED BY YOUR ACTIONS, SUPERMAN.
MANY NOW DYING BECAUSE OF YOU!
N-NO...!! HOW... HOW COULD THAT BE?
HOW COULD THIS TERRIBLE THING HAVE HAPPENED?
THAT MATTERS LESS NOW THAN HOW IT MAY BE UNDONE.
UNDONE...?
YOU...YOU MEAN THERE'S STILL A CHANCE TO SAVE THESE PEOPLE?
HOW, DEMON?
HOW?!?
LESS "HOW" THAN "WHEN," SUPERMAN.
THE DAMAGE IS DONE. THE ONLY WAY TO SAVE THESE CURSED FOLK IS TO STOP THE HARM BEFORE IT HAPPENED...
...BY THE SPELL OF TEMPUS FRANGIT!
"TEMPUS FRANGIT"?
THAT'S... OLD LATIN. IT MEANS...
"...TIME BREAKER!!!"
11

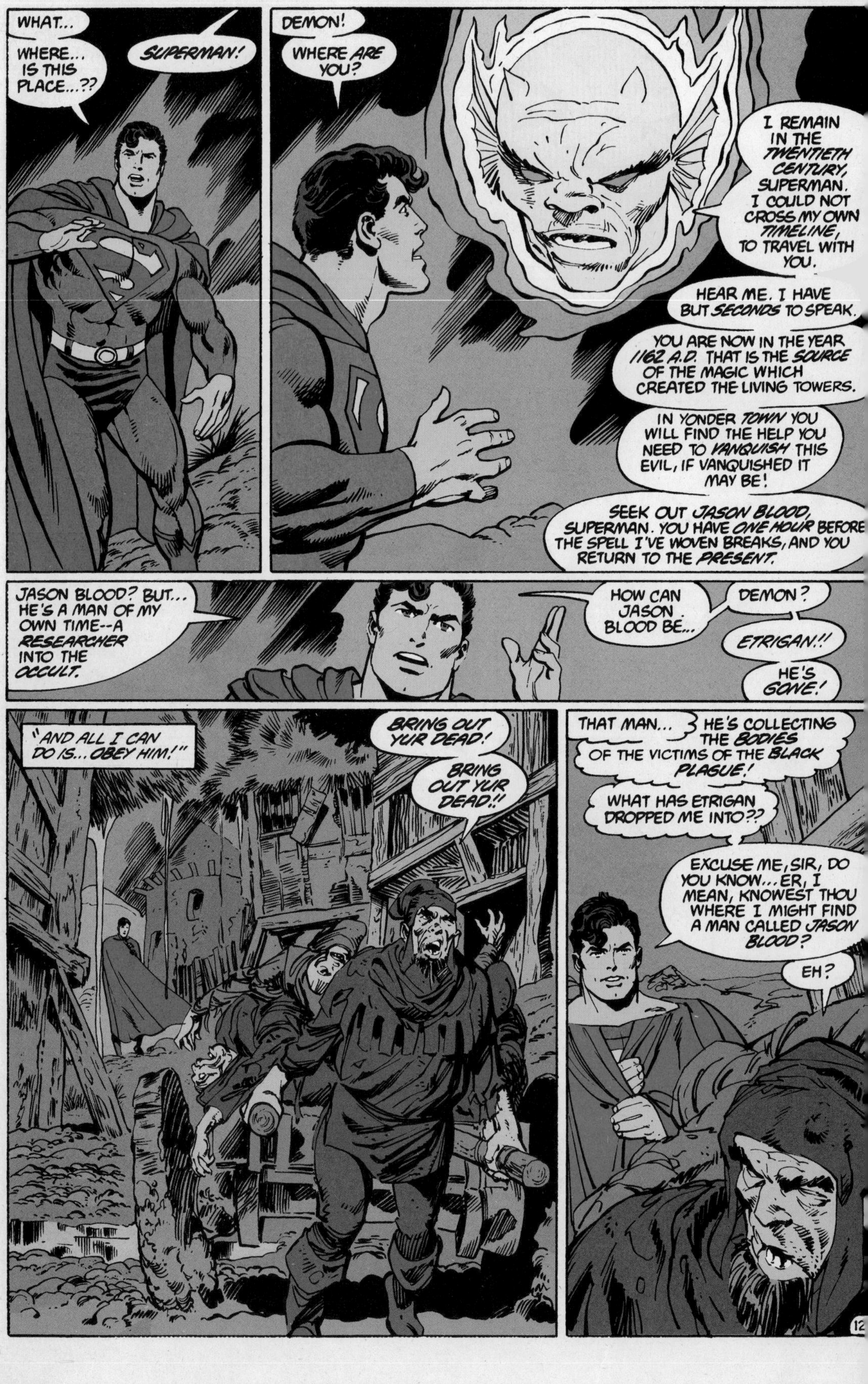
WHAT...
WHERE... IS THIS PLACE...??
SUPERMAN!
DEMON!
WHERE ARE YOU?
I REMAIN IN THE TWENTIETH CENTURY, SUPERMAN. I COULD NOT CROSS MY OWN TIMELINE, TO TRAVEL WITH YOU.
HEAR ME. I HAVE BUT SECONDS TO SPEAK.
YOU ARE NOW IN THE YEAR 1162 A.D. THAT IS THE SOURCE OF THE MAGIC WHICH CREATED THE LIVING TOWERS.
IN YONDER TOWN YOU WILL FIND THE HELP YOU NEED TO VANQUISH THIS EVIL, IF VANQUISHED IT MAY BE!
SEEK OUT JASON BLOOD, SUPERMAN. YOU HAVE ONE HOUR BEFORE THE SPELL I'VE WOVEN BREAKS, AND YOU RETURN TO THE PRESENT.
JASON BLOOD? BUT... HE'S A MAN OF MY OWN TIME--A RESEARCHER INTO THE OCCULT.
HOW CAN JASON BLOOD BE...
DEMON?
ETRIGAN!!
HE'S GONE!
"AND ALL I CAN DO IS... OBEY HIM!"
BRING OUT YUR DEAD!
BRING OUT YUR DEAD!!
THAT MAN...
HE'S COLLECTING THE BODIES OF THE VICTIMS OF THE BLACK PLAGUE!
WHAT HAS ETRIGAN DROPPED ME INTO??
EXCUSE ME, SIR, DO YOU KNOW... ER, I MEAN, KNOWEST THOU WHERE I MIGHT FIND A MAN CALLED JASON BLOOD?
EH?
12

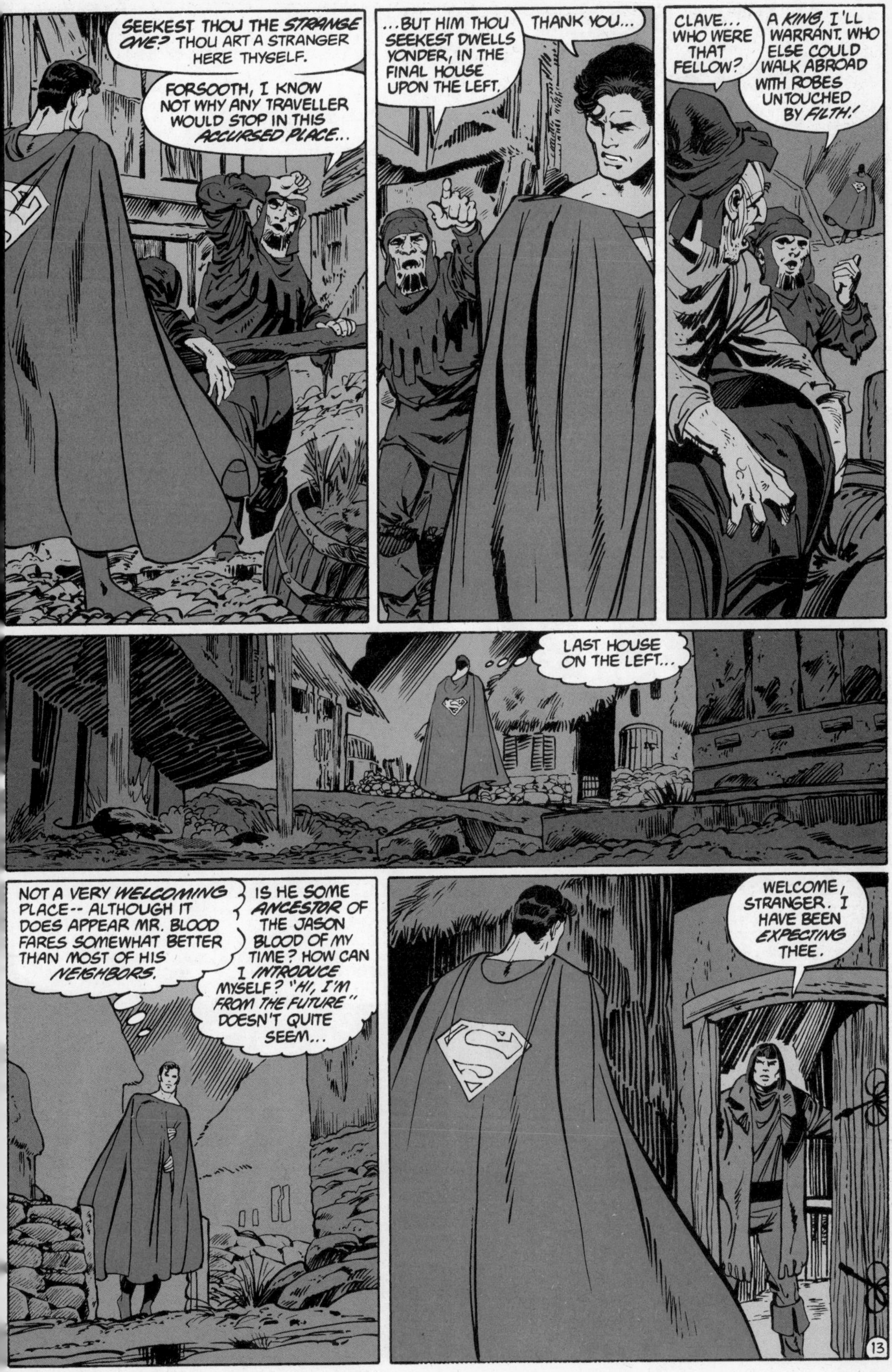

SEEKEST THOU THE STRANGE ONE? THOU ART A STRANGER HERE THYSELF.
FORSOOTH, I KNOW NOT WHY ANY TRAVELLER WOULD STOP IN THIS ACCURSED PLACE...
...BUT HIM THOU SEEKEST DWELLS YONDER, IN THE FINAL HOUSE UPON THE LEFT.
THANK YOU...
CLAVE... WHO WERE THAT FELLOW?
A KING, I'LL WARRANT. WHO ELSE COULD WALK ABROAD WITH ROBES UNTOUCHED BY FILTH!
LAST HOUSE ON THE LEFT...
NOT A VERY WELCOMING PLACE-- ALTHOUGH IT DOES APPEAR MR. BLOOD FARES SOMEWHAT BETTER THAN MOST OF HIS NEIGHBORS.
IS HE SOME ANCESTOR OF THE JASON BLOOD OF MY TIME? HOW CAN I INTRODUCE MYSELF? "HI, I'M FROM THE FUTURE" DOESN'T QUITE SEEM...
WELCOME, STRANGER. I HAVE BEEN EXPECTING THEE.
13

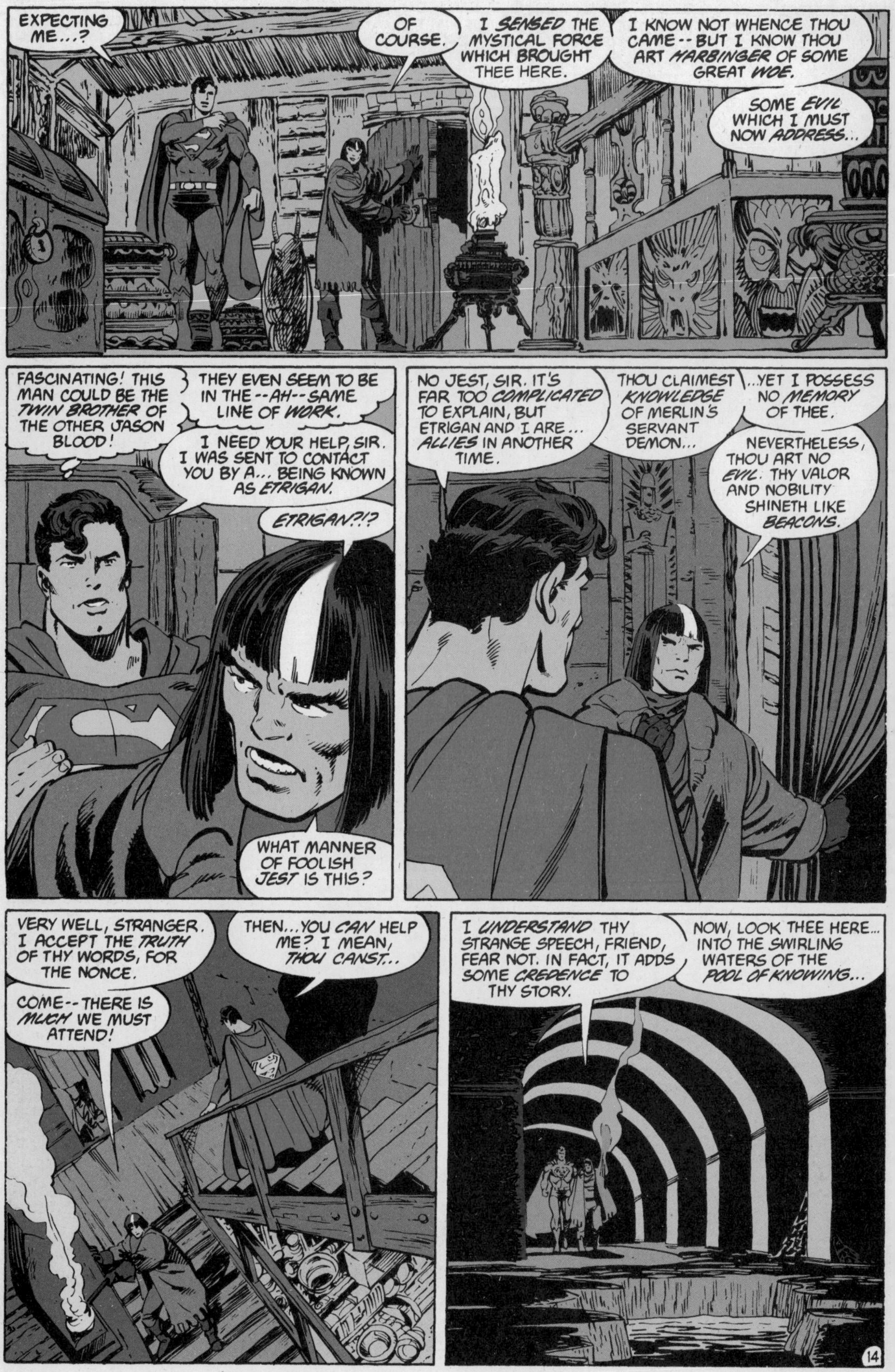
EXPECTING ME...?
OF COURSE.
I SENSED THE MYSTICAL FORCE WHICH BROUGHT THEE HERE.
I KNOW NOT WHENCE THOU CAME--BUT I KNOW THOU ART HARBINGER OF SOME GREAT WOE.
SOME EVIL WHICH I MUST NOW ADDRESS...
FASCINATING! THIS MAN COULD BE THE TWIN BROTHER OF THE OTHER JASON BLOOD!
THEY EVEN SEEM TO BE IN THE--AH--SAME LINE OF WORK.
I NEED YOUR HELP, SIR. I WAS SENT TO CONTACT YOU BY A... BEING KNOWN AS ETRIGAN.
ETRIGAN?!?
WHAT MANNER OF FOOLISH JEST IS THIS?
NO JEST, SIR. IT'S FAR TOO COMPLICATED TO EXPLAIN, BUT ETRIGAN AND I ARE... ALLIES IN ANOTHER TIME.
THOU CLAIMEST KNOWLEDGE OF MERLIN'S SERVANT DEMON...
...YET I POSSESS NO MEMORY OF THEE.
NEVERTHELESS, THOU ART NO EVIL. THY VALOR AND NOBILITY SHINETH LIKE BEACONS.
VERY WELL, STRANGER. I ACCEPT THE TRUTH OF THY WORDS, FOR THE NONCE.
COME--THERE IS MUCH WE MUST ATTEND!
THEN...YOU CAN HELP ME? I MEAN, THOU CANST...
I UNDERSTAND THY STRANGE SPEECH, FRIEND. FEAR NOT. IN FACT, IT ADDS SOME CREDENCE TO THY STORY.
NOW, LOOK THEE HERE... INTO THE SWIRLING WATERS OF THE POOL OF KNOWING...
14

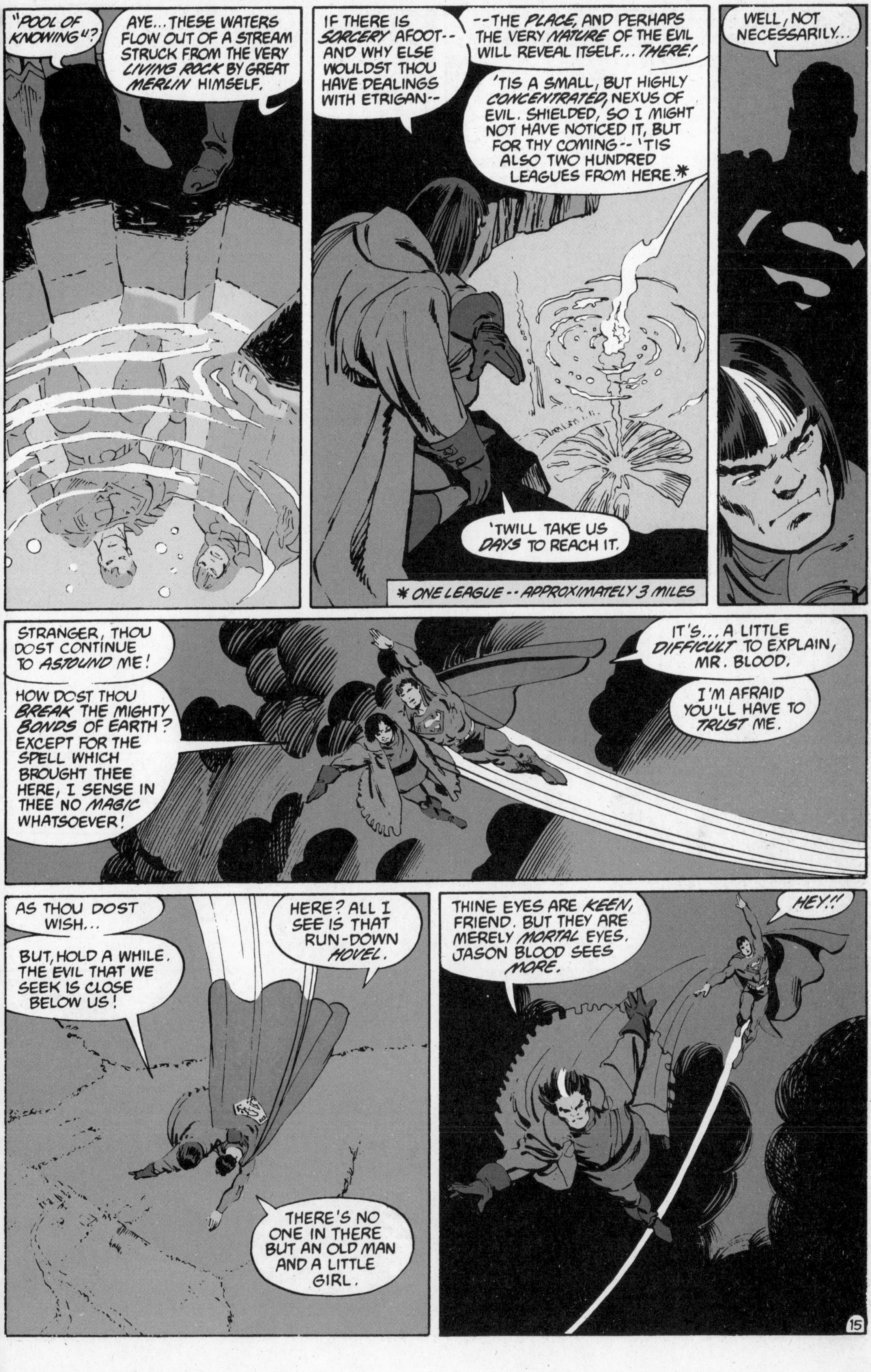

"POOL OF KNOWING"?
AYE... THESE WATERS FLOW OUT OF A STREAM STRUCK FROM THE VERY LIVING ROCK BY GREAT MERLIN HIMSELF.
IF THERE IS SORCERY AFOOT-- AND WHY ELSE WOULDST THOU HAVE DEALINGS WITH ETRIGAN--
--THE PLACE, AND PERHAPS THE VERY NATURE OF THE EVIL WILL REVEAL ITSELF... THERE!
'TIS A SMALL, BUT HIGHLY CONCENTRATED, NEXUS OF EVIL. SHIELDED, SO I MIGHT NOT HAVE NOTICED IT, BUT FOR THY COMING-- 'TIS ALSO TWO HUNDRED LEAGUES FROM HERE.*
'TWILL TAKE US DAYS TO REACH IT.
* ONE LEAGUE -- APPROXIMATELY 3 MILES
WELL, NOT NECESSARILY...
STRANGER, THOU DOST CONTINUE TO ASTOUND ME!
HOW DOST THOU BREAK THE MIGHTY BONDS OF EARTH? EXCEPT FOR THE SPELL WHICH BROUGHT THEE HERE, I SENSE IN THEE NO MAGIC WHATSOEVER!
IT'S... A LITTLE DIFFICULT TO EXPLAIN, MR. BLOOD.
I'M AFRAID YOU'LL HAVE TO TRUST ME.
AS THOU DOST WISH...
BUT, HOLD A WHILE. THE EVIL THAT WE SEEK IS CLOSE BELOW US!
HERE? ALL I SEE IS THAT RUN-DOWN HOVEL.
THERE'S NO ONE IN THERE BUT AN OLD MAN AND A LITTLE GIRL.
THINE EYES ARE KEEN, FRIEND. BUT THEY ARE MERELY MORTAL EYES. JASON BLOOD SEES MORE.
HEY!!
15

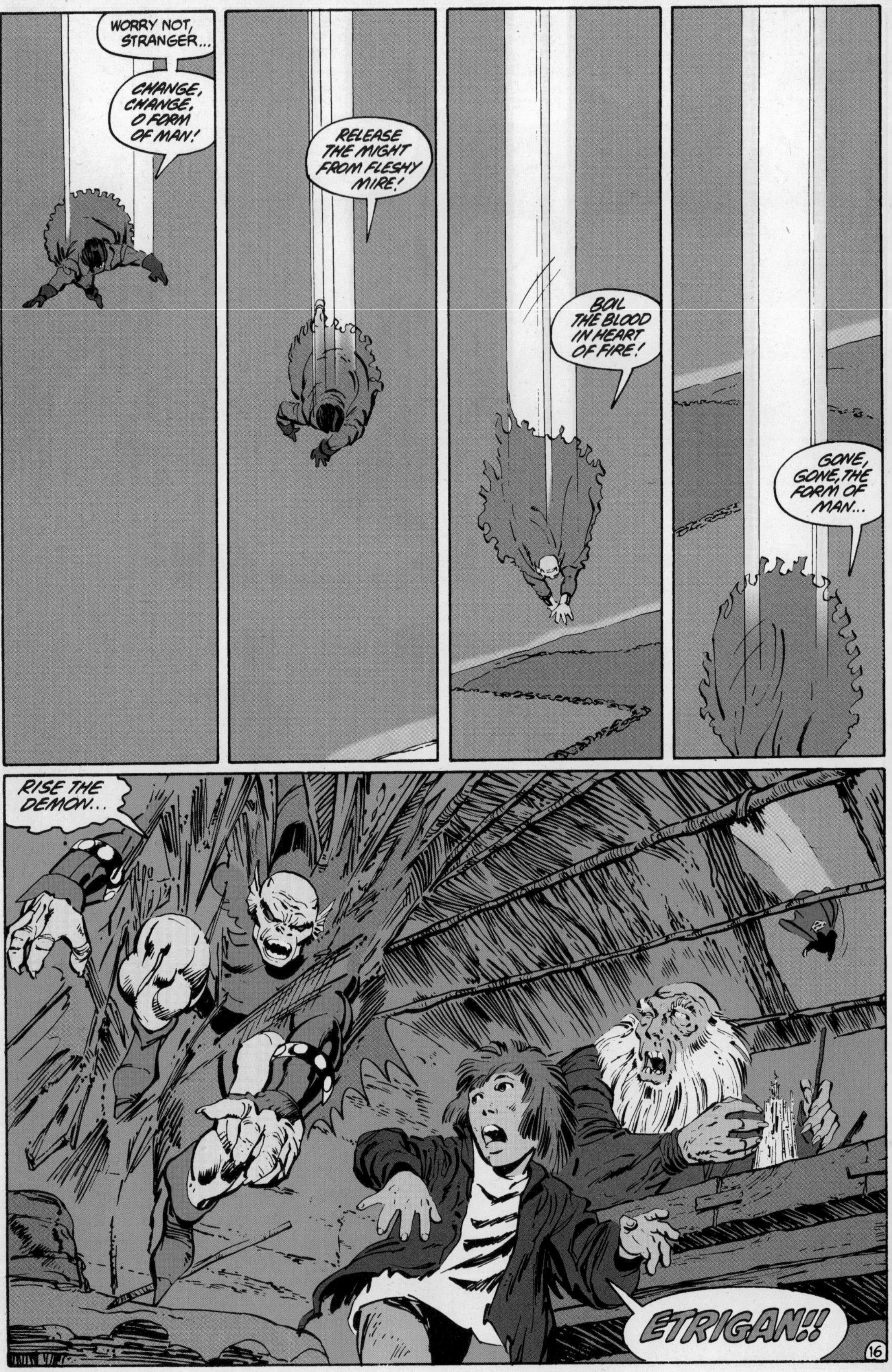
WORRY NOT, STRANGER...
CHANGE, CHANGE, O FORM OF MAN!
RELEASE THE MIGHT FROM FLESHY MIRE!
BOIL THE BLOOD IN HEART OF FIRE!
GONE, GONE, THE FORM OF MAN...
RISE THE DEMON...
ETRIGAN!!
16

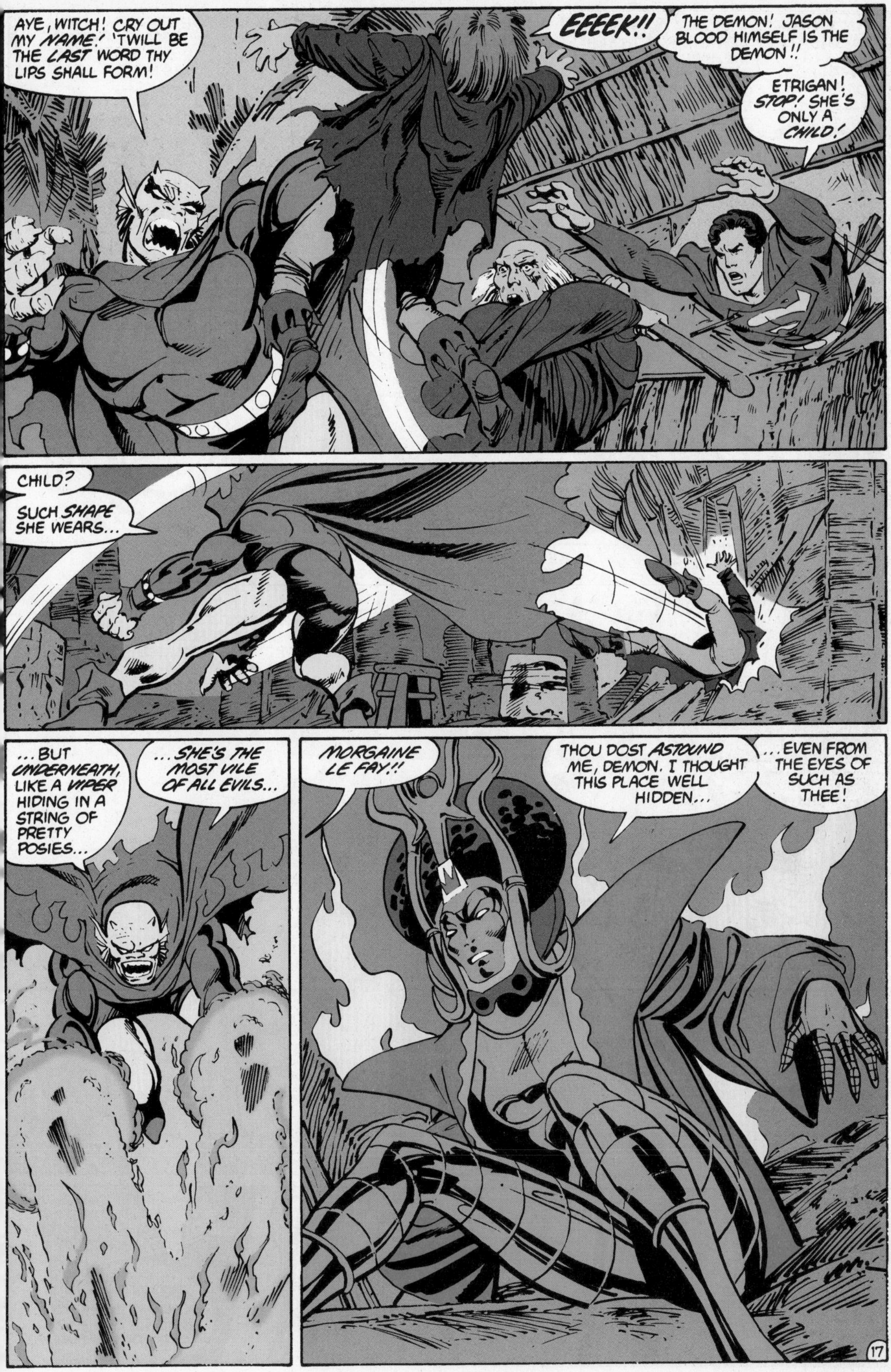
AYE, WITCH! CRY OUT MY NAME! 'TWILL BE THE LAST WORD THY LIPS SHALL FORM!
EEEEK!!
THE DEMON! JASON BLOOD HIMSELF IS THE DEMON!!
ETRIGAN! STOP! SHE'S ONLY A CHILD!
CHILD?
SUCH SHAPE SHE WEARS...
...BUT UNDERNEATH, LIKE A VIPER HIDING IN A STRING OF PRETTY POSIES...
...SHE'S THE MOST VILE OF ALL EVILS...
MORGAINE LE FAY!!
THOU DOST ASTOUND ME, DEMON. I THOUGHT THIS PLACE WELL HIDDEN...
...EVEN FROM THE EYES OF SUCH AS THEE!
17

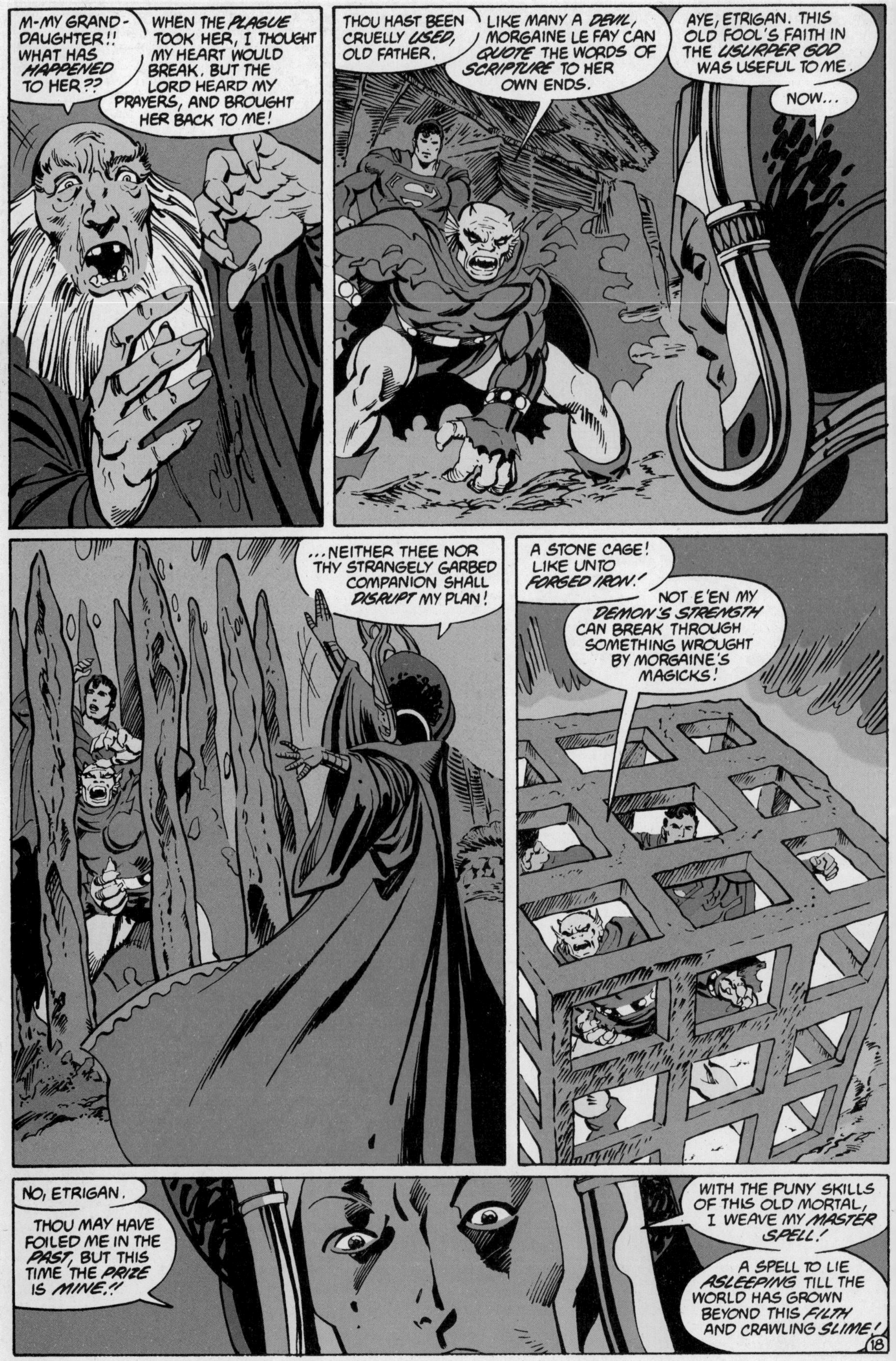

M-MY GRAND-DAUGHTER!! WHAT HAS HAPPENED TO HER??
WHEN THE PLAGUE TOOK HER, I THOUGHT MY HEART WOULD BREAK. BUT THE LORD HEARD MY PRAYERS, AND BROUGHT HER BACK TO ME!
THOU HAST BEEN CRUELLY USED, OLD FATHER.
LIKE MANY A DEVIL, MORGAINE LE FAY CAN QUOTE THE WORDS OF SCRIPTURE TO HER OWN ENDS.
AYE, ETRIGAN. THIS OLD FOOL'S FAITH IN THE USURPER GOD WAS USEFUL TO ME.
NOW...
...NEITHER THEE NOR THY STRANGELY GARBED COMPANION SHALL DISRUPT MY PLAN!
A STONE CAGE! LIKE UNTO FORGED IRON!
NOT E'EN MY DEMON'S STRENGTH CAN BREAK THROUGH SOMETHING WROUGHT BY MORGAINE'S MAGICKS!
NO, ETRIGAN.
THOU MAY HAVE FOILED ME IN THE PAST, BUT THIS TIME THE PRIZE IS MINE!!
WITH THE PUNY SKILLS OF THIS OLD MORTAL, I WEAVE MY MASTER SPELL!
A SPELL TO LIE ASLEEPING TILL THE WORLD HAS GROWN BEYOND THIS FILTH AND CRAWLING SLIME!
18

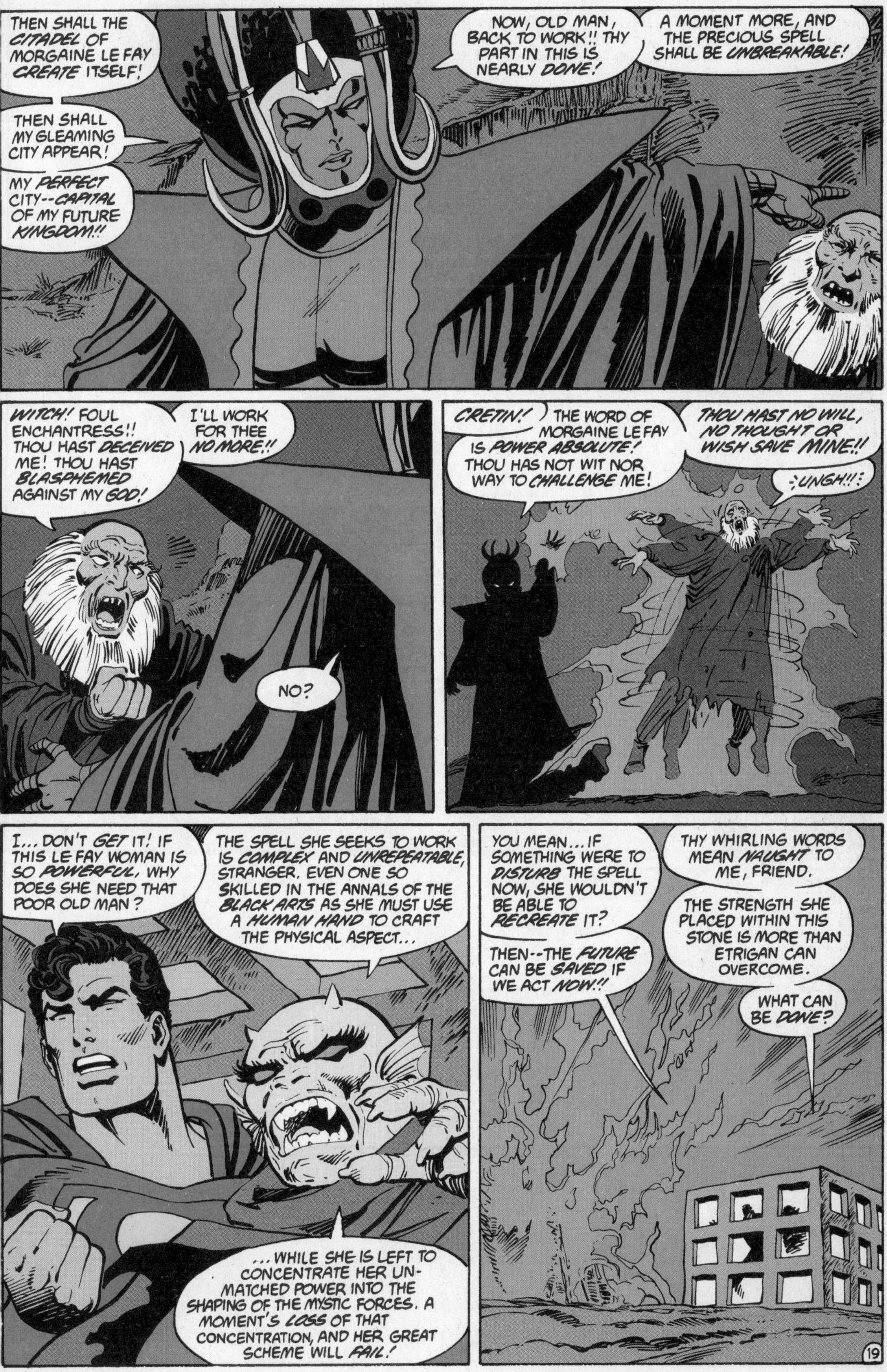

THEN SHALL THE CITADEL OF MORGAINE LE FAY CREATE ITSELF!
THEN SHALL MY GLEAMING CITY APPEAR!
MY PERFECT CITY--CAPITAL OF MY FUTURE KINGDOM!!
NOW, OLD MAN, BACK TO WORK!! THY PART IN THIS IS NEARLY DONE!
A MOMENT MORE, AND THE PRECIOUS SPELL SHALL BE UNBREAKABLE!
WITCH! FOUL ENCHANTRESS!! THOU HAST DECEIVED ME! THOU HAST BLASPHEMED AGAINST MY GOD!
I'LL WORK FOR THEE NO MORE!!
NO?
CRETIN!
THE WORD OF MORGAINE LE FAY IS POWER ABSOLUTE! THOU HAS NOT WIT NOR WAY TO CHALLENGE ME!
THOU HAST NO WILL, NO THOUGHT OR WISH SAVE MINE!!
UNGH!!
I... DON'T GET IT! IF THIS LE FAY WOMAN IS SO POWERFUL, WHY DOES SHE NEED THAT POOR OLD MAN?
THE SPELL SHE SEEKS TO WORK IS COMPLEX AND UNREPEATABLE, STRANGER. EVEN ONE SO SKILLED IN THE ANNALS OF THE BLACK ARTS AS SHE MUST USE A HUMAN HAND TO CRAFT THE PHYSICAL ASPECT...
...WHILE SHE IS LEFT TO CONCENTRATE HER UNMATCHED POWER INTO THE SHAPING OF THE MYSTIC FORCES. A MOMENT'S LOSS OF THAT CONCENTRATION, AND HER GREAT SCHEME WILL FAIL!
YOU MEAN... IF SOMETHING WERE TO DISTURB THE SPELL NOW, SHE WOULDN'T BE ABLE TO RECREATE IT?
THEN--THE FUTURE CAN BE SAVED IF WE ACT NOW!!
THY WHIRLING WORDS MEAN NAUGHT TO ME, FRIEND.
THE STRENGTH SHE PLACED WITHIN THIS STONE IS MORE THAN ETRIGAN CAN OVERCOME.
WHAT CAN BE DONE?
19

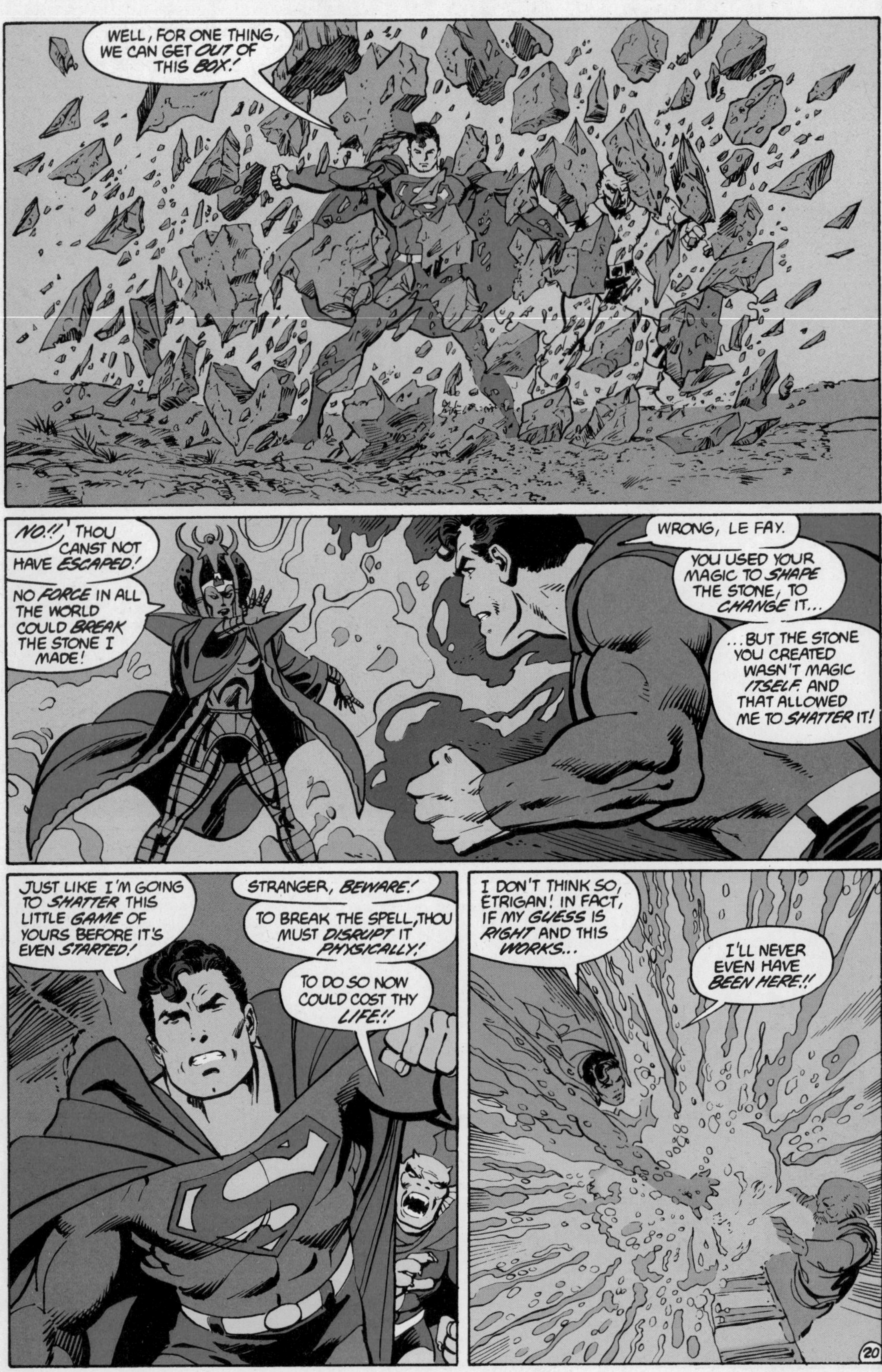
WELL, FOR ONE THING, WE CAN GET OUT OF THIS BOX!
NO!! THOU CANST NOT HAVE ESCAPED!
NO FORCE IN ALL THE WORLD COULD BREAK THE STONE I MADE!
WRONG, LE FAY.
YOU USED YOUR MAGIC TO SHAPE THE STONE, TO CHANGE IT...
...BUT THE STONE YOU CREATED WASN'T MAGIC ITSELF. AND THAT ALLOWED ME TO SHATTER IT!
JUST LIKE I'M GOING TO SHATTER THIS LITTLE GAME OF YOURS BEFORE IT'S EVEN STARTED!
STRANGER, BEWARE!
TO BREAK THE SPELL, THOU MUST DISRUPT IT PHYSICALLY!
TO DO SO NOW COULD COST THY LIFE!!
I DON'T THINK SO, ETRIGAN! IN FACT, IF MY GUESS IS RIGHT AND THIS WORKS...
I'LL NEVER EVEN HAVE BEEN HERE!!
20

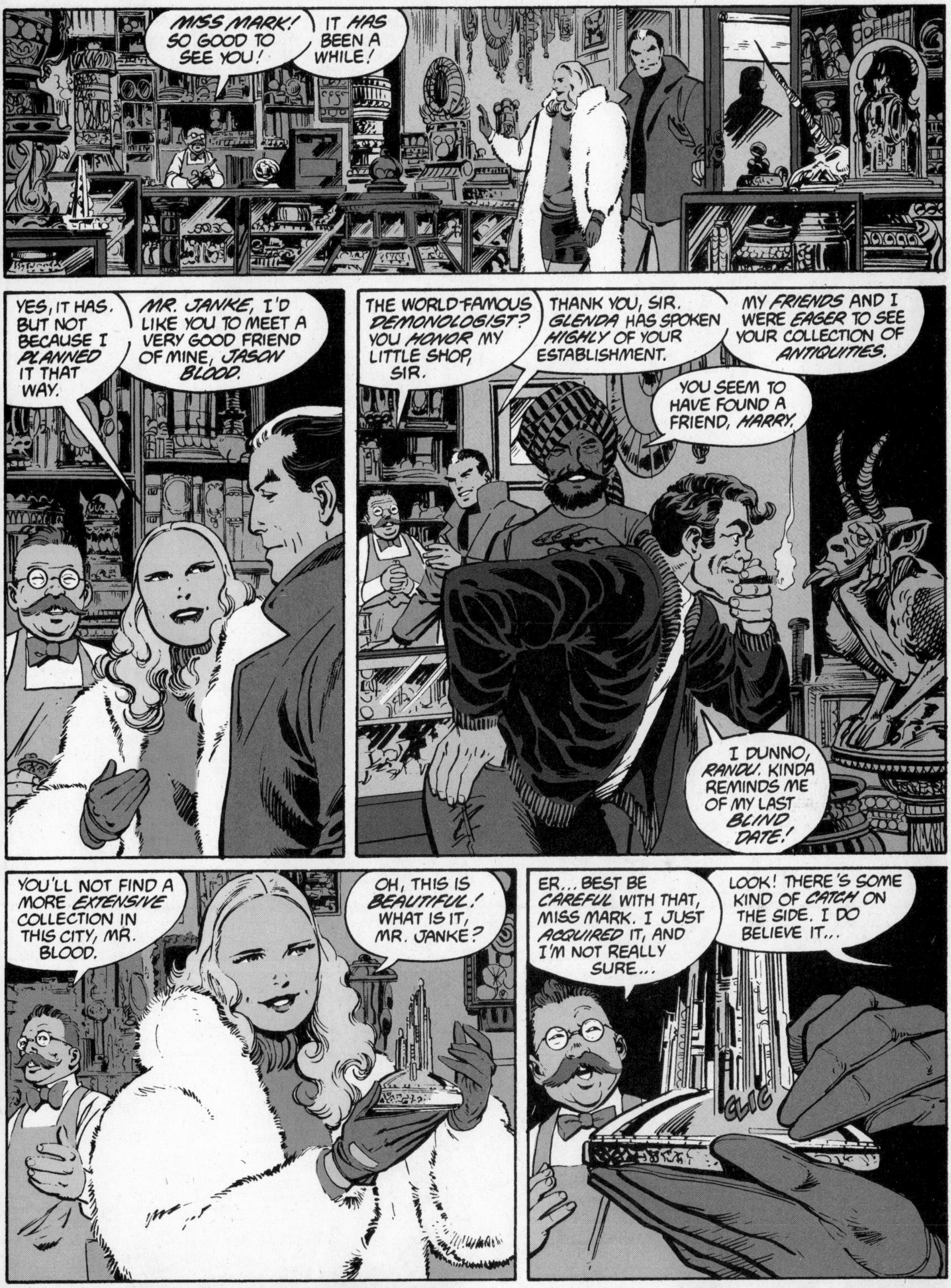
MISS MARK! SO GOOD TO SEE YOU!
IT HAS BEEN A WHILE!
YES, IT HAS. BUT NOT BECAUSE I PLANNED IT THAT WAY.
MR. JANKE, I'D LIKE YOU TO MEET A VERY GOOD FRIEND OF MINE, JASON BLOOD.
THE WORLD-FAMOUS DEMONOLOGIST? YOU HONOR MY LITTLE SHOP, SIR.
THANK YOU, SIR. GLENDA HAS SPOKEN HIGHLY OF YOUR ESTABLISHMENT.
MY FRIENDS AND I WERE EAGER TO SEE YOUR COLLECTION OF ANTIQUITIES.
YOU SEEM TO HAVE FOUND A FRIEND, HARRY.
I DUNNO, RANDU. KINDA REMINDS ME OF MY LAST BLIND DATE!
YOU'LL NOT FIND A MORE EXTENSIVE COLLECTION IN THIS CITY, MR. BLOOD.
OH, THIS IS BEAUTIFUL! WHAT IS IT, MR. JANKE?
ER... BEST BE CAREFUL WITH THAT, MISS MARK. I JUST ACQUIRED IT, AND I'M NOT REALLY SURE...
LOOK! THERE'S SOME KIND OF CATCH ON THE SIDE. I DO BELIEVE IT...
CLIC
...OPENS...
OH...
WHAT A DISAPPOINTMENT!
IT'S EMPTY!
21

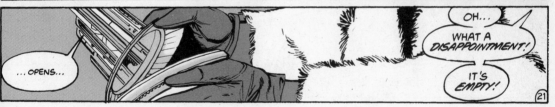

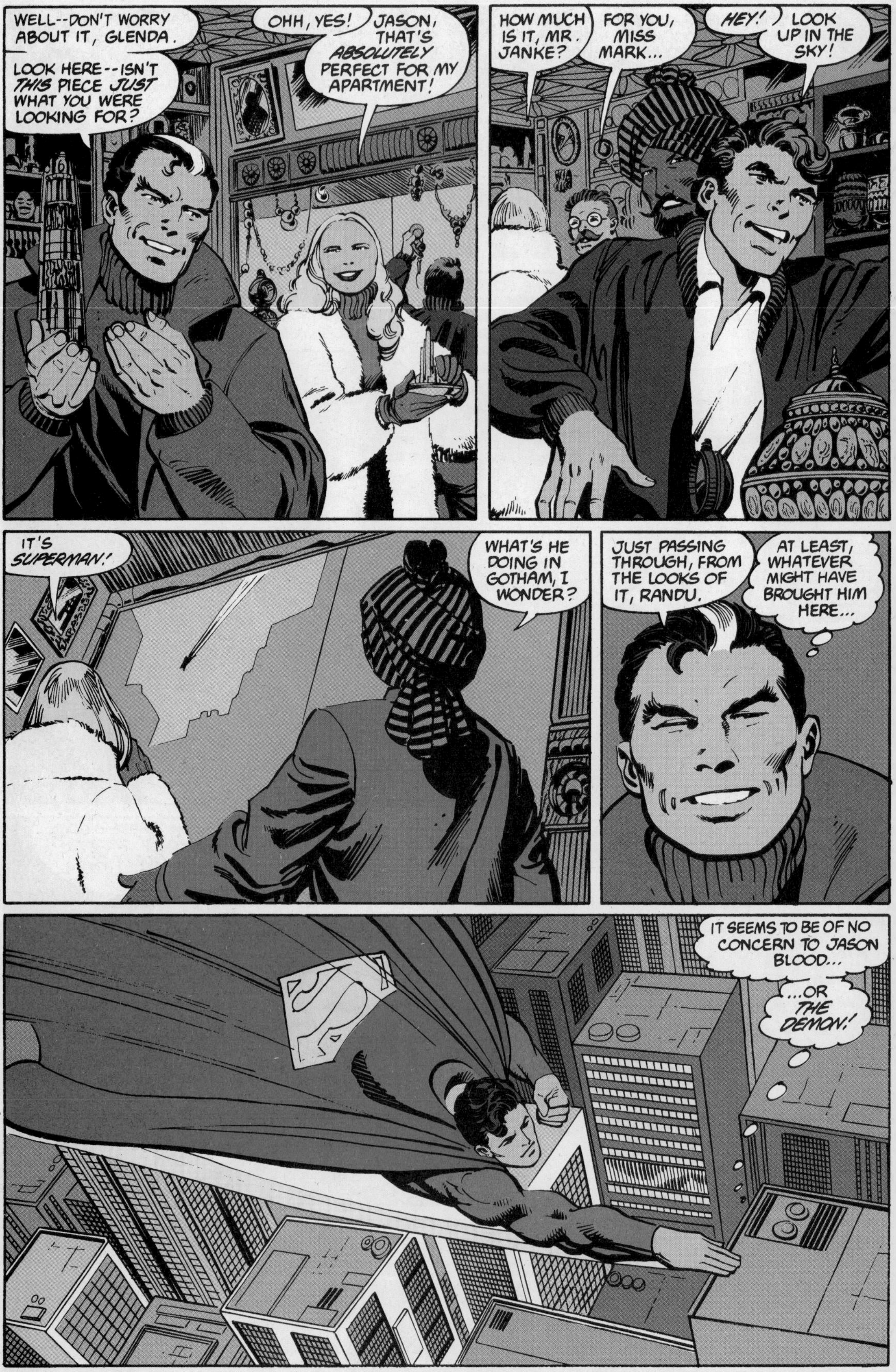
WELL--DON'T WORRY ABOUT IT, GLENDA.
LOOK HERE--ISN'T THIS PIECE JUST WHAT YOU WERE LOOKING FOR?
OHH, YES!
JASON, THAT'S ABSOLUTELY PERFECT FOR MY APARTMENT!
HOW MUCH IS IT, MR. JANKE?
FOR YOU, MISS MARK...
HEY!
LOOK UP IN THE SKY!
IT'S SUPERMAN!
WHAT'S HE DOING IN GOTHAM, I WONDER?
JUST PASSING THROUGH, FROM THE LOOKS OF IT, RANDU.
AT LEAST, WHATEVER MIGHT HAVE BROUGHT HIM HERE...
IT SEEMS TO BE OF NO CONCERN TO JASON BLOOD...
...OR THE DEMON!

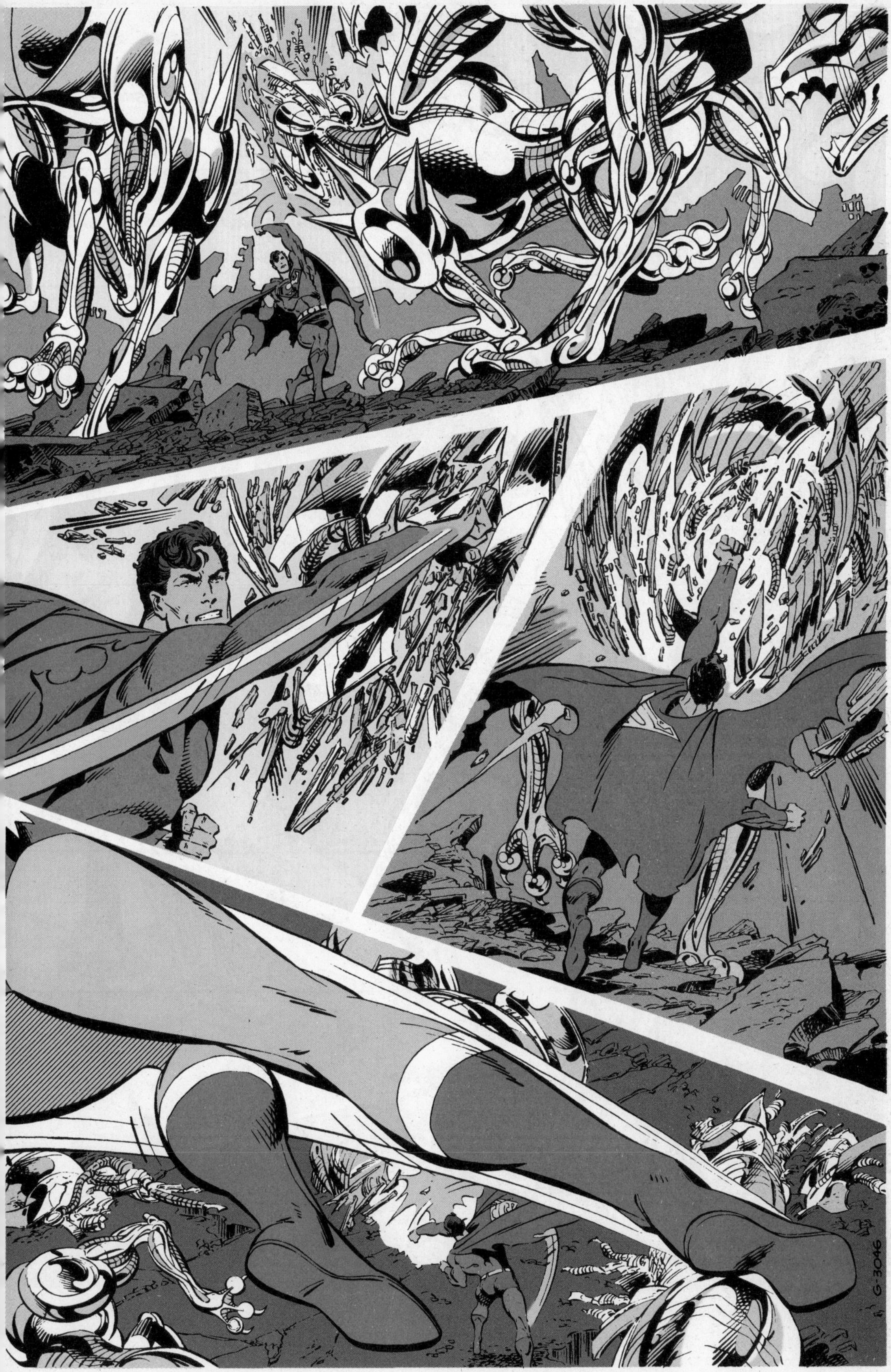
G-3046

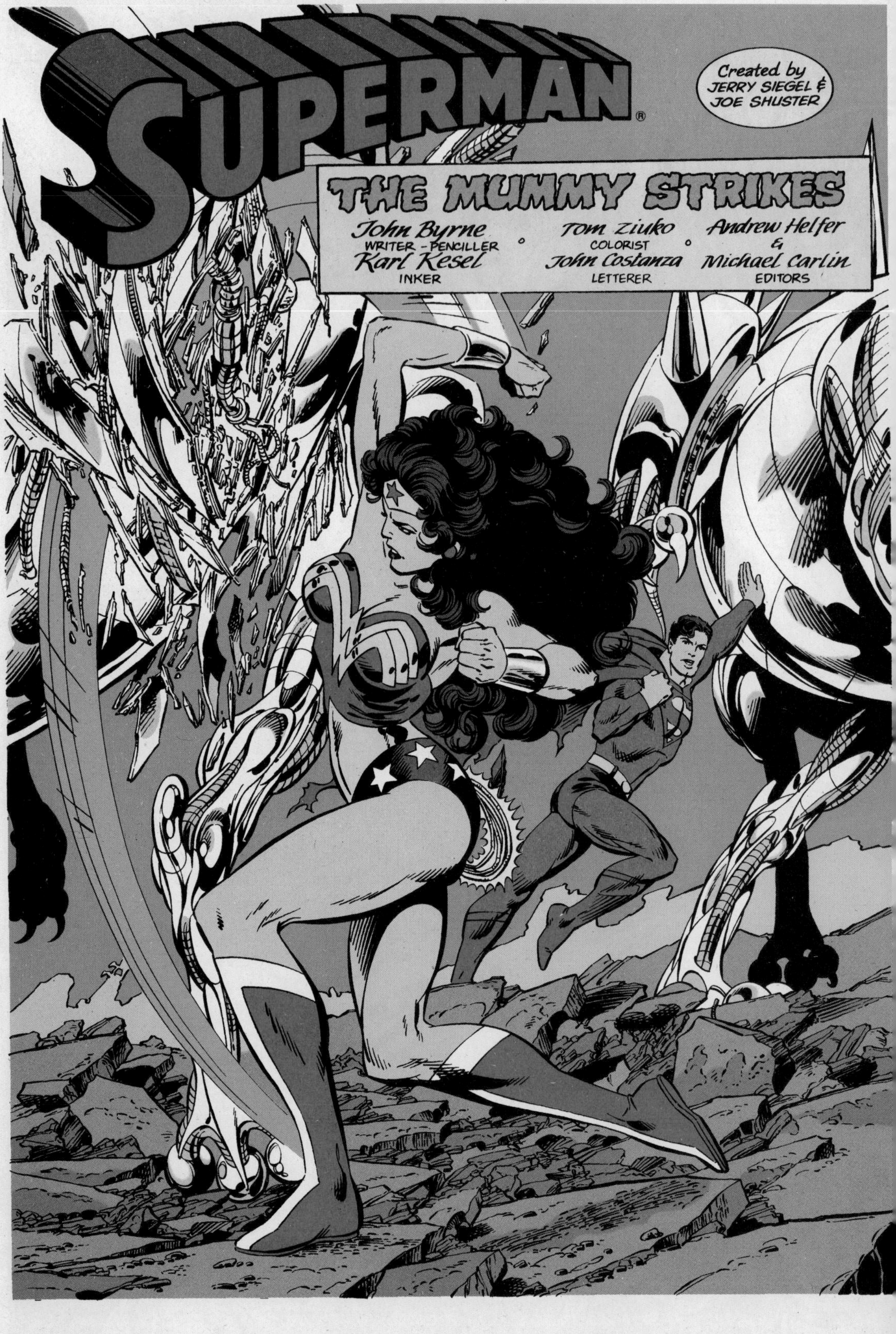
SUPERMAN
Created by JERRY SIEGEL & JOE SHUSTER
THE MUMMY STRIKES
John Byrne WRITER - PENCILLER
Karl Kesel INKER
Tom Ziuko COLORIST
John Costanza LETTERER
Andrew Helfer & Michael Carlin EDITORS

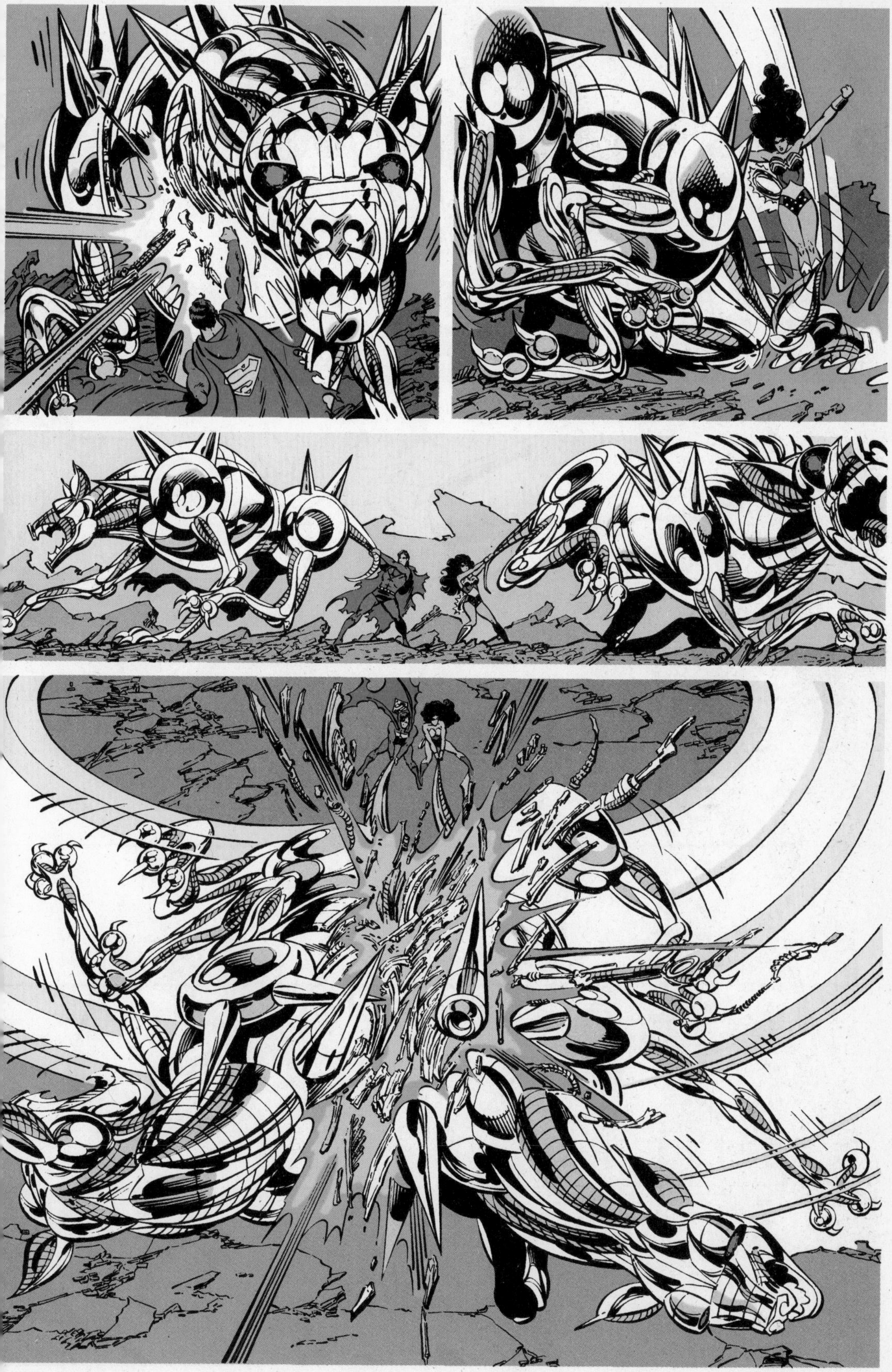

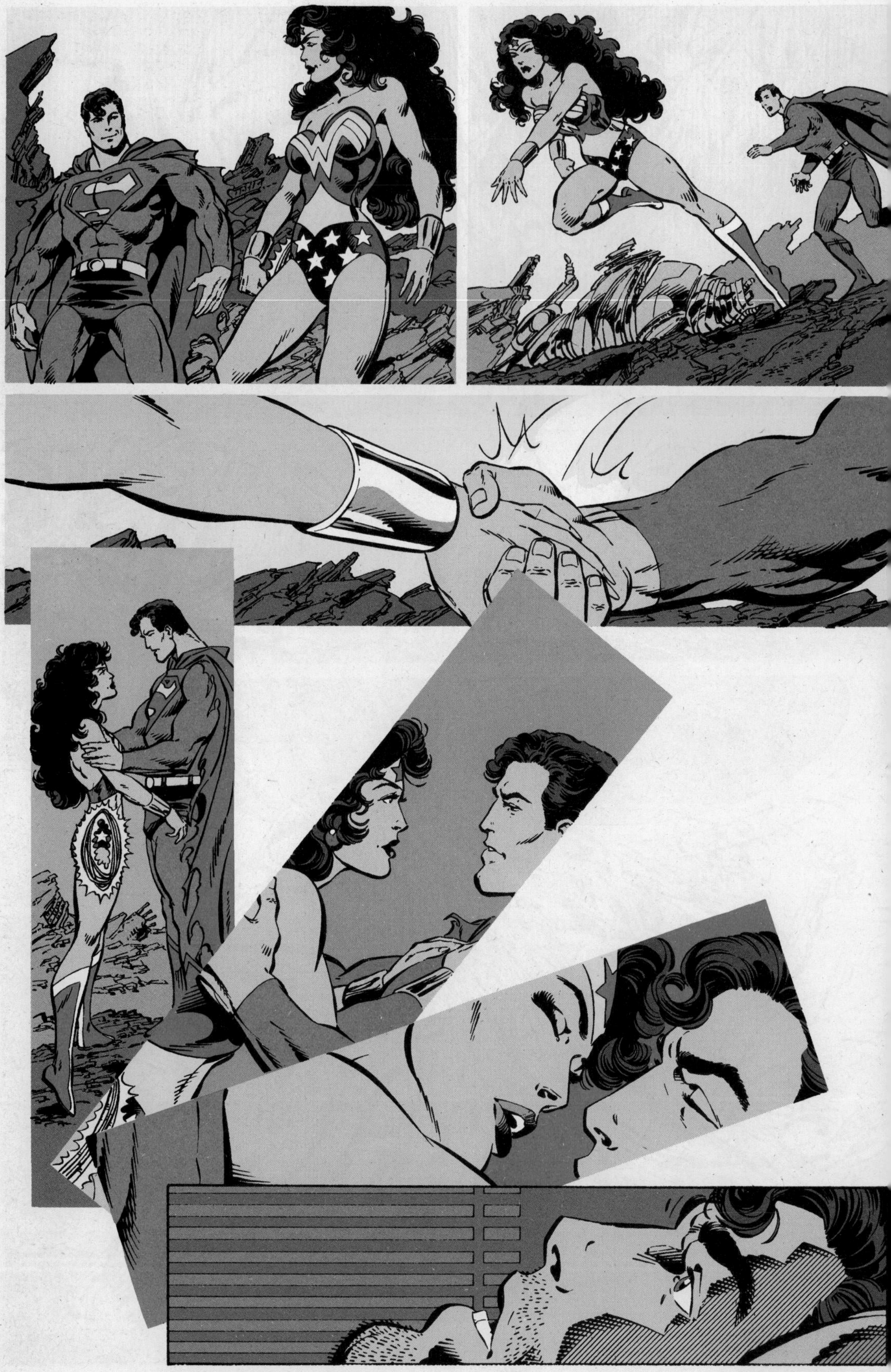

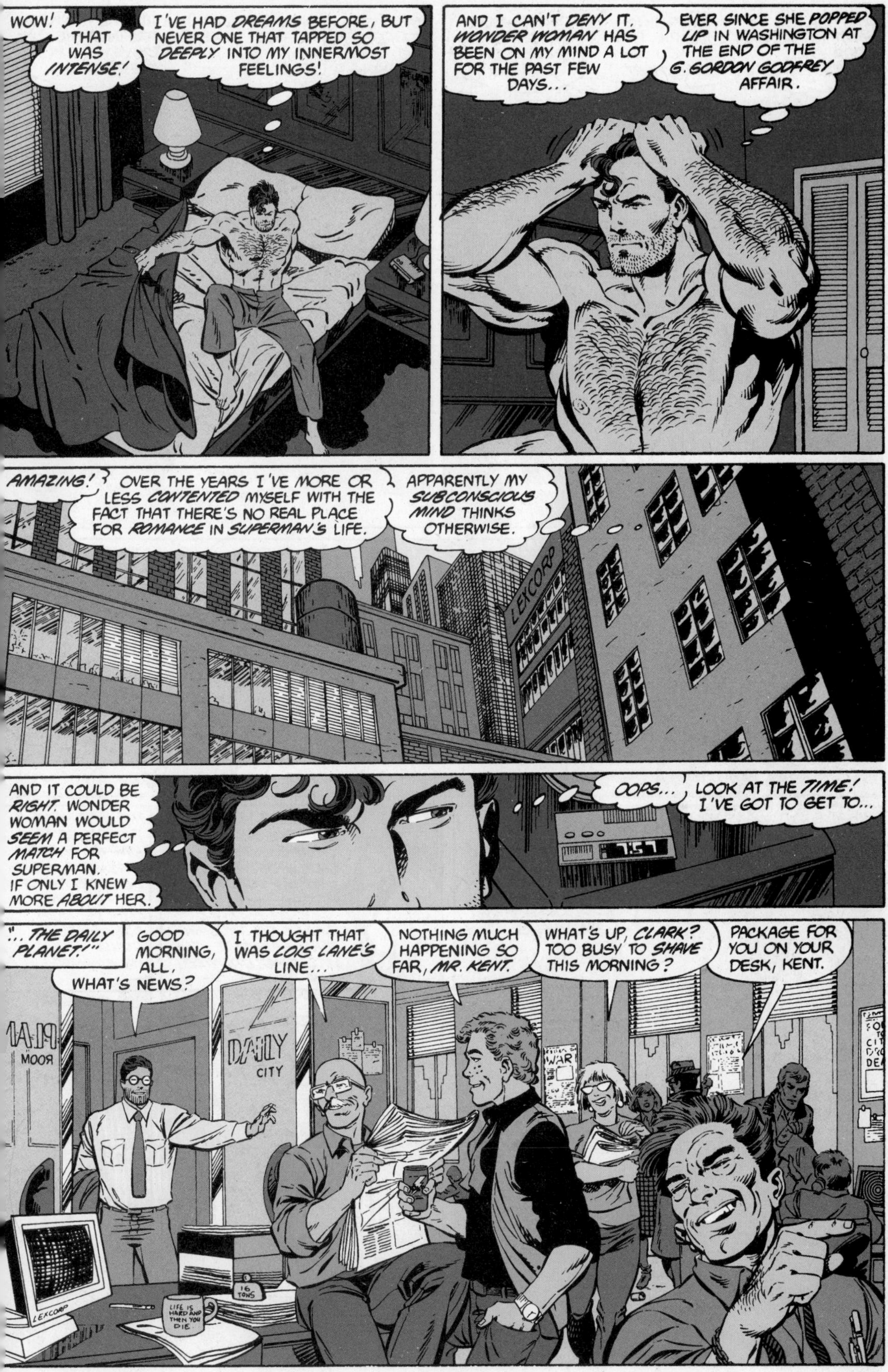
WOW! THAT WAS INTENSE!
I'VE HAD DREAMS BEFORE, BUT NEVER ONE THAT TAPPED SO DEEPLY INTO MY INNERMOST FEELINGS!
AND I CAN'T DENY IT. WONDER WOMAN HAS BEEN ON MY MIND A LOT FOR THE PAST FEW DAYS...
EVER SINCE SHE POPPED UP IN WASHINGTON AT THE END OF THE G. GORDON GODFREY AFFAIR.
AMAZING!
OVER THE YEARS I'VE MORE OR LESS CONTENTED MYSELF WITH THE FACT THAT THERE'S NO REAL PLACE FOR ROMANCE IN SUPERMAN'S LIFE.
APPARENTLY MY SUBCONSCIOUS MIND THINKS OTHERWISE.
LEXCORP
AND IT COULD BE RIGHT. WONDER WOMAN WOULD SEEM A PERFECT MATCH FOR SUPERMAN. IF ONLY I KNEW MORE ABOUT HER.
OOPS...
LOOK AT THE TIME! I'VE GOT TO GET TO...
7:57
"...THE DAILY PLANET!"
GOOD MORNING, ALL. WHAT'S NEWS?
I THOUGHT THAT WAS LOIS LANE'S LINE...
NOTHING MUCH HAPPENING SO FAR, MR. KENT.
WHAT'S UP, CLARK? TOO BUSY TO SHAVE THIS MORNING?
PACKAGE FOR YOU ON YOUR DESK, KENT.
DAILY
CITY
ROOM
WAR
16 TONS
LIFE IS HARD AND THEN YOU DIE
LEXCORP

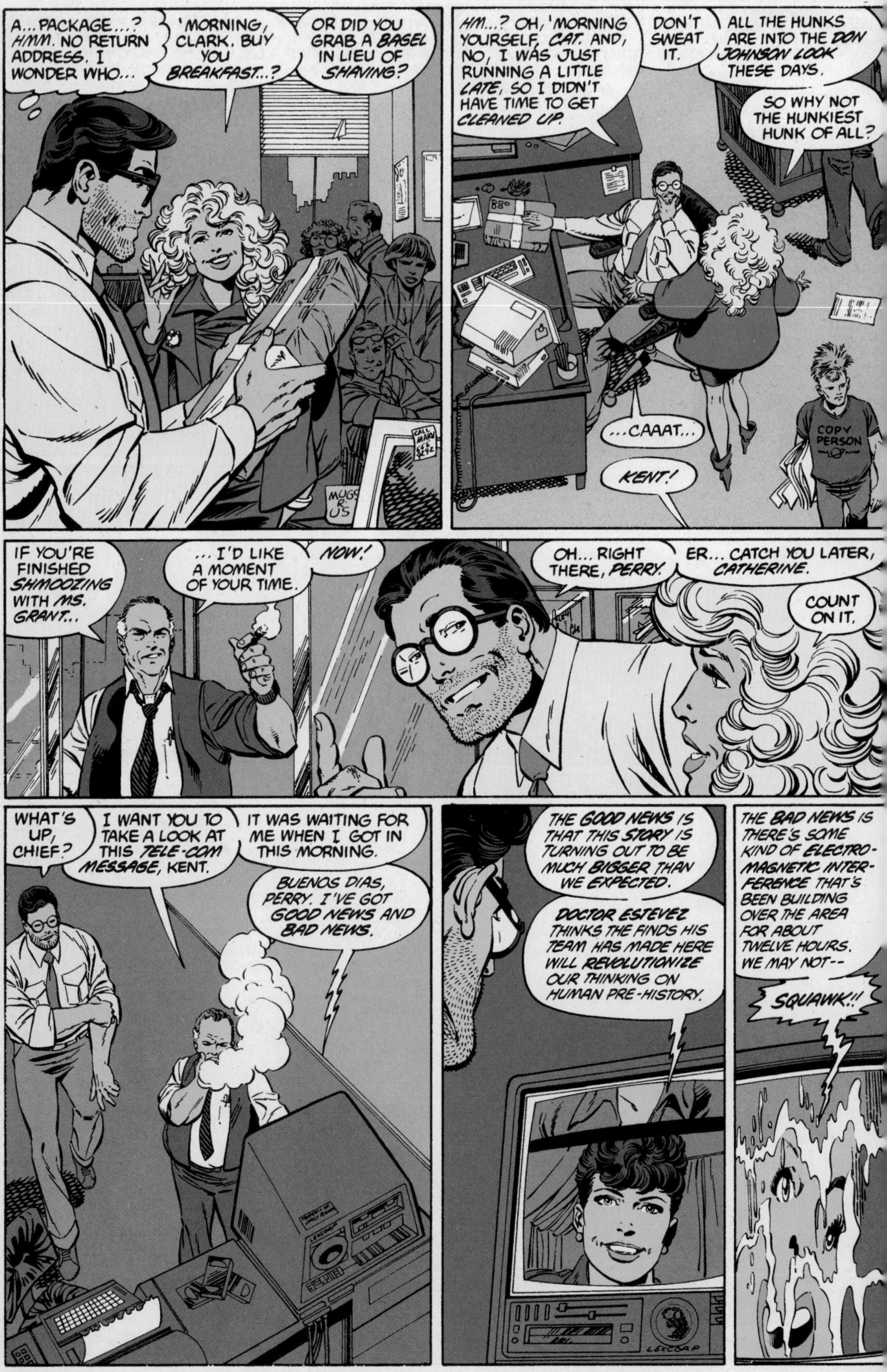

A...PACKAGE...? HMM. NO RETURN ADDRESS. I WONDER WHO...
'MORNING, CLARK. BUY YOU BREAKFAST...?
OR DID YOU GRAB A BAGEL IN LIEU OF SHAVING?
CALL MARY 555-9292
MUGS R US
HM...? OH, 'MORNING YOURSELF, CAT. AND, NO, I WAS JUST RUNNING A LITTLE LATE, SO I DIDN'T HAVE TIME TO GET CLEANED UP.
DON'T SWEAT IT.
ALL THE HUNKS ARE INTO THE DON JOHNSON LOOK THESE DAYS.
SO WHY NOT THE HUNKIEST HUNK OF ALL?
...CAAAT...
KENT!
COPY PERSON
IF YOU'RE FINISHED SHMOOZING WITH MS. GRANT...
...I'D LIKE A MOMENT OF YOUR TIME.
NOW!
OH...RIGHT THERE, PERRY.
ER...CATCH YOU LATER, CATHERINE.
COUNT ON IT.
WHAT'S UP, CHIEF?
I WANT YOU TO TAKE A LOOK AT THIS TELE-COM MESSAGE, KENT.
IT WAS WAITING FOR ME WHEN I GOT IN THIS MORNING.
BUENOS DIAS, PERRY. I'VE GOT GOOD NEWS AND BAD NEWS.
LEXCORP
THE GOOD NEWS IS THAT THIS STORY IS TURNING OUT TO BE MUCH BIGGER THAN WE EXPECTED.
DOCTOR ESTEVEZ THINKS THE FINDS HIS TEAM HAS MADE HERE WILL REVOLUTIONIZE OUR THINKING ON HUMAN PRE-HISTORY.
LEXCORP
THE BAD NEWS IS THERE'S SOME KIND OF ELECTRO-MAGNETIC INTER-FERENCE THAT'S BEEN BUILDING OVER THE AREA FOR ABOUT TWELVE HOURS. WE MAY NOT--
SQUAWK!!

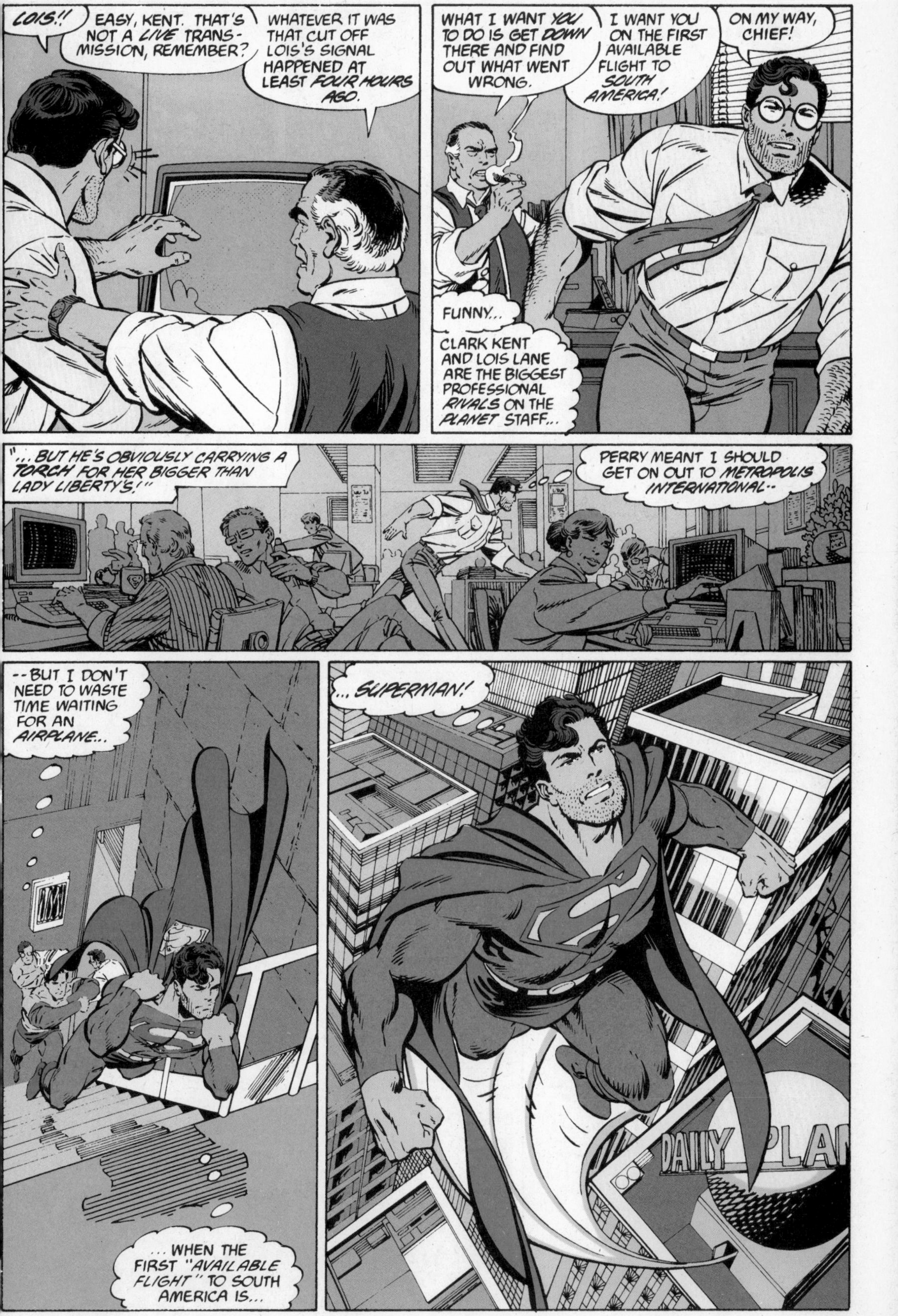
LOIS!!
EASY, KENT. THAT'S NOT A LIVE TRANSMISSION, REMEMBER?
WHATEVER IT WAS THAT CUT OFF LOIS'S SIGNAL HAPPENED AT LEAST FOUR HOURS AGO.
WHAT I WANT YOU TO DO IS GET DOWN THERE AND FIND OUT WHAT WENT WRONG.
I WANT YOU ON THE FIRST AVAILABLE FLIGHT TO SOUTH AMERICA!
ON MY WAY, CHIEF!
FUNNY...
CLARK KENT AND LOIS LANE ARE THE BIGGEST PROFESSIONAL RIVALS ON THE PLANET STAFF...
"...BUT HE'S OBVIOUSLY CARRYING A TORCH FOR HER BIGGER THAN LADY LIBERTY'S!"
PERRY MEANT I SHOULD GET ON OUT TO METROPOLIS INTERNATIONAL--
--BUT I DON'T NEED TO WASTE TIME WAITING FOR AN AIRPLANE...
...WHEN THE FIRST "AVAILABLE FLIGHT" TO SOUTH AMERICA IS...
...SUPERMAN!

IT'S NEARLY *TWELVE THOUSAND MILES* FROM METROPOLIS TO *COSTA DEL MARCO,* WHERE LOIS IS.

THE FASTEST WAY I CAN GET THERE IS TO BORROW A *PAGE* FROM MISSILE TRAJECTORY PROGRAMMING.

A *SUBORBITAL* PATH TAKES ME *UP* OUT OF EARTH'S ATMOSPHERE FOR A FEW SECONDS--

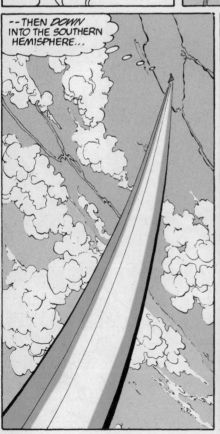

--THEN *DOWN* INTO THE SOUTHERN HEMISPHERE...

...ALMOST *ON TOP* OF LOIS'S POSITION.

HMM-- EVERYTHING LOOKS *OKAY* DOWN BELOW.

I'D BETTER DO A *SUPER-SPEED* RECONNOITER BEFORE I *REVEAL* MYSELF.

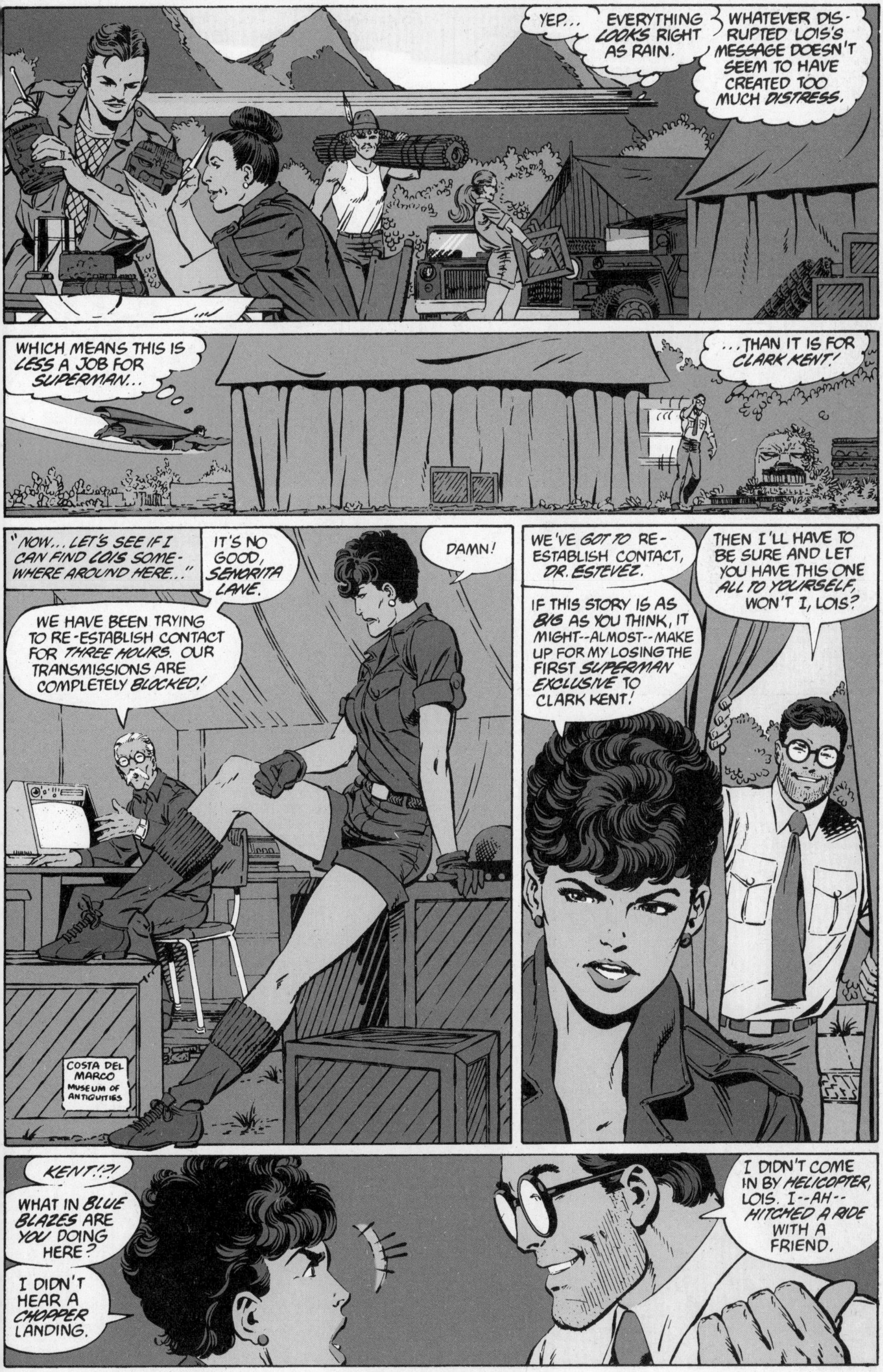
YEP... EVERYTHING LOOKS RIGHT AS RAIN.
WHATEVER DIS-RUPTED LOIS'S MESSAGE DOESN'T SEEM TO HAVE CREATED TOO MUCH DISTRESS.
WHICH MEANS THIS IS LESS A JOB FOR SUPERMAN...
...THAN IT IS FOR CLARK KENT!
"NOW... LET'S SEE IF I CAN FIND LOIS SOMEWHERE AROUND HERE..."
IT'S NO GOOD, SENORITA LANE.
WE HAVE BEEN TRYING TO RE-ESTABLISH CONTACT FOR THREE HOURS. OUR TRANSMISSIONS ARE COMPLETELY BLOCKED!
DAMN!
COSTA DEL MARCO MUSEUM OF ANTIQUITIES
WE'VE GOT TO RE-ESTABLISH CONTACT, DR. ESTEVEZ.
IF THIS STORY IS AS BIG AS YOU THINK, IT MIGHT--ALMOST--MAKE UP FOR MY LOSING THE FIRST SUPERMAN EXCLUSIVE TO CLARK KENT!
THEN I'LL HAVE TO BE SURE AND LET YOU HAVE THIS ONE ALL TO YOURSELF, WON'T I, LOIS?
KENT!?!
WHAT IN BLUE BLAZES ARE YOU DOING HERE?
I DIDN'T HEAR A CHOPPER LANDING.
I DIDN'T COME IN BY HELICOPTER, LOIS. I--AH--HITCHED A RIDE WITH A FRIEND.

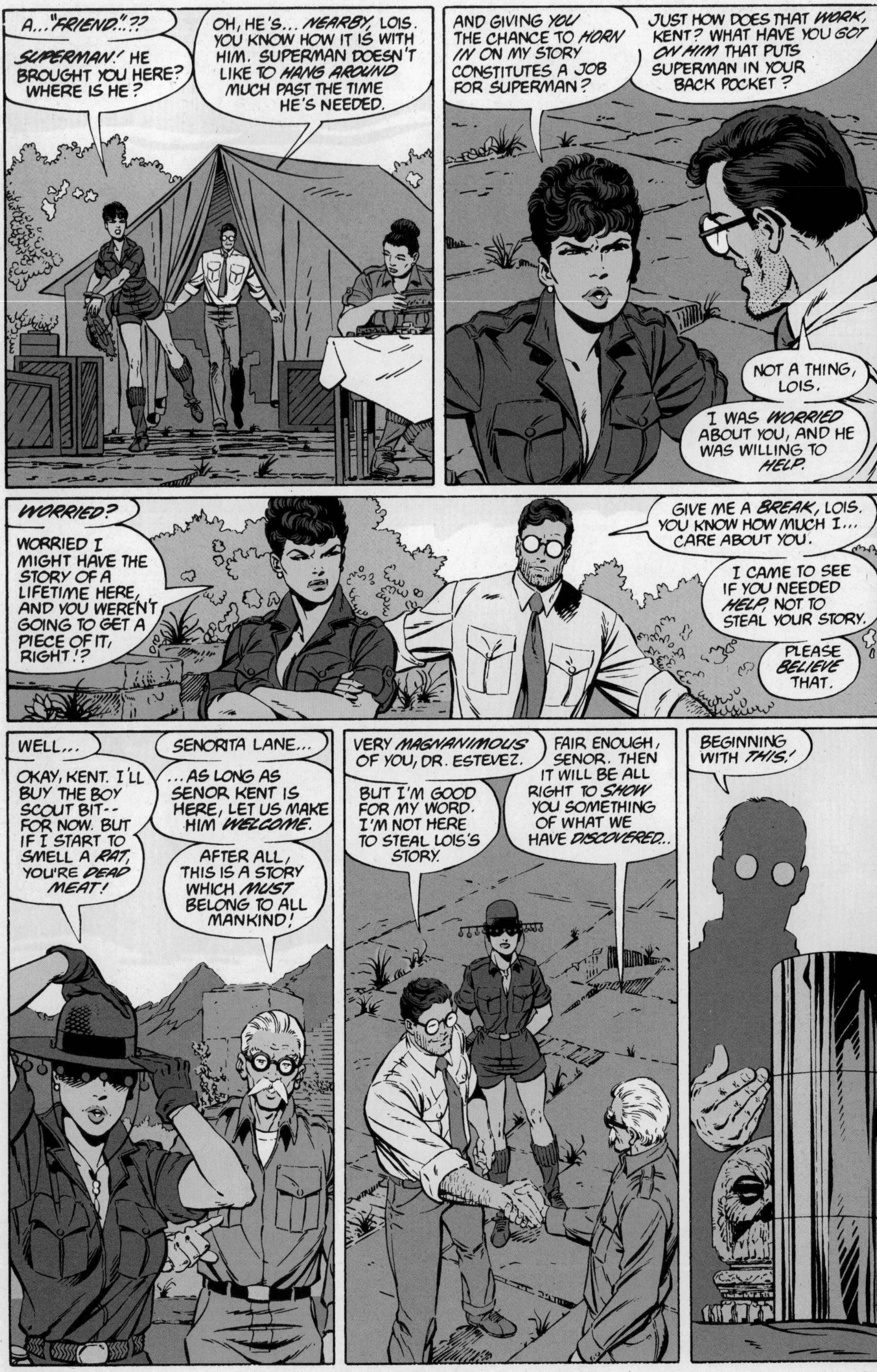

A..."FRIEND"...??
SUPERMAN! HE BROUGHT YOU HERE? WHERE IS HE?
OH, HE'S... NEARBY, LOIS. YOU KNOW HOW IT IS WITH HIM. SUPERMAN DOESN'T LIKE TO HANG AROUND MUCH PAST THE TIME HE'S NEEDED.
AND GIVING YOU THE CHANCE TO HORN IN ON MY STORY CONSTITUTES A JOB FOR SUPERMAN?
JUST HOW DOES THAT WORK, KENT? WHAT HAVE YOU GOT ON HIM THAT PUTS SUPERMAN IN YOUR BACK POCKET?
NOT A THING, LOIS.
I WAS WORRIED ABOUT YOU, AND HE WAS WILLING TO HELP.
WORRIED?
WORRIED I MIGHT HAVE THE STORY OF A LIFETIME HERE, AND YOU WEREN'T GOING TO GET A PIECE OF IT, RIGHT!?
GIVE ME A BREAK, LOIS. YOU KNOW HOW MUCH I... CARE ABOUT YOU.
I CAME TO SEE IF YOU NEEDED HELP, NOT TO STEAL YOUR STORY.
PLEASE BELIEVE THAT.
WELL...
OKAY, KENT. I'LL BUY THE BOY SCOUT BIT-- FOR NOW. BUT IF I START TO SMELL A RAT, YOU'RE DEAD MEAT!
SENORITA LANE...
...AS LONG AS SENOR KENT IS HERE, LET US MAKE HIM WELCOME.
AFTER ALL, THIS IS A STORY WHICH MUST BELONG TO ALL MANKIND!
VERY MAGNANIMOUS OF YOU, DR. ESTEVEZ.
BUT I'M GOOD FOR MY WORD. I'M NOT HERE TO STEAL LOIS'S STORY.
FAIR ENOUGH, SENOR. THEN IT WILL BE ALL RIGHT TO SHOW YOU SOMETHING OF WHAT WE HAVE DISCOVERED...
BEGINNING WITH THIS!

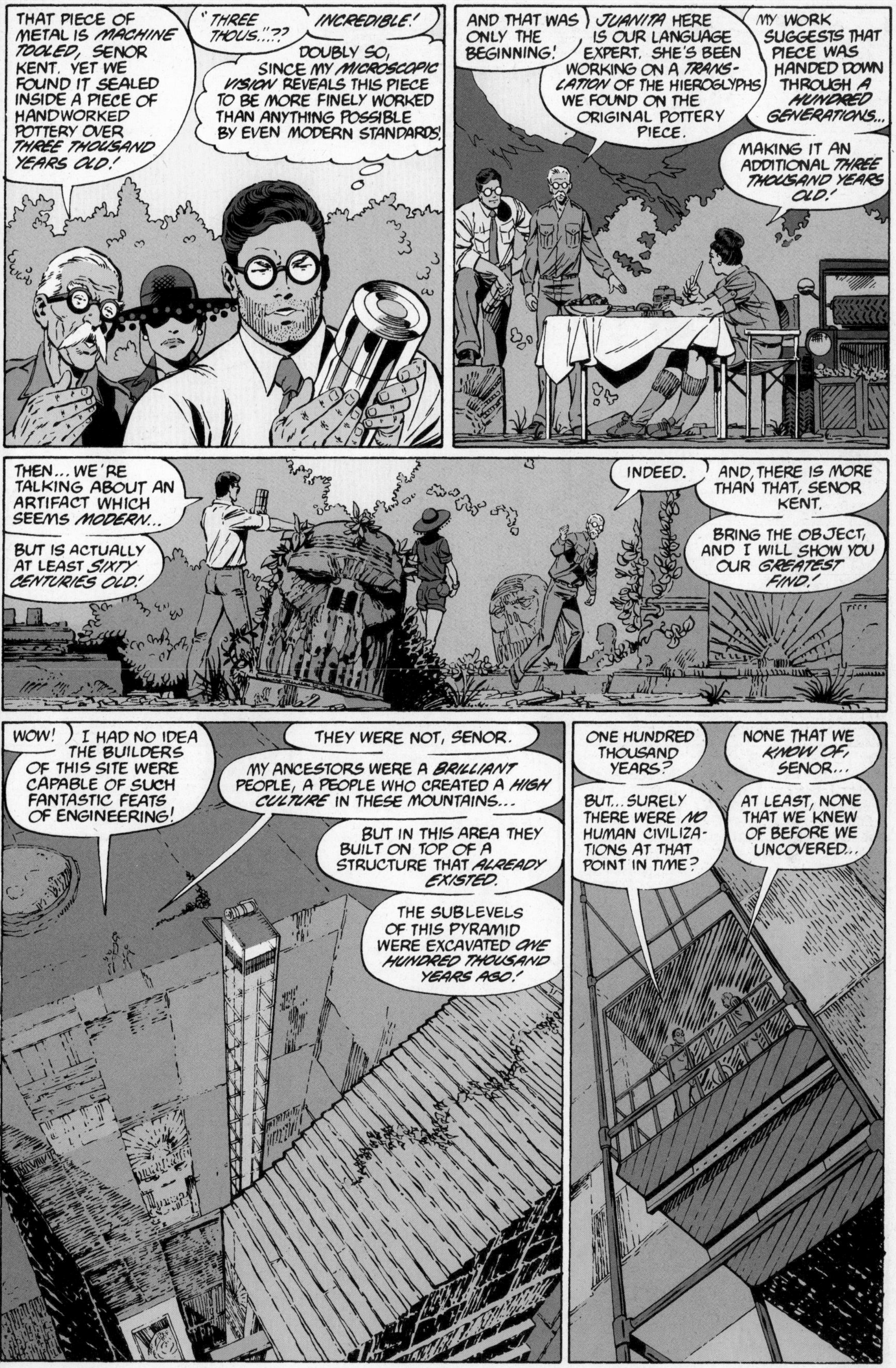
THAT PIECE OF METAL IS MACHINE TOOLED, SENOR KENT. YET WE FOUND IT SEALED INSIDE A PIECE OF HANDWORKED POTTERY OVER THREE THOUSAND YEARS OLD!
"THREE THOUS..."??
INCREDIBLE!
DOUBLY SO, SINCE MY MICROSCOPIC VISION REVEALS THIS PIECE TO BE MORE FINELY WORKED THAN ANYTHING POSSIBLE BY EVEN MODERN STANDARDS!
AND THAT WAS ONLY THE BEGINNING!
JUANITA HERE IS OUR LANGUAGE EXPERT. SHE'S BEEN WORKING ON A TRANSLATION OF THE HIEROGLYPHS WE FOUND ON THE ORIGINAL POTTERY PIECE.
MY WORK SUGGESTS THAT PIECE WAS HANDED DOWN THROUGH A HUNDRED GENERATIONS...
MAKING IT AN ADDITIONAL THREE THOUSAND YEARS OLD!
THEN... WE'RE TALKING ABOUT AN ARTIFACT WHICH SEEMS MODERN...
BUT IS ACTUALLY AT LEAST SIXTY CENTURIES OLD!
INDEED.
AND, THERE IS MORE THAN THAT, SENOR KENT.
BRING THE OBJECT, AND I WILL SHOW YOU OUR GREATEST FIND!
WOW! I HAD NO IDEA THE BUILDERS OF THIS SITE WERE CAPABLE OF SUCH FANTASTIC FEATS OF ENGINEERING!
THEY WERE NOT, SENOR.
MY ANCESTORS WERE A BRILLIANT PEOPLE, A PEOPLE WHO CREATED A HIGH CULTURE IN THESE MOUNTAINS...
BUT IN THIS AREA THEY BUILT ON TOP OF A STRUCTURE THAT ALREADY EXISTED.
THE SUBLEVELS OF THIS PYRAMID WERE EXCAVATED ONE HUNDRED THOUSAND YEARS AGO!
ONE HUNDRED THOUSAND YEARS?
BUT... SURELY THERE WERE NO HUMAN CIVILIZATIONS AT THAT POINT IN TIME?
NONE THAT WE KNOW OF, SENOR...
AT LEAST, NONE THAT WE KNEW OF BEFORE WE UNCOVERED...

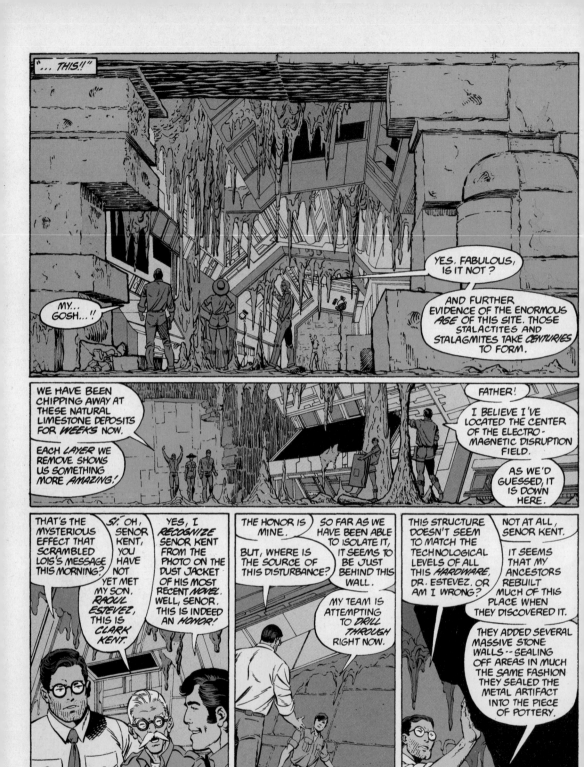

"... THIS!!"

YES, FABULOUS, IS IT NOT?

AND FURTHER EVIDENCE OF THE ENORMOUS *AGE* OF THIS SITE. THOSE STALACTITES AND STALAGMITES TAKE *CENTURIES* TO FORM.

MY... GOSH...!!

WE HAVE BEEN CHIPPING AWAY AT THESE NATURAL LIMESTONE DEPOSITS FOR *WEEKS* NOW.

EACH *LAYER* WE REMOVE SHOWS US SOMETHING MORE *AMAZING!*

FATHER!

I BELIEVE I'VE LOCATED THE CENTER OF THE ELECTRO-MAGNETIC DISRUPTION FIELD.

AS WE'D GUESSED, IT IS DOWN HERE.

THAT'S THE MYSTERIOUS EFFECT THAT SCRAMBLED LOIS'S MESSAGE THIS MORNING?

SÍ: OH, SENOR KENT, YOU HAVE NOT YET MET MY SON, *RAOUL ESTEVEZ,* THIS IS *CLARK KENT.*

YES, I *RECOGNIZE* SENOR KENT FROM THE PHOTO ON THE DUST JACKET OF HIS MOST RECENT *NOVEL.* WELL, SENOR. THIS IS INDEED AN *HONOR!*

THE HONOR IS MINE.

BUT, WHERE IS THE SOURCE OF THIS DISTURBANCE?

SO FAR AS WE HAVE BEEN ABLE TO ISOLATE IT, IT SEEMS TO BE JUST BEHIND THIS WALL.

MY TEAM IS ATTEMPTING TO *DRILL THROUGH* RIGHT NOW.

THIS STRUCTURE DOESN'T SEEM TO MATCH THE TECHNOLOGICAL LEVELS OF ALL THIS *HARDWARE,* DR. ESTEVEZ, OR AM I WRONG?

NOT AT ALL, SENOR KENT.

IT SEEMS THAT MY ANCESTORS REBUILT MUCH OF THIS PLACE WHEN THEY DISCOVERED IT.

THEY ADDED SEVERAL MASSIVE STONE WALLS -- SEALING OFF AREAS IN MUCH THE SAME FASHION THEY SEALED THE METAL ARTIFACT INTO THE PIECE OF POTTERY.

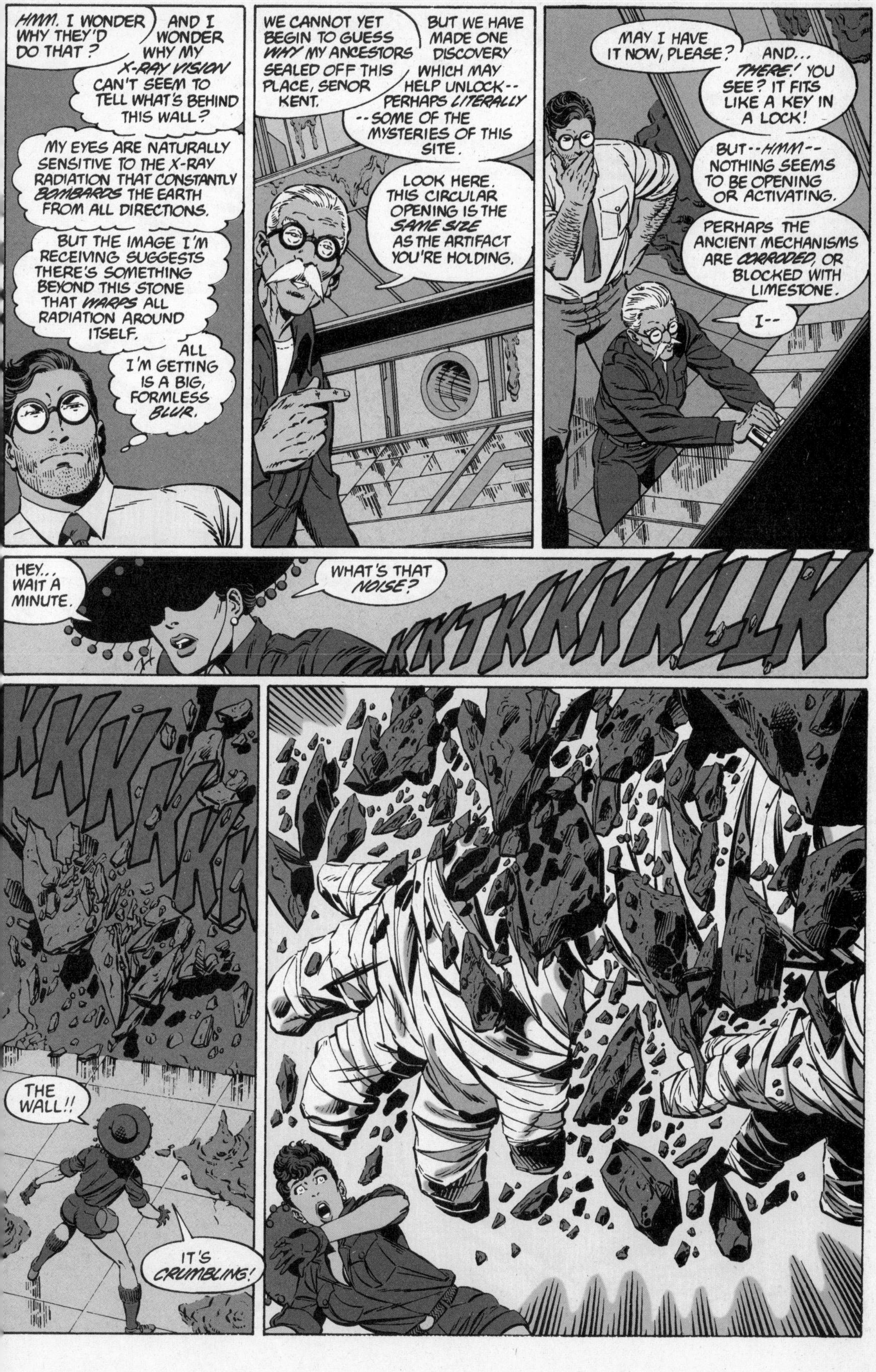

HMM. I WONDER WHY THEY'D DO THAT?
AND I WONDER WHY MY X-RAY VISION CAN'T SEEM TO TELL WHAT'S BEHIND THIS WALL?
MY EYES ARE NATURALLY SENSITIVE TO THE X-RAY RADIATION THAT CONSTANTLY BOMBARDS THE EARTH FROM ALL DIRECTIONS.
BUT THE IMAGE I'M RECEIVING SUGGESTS THERE'S SOMETHING BEYOND THIS STONE THAT WARPS ALL RADIATION AROUND ITSELF.
ALL I'M GETTING IS A BIG, FORMLESS BLUR.
WE CANNOT YET BEGIN TO GUESS WHY MY ANCESTORS SEALED OFF THIS PLACE, SENOR KENT.
BUT WE HAVE MADE ONE DISCOVERY WHICH MAY HELP UNLOCK-- PERHAPS LITERALLY --SOME OF THE MYSTERIES OF THIS SITE.
LOOK HERE. THIS CIRCULAR OPENING IS THE SAME SIZE AS THE ARTIFACT YOU'RE HOLDING.
MAY I HAVE IT NOW, PLEASE?
AND... THERE! YOU SEE? IT FITS LIKE A KEY IN A LOCK!
BUT--HMM-- NOTHING SEEMS TO BE OPENING OR ACTIVATING.
PERHAPS THE ANCIENT MECHANISMS ARE CORRODED, OR BLOCKED WITH LIMESTONE.
I--
HEY... WAIT A MINUTE.
WHAT'S THAT NOISE?
KKTKKKKKKLLK
KKKKKKK
THE WALL!!
IT'S CRUMBLING!

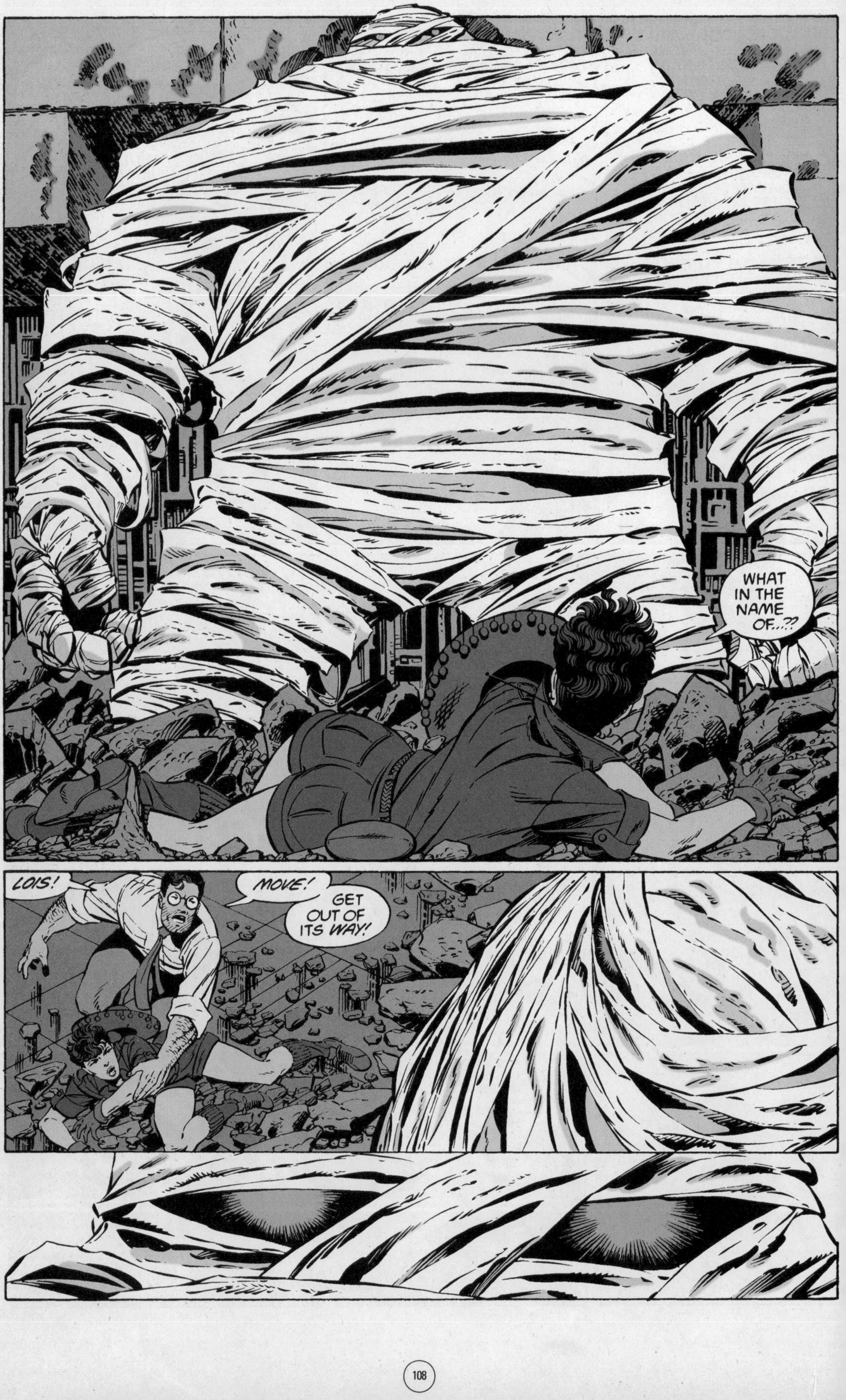

WHAT IN THE NAME OF...??
LOIS!
MOVE!
GET OUT OF ITS WAY!

WHAT... WHAT *IS* THAT THING? I'VE NEVER SEEN ANYTHING *LIKE* IT!!

DON'T WORRY ABOUT *THAT,* DOCTOR!

JUST GET YOUR PEOPLE *CLEAR!*

WHATEVER THAT CREATURE IS...

IT'S OBVIOUSLY OUT FOR *BLOOD!*

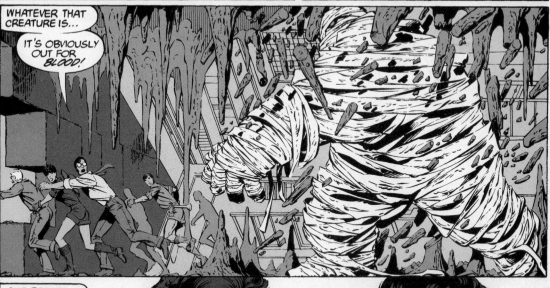

AND BEFORE IT *GETS* ANY...

...I'VE GOT TO FIND A WAY TO USE MY *SUPER-POWERS*...

...WITHOUT REVEALING MY *SECRET IDENTITY!*

SO THE *FIRST* THING I'VE GOT TO DO IS *SEPARATE* MYSELF FROM LOIS AND THE OTHERS.

AND A BIT OF *HEAT VISION* "CARVING" SHOULD EFFECTIVELY...

...BRING DOWN THE *ROOF!*

LOIS! LOOK OUT!

WHAT...?!?

KENT!!

CLARK!!!

NOW... LET'S SEE WHAT WE CAN *DO* ABOUT TALL, WRAPPED AND LUMPY HERE.

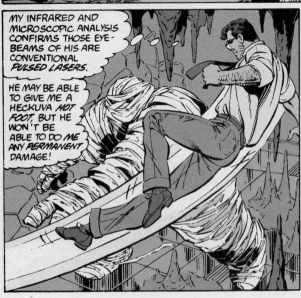

MY INFRARED AND MICROSCOPIC ANALYSIS CONFIRMS THOSE EYE-BEAMS OF HIS ARE CONVENTIONAL *PULSED LASERS.*

HE MAY BE ABLE TO GIVE ME A HECKUVA *HOT FOOT,* BUT HE WON'T BE ABLE TO DO *ME* ANY *PERMANENT* DAMAGE!

UH-OH. LOOKS LIKE *FLYING* WASN'T SUCH A BRIGHT IDEA.

OUR BOY *LEARNS* BY EXAMPLE!

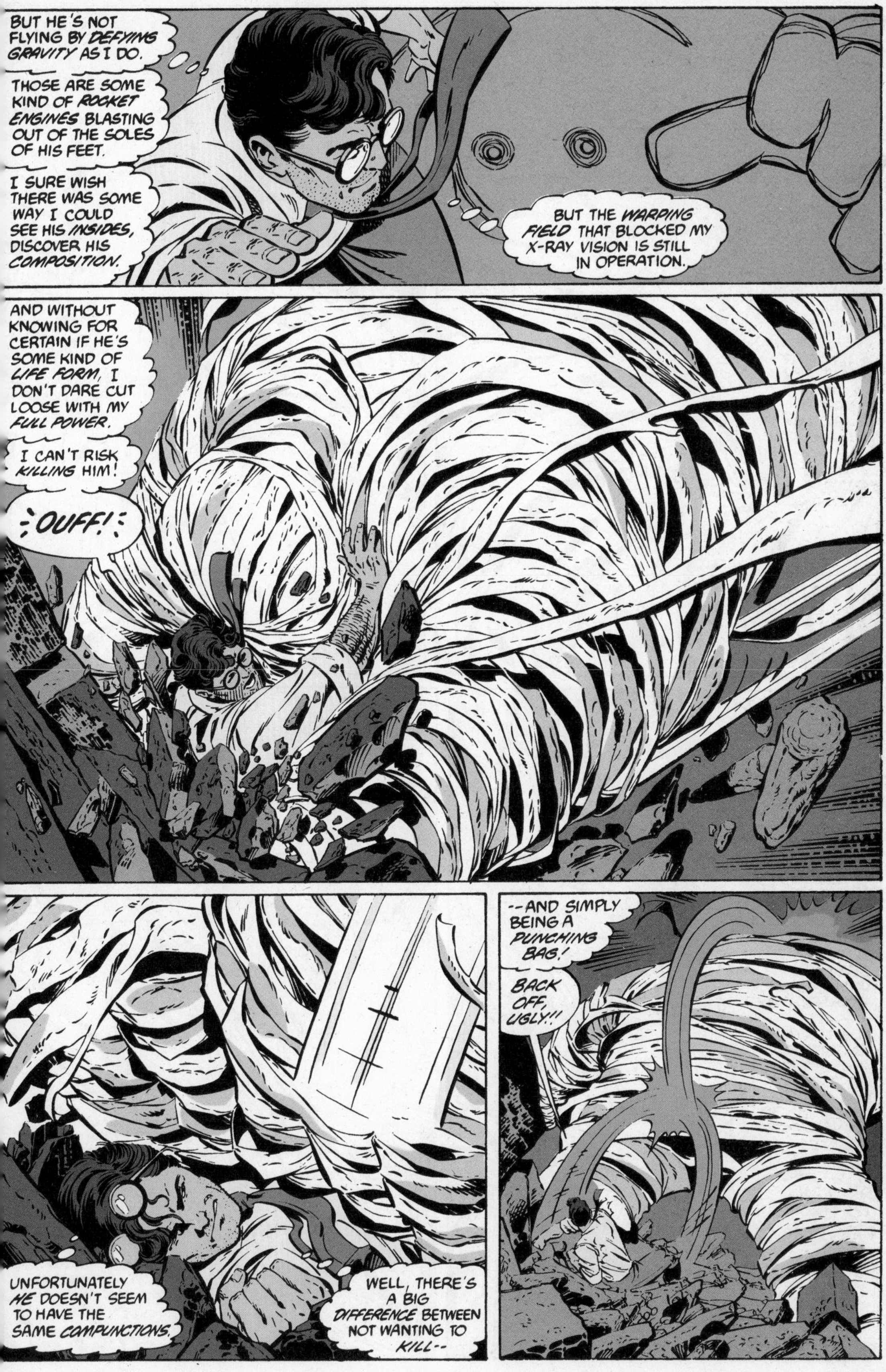
BUT HE'S NOT FLYING BY DEFYING GRAVITY AS I DO.
THOSE ARE SOME KIND OF ROCKET ENGINES BLASTING OUT OF THE SOLES OF HIS FEET.
I SURE WISH THERE WAS SOME WAY I COULD SEE HIS INSIDES, DISCOVER HIS COMPOSITION.
BUT THE WARPING FIELD THAT BLOCKED MY X-RAY VISION IS STILL IN OPERATION.
AND WITHOUT KNOWING FOR CERTAIN IF HE'S SOME KIND OF LIFE FORM, I DON'T DARE CUT LOOSE WITH MY FULL POWER.
I CAN'T RISK KILLING HIM!
OUFF!
UNFORTUNATELY HE DOESN'T SEEM TO HAVE THE SAME COMPUNCTIONS.
WELL, THERE'S A BIG DIFFERENCE BETWEEN NOT WANTING TO KILL--
--AND SIMPLY BEING A PUNCHING BAG!
BACK OFF, UGLY!!

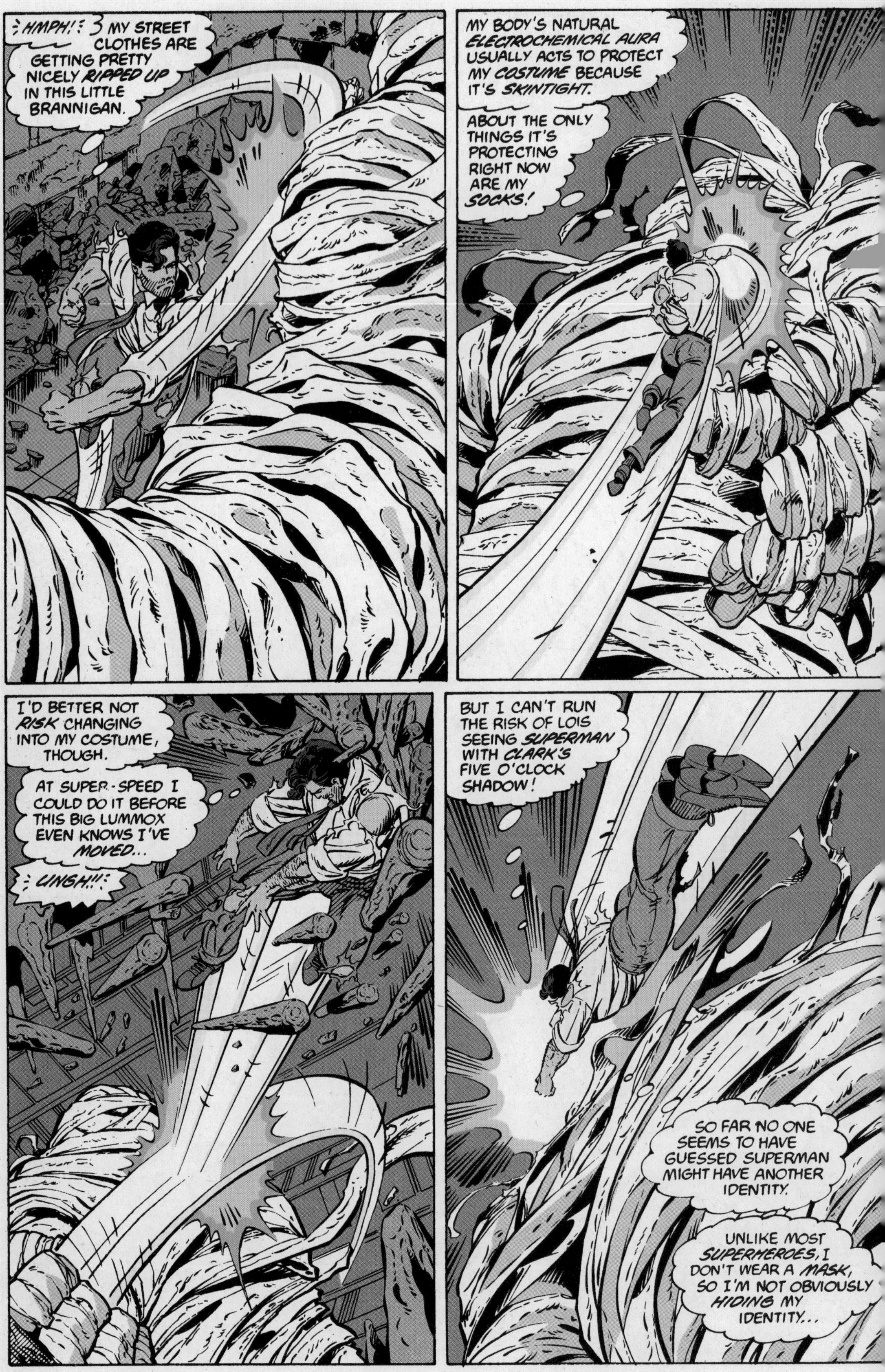

HMPH!! MY STREET CLOTHES ARE GETTING PRETTY NICELY RIPPED UP IN THIS LITTLE BRANNIGAN.
MY BODY'S NATURAL ELECTROCHEMICAL AURA USUALLY ACTS TO PROTECT MY COSTUME BECAUSE IT'S SKINTIGHT.
ABOUT THE ONLY THINGS IT'S PROTECTING RIGHT NOW ARE MY SOCKS!
I'D BETTER NOT RISK CHANGING INTO MY COSTUME, THOUGH.
AT SUPER-SPEED I COULD DO IT BEFORE THIS BIG LUMMOX EVEN KNOWS I'VE MOVED...
UNGH!!!
BUT I CAN'T RUN THE RISK OF LOIS SEEING SUPERMAN WITH CLARK'S FIVE O'CLOCK SHADOW!
SO FAR NO ONE SEEMS TO HAVE GUESSED SUPERMAN MIGHT HAVE ANOTHER IDENTITY.
UNLIKE MOST SUPERHEROES, I DON'T WEAR A MASK, SO I'M NOT OBVIOUSLY HIDING MY IDENTITY...

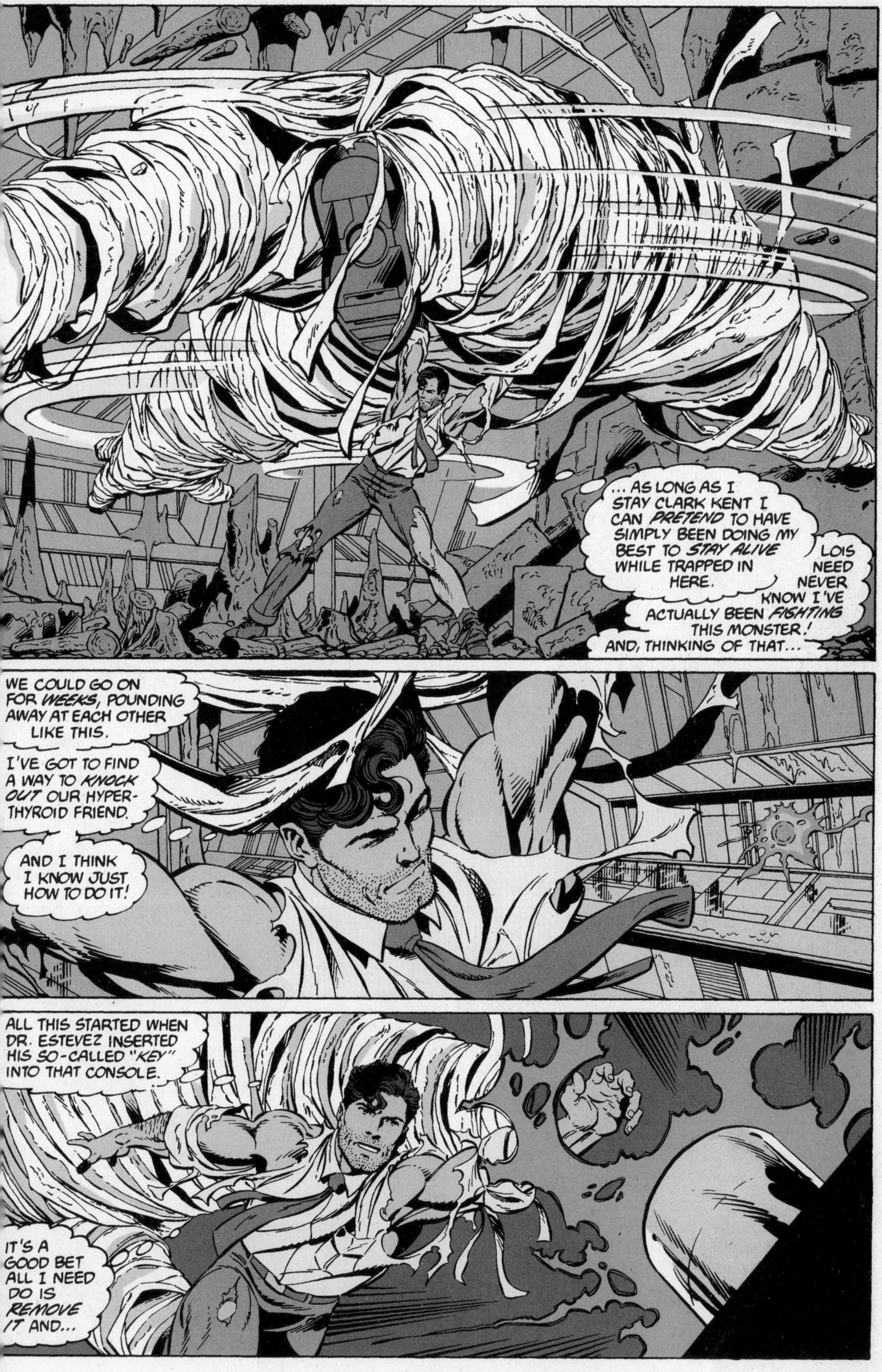
...AS LONG AS I STAY CLARK KENT I CAN PRETEND TO HAVE SIMPLY BEEN DOING MY BEST TO STAY ALIVE WHILE TRAPPED IN HERE.
LOIS NEED NEVER KNOW I'VE ACTUALLY BEEN FIGHTING THIS MONSTER! AND, THINKING OF THAT...
WE COULD GO ON FOR WEEKS, POUNDING AWAY AT EACH OTHER LIKE THIS.
I'VE GOT TO FIND A WAY TO KNOCK OUT OUR HYPER-THYROID FRIEND.
AND I THINK I KNOW JUST HOW TO DO IT!
ALL THIS STARTED WHEN DR. ESTEVEZ INSERTED HIS SO-CALLED "KEY" INTO THAT CONSOLE.
IT'S A GOOD BET ALL I NEED DO IS REMOVE IT AND...

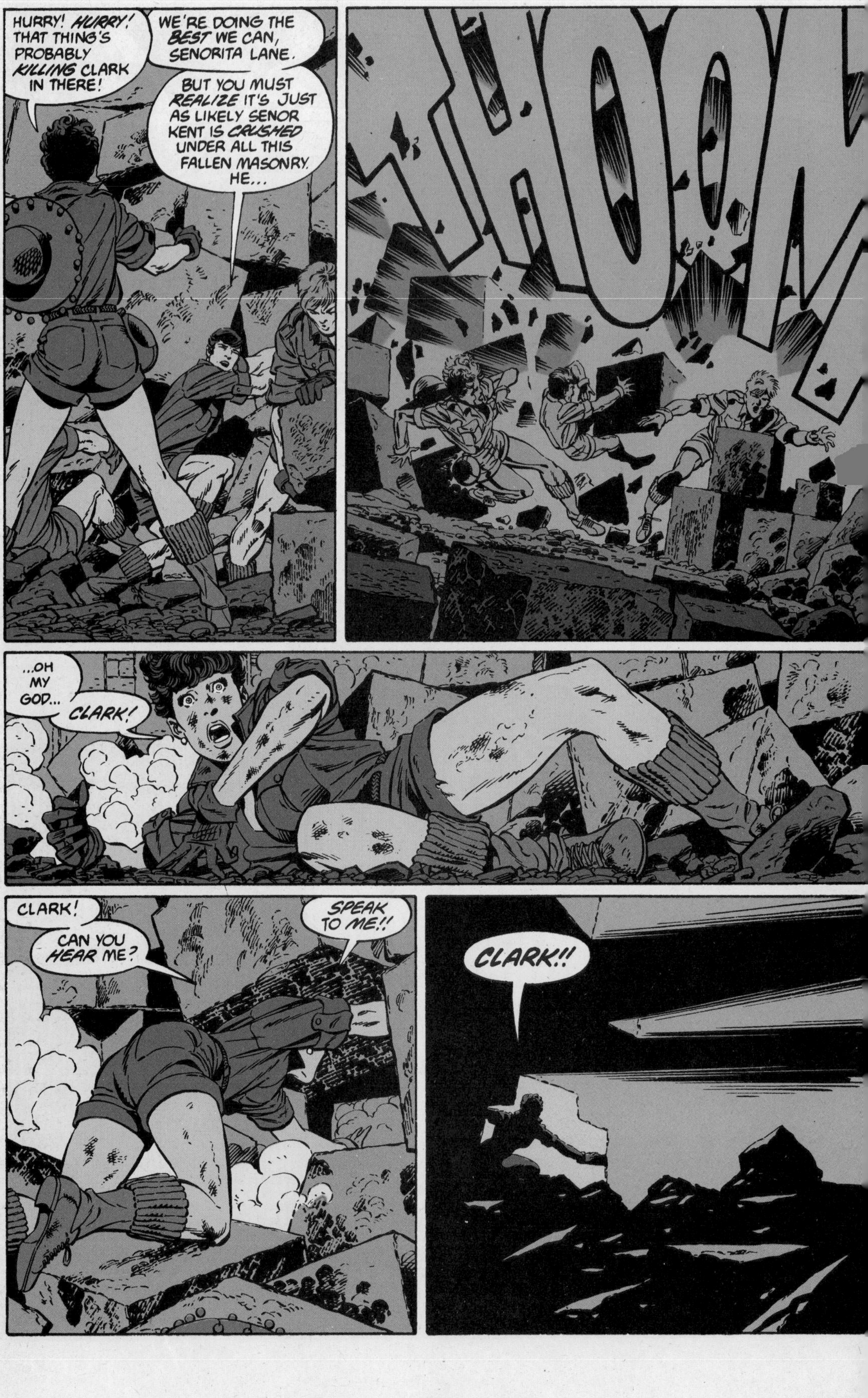
HURRY! HURRY! THAT THING'S PROBABLY KILLING CLARK IN THERE!
WE'RE DOING THE BEST WE CAN, SENORITA LANE.
BUT YOU MUST REALIZE IT'S JUST AS LIKELY SENOR KENT IS CRUSHED UNDER ALL THIS FALLEN MASONRY. HE...
THOOM
...OH MY GOD... CLARK!
CLARK!
CAN YOU HEAR ME?
SPEAK TO ME!!
CLARK!!

CLARK!!

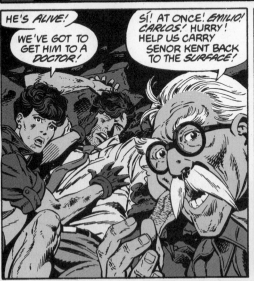

HE'S ALIVE! WE'VE GOT TO GET HIM TO A DOCTOR!

SÍ! AT ONCE! EMILIO! CARLOS! HURRY! HELP US CARRY SENOR KENT BACK TO THE SURFACE!

BE CAREFUL! HE MAY HAVE INTERNAL INJURIES!

RAOUL? ARE YOU COMING? THIS PLACE IS NOT SAFE!

IN A MOMENT, FATHER. I WANT TO CHECK SOMETHING.

THAT EXPLOSION-- OR WHATEVER IT WAS-- SEEMS TO HAVE KNOCKED DOWN ALL THE MASONRY AND NATURAL ROCK FORMATIONS.

BUT IT DOESN'T SEEM TO HAVE HARMED THE MACHINERY.

NOT SURPRISING. TO HAVE SURVIVED ALL THESE CENTURIES THESE PANELS MUST BE NEARLY INDESTRUCTIBLE!

BUT...

WHERE IS THAT MUMMY CREA--

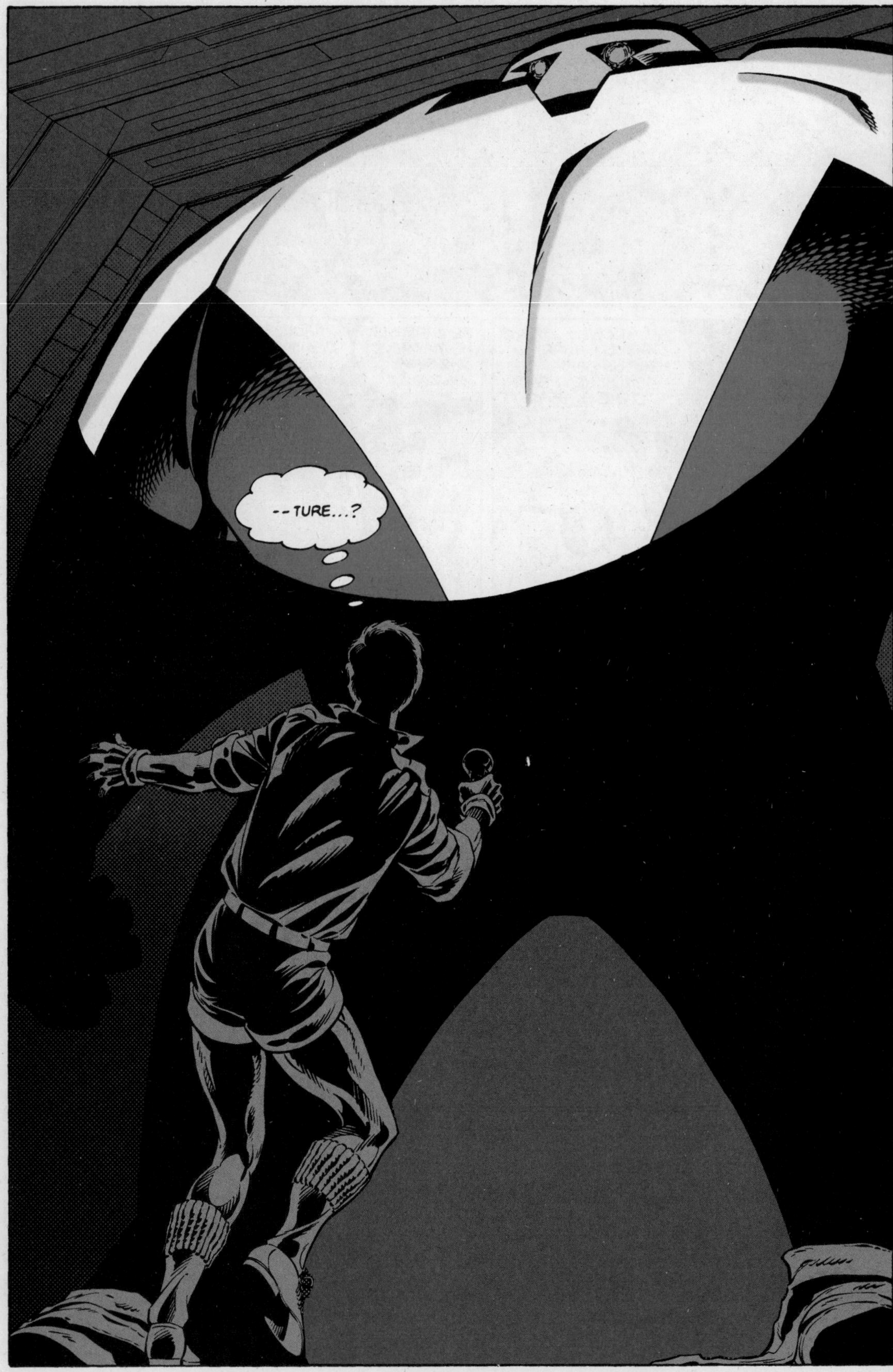
--TURE...?

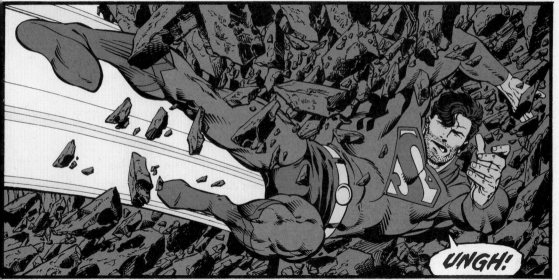

UNGH!

OUHF!!

G-3091

BOY! THIS ISN'T GOING WELL AT ALL...IS IT?

AND HERE I DIDN'T THINK THINGS COULD GET ANY WORSE THAN WHEN I WOKE UP THIS MORNING...

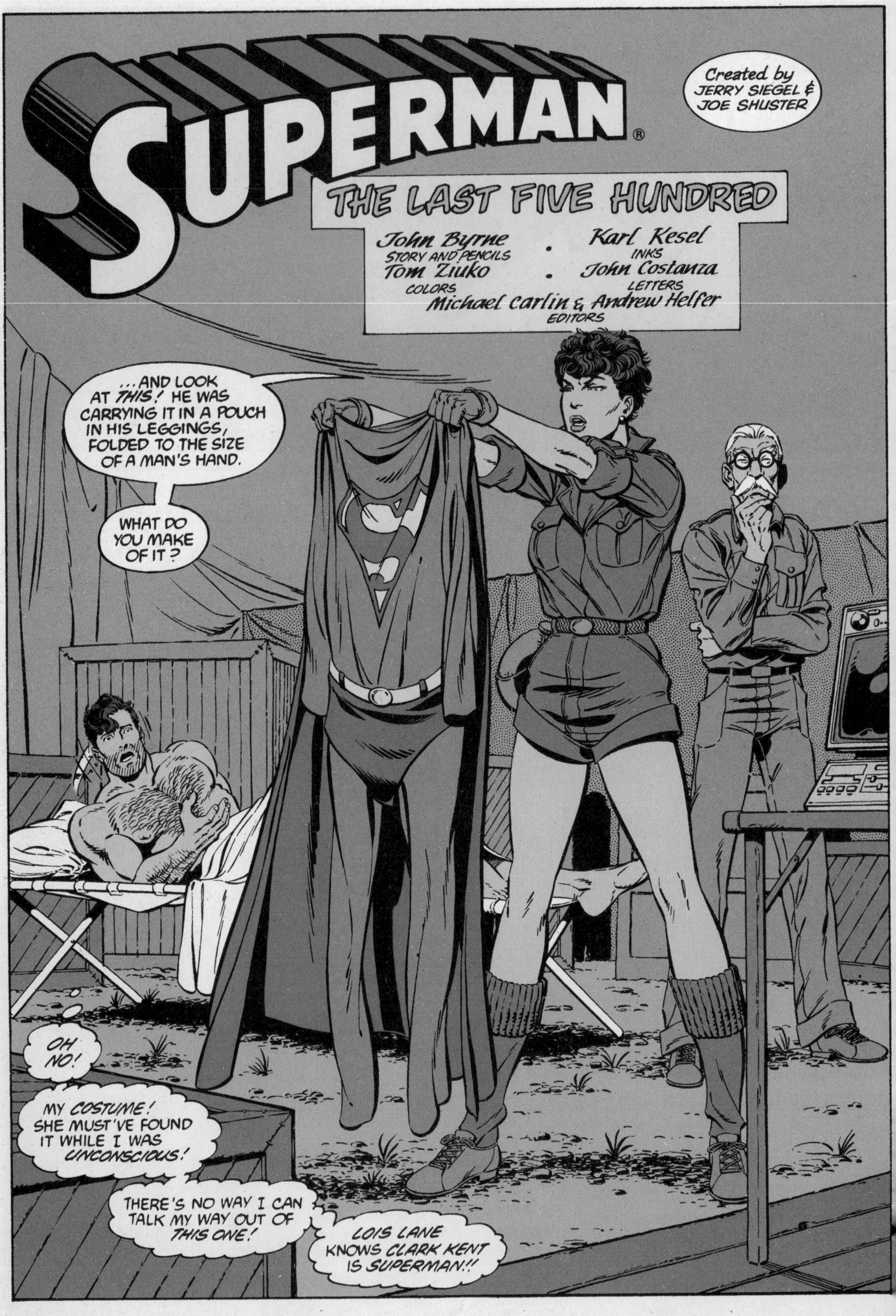
SUPERMAN®
Created by JERRY SIEGEL & JOE SHUSTER
THE LAST FIVE HUNDRED
John Byrne STORY AND PENCILS • Karl Kesel INKS
Tom Ziuko COLORS • John Costanza LETTERS
Michael Carlin & Andrew Helfer EDITORS
...AND LOOK AT THIS! HE WAS CARRYING IT IN A POUCH IN HIS LEGGINGS, FOLDED TO THE SIZE OF A MAN'S HAND.
WHAT DO YOU MAKE OF IT?
OH NO!
MY COSTUME! SHE MUST'VE FOUND IT WHILE I WAS UNCONSCIOUS!
THERE'S NO WAY I CAN TALK MY WAY OUT OF THIS ONE!
LOIS LANE KNOWS CLARK KENT IS SUPERMAN!!

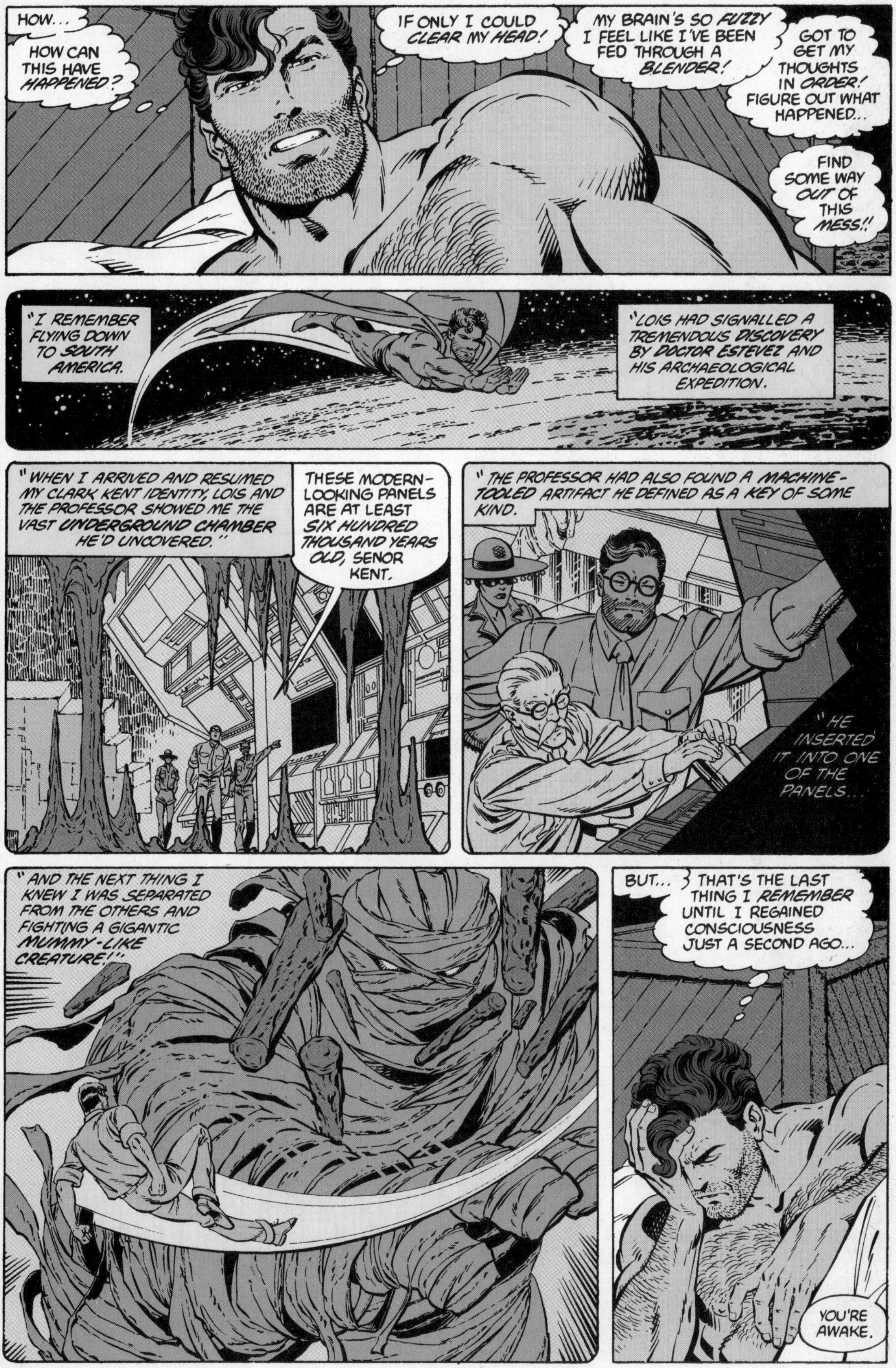
HOW... HOW CAN THIS HAVE HAPPENED?
IF ONLY I COULD CLEAR MY HEAD!
MY BRAIN'S SO FUZZY I FEEL LIKE I'VE BEEN FED THROUGH A BLENDER!
GOT TO GET MY THOUGHTS IN ORDER! FIGURE OUT WHAT HAPPENED...
FIND SOME WAY OUT OF THIS MESS!!
"I REMEMBER FLYING DOWN TO SOUTH AMERICA.
"LOIS HAD SIGNALLED A TREMENDOUS DISCOVERY BY DOCTOR ESTEVEZ AND HIS ARCHAEOLOGICAL EXPEDITION.
"WHEN I ARRIVED AND RESUMED MY CLARK KENT IDENTITY, LOIS AND THE PROFESSOR SHOWED ME THE VAST UNDERGROUND CHAMBER HE'D UNCOVERED."
THESE MODERN-LOOKING PANELS ARE AT LEAST SIX HUNDRED THOUSAND YEARS OLD, SENOR KENT.
"THE PROFESSOR HAD ALSO FOUND A MACHINE-TOOLED ARTIFACT HE DEFINED AS A KEY OF SOME KIND.
"HE INSERTED IT INTO ONE OF THE PANELS...
"AND THE NEXT THING I KNEW I WAS SEPARATED FROM THE OTHERS AND FIGHTING A GIGANTIC MUMMY-LIKE CREATURE!"
BUT... THAT'S THE LAST THING I REMEMBER UNTIL I REGAINED CONSCIOUSNESS JUST A SECOND AGO...
YOU'RE AWAKE.

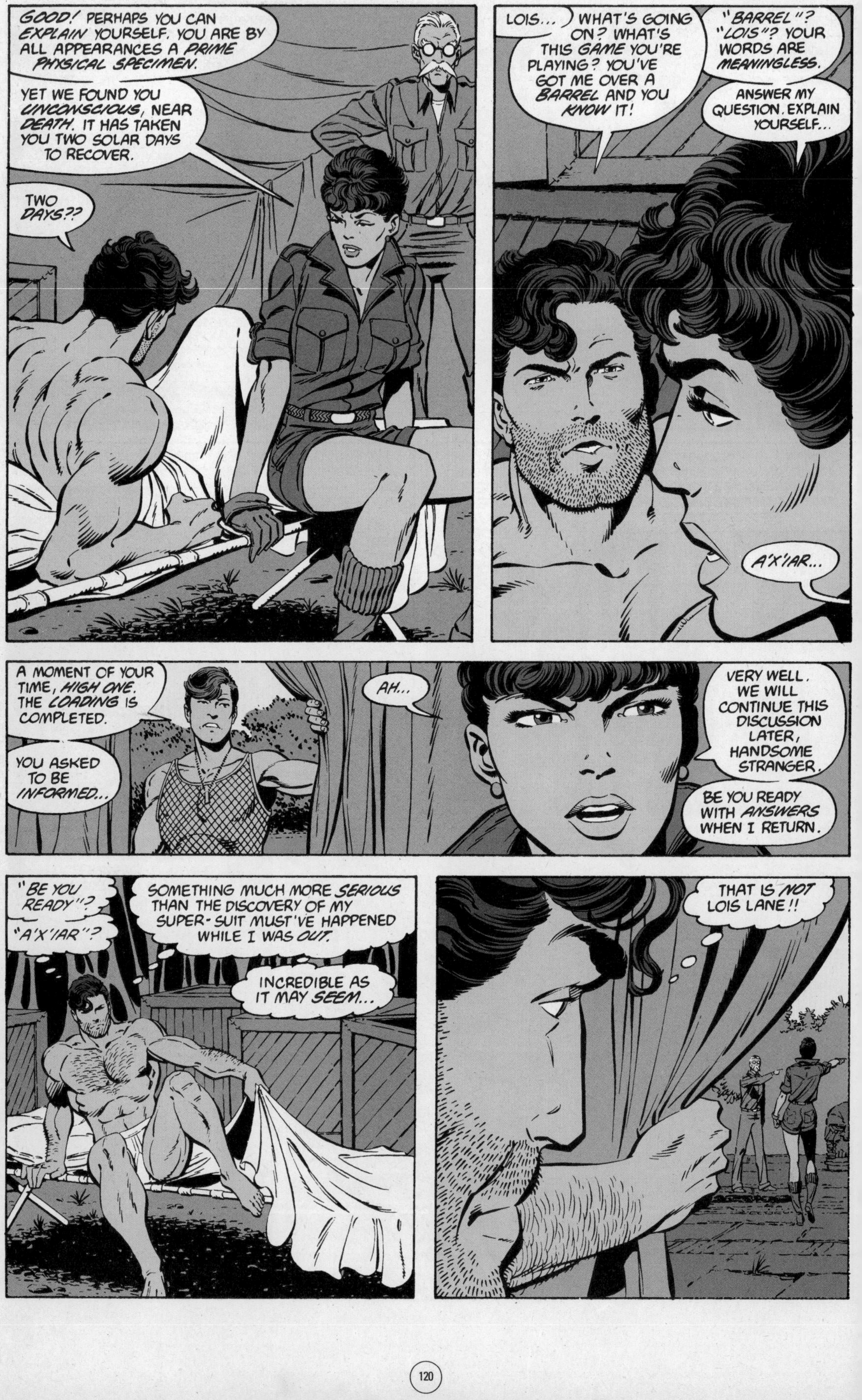
GOOD! PERHAPS YOU CAN EXPLAIN YOURSELF. YOU ARE BY ALL APPEARANCES A PRIME PHYSICAL SPECIMEN.
YET WE FOUND YOU UNCONSCIOUS, NEAR DEATH. IT HAS TAKEN YOU TWO SOLAR DAYS TO RECOVER.
TWO DAYS??
LOIS...
WHAT'S GOING ON? WHAT'S THIS GAME YOU'RE PLAYING? YOU'VE GOT ME OVER A BARREL AND YOU KNOW IT!
"BARREL"? "LOIS"? YOUR WORDS ARE MEANINGLESS.
ANSWER MY QUESTION. EXPLAIN YOURSELF...
A'X'IAR...
A MOMENT OF YOUR TIME, HIGH ONE. THE LOADING IS COMPLETED.
YOU ASKED TO BE INFORMED...
AH...
VERY WELL. WE WILL CONTINUE THIS DISCUSSION LATER, HANDSOME STRANGER.
BE YOU READY WITH ANSWERS WHEN I RETURN.
"BE YOU READY"?
"A'X'IAR"?
SOMETHING MUCH MORE SERIOUS THAN THE DISCOVERY OF MY SUPER-SUIT MUST'VE HAPPENED WHILE I WAS OUT.
INCREDIBLE AS IT MAY SEEM...
THAT IS NOT LOIS LANE!!

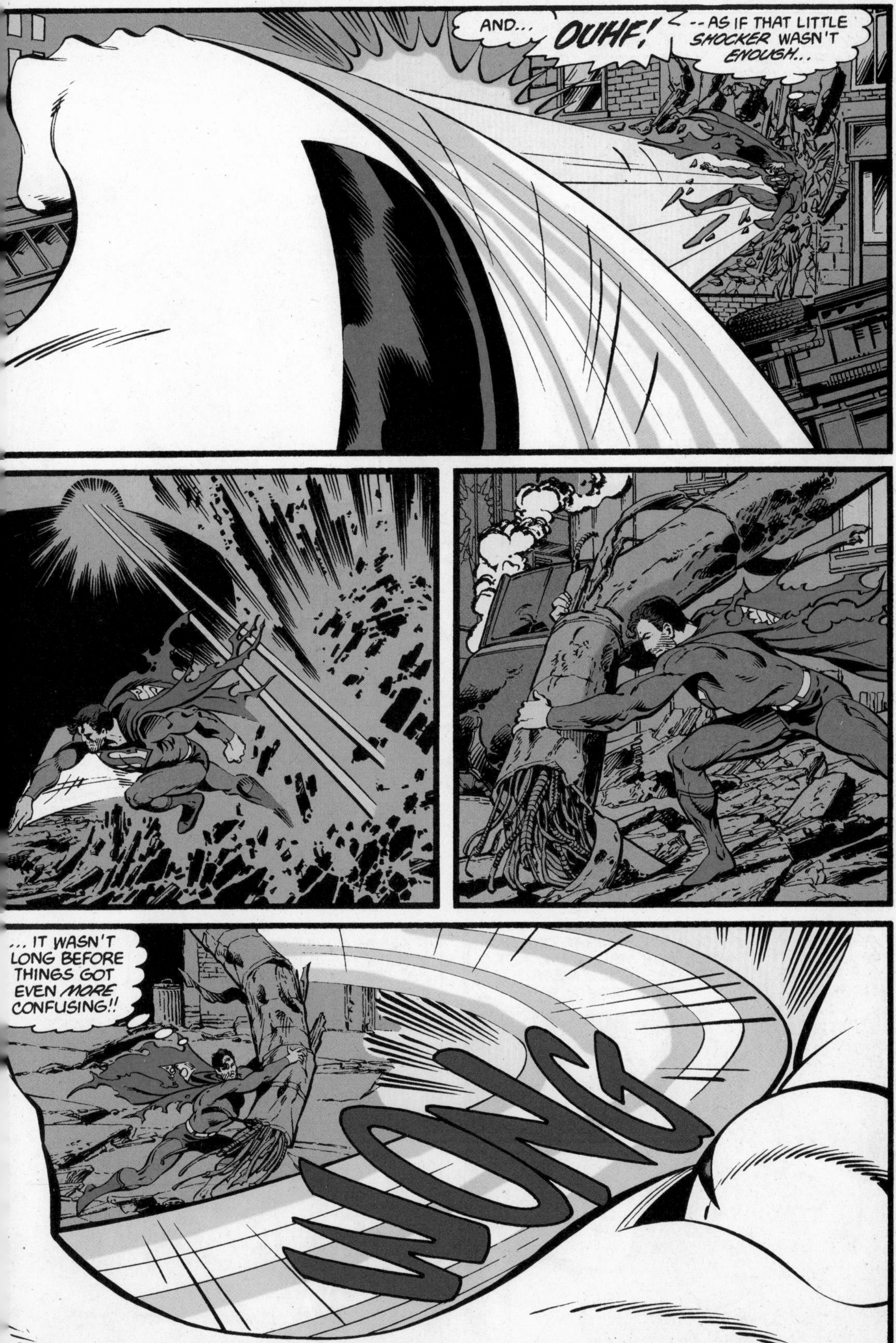
AND...
OUHF!
--AS IF THAT LITTLE SHOCKER WASN'T ENOUGH...
...IT WASN'T LONG BEFORE THINGS GOT EVEN MORE CONFUSING!!
WONG

THERE'S NO SIGN OF THE *REAL* LOIS ANYWHERE WITHIN RANGE OF MY *TELESCOPIC VISION.*

I'D BETTER NOT *ACT* AGAINST THE IMPOSTOR UNTIL I CAN BE SURE OF LOIS' SAFETY.

NOW LET'S SEE WHAT *MY SUPER-SENSES* CAN DISCOVER FOR ME ABOUT THE *TRUE* IDENTITY OF THIS WOMAN...

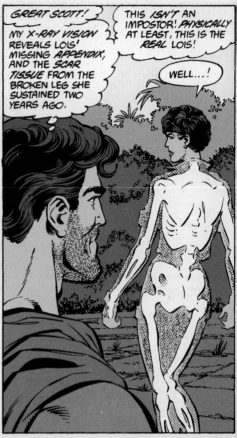

GREAT *SCOTT!* MY *X-RAY VISION* REVEALS LOIS' MISSING *APPENDIX,* AND THE *SCAR TISSUE* FROM THE BROKEN LEG SHE SUSTAINED TWO YEARS AGO.

THIS *ISN'T* AN IMPOSTOR! *PHYSICALLY* AT LEAST, THIS IS THE *REAL* LOIS!

WELL...!

WHAT A *MAGNIFICENT* TRANSFORMATION.

YOU LOOK *BORN* TO WEAR THE GARMENT, STRANGER.

VERY IMPRESSIVE...

...ER...

A'X'IAR!

IF YOU ARE NOT *TOO* BUSY...

DO NOT TAKE THAT TONE OF VOICE WITH ME, *E'V'EN!* NOT SO LONG AS YOU WEAR *THAT* PATHETIC FORM!

IT SEEMS A HALF A MILLION YEARS HAS NOT *MELLOWED* YOU, A'X'IAR. YOUR TONGUE IS AS *SHARP* AS EVER IT WAS!

SHARPER, OLD MAN. MIND IT DOES NOT *CUT* YOU!

"...*WEAR THAT...FORM"*?

OF COURSE!!

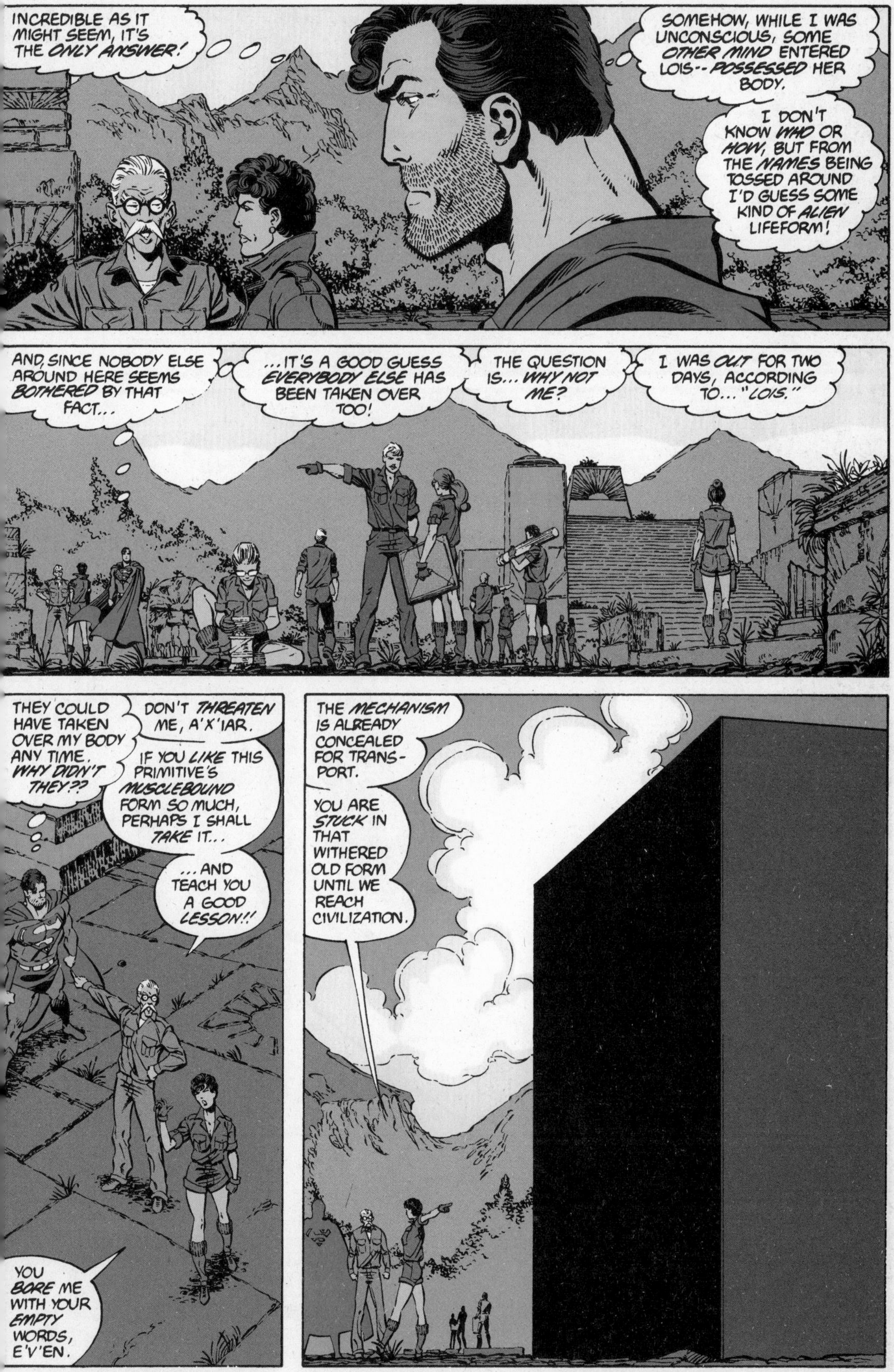
INCREDIBLE AS IT MIGHT SEEM, IT'S THE ONLY ANSWER!
SOMEHOW, WHILE I WAS UNCONSCIOUS, SOME OTHER MIND ENTERED LOIS-- POSSESSED HER BODY.
I DON'T KNOW WHO OR HOW, BUT FROM THE NAMES BEING TOSSED AROUND I'D GUESS SOME KIND OF ALIEN LIFEFORM!
AND, SINCE NOBODY ELSE AROUND HERE SEEMS BOTHERED BY THAT FACT...
...IT'S A GOOD GUESS EVERYBODY ELSE HAS BEEN TAKEN OVER TOO!
THE QUESTION IS... WHY NOT ME?
I WAS OUT FOR TWO DAYS, ACCORDING TO... "LOIS."
THEY COULD HAVE TAKEN OVER MY BODY ANY TIME. WHY DIDN'T THEY??
DON'T THREATEN ME, A'X'IAR.
IF YOU LIKE THIS PRIMITIVE'S MUSCLEBOUND FORM SO MUCH, PERHAPS I SHALL TAKE IT...
...AND TEACH YOU A GOOD LESSON!!
YOU BORE ME WITH YOUR EMPTY WORDS, E'V'EN.
THE MECHANISM IS ALREADY CONCEALED FOR TRANS-PORT.
YOU ARE STUCK IN THAT WITHERED OLD FORM UNTIL WE REACH CIVILIZATION.

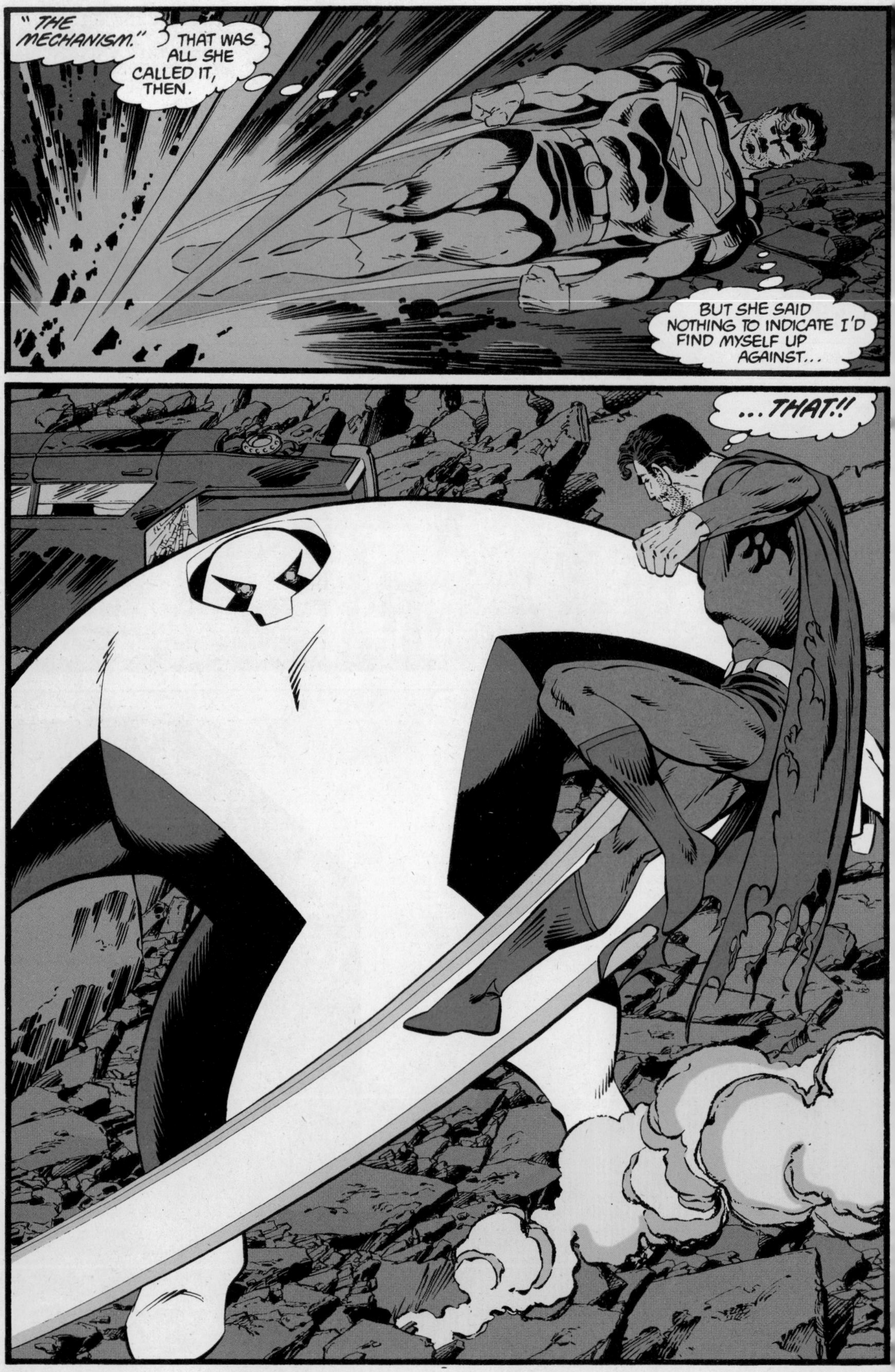
"THE MECHANISM." THAT WAS ALL SHE CALLED IT, THEN.
BUT SHE SAID NOTHING TO INDICATE I'D FIND MYSELF UP AGAINST...
...THAT!!

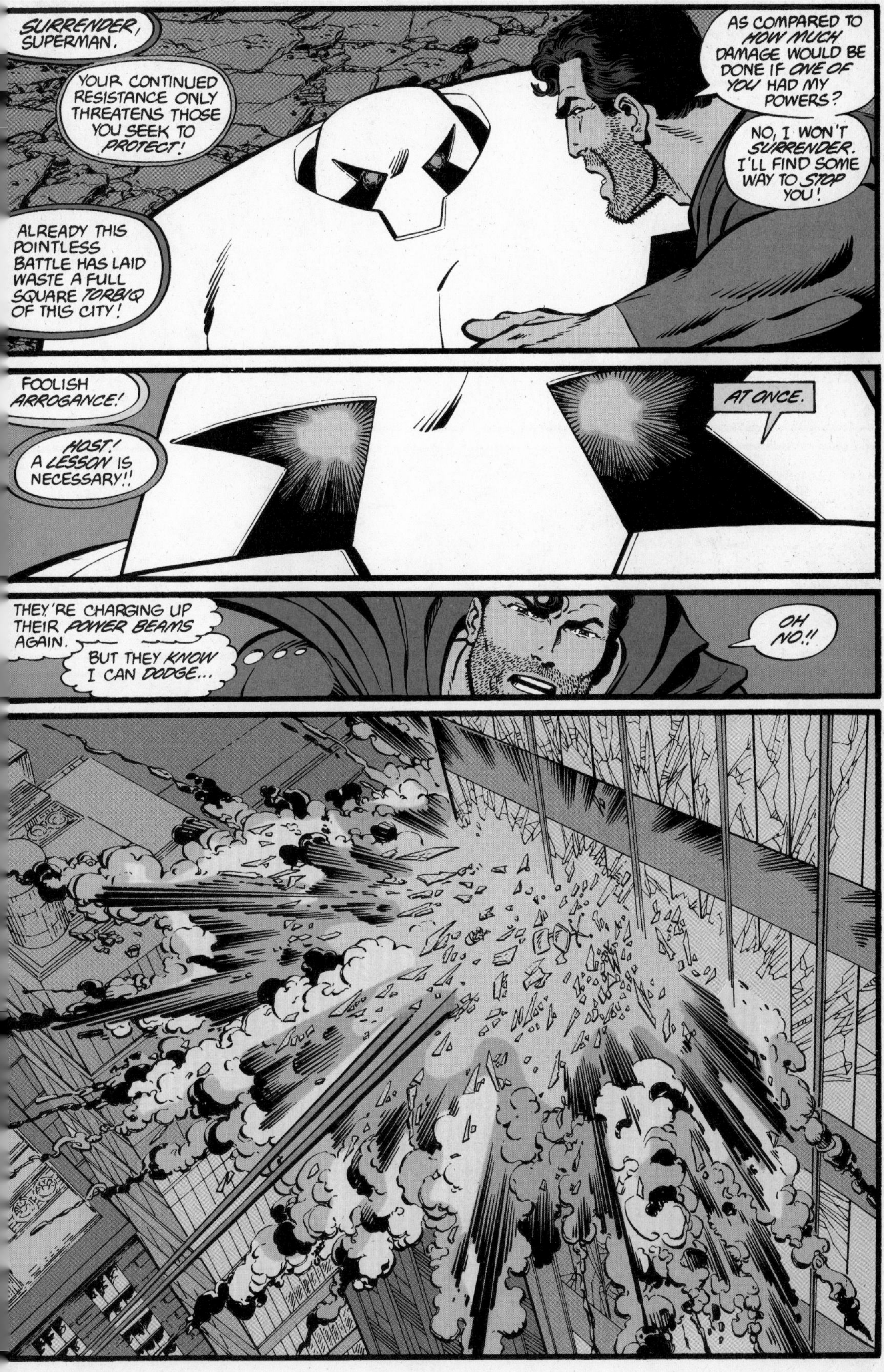
SURRENDER, SUPERMAN.
YOUR CONTINUED RESISTANCE ONLY THREATENS THOSE YOU SEEK TO PROTECT!
ALREADY THIS POINTLESS BATTLE HAS LAID WASTE A FULL SQUARE TORBIQ OF THIS CITY!
AS COMPARED TO HOW MUCH DAMAGE WOULD BE DONE IF ONE OF YOU HAD MY POWERS?
NO, I WON'T SURRENDER. I'LL FIND SOME WAY TO STOP YOU!
FOOLISH ARROGANCE!
HOST! A LESSON IS NECESSARY!!
AT ONCE.
THEY'RE CHARGING UP THEIR POWER BEAMS AGAIN.
BUT THEY KNOW I CAN DODGE...
OH NO!!

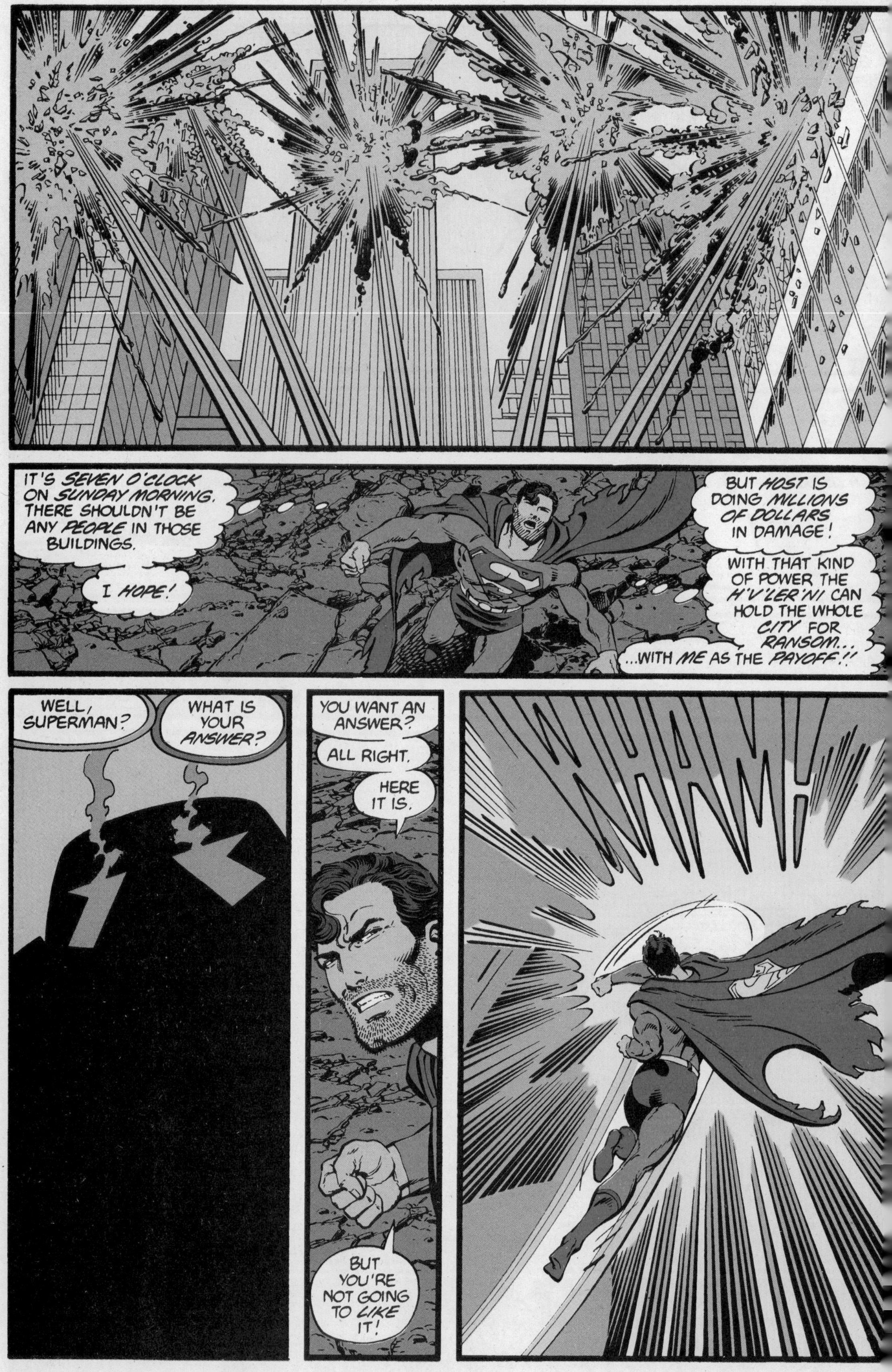
IT'S SEVEN O'CLOCK ON SUNDAY MORNING. THERE SHOULDN'T BE ANY PEOPLE IN THOSE BUILDINGS.
I HOPE!
BUT HOST IS DOING MILLIONS OF DOLLARS IN DAMAGE!
WITH THAT KIND OF POWER THE H'V'LER'NI CAN HOLD THE WHOLE CITY FOR RANSOM...
...WITH ME AS THE PAYOFF!!
WELL, SUPERMAN?
WHAT IS YOUR ANSWER?
YOU WANT AN ANSWER?
ALL RIGHT.
HERE IT IS.
BUT YOU'RE NOT GOING TO LIKE IT!
WHAMM

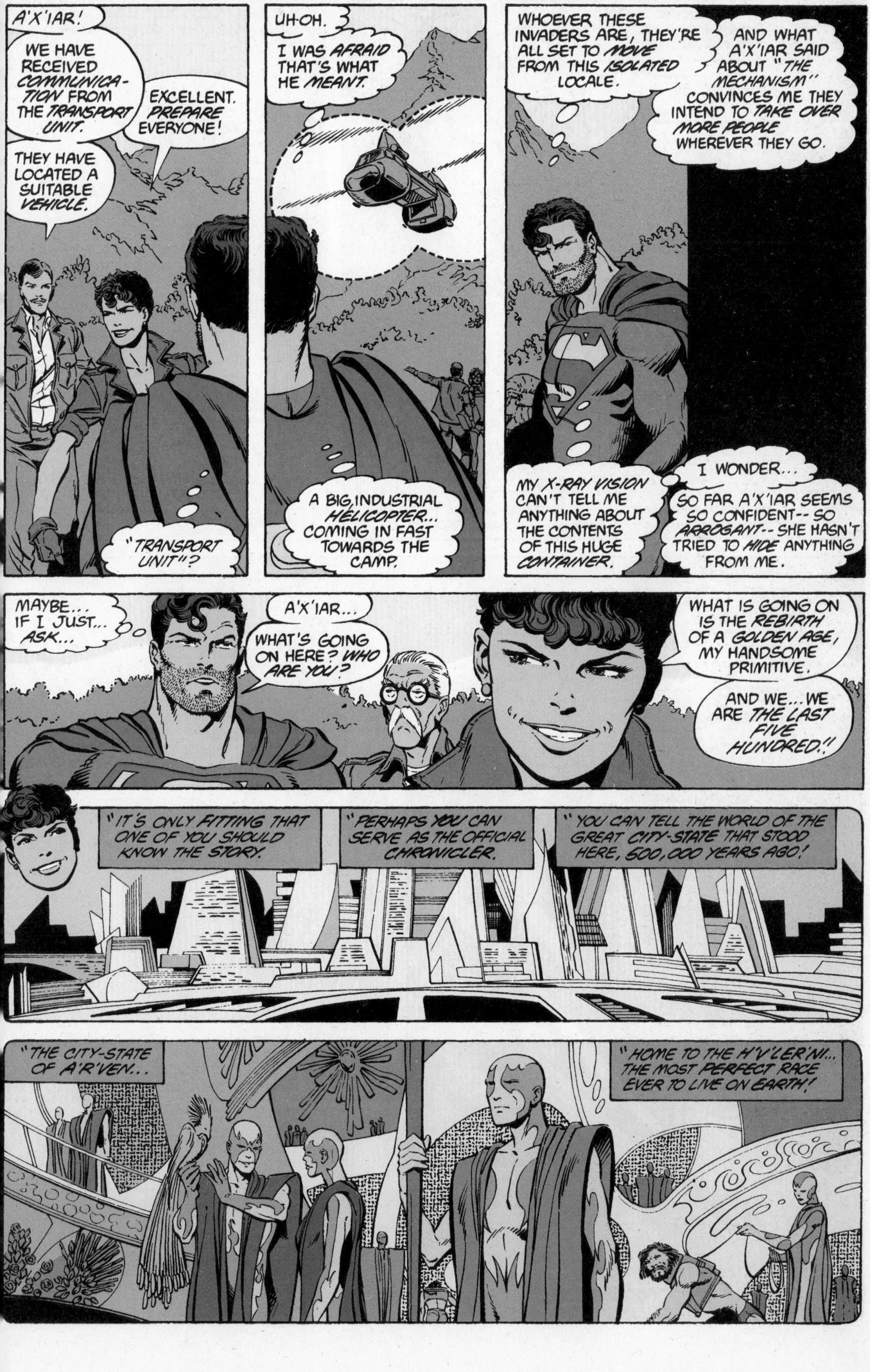
A'X'IAR!
WE HAVE RECEIVED COMMUNICATION FROM THE TRANSPORT UNIT.
THEY HAVE LOCATED A SUITABLE VEHICLE.
EXCELLENT. PREPARE EVERYONE!
"TRANSPORT UNIT"?
UH-OH.
I WAS AFRAID THAT'S WHAT HE MEANT.
A BIG INDUSTRIAL HELICOPTER... COMING IN FAST TOWARDS THE CAMP.
WHOEVER THESE INVADERS ARE, THEY'RE ALL SET TO MOVE FROM THIS ISOLATED LOCALE.
AND WHAT A'X'IAR SAID ABOUT "THE MECHANISM" CONVINCES ME THEY INTEND TO TAKE OVER MORE PEOPLE WHEREVER THEY GO.
MY X-RAY VISION CAN'T TELL ME ANYTHING ABOUT THE CONTENTS OF THIS HUGE CONTAINER.
I WONDER...
SO FAR A'X'IAR SEEMS SO CONFIDENT-- SO ARROGANT-- SHE HASN'T TRIED TO HIDE ANYTHING FROM ME.
MAYBE... IF I JUST... ASK...
A'X'IAR...
WHAT'S GOING ON HERE? WHO ARE YOU?
WHAT IS GOING ON IS THE REBIRTH OF A GOLDEN AGE, MY HANDSOME PRIMITIVE.
AND WE... WE ARE THE LAST FIVE HUNDRED!
"IT'S ONLY FITTING THAT ONE OF YOU SHOULD KNOW THE STORY.
"PERHAPS YOU CAN SERVE AS THE OFFICIAL CHRONICLER.
"YOU CAN TELL THE WORLD OF THE GREAT CITY-STATE THAT STOOD HERE, 500,000 YEARS AGO!
"THE CITY-STATE OF A'R'VEN...
"HOME TO THE H'V'LER'NI... THE MOST PERFECT RACE EVER TO LIVE ON EARTH!

"FOR TEN *CENTURIES* THE CITY THRIVED IN THE RAREFIED AIR OF THESE HIGH MOUNTAINS.

"UNTIL, ONE DAY...

" A TERRIBLE *PLAGUE* STRUCK, INSTANTLY, EXPLOSIVELY, UTTERLY WITHOUT WARNING.

"WITHIN TEN DAYS FORTY THOUSAND H'V'LER'NI LAY *DEAD!!*

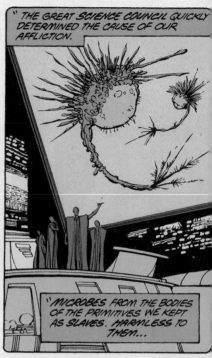

" THE GREAT *SCIENCE* COUNCIL QUICKLY DETERMINED THE CAUSE OF OUR AFFLICTION.

"MICROBES FROM THE BODIES OF THE PRIMITIVES WE KEPT AS SLAVES. HARMLESS TO THEM...

.."BUT AGAINST WHICH OUR *PERFECT*-- AND PERFECTLY GERM-FREE-- BODIES HAD *NO DEFENSE.'*

"NATURALLY WE *SLAUGHTERED* ALL THE SLAVES IMMEDIATELY! BUT IT WAS TOO LATE FOR SUCH CLEANSING MEASURES.

" THE SCIENCE COUNCIL TURNED TO THE *SALVATION* OF THE H'V'LER'NI THAT REMAINED.

"THEIR SOLUTION: *ABANDON EARTH!* WE H'V'LER'NI WOULD LEAVE THE PLANET OF OUR BIRTH FOR ALL TIME!

" IN THE DREAMLESS SLEEP OF *SUSPENDED ANIMATION* TWENTY MILLION OF US SET SAIL INTO THE DEPTHS OF SPACE FAR BEYOND OUR SOLAR SYSTEM. TWENTY MILLION...

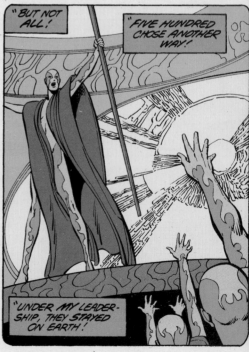

"BUT NOT *ALL!*

"FIVE HUNDRED CHOSE ANOTHER WAY!

"UNDER MY *LEADER-SHIP,* THEY STAYED ON EARTH!

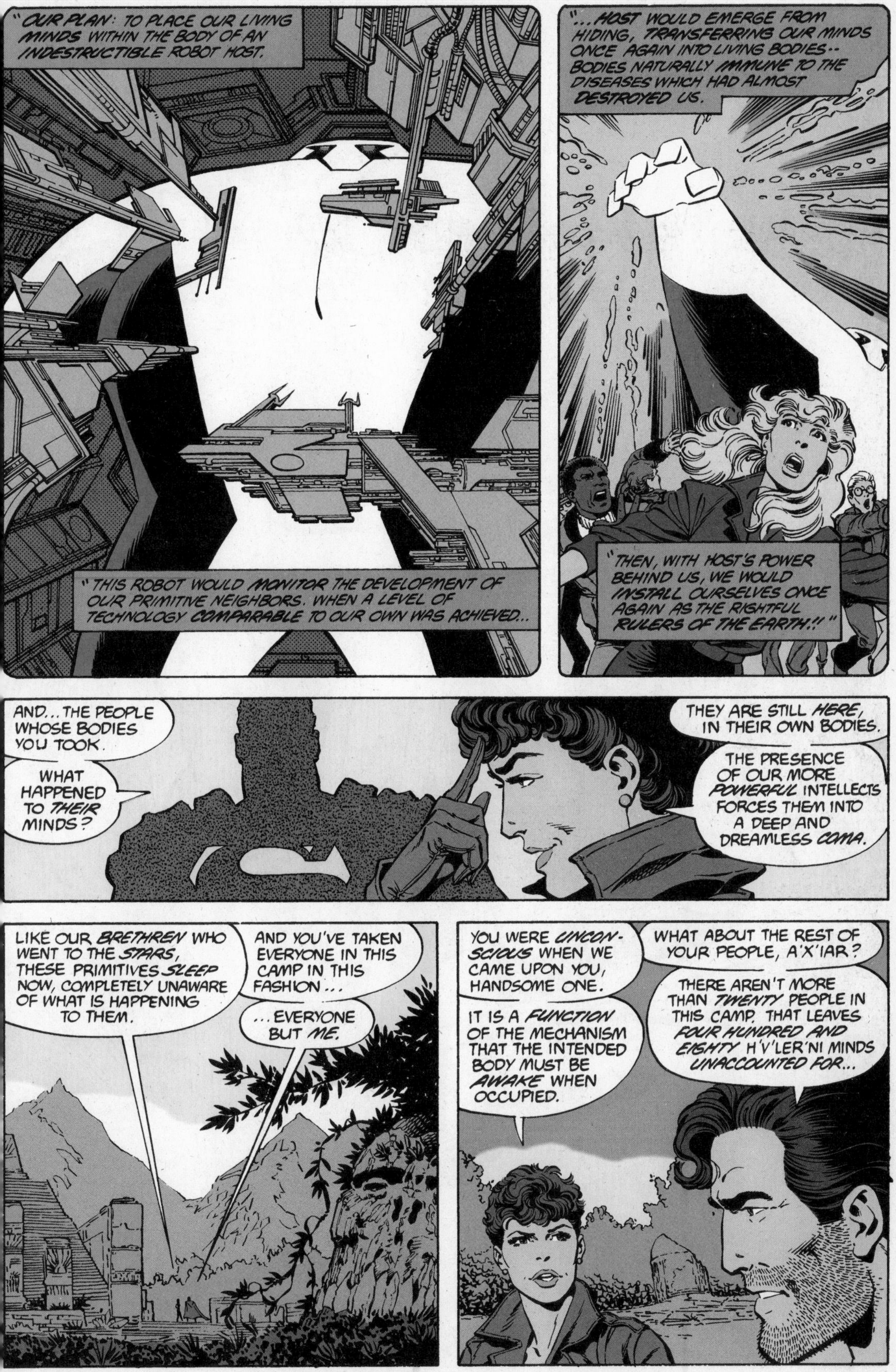
"OUR PLAN: TO PLACE OUR LIVING MINDS WITHIN THE BODY OF AN INDESTRUCTIBLE ROBOT HOST.
"THIS ROBOT WOULD MONITOR THE DEVELOPMENT OF OUR PRIMITIVE NEIGHBORS. WHEN A LEVEL OF TECHNOLOGY COMPARABLE TO OUR OWN WAS ACHIEVED...
"...HOST WOULD EMERGE FROM HIDING, TRANSFERRING OUR MINDS ONCE AGAIN INTO LIVING BODIES-- BODIES NATURALLY IMMUNE TO THE DISEASES WHICH HAD ALMOST DESTROYED US.
"THEN, WITH HOST'S POWER BEHIND US, WE WOULD INSTALL OURSELVES ONCE AGAIN AS THE RIGHTFUL RULERS OF THE EARTH!!"
AND... THE PEOPLE WHOSE BODIES YOU TOOK.
WHAT HAPPENED TO THEIR MINDS?
THEY ARE STILL HERE, IN THEIR OWN BODIES.
THE PRESENCE OF OUR MORE POWERFUL INTELLECTS FORCES THEM INTO A DEEP AND DREAMLESS COMA.
LIKE OUR BRETHREN WHO WENT TO THE STARS, THESE PRIMITIVES SLEEP NOW, COMPLETELY UNAWARE OF WHAT IS HAPPENING TO THEM.
AND YOU'VE TAKEN EVERYONE IN THIS CAMP IN THIS FASHION...
...EVERYONE BUT ME.
YOU WERE UNCON-SCIOUS WHEN WE CAME UPON YOU, HANDSOME ONE.
IT IS A FUNCTION OF THE MECHANISM THAT THE INTENDED BODY MUST BE AWAKE WHEN OCCUPIED.
WHAT ABOUT THE REST OF YOUR PEOPLE, A'X'IAR?
THERE AREN'T MORE THAN TWENTY PEOPLE IN THIS CAMP. THAT LEAVES FOUR HUNDRED AND EIGHTY H'V'LER'NI MINDS UNACCOUNTED FOR...

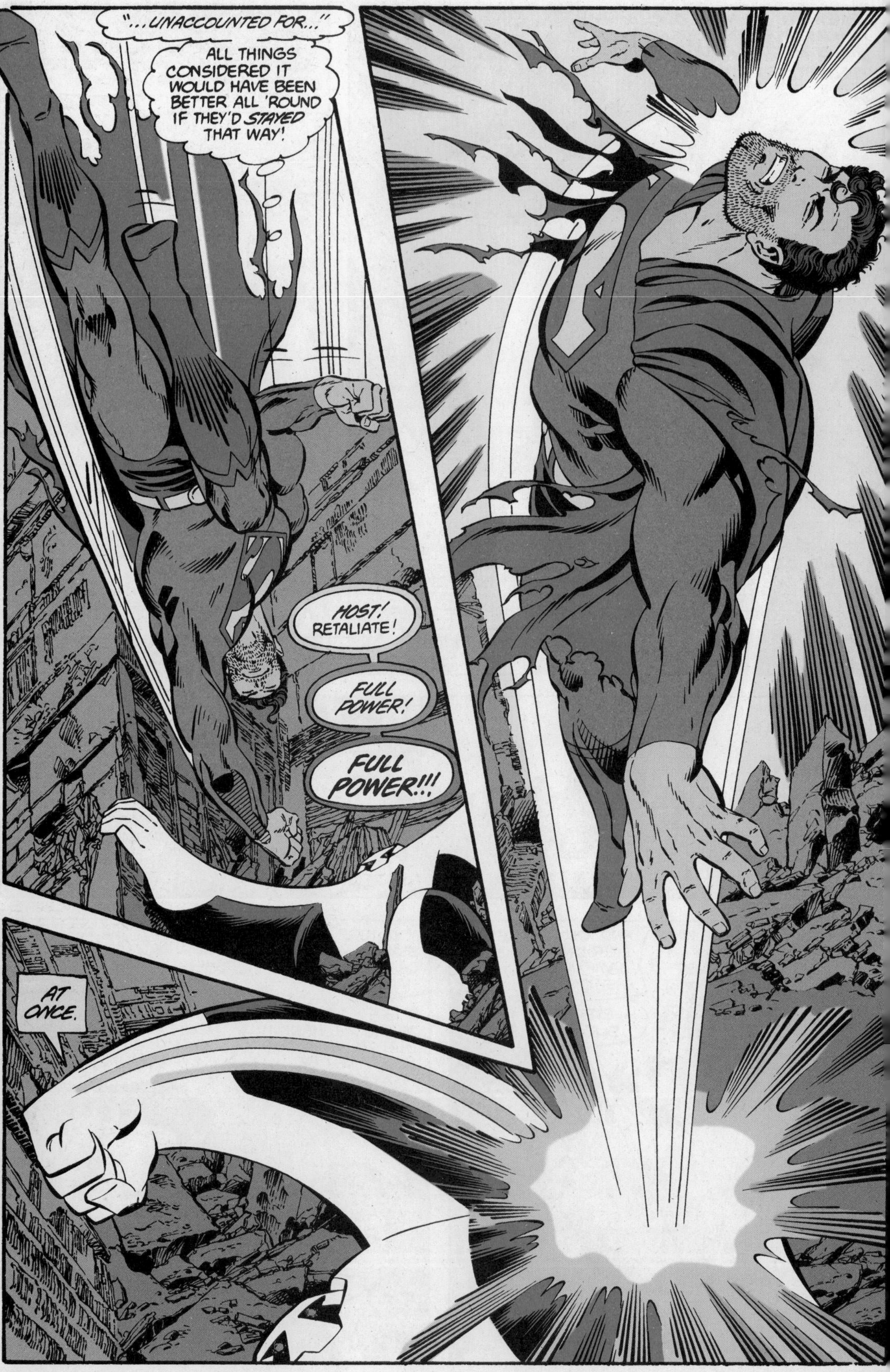
"...UNACCOUNTED FOR..."
ALL THINGS CONSIDERED IT WOULD HAVE BEEN BETTER ALL 'ROUND IF THEY'D STAYED THAT WAY!
HOST! RETALIATE!
FULL POWER!
FULL POWER!!!
AT ONCE.

...ONCE THE MECHANISM HAS BEEN SECRETLY INSTALLED IN THE CENTER OF A MORE *POPULOUS* REGION, OUR PLAN OF *CONQUEST* CAN BEGIN!

I SHALL RULE THE WORLD ONCE MORE!!

WELL... SORRY TO THROW A *WET BLANKET* ON YOUR PLANS, A'X'IAR, BUT I THINK IT'S HIGH TIME I PUT A *STOP* TO ALL THIS.

"...PUT A STOP..."? AND JUST *HOW* DO YOU PROPOSE TO DO *THAT*, PRIMITIVE?

WELL, TO BEGIN WITH... I THINK I'LL HAVE A BETTER LOOK AT THIS "HOST" OF YOURS.

RUNCK

KRUNCH

KRRRAKK!

AS I THOUGHT.

FROM THE *SIZE* AND *SHAPE* I'D GUESS *THIS* IS THE *MUMMY* I FOUGHT EARLIER.

SOMETIME IN ITS *500,000* YEARS THE *LOCAL NATIVES* MUST'VE *FOUND* ITS HIDING PLACE, AND WRAPPED IT LIKE A *DEAD KING!*

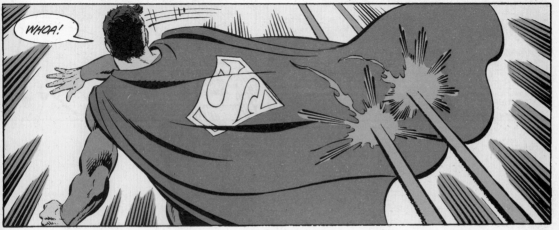

WHOA!

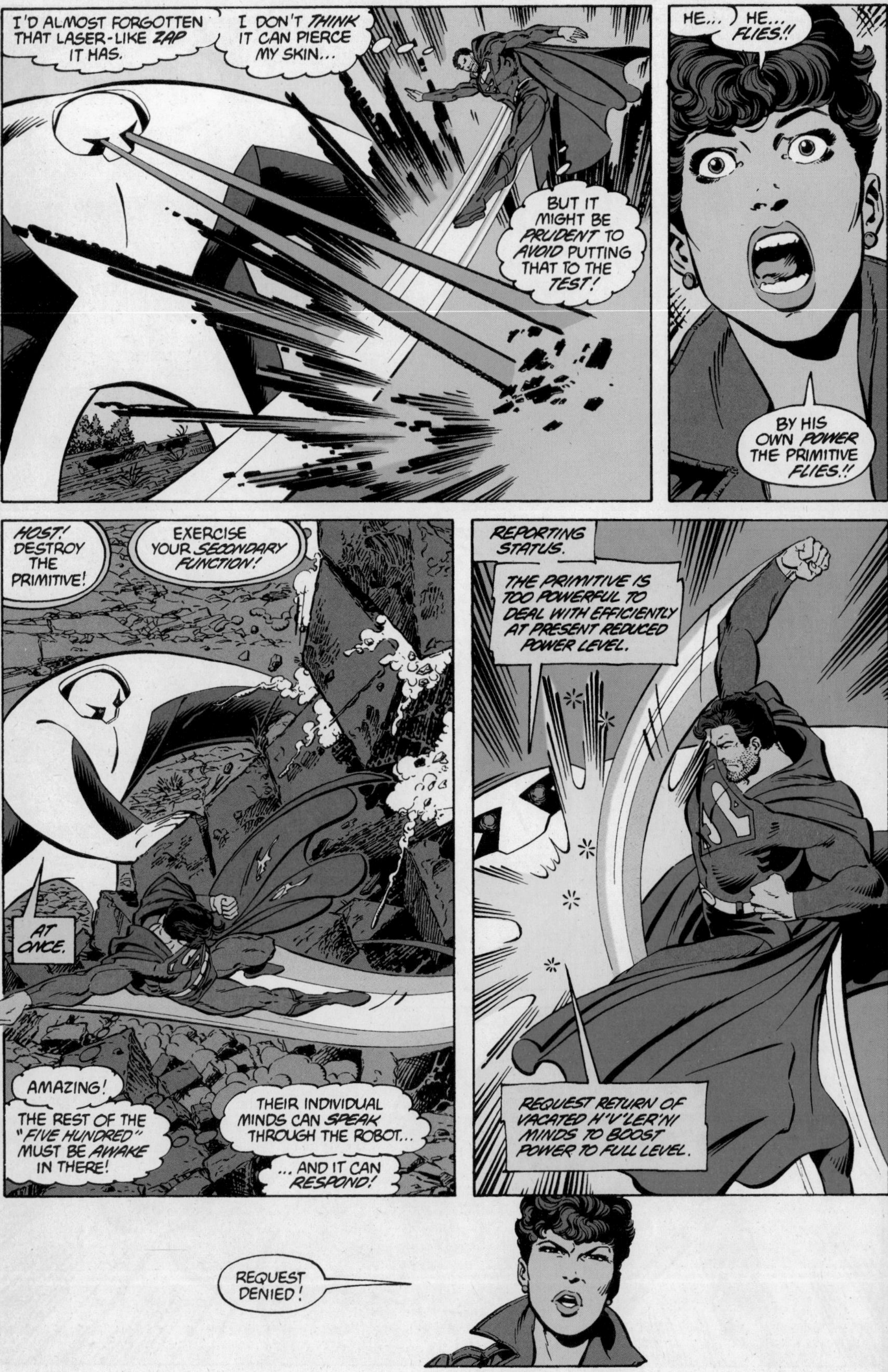
I'D ALMOST FORGOTTEN THAT LASER-LIKE *ZAP* IT HAS.
I DON'T *THINK* IT CAN PIERCE MY SKIN...
BUT IT MIGHT BE *PRUDENT* TO *AVOID* PUTTING THAT TO THE *TEST!*
HE... HE... *FLIES!!*
BY HIS OWN *POWER* THE PRIMITIVE *FLIES!!*
HOST! DESTROY THE PRIMITIVE!
EXERCISE YOUR *SECONDARY FUNCTION!*
AT ONCE.
AMAZING!
THE REST OF THE *"FIVE HUNDRED"* MUST BE *AWAKE* IN THERE!
THEIR INDIVIDUAL MINDS CAN *SPEAK* THROUGH THE ROBOT...
...AND IT CAN *RESPOND!*
REPORTING STATUS.
THE PRIMITIVE IS TOO POWERFUL TO DEAL WITH EFFICIENTLY AT PRESENT REDUCED POWER LEVEL.
REQUEST RETURN OF VACATED H'V'LER'NI MINDS TO BOOST POWER TO FULL LEVEL.
REQUEST DENIED!

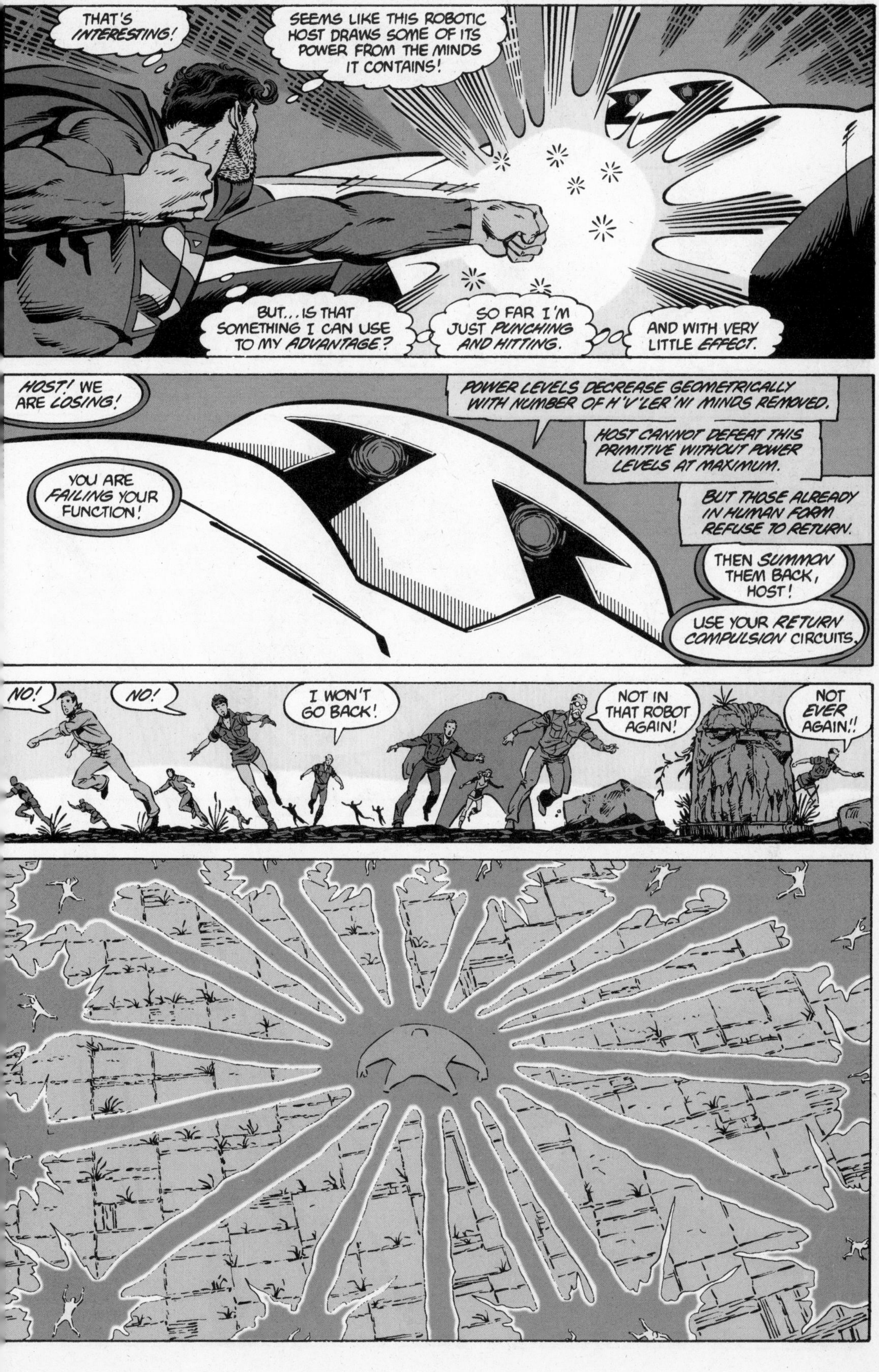

THAT'S INTERESTING!
SEEMS LIKE THIS ROBOTIC HOST DRAWS SOME OF ITS POWER FROM THE MINDS IT CONTAINS!
BUT... IS THAT SOMETHING I CAN USE TO MY ADVANTAGE?
SO FAR I'M JUST PUNCHING AND HITTING.
AND WITH VERY LITTLE EFFECT.
HOST! WE ARE LOSING!
YOU ARE FAILING YOUR FUNCTION!
POWER LEVELS DECREASE GEOMETRICALLY WITH NUMBER OF H'V'LER'NI MINDS REMOVED.
HOST CANNOT DEFEAT THIS PRIMITIVE WITHOUT POWER LEVELS AT MAXIMUM.
BUT THOSE ALREADY IN HUMAN FORM REFUSE TO RETURN.
THEN SUMMON THEM BACK, HOST!
USE YOUR RETURN COMPULSION CIRCUITS.
NO!
NO!
I WON'T GO BACK!
NOT IN THAT ROBOT AGAIN!
NOT EVER AGAIN!!

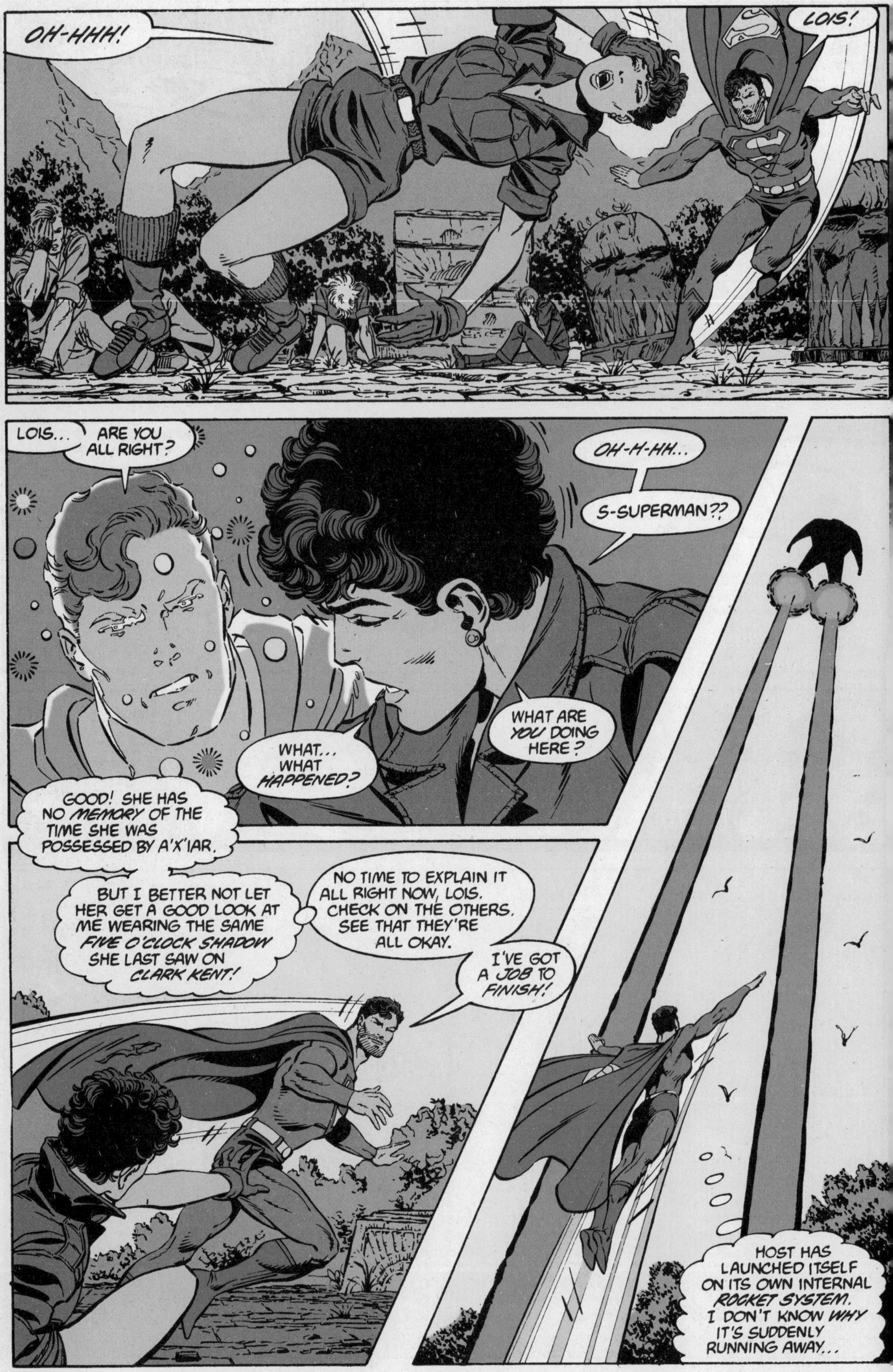
OH-HHH!
LOIS!
LOIS... ARE YOU ALL RIGHT?
OH-H-HH...
S-SUPERMAN??
WHAT... WHAT HAPPENED?
WHAT ARE YOU DOING HERE?
GOOD! SHE HAS NO MEMORY OF THE TIME SHE WAS POSSESSED BY A'X'IAR.
BUT I BETTER NOT LET HER GET A GOOD LOOK AT ME WEARING THE SAME FIVE O'CLOCK SHADOW SHE LAST SAW ON CLARK KENT!
NO TIME TO EXPLAIN IT ALL RIGHT NOW, LOIS. CHECK ON THE OTHERS. SEE THAT THEY'RE ALL OKAY.
I'VE GOT A JOB TO FINISH!
HOST HAS LAUNCHED ITSELF ON ITS OWN INTERNAL ROCKET SYSTEM. I DON'T KNOW WHY IT'S SUDDENLY RUNNING AWAY...

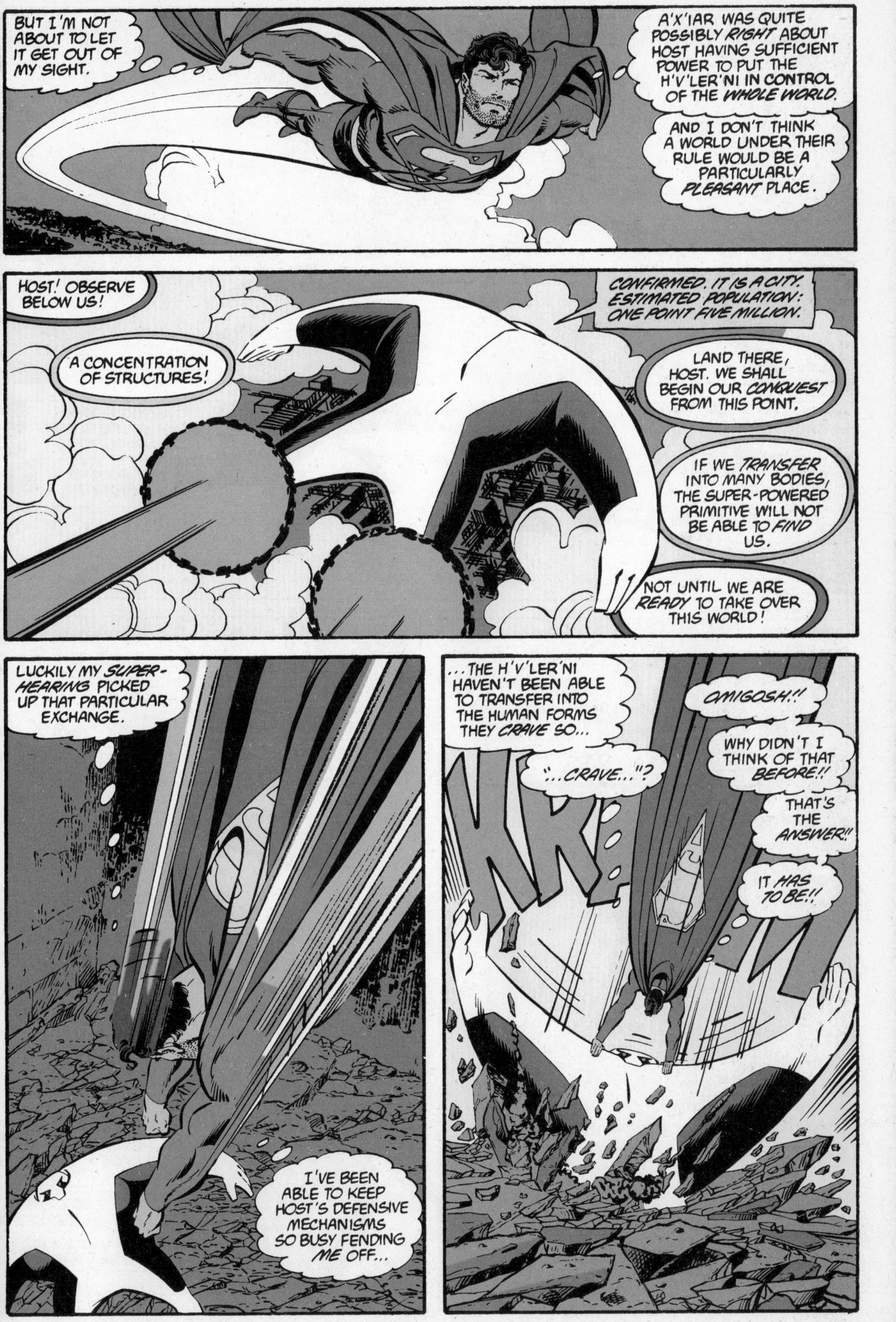
BUT I'M NOT ABOUT TO LET IT GET OUT OF MY SIGHT.
A'X'IAR WAS QUITE POSSIBLY RIGHT ABOUT HOST HAVING SUFFICIENT POWER TO PUT THE H'V'LER'NI IN CONTROL OF THE WHOLE WORLD.
AND I DON'T THINK A WORLD UNDER THEIR RULE WOULD BE A PARTICULARLY PLEASANT PLACE.
HOST! OBSERVE BELOW US!
A CONCENTRATION OF STRUCTURES!
CONFIRMED. IT IS A CITY. ESTIMATED POPULATION: ONE POINT FIVE MILLION.
LAND THERE, HOST. WE SHALL BEGIN OUR CONQUEST FROM THIS POINT.
IF WE TRANSFER INTO MANY BODIES, THE SUPER-POWERED PRIMITIVE WILL NOT BE ABLE TO FIND US.
NOT UNTIL WE ARE READY TO TAKE OVER THIS WORLD!
LUCKILY MY SUPER-HEARING PICKED UP THAT PARTICULAR EXCHANGE.
I'VE BEEN ABLE TO KEEP HOST'S DEFENSIVE MECHANISMS SO BUSY FENDING ME OFF...
...THE H'V'LER'NI HAVEN'T BEEN ABLE TO TRANSFER INTO THE HUMAN FORMS THEY CRAVE SO...
"...CRAVE..."?
OMIGOSH!!
WHY DIDN'T I THINK OF THAT BEFORE!!
THAT'S THE ANSWER!!
IT HAS TO BE!!

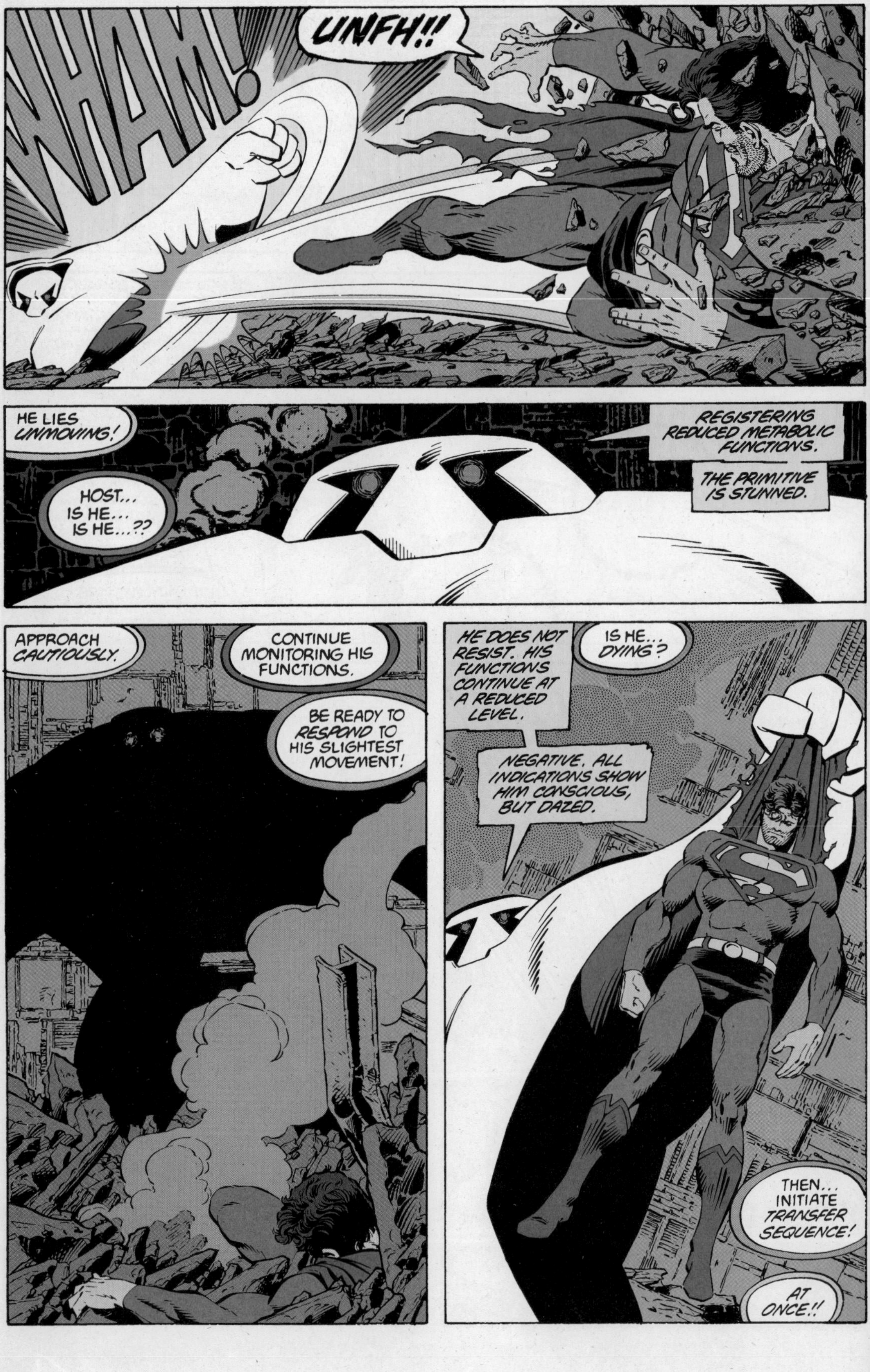
WHAM!
UNFH!!
HE LIES UNMOVING!
REGISTERING REDUCED METABOLIC FUNCTIONS.
THE PRIMITIVE IS STUNNED.
HOST... IS HE... IS HE...??
APPROACH CAUTIOUSLY.
CONTINUE MONITORING HIS FUNCTIONS.
BE READY TO RESPOND TO HIS SLIGHTEST MOVEMENT!
HE DOES NOT RESIST. HIS FUNCTIONS CONTINUE AT A REDUCED LEVEL.
IS HE... DYING?
NEGATIVE. ALL INDICATIONS SHOW HIM CONSCIOUS, BUT DAZED.
THEN... INITIATE TRANSFER SEQUENCE!
AT ONCE!!

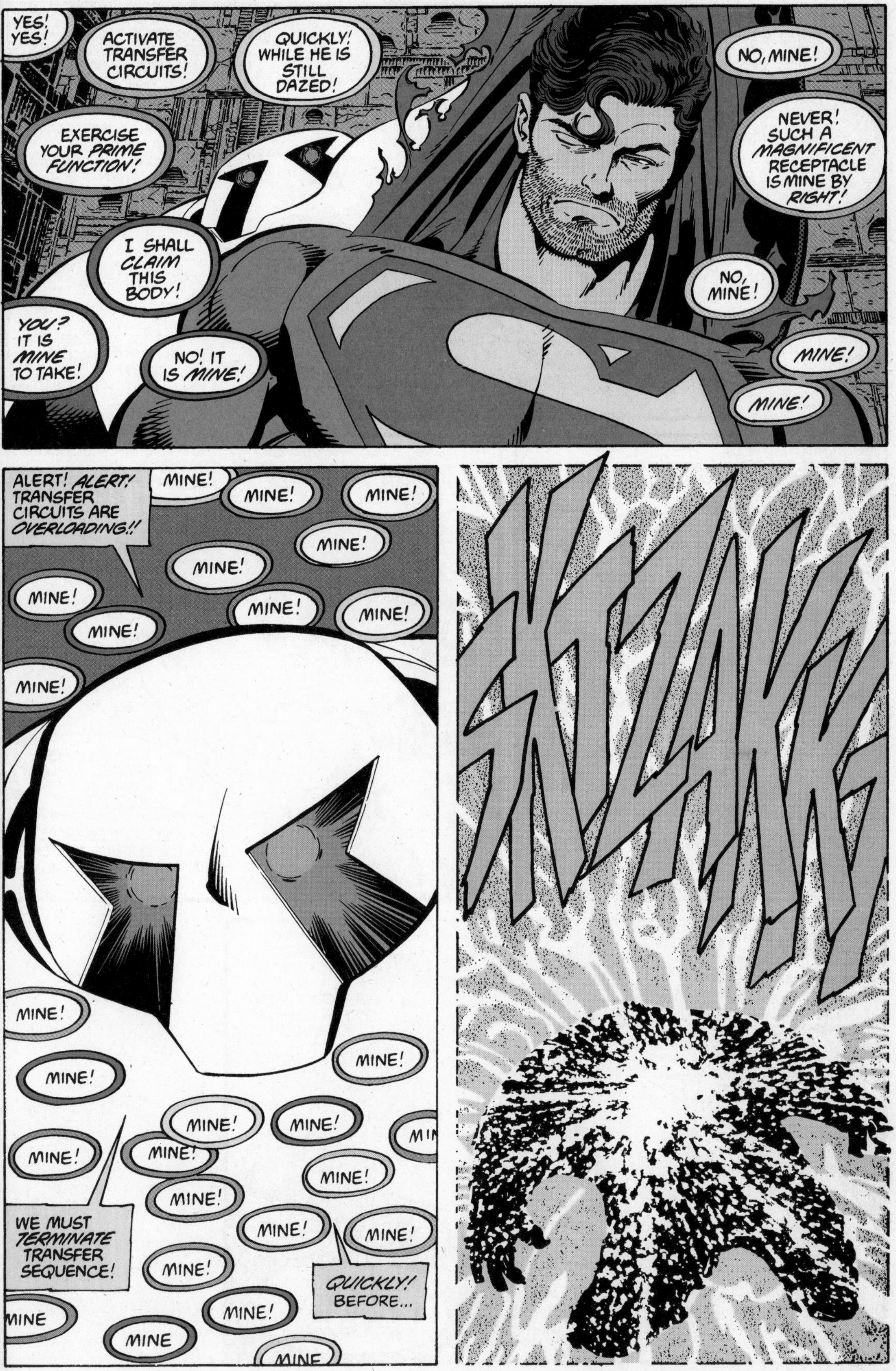

YES! YES!
ACTIVATE TRANSFER CIRCUITS!
QUICKLY! WHILE HE IS STILL DAZED!
NO, MINE!
EXERCISE YOUR *PRIME FUNCTION!*
NEVER! SUCH A *MAGNIFICENT* RECEPTACLE IS MINE BY *RIGHT!*
I SHALL *CLAIM* THIS BODY!
NO, MINE!
YOU? IT IS *MINE* TO TAKE!
NO! IT IS *MINE!*
MINE!
MINE!
ALERT! *ALERT!* TRANSFER CIRCUITS ARE *OVERLOADING!!*
MINE!
MINE!
MINE!
MINE!
MINE!
MINE!
MINE!
MINE!
MINE!
MINE!
MINE!
MINE!
MINE!
MINE!
MINE!
MINE!
MINE!
MINE!
MINE!
WE MUST *TERMINATE* TRANSFER SEQUENCE!
MINE!
MINE!
MINE!
QUICKLY! BEFORE...
MINE!
MINE

SO YOU JUST...FAKED HIM OUT AND HE...BLEW UP?

MM. A MASSIVE SHORT CIRCUIT OF ALL ITS INTERNAL SYSTEMS. EVERYTHING WAS SUBORDINATE TO THE TRANSFER CIRCUITS, IT SEEMS.

I'LL CONFESS IT WAS A LITTLE MORE EXPLOSIVE THAN I'D EXPECTED.

I'D GUESSED THE EFFECT MIGHT BE SIMPLY TO FUSE THE TRANSFER CIRCUITS, TRAPPING THE H'V'LER'NI.

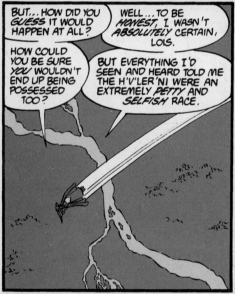

BUT...HOW DID YOU GUESS IT WOULD HAPPEN AT ALL?

HOW COULD YOU BE SURE YOU WOULDN'T END UP BEING POSSESSED TOO?

WELL...TO BE HONEST, I WASN'T ABSOLUTELY CERTAIN, LOIS.

BUT EVERYTHING I'D SEEN AND HEARD TOLD ME THE H'V'LER'NI WERE AN EXTREMELY PETTY AND SELFISH RACE.

THEY ENSLAVED "PRIMITIVES."

THEY REFUSED TO HELP EVEN EACH OTHER...

AND A'X'IAR'S BUNCH SEEMED TO REPRESENT THE VERY WORST OF THE LOT!!

AND ALL THIS HAPPENED WHILE I WAS IN LA-LA LAND!

OH, WELL...AT LEAST YOU GAVE THE DETAILS TO ME, AND NOT YOUR BUDDY CLARK KENT.

HOW IS HE, BY THE WAY?

YOU TOLD ME YOU FLEW HIM BACK TO METROPOLIS, BUT THE LAST TIME I SAW HIM HE WAS IN ROUGH SHAPE.

OHH...

CLARK'S A PRETTY RESILIENT SORT OF GUY, LOIS. IT WAS TOUCH-AND-GO FOR A WHILE THERE...

BUT...THE NEXT TIME YOU SEE HIM I'M SURE HE'LL BE JUST FINE...

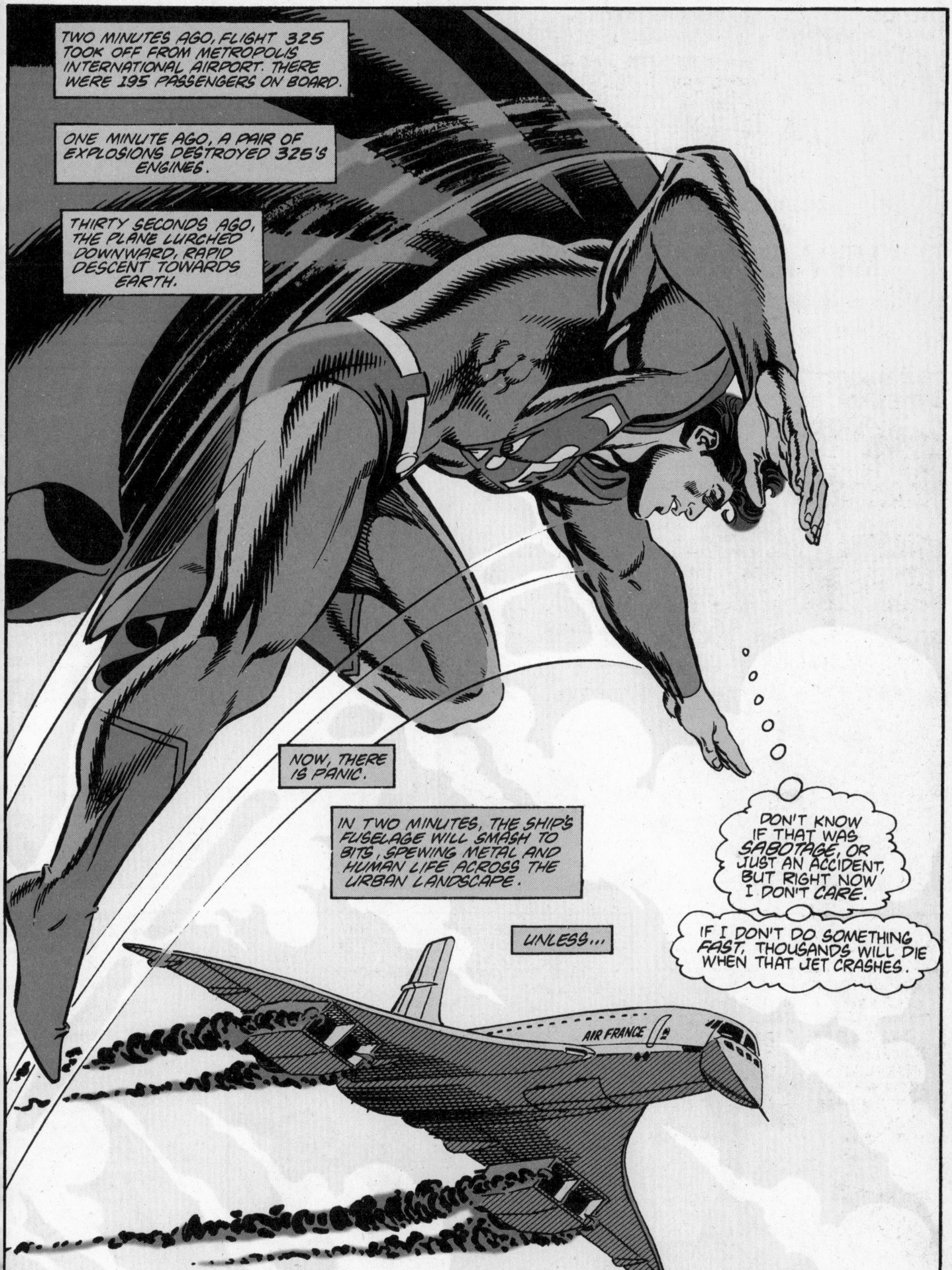
TWO MINUTES AGO, FLIGHT 325 TOOK OFF FROM METROPOLIS INTERNATIONAL AIRPORT. THERE WERE 195 PASSENGERS ON BOARD.
ONE MINUTE AGO, A PAIR OF EXPLOSIONS DESTROYED 325'S ENGINES.
THIRTY SECONDS AGO, THE PLANE LURCHED DOWNWARD, RAPID DESCENT TOWARDS EARTH.
NOW, THERE IS PANIC.
IN TWO MINUTES, THE SHIP'S FUSELAGE WILL SMASH TO BITS, SPEWING METAL AND HUMAN LIFE ACROSS THE URBAN LANDSCAPE.
UNLESS...
DON'T KNOW IF THAT WAS SABOTAGE, OR JUST AN ACCIDENT, BUT RIGHT NOW I DON'T CARE.
IF I DON'T DO SOMETHING FAST, THOUSANDS WILL DIE WHEN THAT JET CRASHES.
AIR FRANCE
1

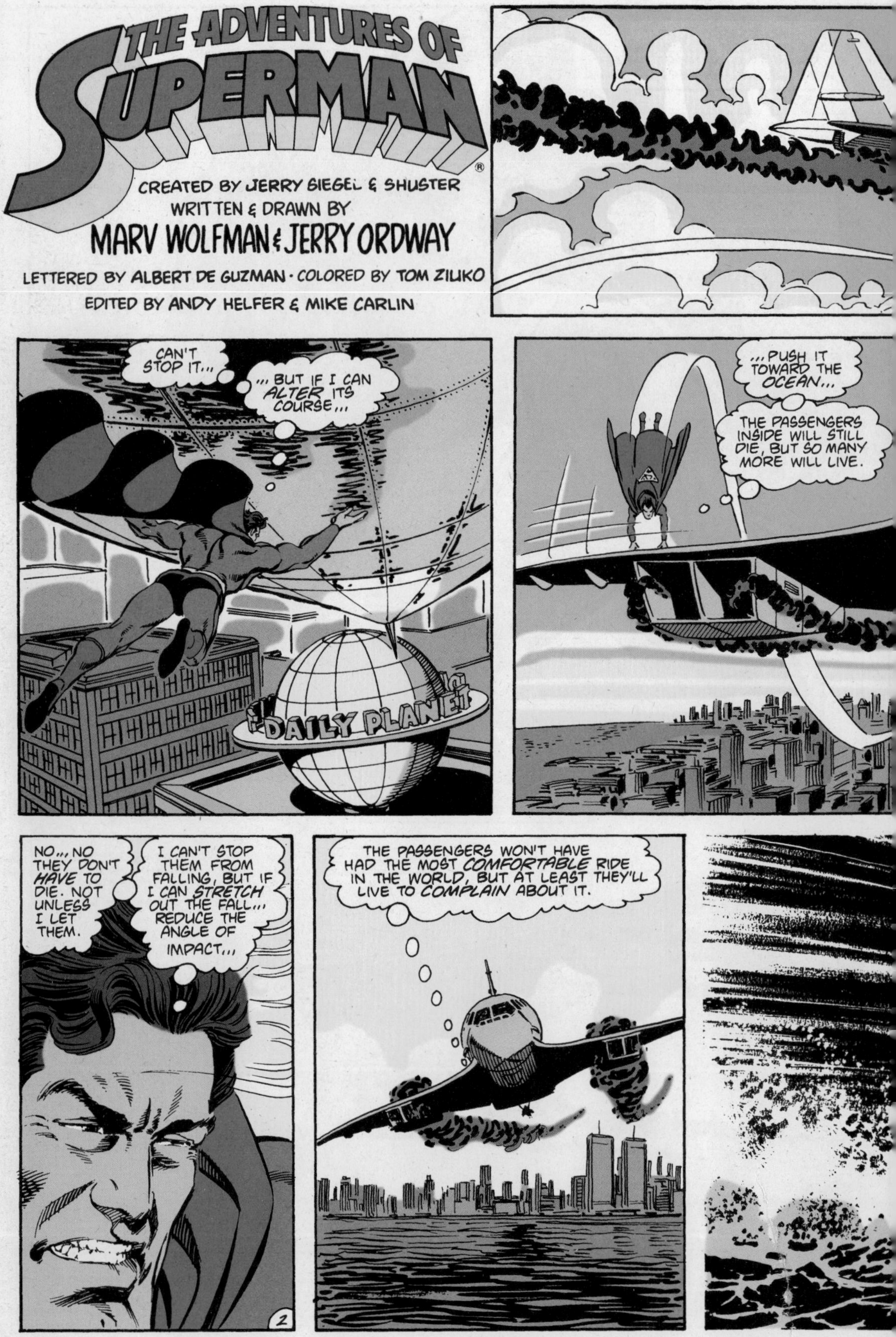
THE ADVENTURES OF SUPERMAN®
CREATED BY JERRY SIEGEL & SHUSTER
WRITTEN & DRAWN BY
MARV WOLFMAN & JERRY ORDWAY
LETTERED BY ALBERT DE GUZMAN · COLORED BY TOM ZIUKO
EDITED BY ANDY HELFER & MIKE CARLIN
CAN'T STOP IT...
...BUT IF I CAN ALTER ITS COURSE...
DAILY PLANET
...PUSH IT TOWARD THE OCEAN...
THE PASSENGERS INSIDE WILL STILL DIE, BUT SO MANY MORE WILL LIVE.
NO... NO THEY DON'T HAVE TO DIE. NOT UNLESS I LET THEM.
I CAN'T STOP THEM FROM FALLING, BUT IF I CAN STRETCH OUT THE FALL... REDUCE THE ANGLE OF IMPACT...
2
THE PASSENGERS WON'T HAVE HAD THE MOST COMFORTABLE RIDE IN THE WORLD, BUT AT LEAST THEY'LL LIVE TO COMPLAIN ABOUT IT.

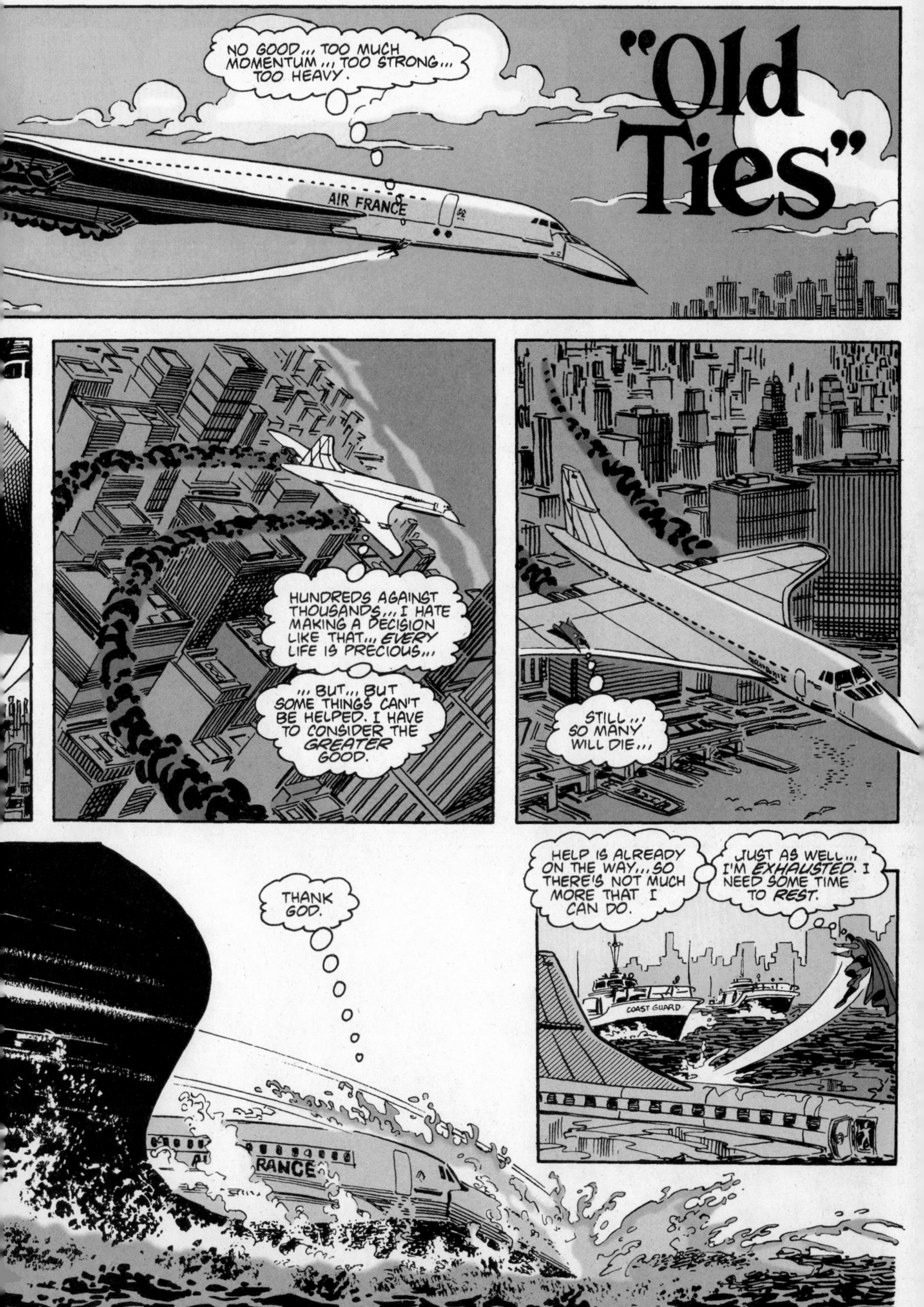

NO GOOD... TOO MUCH MOMENTUM... TOO STRONG... TOO HEAVY.
"Old Ties"
AIR FRANCE
HUNDREDS AGAINST THOUSANDS... I HATE MAKING A DECISION LIKE THAT... EVERY LIFE IS PRECIOUS...
... BUT... BUT SOME THINGS CAN'T BE HELPED. I HAVE TO CONSIDER THE GREATER GOOD.
STILL... SO MANY WILL DIE...
THANK GOD.
RANCE
HELP IS ALREADY ON THE WAY... SO THERE'S NOT MUCH MORE THAT I CAN DO.
JUST AS WELL... I'M EXHAUSTED. I NEED SOME TIME TO REST.
COAST GUARD
3

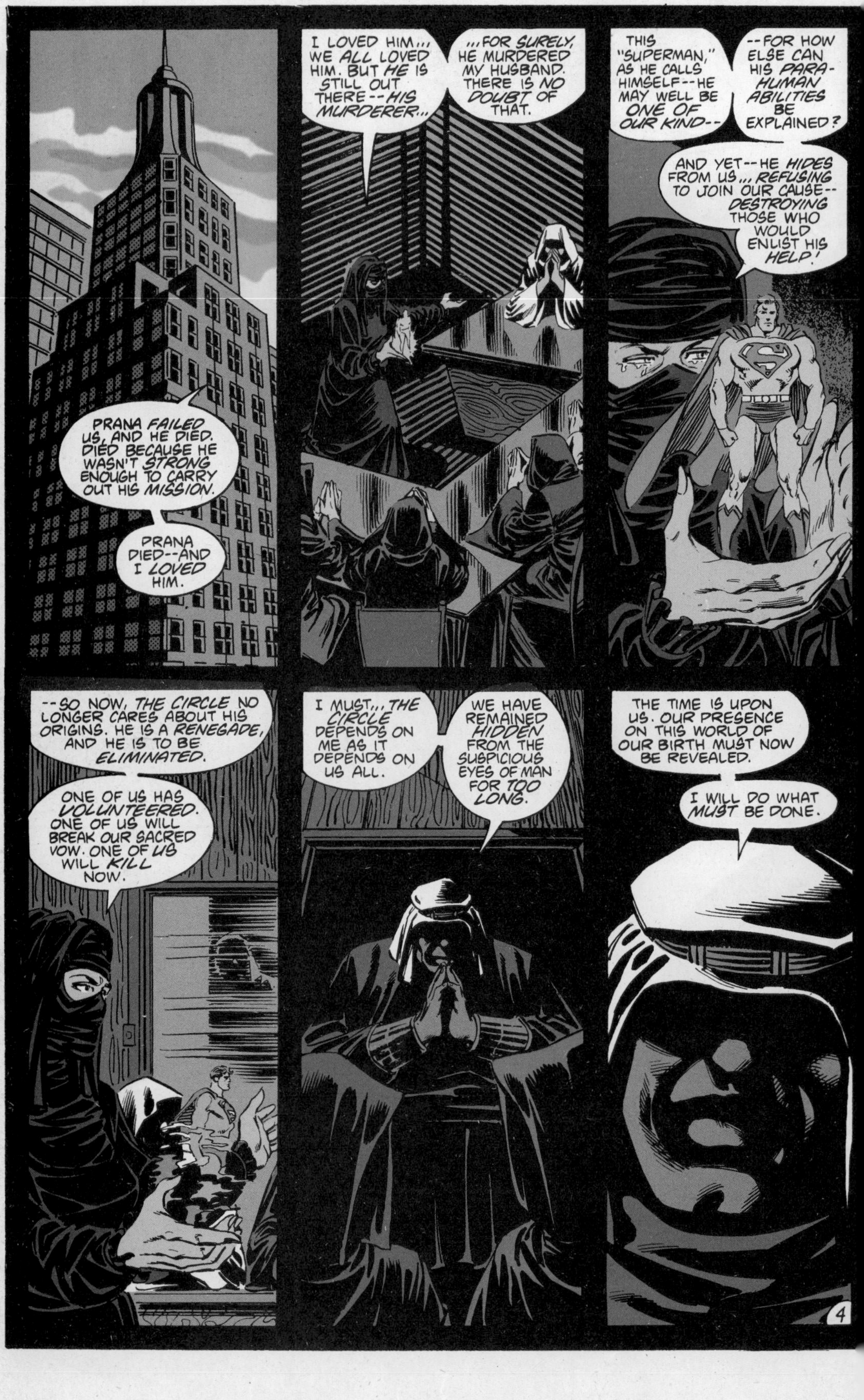
PRANA FAILED US, AND HE DIED. DIED BECAUSE HE WASN'T STRONG ENOUGH TO CARRY OUT HIS MISSION.
PRANA DIED--AND I LOVED HIM.
I LOVED HIM... WE ALL LOVED HIM. BUT HE IS STILL OUT THERE--HIS MURDERER...
...FOR SURELY, HE MURDERED MY HUSBAND. THERE IS NO DOUBT OF THAT.
THIS "SUPERMAN," AS HE CALLS HIMSELF--HE MAY WELL BE ONE OF OUR KIND--
--FOR HOW ELSE CAN HIS PARA-HUMAN ABILITIES BE EXPLAINED?
AND YET--HE HIDES FROM US... REFUSING TO JOIN OUR CAUSE--DESTROYING THOSE WHO WOULD ENLIST HIS HELP!
--SO NOW, THE CIRCLE NO LONGER CARES ABOUT HIS ORIGINS. HE IS A RENEGADE, AND HE IS TO BE ELIMINATED.
ONE OF US HAS VOLUNTEERED. ONE OF US WILL BREAK OUR SACRED VOW. ONE OF US WILL KILL NOW.
I MUST... THE CIRCLE DEPENDS ON ME AS IT DEPENDS ON US ALL.
WE HAVE REMAINED HIDDEN FROM THE SUSPICIOUS EYES OF MAN FOR TOO LONG.
THE TIME IS UPON US. OUR PRESENCE ON THIS WORLD OF OUR BIRTH MUST NOW BE REVEALED.
I WILL DO WHAT MUST BE DONE.
4

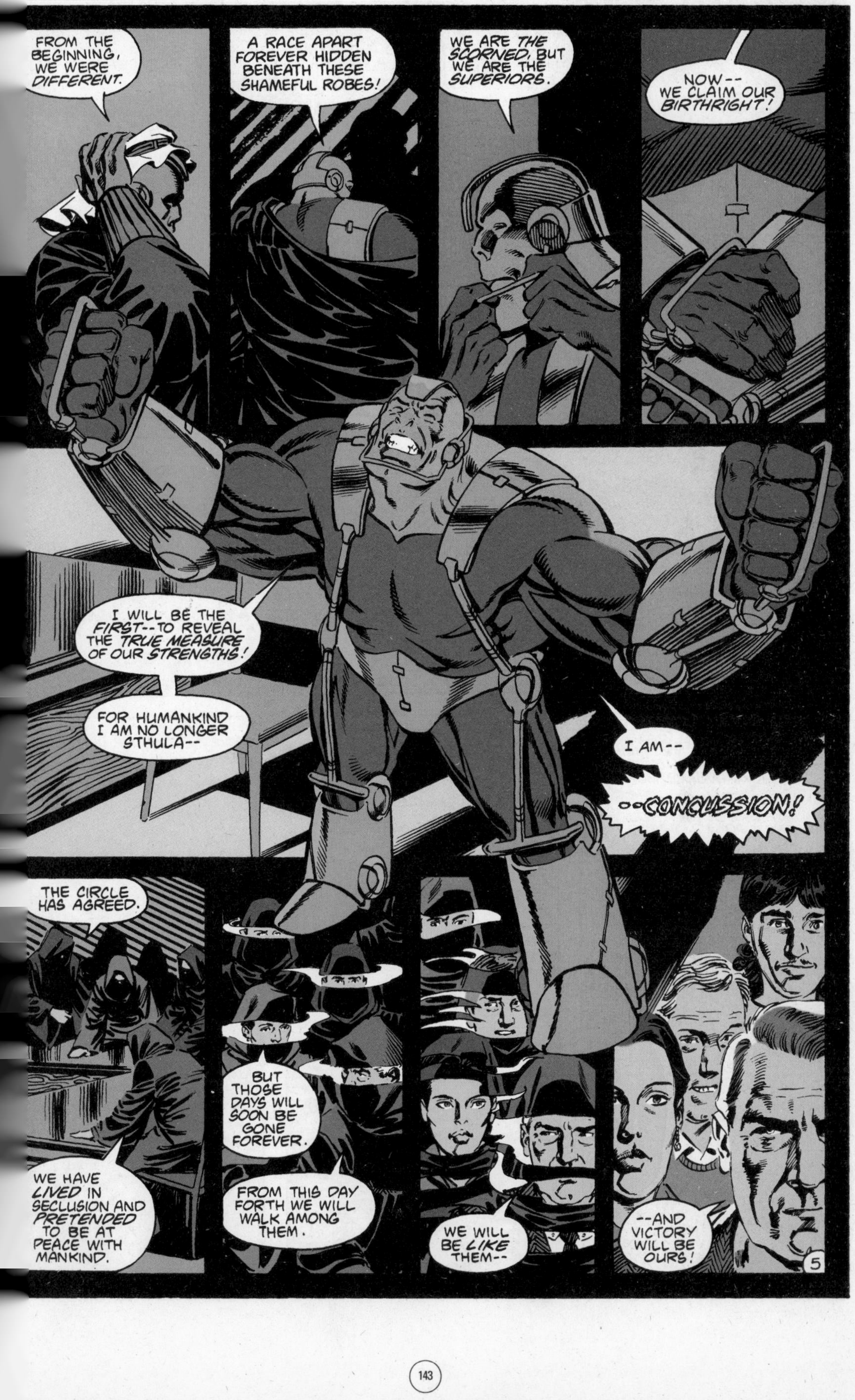

FROM THE BEGINNING, WE WERE DIFFERENT.
A RACE APART FOREVER HIDDEN BENEATH THESE SHAMEFUL ROBES!
WE ARE THE SCORNED, BUT WE ARE THE SUPERIORS.
NOW-- WE CLAIM OUR BIRTHRIGHT!
I WILL BE THE FIRST--TO REVEAL THE TRUE MEASURE OF OUR STRENGTHS!
FOR HUMANKIND I AM NO LONGER STHULA--
I AM--
--CONCUSSION!
THE CIRCLE HAS AGREED.
WE HAVE LIVED IN SECLUSION AND PRETENDED TO BE AT PEACE WITH MANKIND.
BUT THOSE DAYS WILL SOON BE GONE FOREVER.
FROM THIS DAY FORTH WE WILL WALK AMONG THEM.
WE WILL BE LIKE THEM--
--AND VICTORY WILL BE OURS!
5

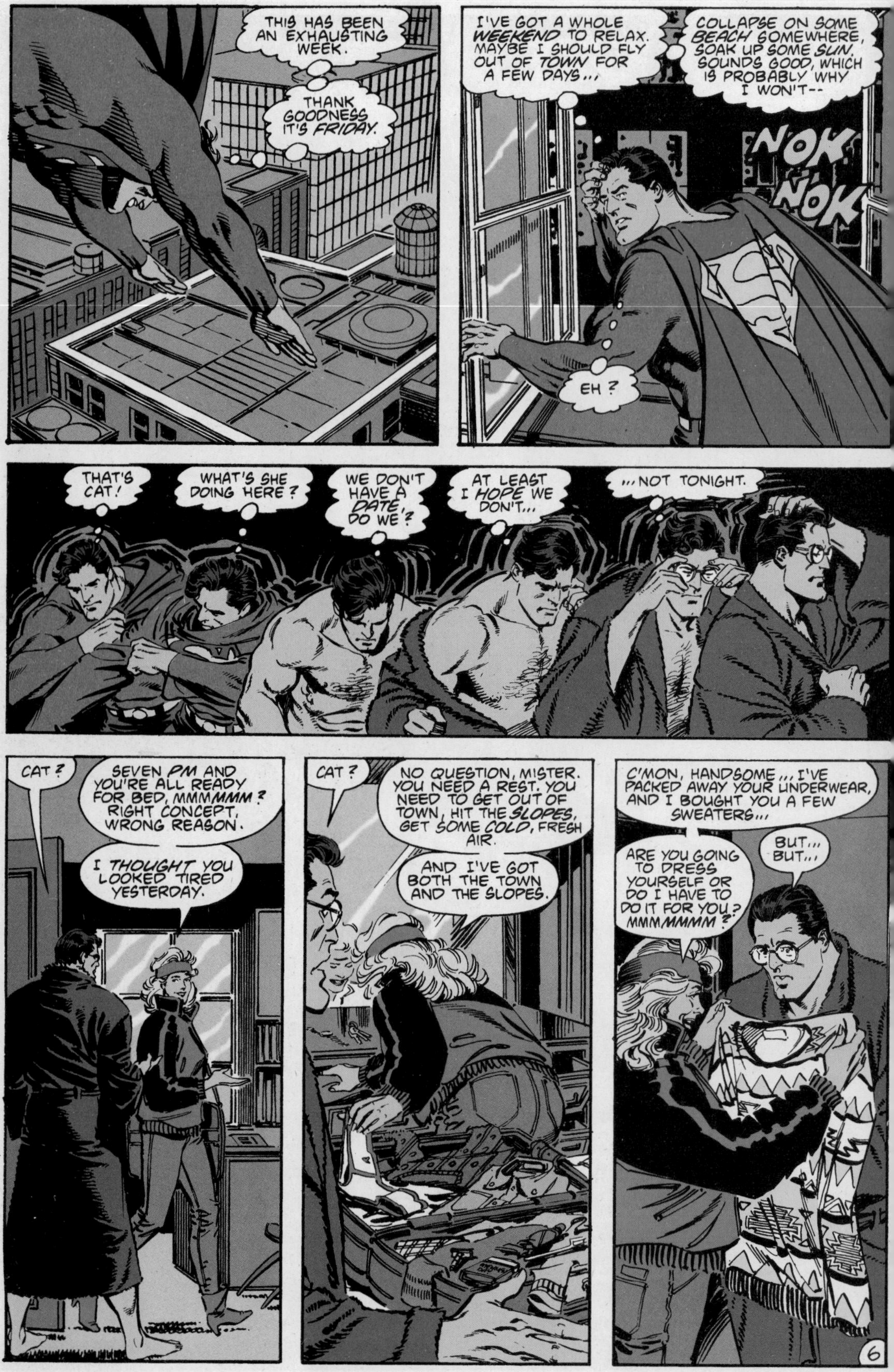

THIS HAS BEEN AN EXHAUSTING WEEK.
THANK GOODNESS IT'S FRIDAY.
I'VE GOT A WHOLE WEEKEND TO RELAX. MAYBE I SHOULD FLY OUT OF TOWN FOR A FEW DAYS...
COLLAPSE ON SOME BEACH SOMEWHERE, SOAK UP SOME SUN. SOUNDS GOOD, WHICH IS PROBABLY WHY I WON'T--
NOK NOK
EH ?
THAT'S CAT!
WHAT'S SHE DOING HERE?
WE DON'T HAVE A DATE, DO WE?
AT LEAST I HOPE WE DON'T...
...NOT TONIGHT.
CAT?
SEVEN PM AND YOU'RE ALL READY FOR BED, MMMMMM? RIGHT CONCEPT, WRONG REASON.
I THOUGHT YOU LOOKED TIRED YESTERDAY.
CAT?
NO QUESTION, MISTER. YOU NEED A REST. YOU NEED TO GET OUT OF TOWN, HIT THE SLOPES, GET SOME COLD, FRESH AIR.
AND I'VE GOT BOTH THE TOWN AND THE SLOPES.
C'MON, HANDSOME... I'VE PACKED AWAY YOUR UNDERWEAR, AND I BOUGHT YOU A FEW SWEATERS...
ARE YOU GOING TO DRESS YOURSELF OR DO I HAVE TO DO IT FOR YOU? MMMMMMM?
BUT... BUT...
6

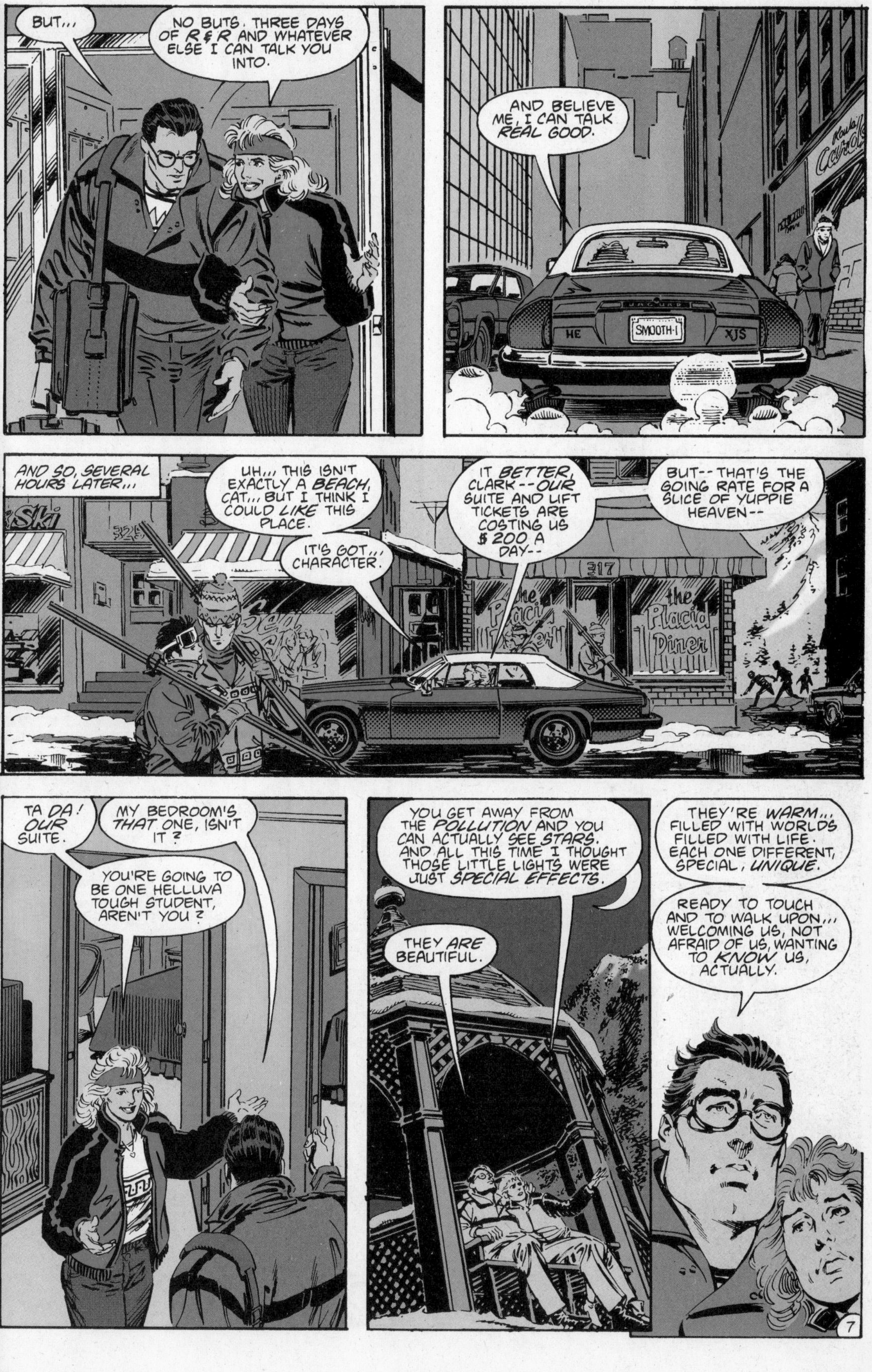

BUT...
NO BUTS. THREE DAYS OF R & R AND WHATEVER ELSE I CAN TALK YOU INTO.
AND BELIEVE ME, I CAN TALK REAL GOOD.
SMOOTH-1
AND SO, SEVERAL HOURS LATER...
UH... THIS ISN'T EXACTLY A BEACH, CAT... BUT I THINK I COULD LIKE THIS PLACE.
IT'S GOT... CHARACTER.
IT BETTER, CLARK--OUR SUITE AND LIFT TICKETS ARE COSTING US $200 A DAY--
BUT--THAT'S THE GOING RATE FOR A SLICE OF YUPPIE HEAVEN--
the Placid Diner
TA DA! OUR SUITE.
MY BEDROOM'S THAT ONE, ISN'T IT?
YOU'RE GOING TO BE ONE HELLUVA TOUGH STUDENT, AREN'T YOU?
YOU GET AWAY FROM THE POLLUTION AND YOU CAN ACTUALLY SEE STARS. AND ALL THIS TIME I THOUGHT THOSE LITTLE LIGHTS WERE JUST SPECIAL EFFECTS.
THEY ARE BEAUTIFUL.
THEY'RE WARM... FILLED WITH WORLDS FILLED WITH LIFE. EACH ONE DIFFERENT, SPECIAL, UNIQUE.
READY TO TOUCH AND TO WALK UPON... WELCOMING US, NOT AFRAID OF US, WANTING TO KNOW US, ACTUALLY.
7

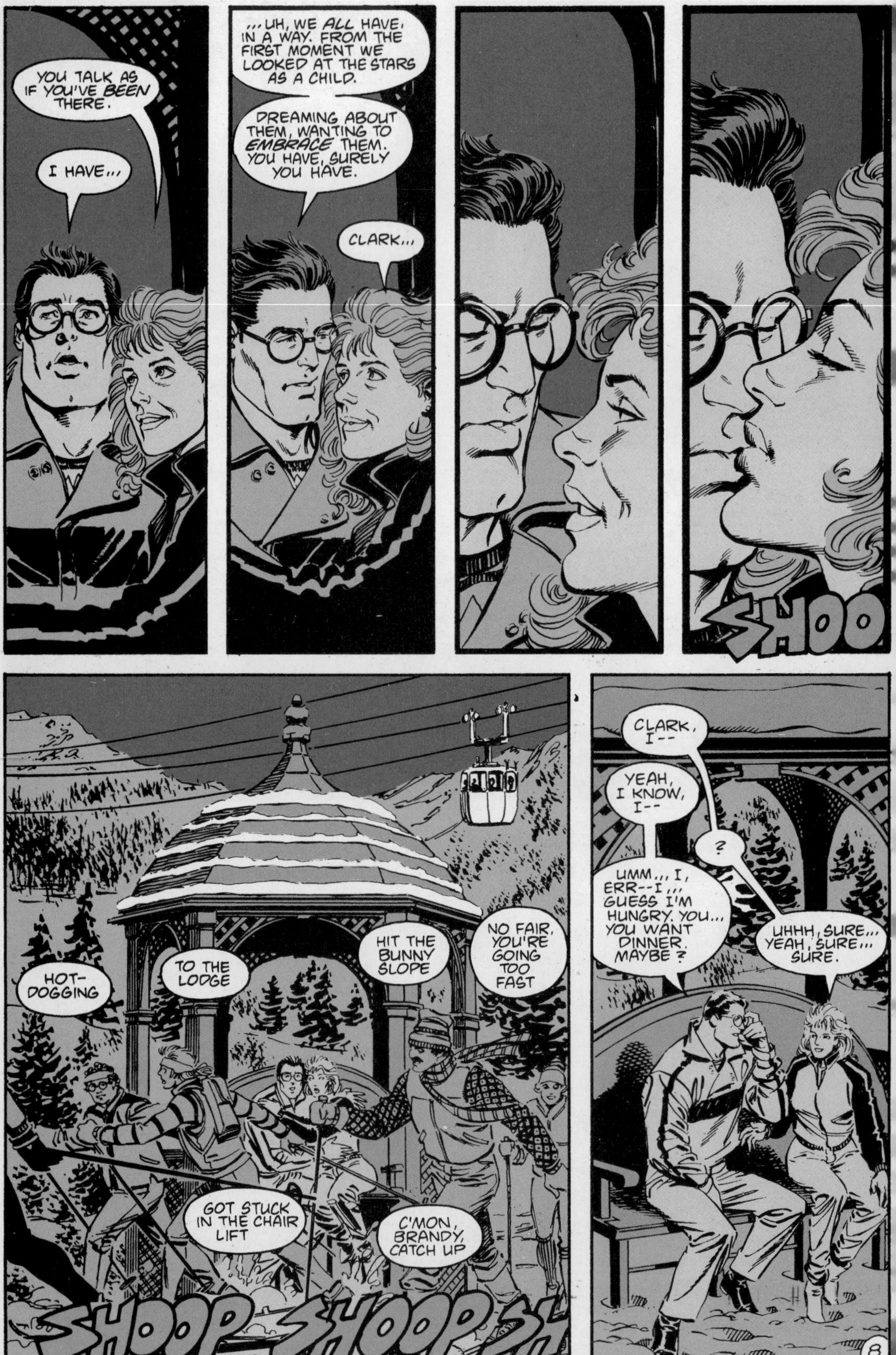

YOU TALK AS IF YOU'VE BEEN THERE.
I HAVE...
...UH, WE ALL HAVE, IN A WAY. FROM THE FIRST MOMENT WE LOOKED AT THE STARS AS A CHILD.
DREAMING ABOUT THEM, WANTING TO EMBRACE THEM. YOU HAVE, SURELY YOU HAVE.
CLARK...
SHOO
HOT-DOGGING
TO THE LODGE
HIT THE BUNNY SLOPE
NO FAIR, YOU'RE GOING TOO FAST
GOT STUCK IN THE CHAIR LIFT
C'MON, BRANDY, CATCH UP
SHOOP SHOOP SH
CLARK, I--
YEAH, I KNOW, I--
?
UMM... I, ERR--I... GUESS I'M HUNGRY. YOU... YOU WANT DINNER, MAYBE ?
UHHH, SURE... YEAH, SURE... SURE.
8

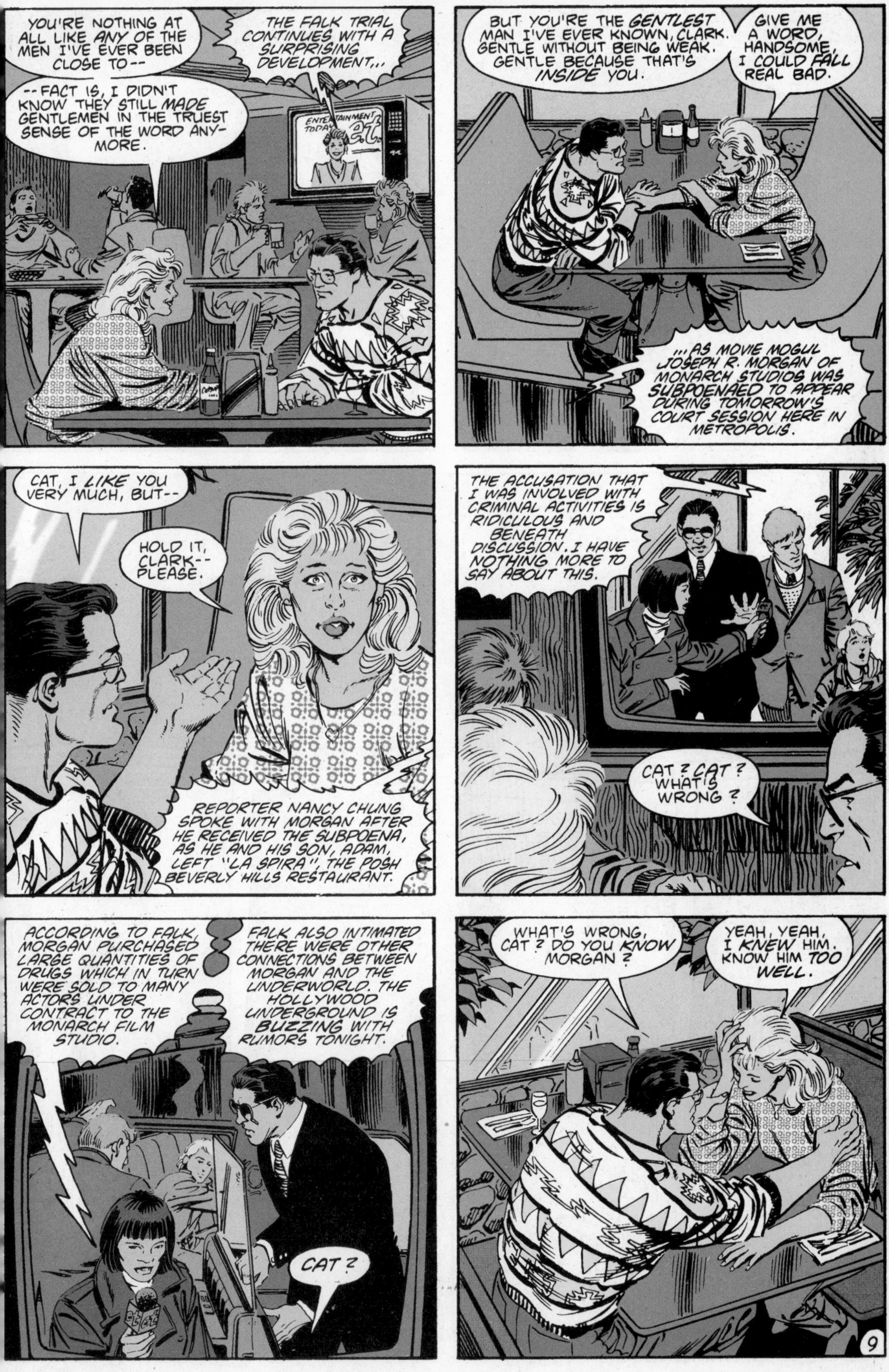

YOU'RE NOTHING AT ALL LIKE ANY OF THE MEN I'VE EVER BEEN CLOSE TO--
THE FALK TRIAL CONTINUES WITH A SURPRISING DEVELOPMENT...
--FACT IS, I DIDN'T KNOW THEY STILL MADE GENTLEMEN IN THE TRUEST SENSE OF THE WORD ANYMORE.
ENTERTAINMENT TODAY
BUT YOU'RE THE GENTLEST MAN I'VE EVER KNOWN, CLARK. GENTLE WITHOUT BEING WEAK. GENTLE BECAUSE THAT'S INSIDE YOU.
GIVE ME A WORD, HANDSOME, I COULD FALL REAL BAD.
...AS MOVIE MOGUL JOSEPH R. MORGAN OF MONARCH STUDIOS WAS SUBPOENAED TO APPEAR DURING TOMORROW'S COURT SESSION HERE IN METROPOLIS.
CAT, I LIKE YOU VERY MUCH, BUT--
HOLD IT, CLARK-- PLEASE.
REPORTER NANCY CHUNG SPOKE WITH MORGAN AFTER HE RECEIVED THE SUBPOENA, AS HE AND HIS SON, ADAM, LEFT "LA SPIRA", THE POSH BEVERLY HILLS RESTAURANT.
THE ACCUSATION THAT I WAS INVOLVED WITH CRIMINAL ACTIVITIES IS RIDICULOUS AND BENEATH DISCUSSION. I HAVE NOTHING MORE TO SAY ABOUT THIS.
CAT? CAT? WHAT'S WRONG?
ACCORDING TO FALK, MORGAN PURCHASED LARGE QUANTITIES OF DRUGS WHICH IN TURN WERE SOLD TO MANY ACTORS UNDER CONTRACT TO THE MONARCH FILM STUDIO.
FALK ALSO INTIMATED THERE WERE OTHER CONNECTIONS BETWEEN MORGAN AND THE UNDERWORLD. THE HOLLYWOOD UNDERGROUND IS BUZZING WITH RUMORS TONIGHT.
CAT?
WHAT'S WRONG, CAT? DO YOU KNOW MORGAN?
YEAH, YEAH, I KNEW HIM. KNOW HIM TOO WELL.
9

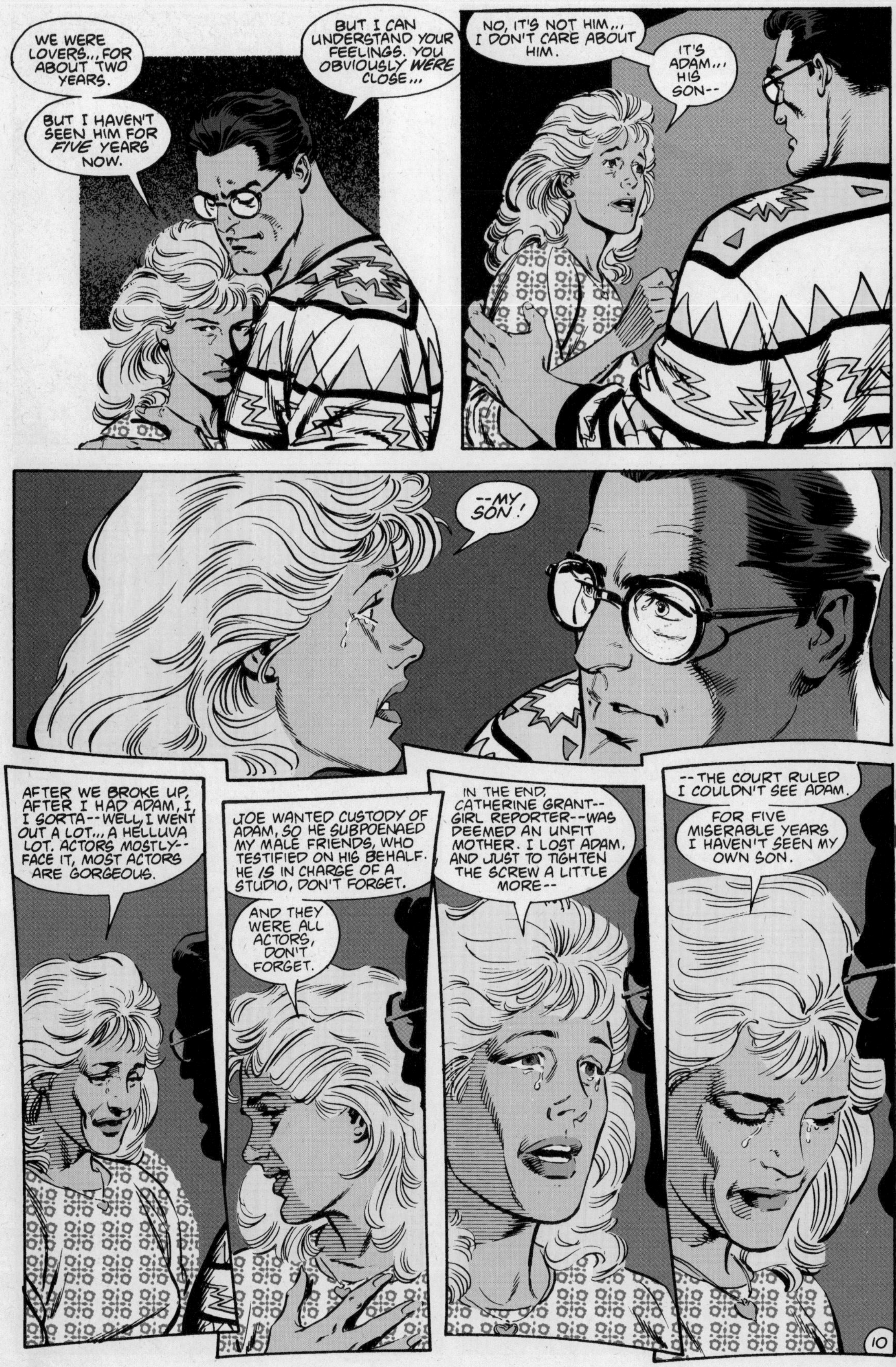
WE WERE LOVERS... FOR ABOUT TWO YEARS.
BUT I HAVEN'T SEEN HIM FOR FIVE YEARS NOW.
BUT I CAN UNDERSTAND YOUR FEELINGS. YOU OBVIOUSLY WERE CLOSE...
NO, IT'S NOT HIM... I DON'T CARE ABOUT HIM.
IT'S ADAM... HIS SON--
--MY SON!
AFTER WE BROKE UP, AFTER I HAD ADAM, I, I SORTA--WELL, I WENT OUT A LOT... A HELLUVA LOT. ACTORS MOSTLY--FACE IT, MOST ACTORS ARE GORGEOUS.
JOE WANTED CUSTODY OF ADAM, SO HE SUBPOENAED MY MALE FRIENDS, WHO TESTIFIED ON HIS BEHALF. HE IS IN CHARGE OF A STUDIO, DON'T FORGET.
AND THEY WERE ALL ACTORS, DON'T FORGET.
IN THE END, CATHERINE GRANT--GIRL REPORTER--WAS DEEMED AN UNFIT MOTHER. I LOST ADAM, AND JUST TO TIGHTEN THE SCREW A LITTLE MORE--
--THE COURT RULED I COULDN'T SEE ADAM.
FOR FIVE MISERABLE YEARS I HAVEN'T SEEN MY OWN SON.
10

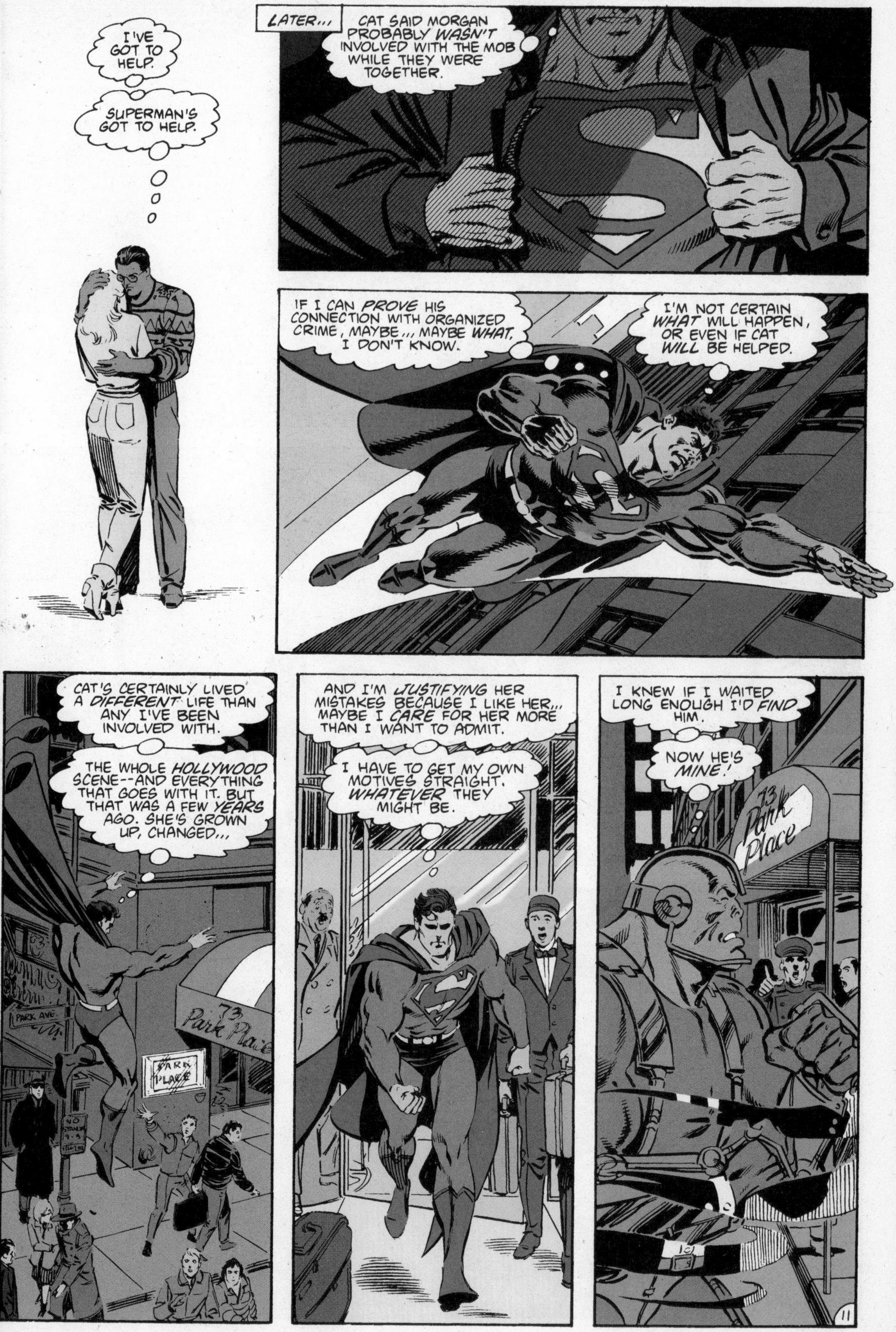
I'VE GOT TO HELP.
SUPERMAN'S GOT TO HELP.
LATER...
CAT SAID MORGAN PROBABLY WASN'T INVOLVED WITH THE MOB WHILE THEY WERE TOGETHER.
IF I CAN PROVE HIS CONNECTION WITH ORGANIZED CRIME, MAYBE... MAYBE WHAT. I DON'T KNOW.
I'M NOT CERTAIN WHAT WILL HAPPEN, OR EVEN IF CAT WILL BE HELPED.
CAT'S CERTAINLY LIVED A DIFFERENT LIFE THAN ANY I'VE BEEN INVOLVED WITH.
THE WHOLE HOLLYWOOD SCENE--AND EVERYTHING THAT GOES WITH IT. BUT THAT WAS A FEW YEARS AGO. SHE'S GROWN UP, CHANGED...
PARK AVE.
73 Park Place
PARK PLACE
AND I'M JUSTIFYING HER MISTAKES BECAUSE I LIKE HER... MAYBE I CARE FOR HER MORE THAN I WANT TO ADMIT.
I HAVE TO GET MY OWN MOTIVES STRAIGHT. WHATEVER THEY MIGHT BE.
I KNEW IF I WAITED LONG ENOUGH I'D FIND HIM.
NOW HE'S MINE!
73 Park Place
11

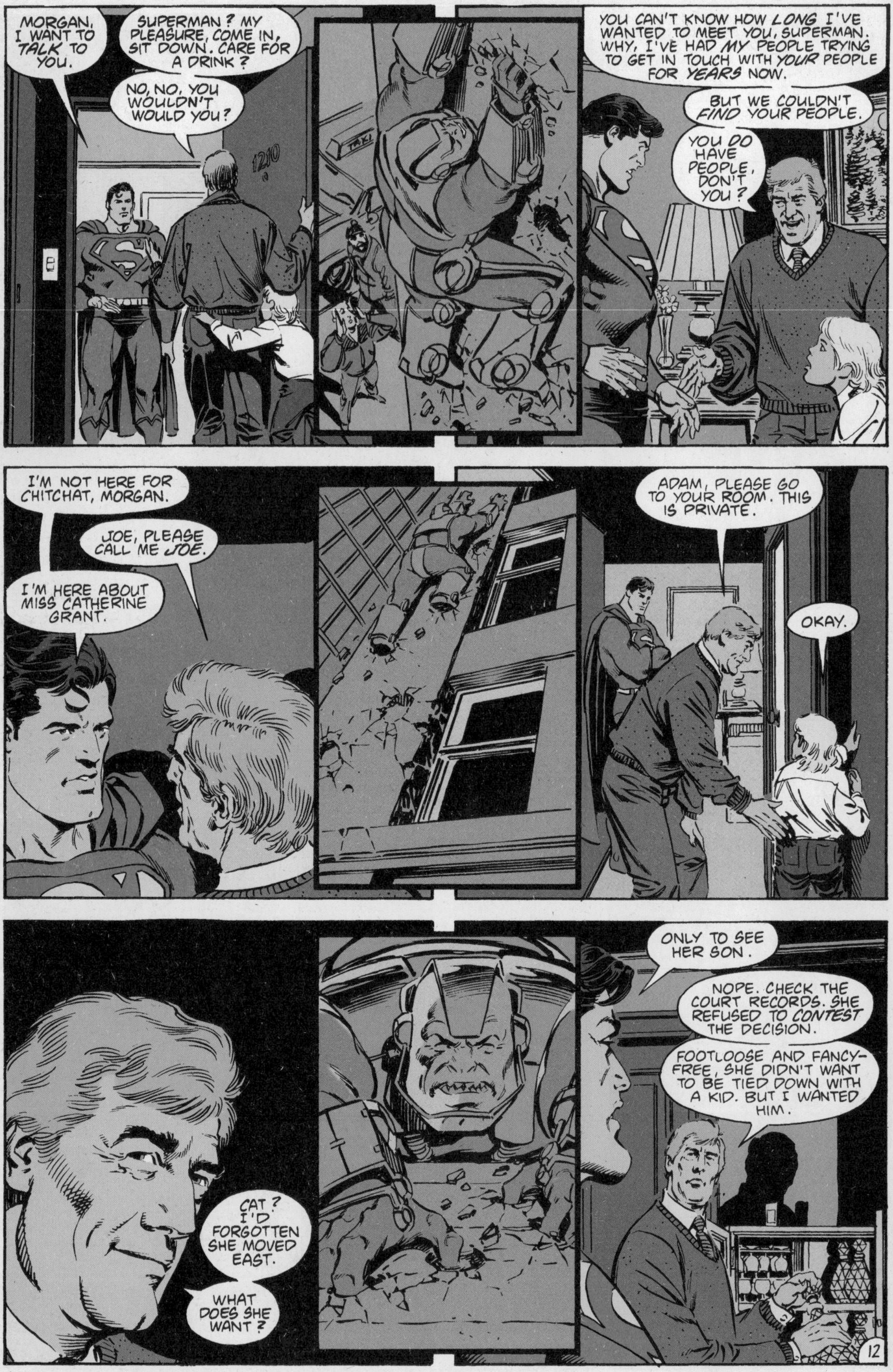
MORGAN, I WANT TO TALK TO YOU.
SUPERMAN? MY PLEASURE, COME IN, SIT DOWN. CARE FOR A DRINK?
NO, NO. YOU WOULDN'T WOULD YOU?
1210
TAXI
YOU CAN'T KNOW HOW LONG I'VE WANTED TO MEET YOU, SUPERMAN. WHY, I'VE HAD MY PEOPLE TRYING TO GET IN TOUCH WITH YOUR PEOPLE FOR YEARS NOW.
BUT WE COULDN'T FIND YOUR PEOPLE.
YOU DO HAVE PEOPLE, DON'T YOU?
I'M NOT HERE FOR CHITCHAT, MORGAN.
JOE, PLEASE CALL ME JOE.
I'M HERE ABOUT MISS CATHERINE GRANT.
ADAM, PLEASE GO TO YOUR ROOM. THIS IS PRIVATE.
OKAY.
CAT? I'D FORGOTTEN SHE MOVED EAST.
WHAT DOES SHE WANT?
ONLY TO SEE HER SON.
NOPE. CHECK THE COURT RECORDS. SHE REFUSED TO CONTEST THE DECISION.
FOOTLOOSE AND FANCY-FREE, SHE DIDN'T WANT TO BE TIED DOWN WITH A KID. BUT I WANTED HIM.
12

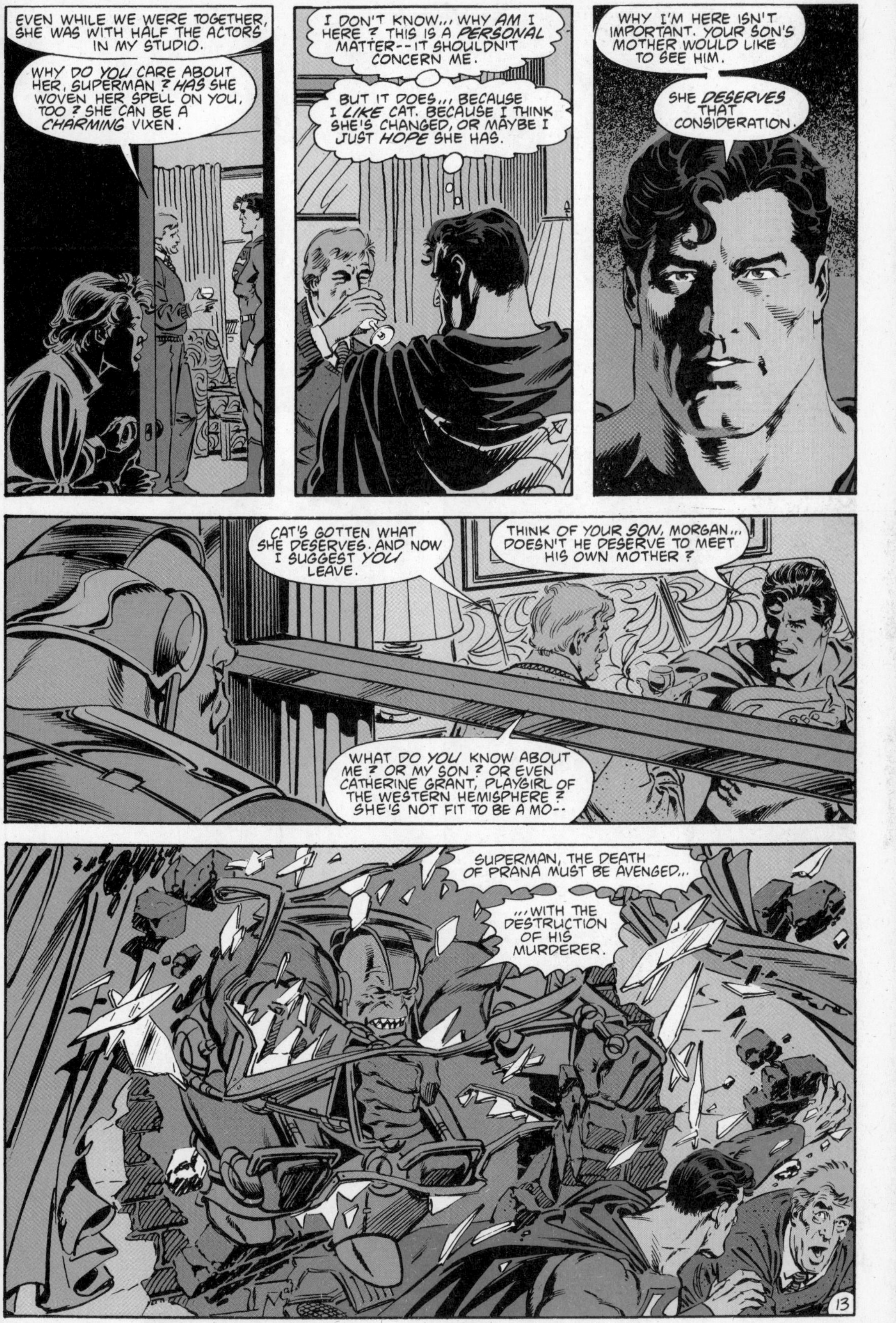
EVEN WHILE WE WERE TOGETHER, SHE WAS WITH HALF THE ACTORS IN MY STUDIO.
WHY DO YOU CARE ABOUT HER, SUPERMAN? HAS SHE WOVEN HER SPELL ON YOU, TOO? SHE CAN BE A CHARMING VIXEN.
I DON'T KNOW... WHY AM I HERE? THIS IS A PERSONAL MATTER--IT SHOULDN'T CONCERN ME.
BUT IT DOES... BECAUSE I LIKE CAT. BECAUSE I THINK SHE'S CHANGED, OR MAYBE I JUST HOPE SHE HAS.
WHY I'M HERE ISN'T IMPORTANT. YOUR SON'S MOTHER WOULD LIKE TO SEE HIM.
SHE DESERVES THAT CONSIDERATION.
CAT'S GOTTEN WHAT SHE DESERVES. AND NOW I SUGGEST YOU LEAVE.
THINK OF YOUR SON, MORGAN... DOESN'T HE DESERVE TO MEET HIS OWN MOTHER?
WHAT DO YOU KNOW ABOUT ME? OR MY SON? OR EVEN CATHERINE GRANT, PLAYGIRL OF THE WESTERN HEMISPHERE? SHE'S NOT FIT TO BE A MO--
SUPERMAN, THE DEATH OF PRANA MUST BE AVENGED...
...WITH THE DESTRUCTION OF HIS MURDERER.
13

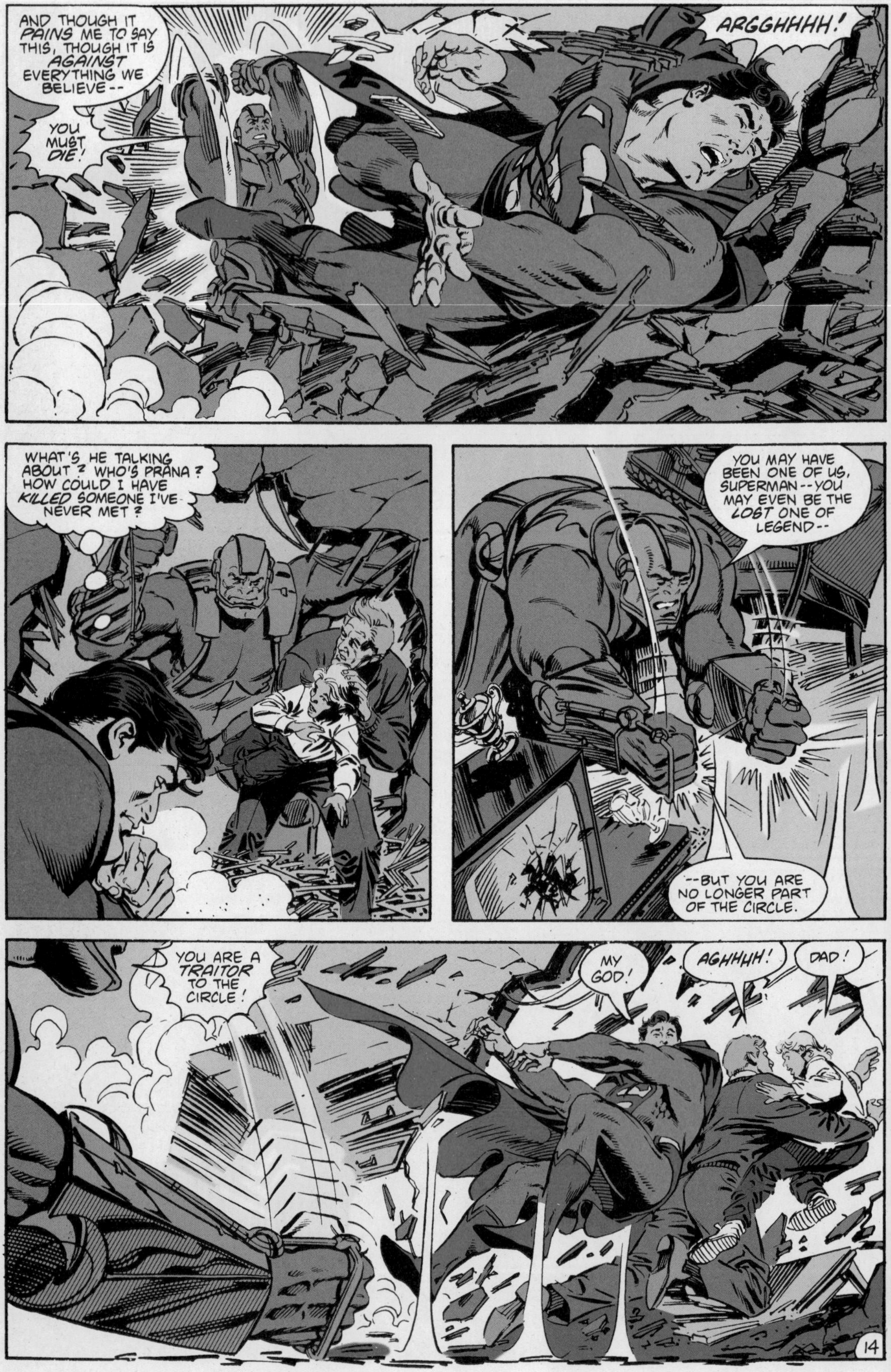

AND THOUGH IT PAINS ME TO SAY THIS, THOUGH IT IS AGAINST EVERYTHING WE BELIEVE--
YOU MUST DIE!
ARGGHHHH!
WHAT'S HE TALKING ABOUT? WHO'S PRANA? HOW COULD I HAVE KILLED SOMEONE I'VE NEVER MET?
YOU MAY HAVE BEEN ONE OF US, SUPERMAN--YOU MAY EVEN BE THE LOST ONE OF LEGEND--
--BUT YOU ARE NO LONGER PART OF THE CIRCLE.
YOU ARE A TRAITOR TO THE CIRCLE!
MY GOD!
AGHHHH!
DAD!
14

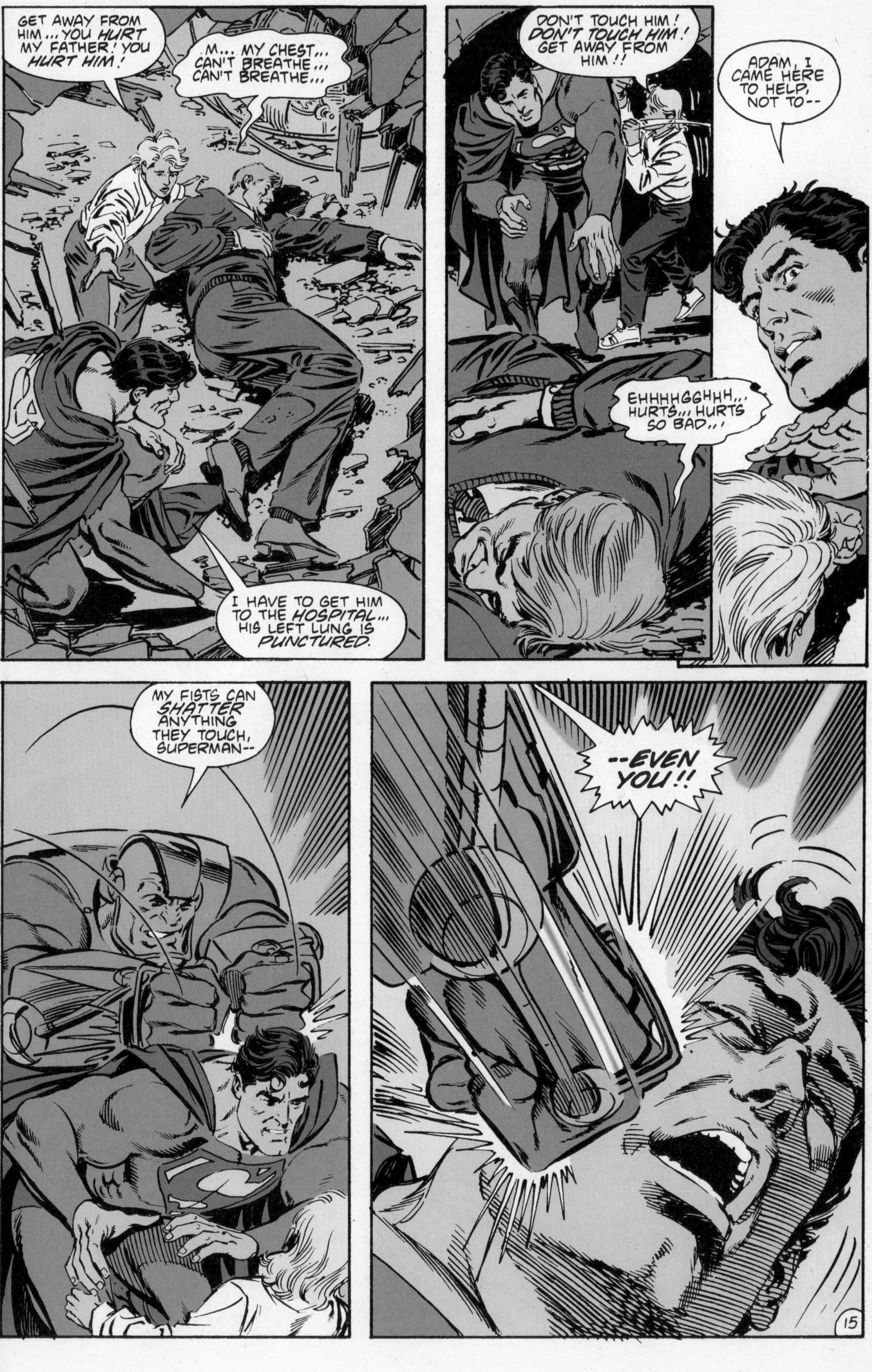

GET AWAY FROM HIM... YOU HURT MY FATHER! YOU HURT HIM!
M... MY CHEST... CAN'T BREATHE... CAN'T BREATHE...
I HAVE TO GET HIM TO THE HOSPITAL... HIS LEFT LUNG IS PUNCTURED.
DON'T TOUCH HIM! DON'T TOUCH HIM! GET AWAY FROM HIM!!
ADAM, I CAME HERE TO HELP, NOT TO--
EHHHHGGHHH... HURTS... HURTS SO BAD...
MY FISTS CAN SHATTER ANYTHING THEY TOUCH, SUPERMAN--
--EVEN YOU!!
15

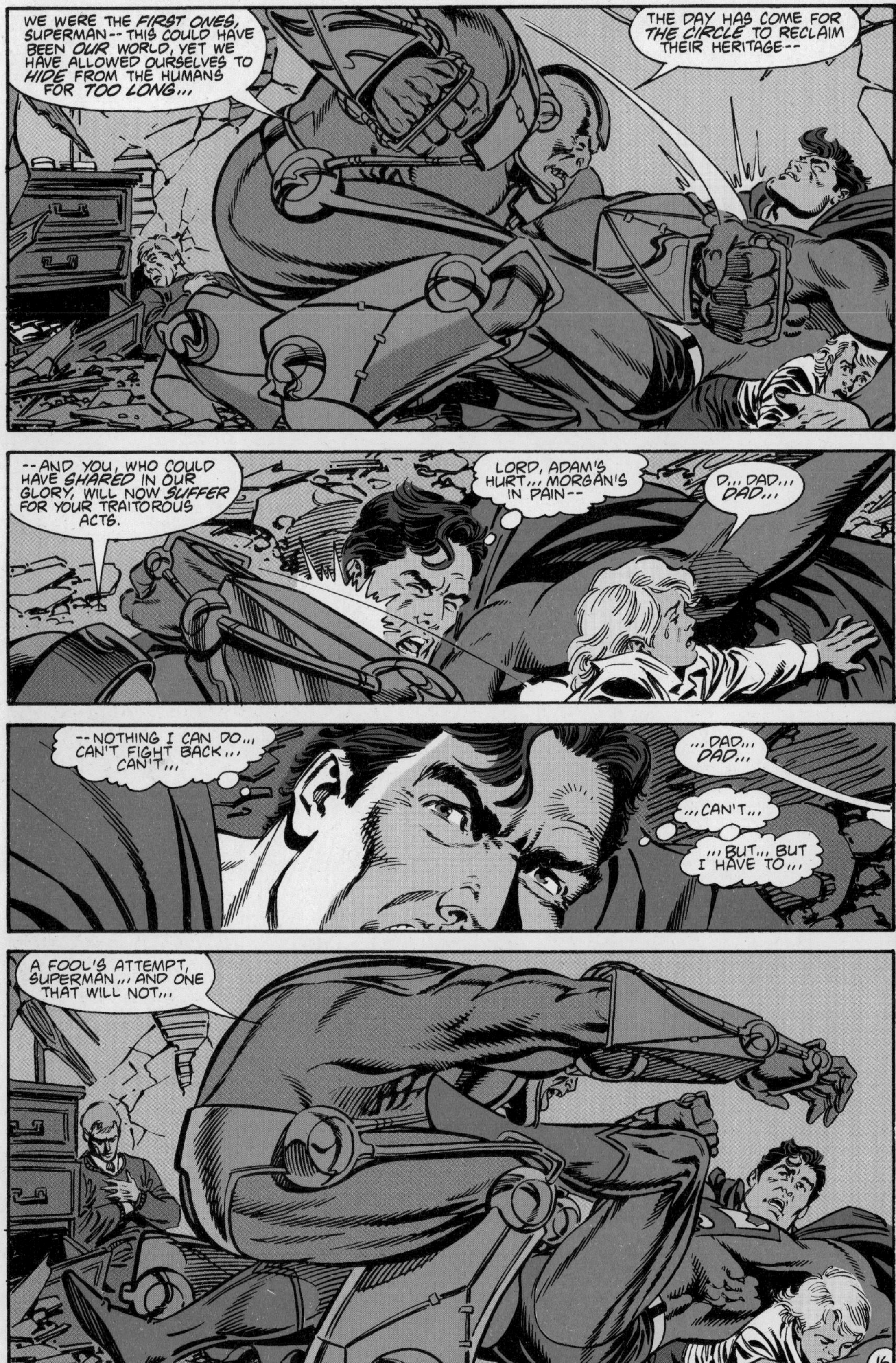
WE WERE THE *FIRST ONES*, SUPERMAN--THIS COULD HAVE BEEN *OUR* WORLD, YET WE HAVE ALLOWED OURSELVES TO *HIDE* FROM THE HUMANS FOR *TOO LONG*...
THE DAY HAS COME FOR *THE CIRCLE* TO RECLAIM THEIR HERITAGE--
--AND YOU, WHO COULD HAVE *SHARED* IN OUR GLORY, WILL NOW *SUFFER* FOR YOUR TRAITOROUS ACTS.
LORD, ADAM'S HURT... MORGAN'S IN PAIN--
D... DAD... *DAD*...
--NOTHING I CAN DO... CAN'T FIGHT BACK... CAN'T...
...DAD... *DAD*...
...CAN'T...
...BUT... BUT I HAVE TO...
A FOOL'S ATTEMPT, SUPERMAN... AND ONE THAT WILL NOT...
16

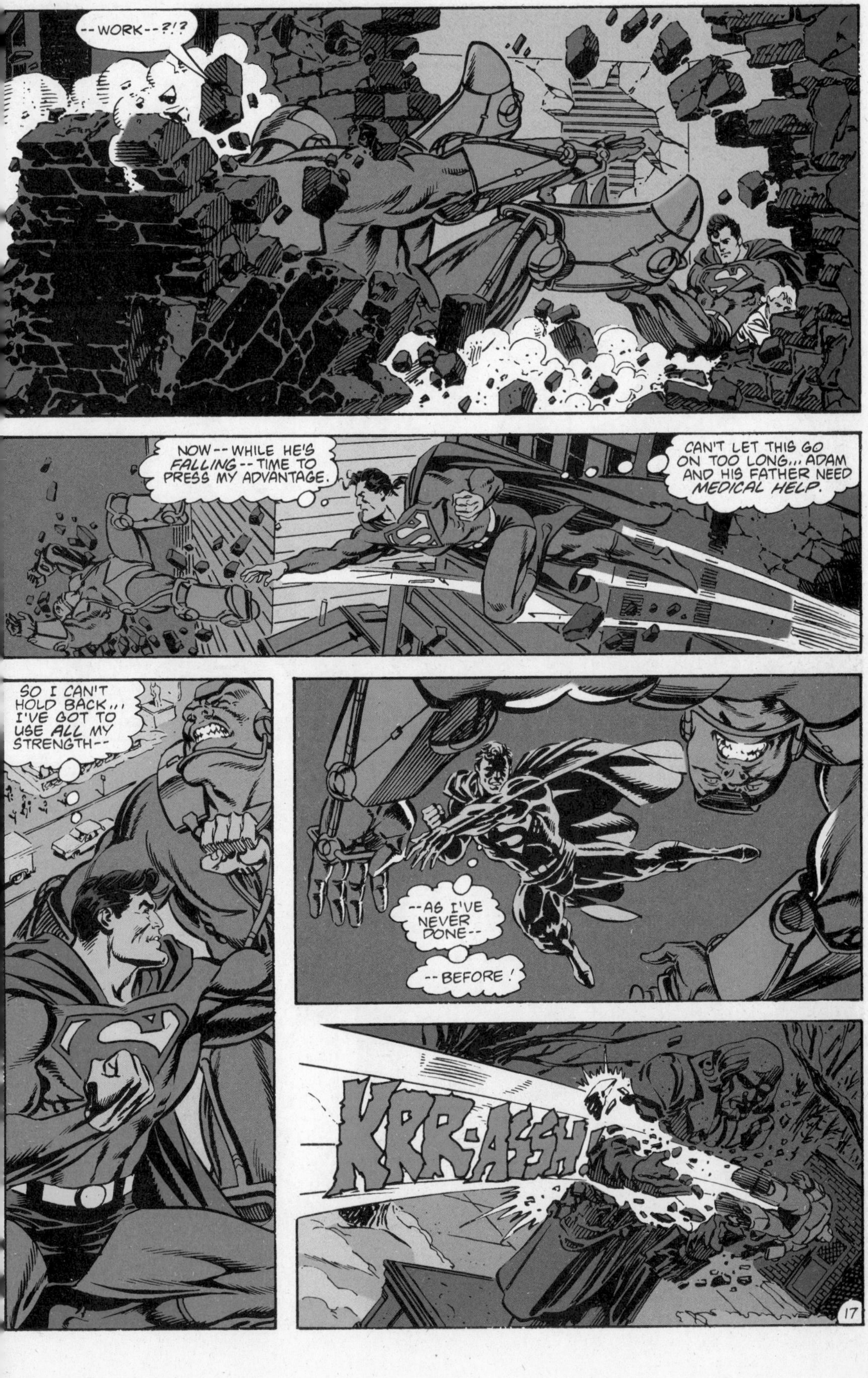
--WORK--?!?
NOW--WHILE HE'S FALLING--TIME TO PRESS MY ADVANTAGE.
CAN'T LET THIS GO ON TOO LONG... ADAM AND HIS FATHER NEED MEDICAL HELP.
SO I CAN'T HOLD BACK... I'VE GOT TO USE ALL MY STRENGTH--
--AS I'VE NEVER DONE--
--BEFORE!
KRR-ASSH!
17

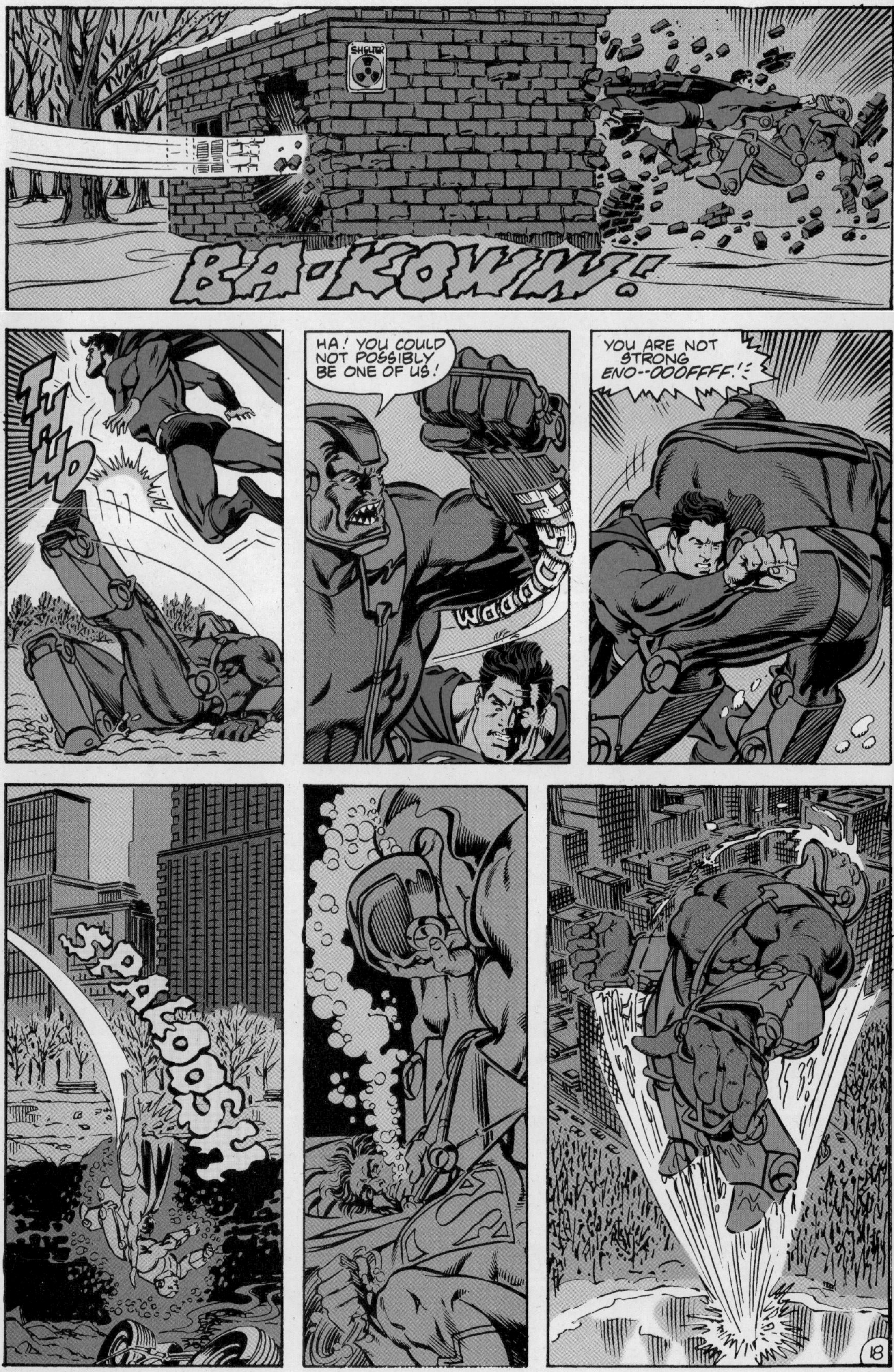
SHELTER
BA-KOWW!
THUD
HA! YOU COULD NOT POSSIBLY BE ONE OF US!
YOU ARE NOT STRONG ENO--OOOFFFF!
SPALOOSH
18

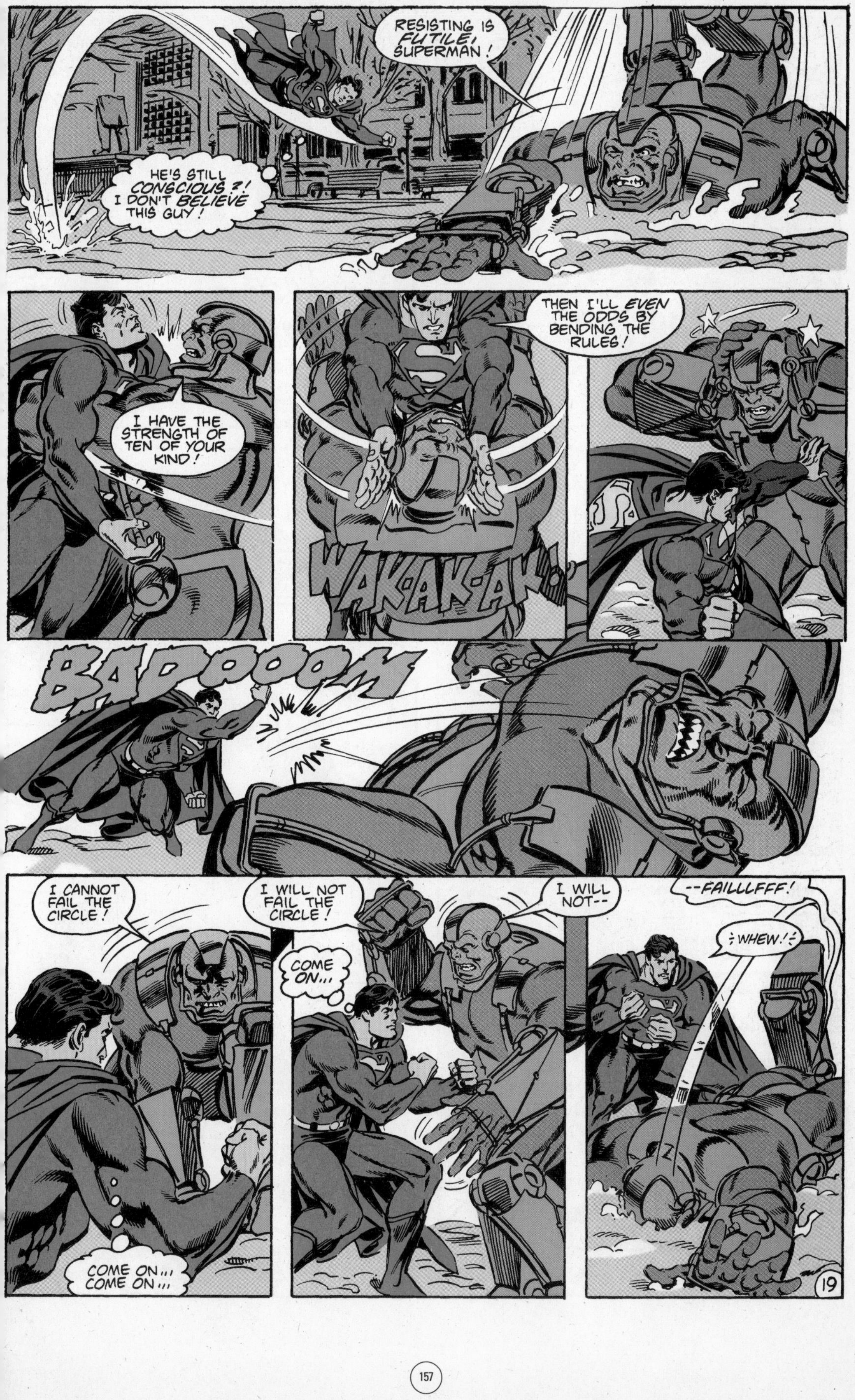
RESISTING IS FUTILE, SUPERMAN!
HE'S STILL CONSCIOUS?! I DON'T BELIEVE THIS GUY!
I HAVE THE STRENGTH OF TEN OF YOUR KIND!
THEN I'LL EVEN THE ODDS BY BENDING THE RULES!
WAK-AK-AK!
BADOOOM
I CANNOT FAIL THE CIRCLE!
COME ON... COME ON...
I WILL NOT FAIL THE CIRCLE!
COME ON...
I WILL NOT--
--FAILLLFFF!
WHEW!
19

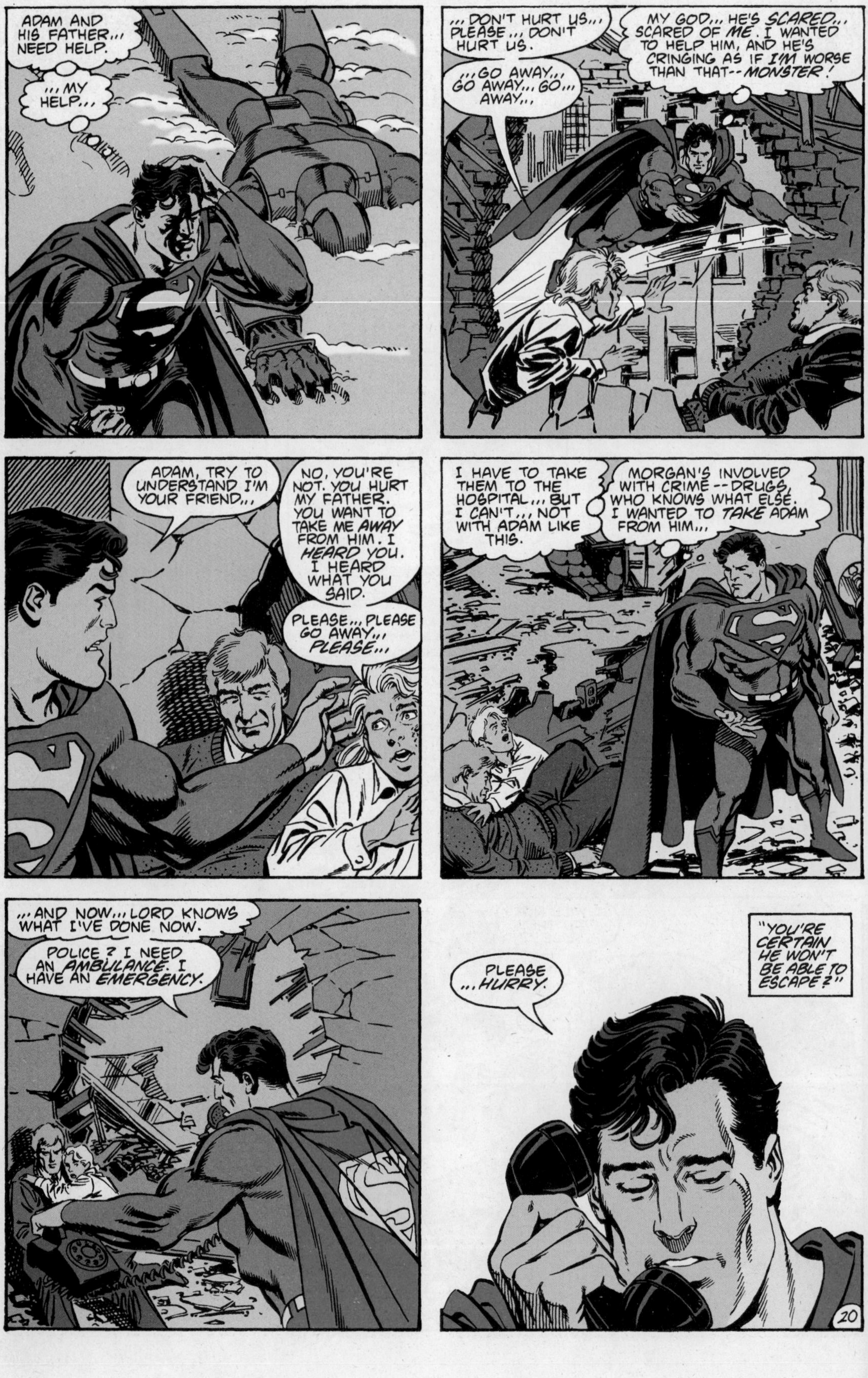
ADAM AND HIS FATHER... NEED HELP.
...MY HELP...
...DON'T HURT US... PLEASE... DON'T HURT US.
...GO AWAY... GO AWAY... GO... AWAY...
MY GOD... HE'S SCARED... SCARED OF ME. I WANTED TO HELP HIM, AND HE'S CRINGING AS IF I'M WORSE THAN THAT--MONSTER!
ADAM, TRY TO UNDERSTAND I'M YOUR FRIEND...
NO, YOU'RE NOT. YOU HURT MY FATHER. YOU WANT TO TAKE ME AWAY FROM HIM. I HEARD YOU. I HEARD WHAT YOU SAID.
PLEASE... PLEASE GO AWAY... PLEASE...
I HAVE TO TAKE THEM TO THE HOSPITAL... BUT I CAN'T... NOT WITH ADAM LIKE THIS.
MORGAN'S INVOLVED WITH CRIME--DRUGS, WHO KNOWS WHAT ELSE. I WANTED TO TAKE ADAM FROM HIM...
...AND NOW... LORD KNOWS WHAT I'VE DONE NOW.
POLICE? I NEED AN AMBULANCE. I HAVE AN EMERGENCY.
PLEASE ...HURRY.
"YOU'RE CERTAIN HE WON'T BE ABLE TO ESCAPE?"
20

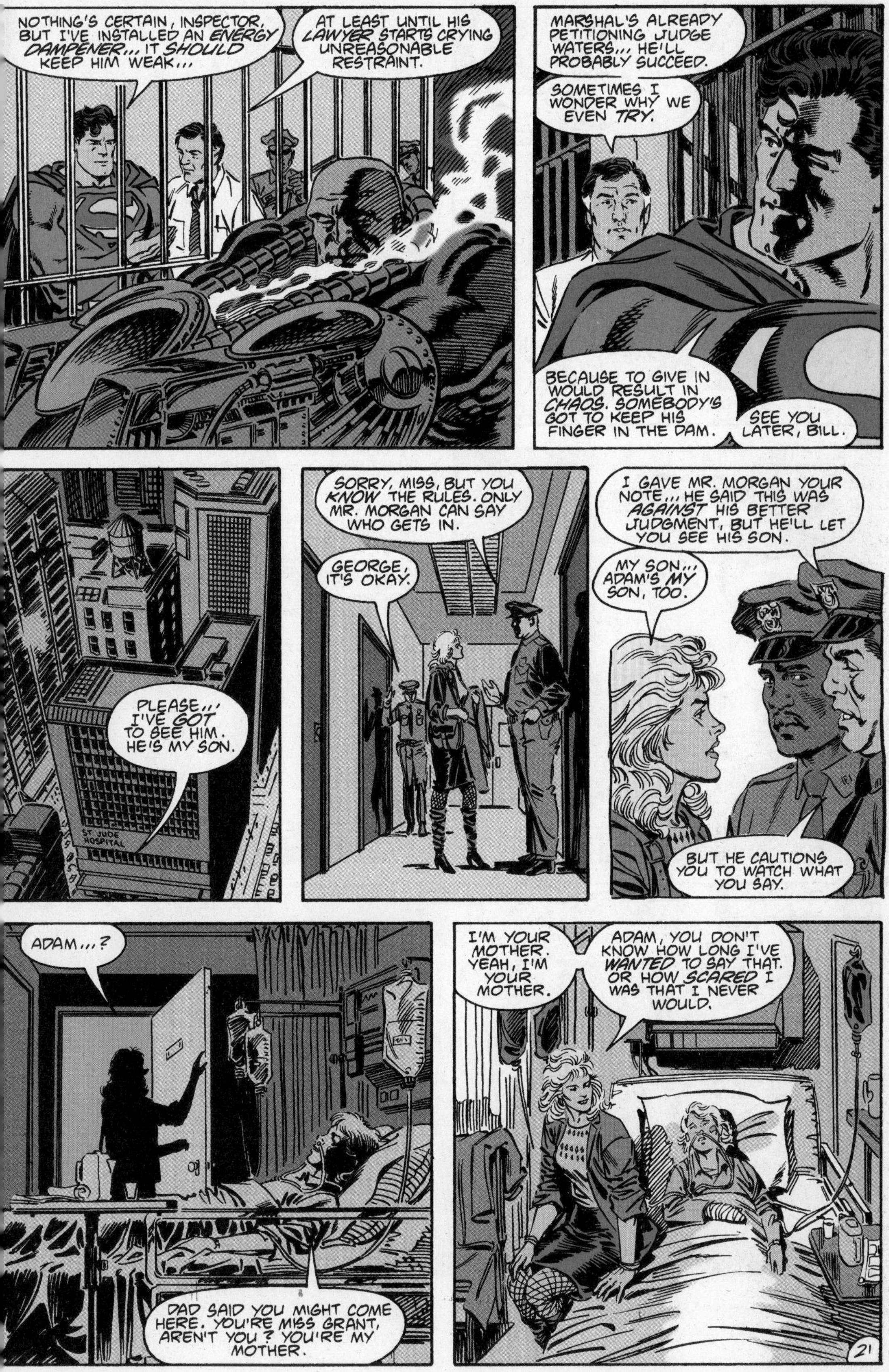
NOTHING'S CERTAIN, INSPECTOR, BUT I'VE INSTALLED AN ENERGY DAMPENER... IT SHOULD KEEP HIM WEAK...
AT LEAST UNTIL HIS LAWYER STARTS CRYING UNREASONABLE RESTRAINT.
MARSHAL'S ALREADY PETITIONING JUDGE WATERS... HE'LL PROBABLY SUCCEED.
SOMETIMES I WONDER WHY WE EVEN TRY.
BECAUSE TO GIVE IN WOULD RESULT IN CHAOS. SOMEBODY'S GOT TO KEEP HIS FINGER IN THE DAM.
SEE YOU LATER, BILL.
ST. JUDE HOSPITAL
PLEASE... I'VE GOT TO SEE HIM. HE'S MY SON.
SORRY, MISS, BUT YOU KNOW THE RULES. ONLY MR. MORGAN CAN SAY WHO GETS IN.
GEORGE, IT'S OKAY.
I GAVE MR. MORGAN YOUR NOTE... HE SAID THIS WAS AGAINST HIS BETTER JUDGMENT, BUT HE'LL LET YOU SEE HIS SON.
MY SON... ADAM'S MY SON, TOO.
BUT HE CAUTIONS YOU TO WATCH WHAT YOU SAY.
ADAM...?
DAD SAID YOU MIGHT COME HERE. YOU'RE MISS GRANT, AREN'T YOU? YOU'RE MY MOTHER.
I'M YOUR MOTHER. YEAH, I'M YOUR MOTHER.
ADAM, YOU DON'T KNOW HOW LONG I'VE WANTED TO SAY THAT. OR HOW SCARED I WAS THAT I NEVER WOULD.
21

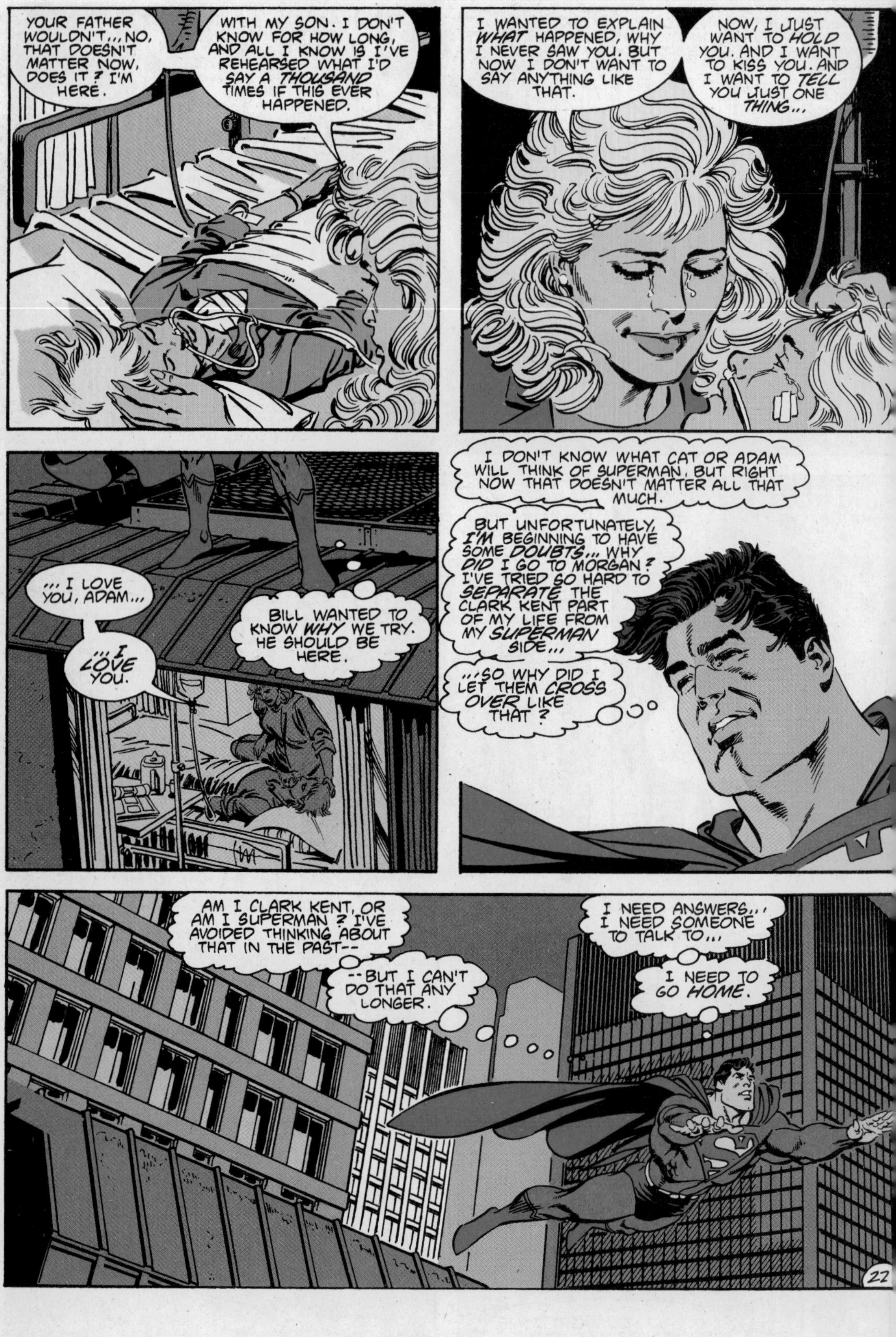

YOUR FATHER WOULDN'T... NO, THAT DOESN'T MATTER NOW, DOES IT? I'M HERE.
WITH MY SON. I DON'T KNOW FOR HOW LONG, AND ALL I KNOW IS I'VE REHEARSED WHAT I'D SAY A THOUSAND TIMES IF THIS EVER HAPPENED.
I WANTED TO EXPLAIN WHAT HAPPENED, WHY I NEVER SAW YOU. BUT NOW I DON'T WANT TO SAY ANYTHING LIKE THAT.
NOW, I JUST WANT TO HOLD YOU. AND I WANT TO KISS YOU. AND I WANT TO TELL YOU JUST ONE THING...
...I LOVE YOU, ADAM...
...I LOVE YOU.
BILL WANTED TO KNOW WHY WE TRY. HE SHOULD BE HERE.
I DON'T KNOW WHAT CAT OR ADAM WILL THINK OF SUPERMAN, BUT RIGHT NOW THAT DOESN'T MATTER ALL THAT MUCH.
BUT UNFORTUNATELY, I'M BEGINNING TO HAVE SOME DOUBTS... WHY DID I GO TO MORGAN? I'VE TRIED SO HARD TO SEPARATE THE CLARK KENT PART OF MY LIFE FROM MY SUPERMAN SIDE...
...SO WHY DID I LET THEM CROSS OVER LIKE THAT?
AM I CLARK KENT, OR AM I SUPERMAN? I'VE AVOIDED THINKING ABOUT THAT IN THE PAST--
--BUT I CAN'T DO THAT ANY LONGER.
I NEED ANSWERS... I NEED SOMEONE TO TALK TO...
I NEED TO GO HOME.
22

I'M GETTING *CLOSER.* THAT ANNOYING *HYPERSONIC* SIGNAL THAT'S BEEN HITTING ME FOR THE PAST *TWENTY MINUTES*...

...ITS SOURCE IS *NEAR* HERE.

VERY NEAR HERE.

SOMEWHERE IN THE MIDDLE OF *THAT MESS.*

LOOKS AS IF THE *POLICE* AND *FIRE DEPARTMENT* ARE HANDLING THE WORST OF IT.

LET'S SEE IF MY *X-RAY VISION* CAN FIND SOMEONE DOWN THERE WHO MIGHT BE *BEHIND* THAT SIGNAL.

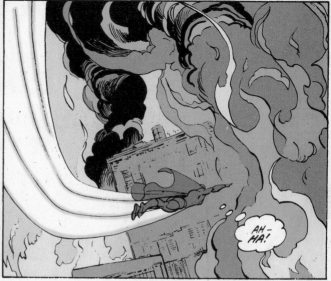

AH-HA!

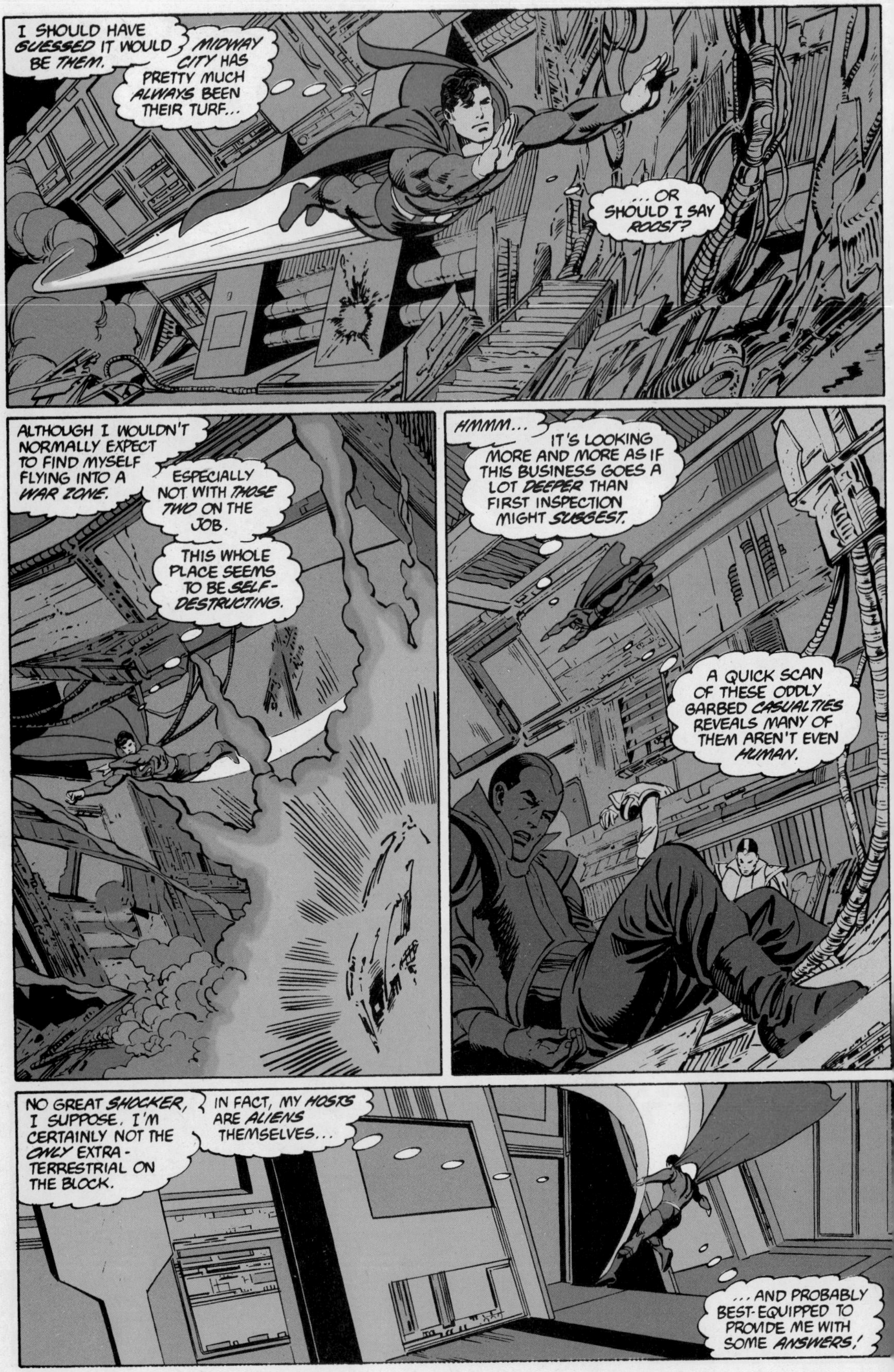
I SHOULD HAVE GUESSED IT WOULD BE THEM.
MIDWAY CITY HAS PRETTY MUCH ALWAYS BEEN THEIR TURF...
...OR SHOULD I SAY ROOST?
ALTHOUGH I WOULDN'T NORMALLY EXPECT TO FIND MYSELF FLYING INTO A WAR ZONE.
ESPECIALLY NOT WITH THOSE TWO ON THE JOB.
THIS WHOLE PLACE SEEMS TO BE SELF-DESTRUCTING.
HMMM...
IT'S LOOKING MORE AND MORE AS IF THIS BUSINESS GOES A LOT DEEPER THAN FIRST INSPECTION MIGHT SUGGEST.
A QUICK SCAN OF THESE ODDLY GARBED CASUALTIES REVEALS MANY OF THEM AREN'T EVEN HUMAN.
NO GREAT SHOCKER, I SUPPOSE. I'M CERTAINLY NOT THE ONLY EXTRA-TERRESTRIAL ON THE BLOCK.
IN FACT, MY HOSTS ARE ALIENS THEMSELVES...
...AND PROBABLY BEST-EQUIPPED TO PROVIDE ME WITH SOME ANSWERS!

SUPERMAN, HAWKMAN and HAWKWOMAN starring in...

ALL WARS MUST END

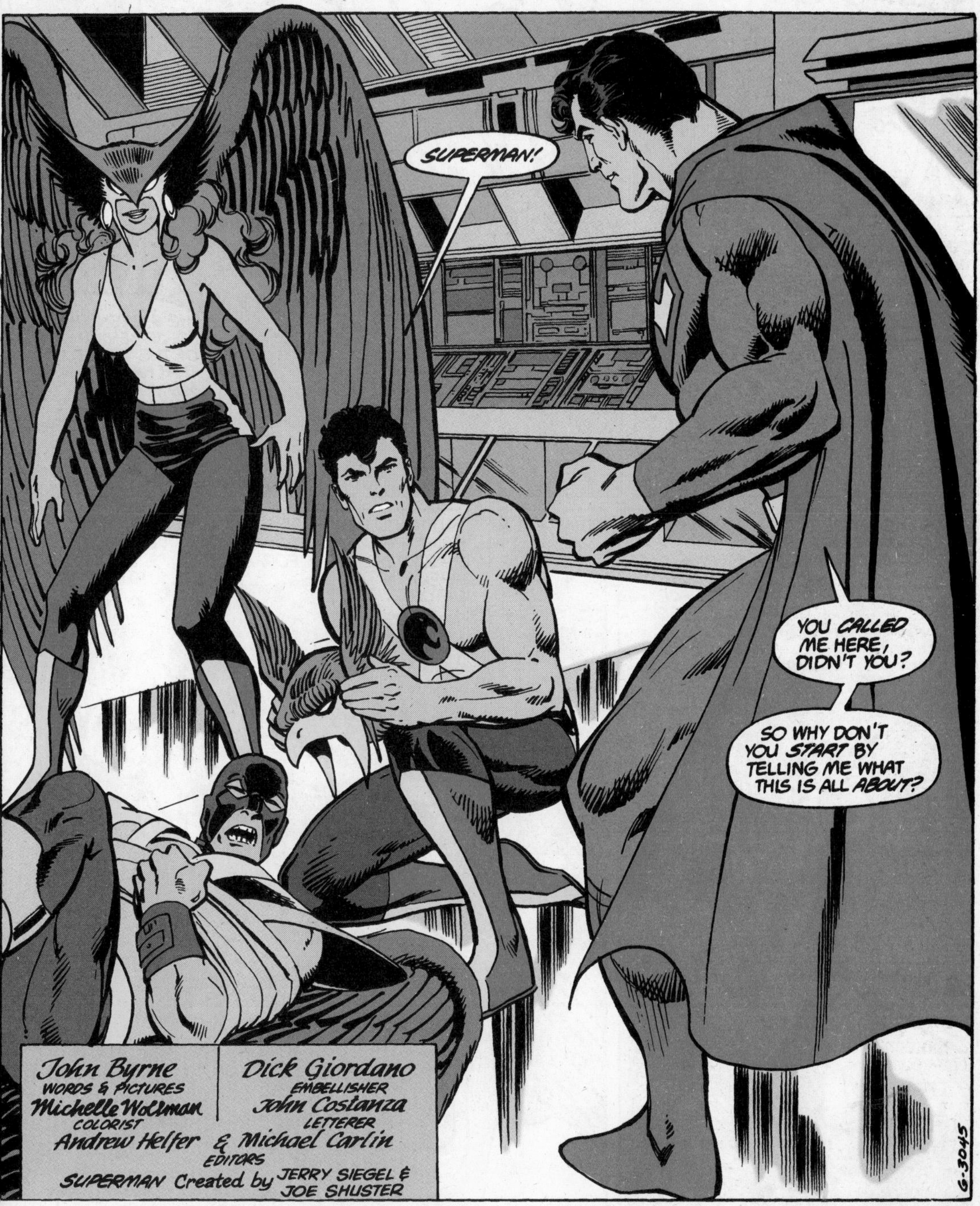

SUPERMAN!
YOU CALLED ME HERE, DIDN'T YOU?
SO WHY DON'T YOU START BY TELLING ME WHAT THIS IS ALL ABOUT?
John Byrne WORDS & PICTURES
Dick Giordano EMBELLISHER
Michelle Wolfman COLORIST
John Costanza LETTERER
Andrew Helfer & Michael Carlin EDITORS
SUPERMAN Created by JERRY SIEGEL & JOE SHUSTER

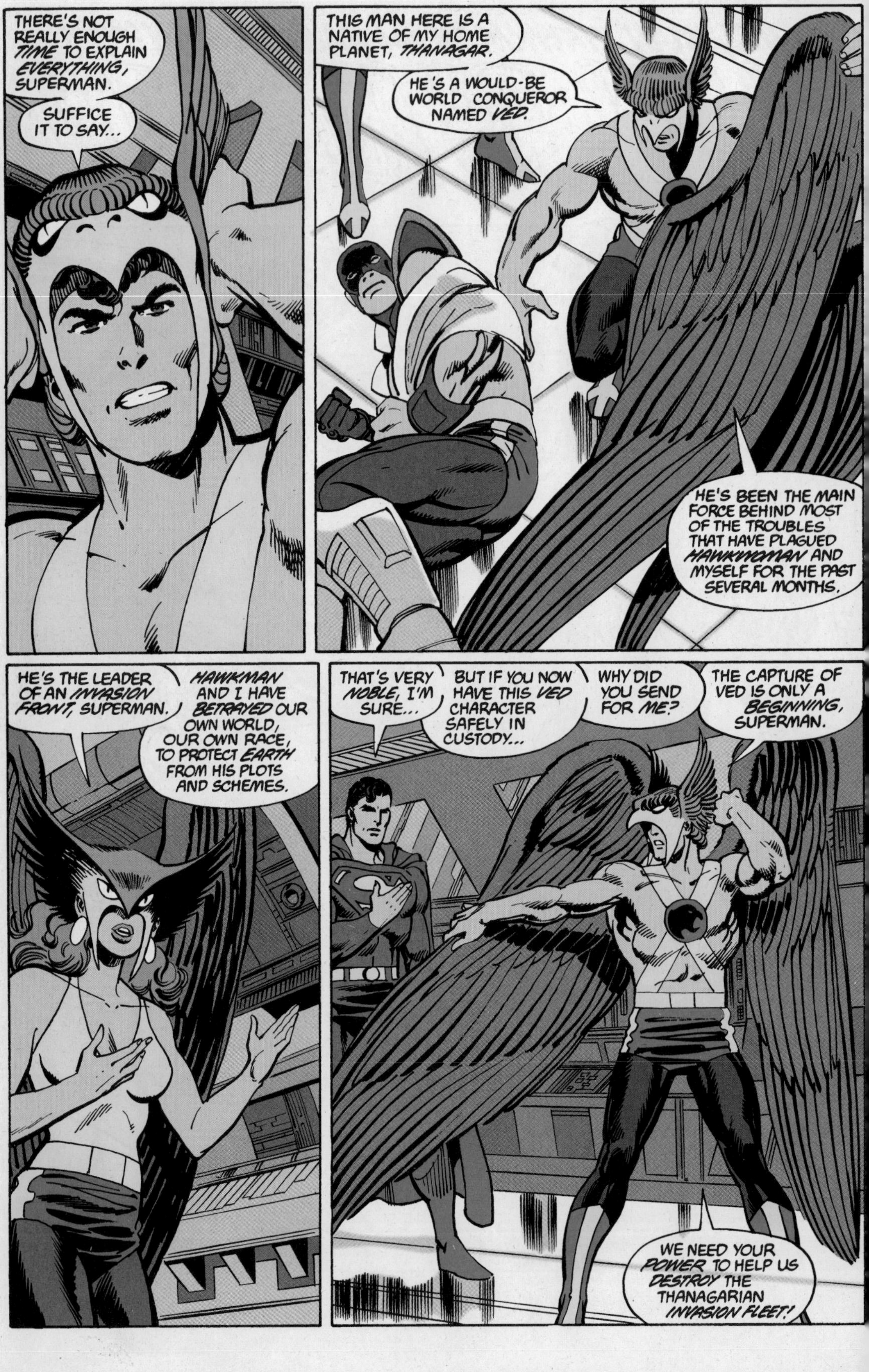
THERE'S NOT REALLY ENOUGH TIME TO EXPLAIN EVERYTHING, SUPERMAN.
SUFFICE IT TO SAY...
THIS MAN HERE IS A NATIVE OF MY HOME PLANET, THANAGAR.
HE'S A WOULD-BE WORLD CONQUEROR NAMED VED.
HE'S BEEN THE MAIN FORCE BEHIND MOST OF THE TROUBLES THAT HAVE PLAGUED HAWKWOMAN AND MYSELF FOR THE PAST SEVERAL MONTHS.
HE'S THE LEADER OF AN INVASION FRONT, SUPERMAN.
HAWKMAN AND I HAVE BETRAYED OUR OWN WORLD, OUR OWN RACE, TO PROTECT EARTH FROM HIS PLOTS AND SCHEMES.
THAT'S VERY NOBLE, I'M SURE...
BUT IF YOU NOW HAVE THIS VED CHARACTER SAFELY IN CUSTODY...
WHY DID YOU SEND FOR ME?
THE CAPTURE OF VED IS ONLY A BEGINNING, SUPERMAN.
WE NEED YOUR POWER TO HELP US DESTROY THE THANAGARIAN INVASION FLEET!

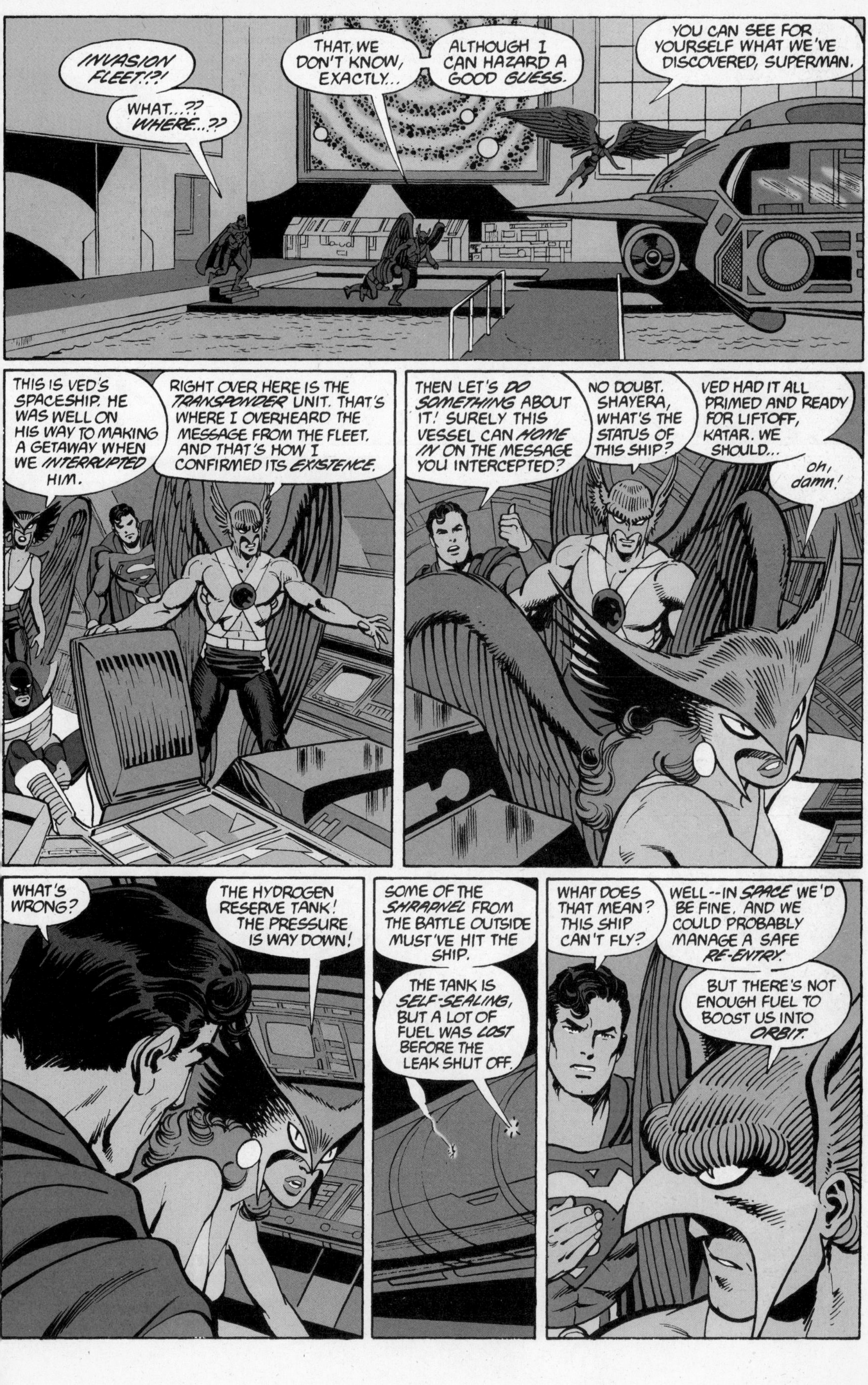
INVASION FLEET!?!
WHAT...?? WHERE...??
THAT, WE DON'T KNOW, EXACTLY...
ALTHOUGH I CAN HAZARD A GOOD GUESS.
YOU CAN SEE FOR YOURSELF WHAT WE'VE DISCOVERED, SUPERMAN.
THIS IS VED'S SPACESHIP. HE WAS WELL ON HIS WAY TO MAKING A GETAWAY WHEN WE INTERRUPTED HIM.
RIGHT OVER HERE IS THE TRANSPONDER UNIT. THAT'S WHERE I OVERHEARD THE MESSAGE FROM THE FLEET. AND THAT'S HOW I CONFIRMED ITS EXISTENCE.
THEN LET'S DO SOMETHING ABOUT IT! SURELY THIS VESSEL CAN HOME IN ON THE MESSAGE YOU INTERCEPTED?
NO DOUBT. SHAYERA, WHAT'S THE STATUS OF THIS SHIP?
VED HAD IT ALL PRIMED AND READY FOR LIFTOFF, KATAR. WE SHOULD...
oh, damn!
WHAT'S WRONG?
THE HYDROGEN RESERVE TANK! THE PRESSURE IS WAY DOWN!
SOME OF THE SHRAPNEL FROM THE BATTLE OUTSIDE MUST'VE HIT THE SHIP.
THE TANK IS SELF-SEALING, BUT A LOT OF FUEL WAS LOST BEFORE THE LEAK SHUT OFF.
WHAT DOES THAT MEAN? THIS SHIP CAN'T FLY?
WELL--IN SPACE WE'D BE FINE, AND WE COULD PROBABLY MANAGE A SAFE RE-ENTRY.
BUT THERE'S NOT ENOUGH FUEL TO BOOST US INTO ORBIT.

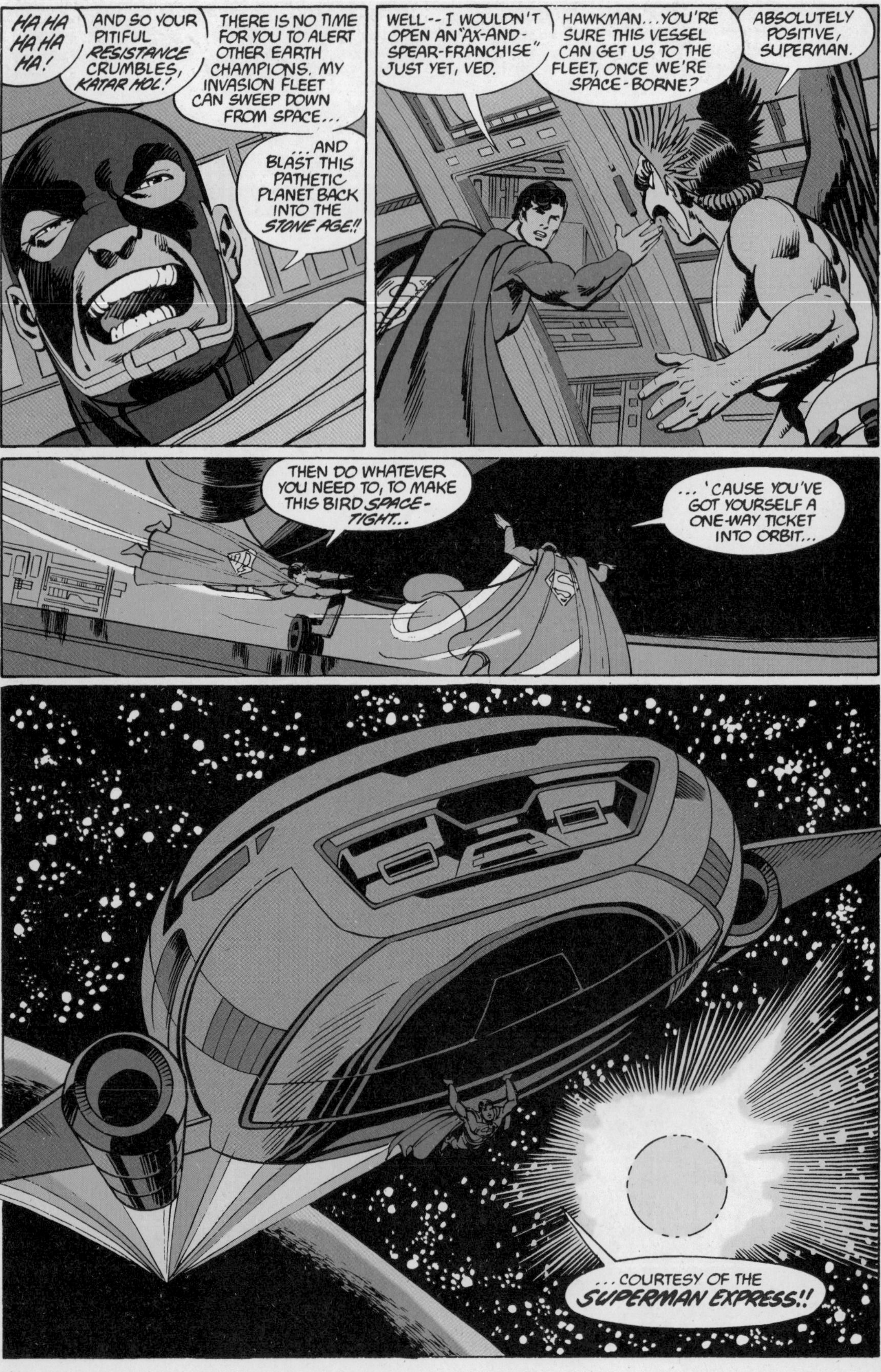

HA HA HA HA HA!
AND SO YOUR PITIFUL RESISTANCE CRUMBLES, KATAR HOL!
THERE IS NO TIME FOR YOU TO ALERT OTHER EARTH CHAMPIONS. MY INVASION FLEET CAN SWEEP DOWN FROM SPACE...
...AND BLAST THIS PATHETIC PLANET BACK INTO THE STONE AGE!!
WELL -- I WOULDN'T OPEN AN "AX-AND-SPEAR-FRANCHISE" JUST YET, VED.
HAWKMAN...YOU'RE SURE THIS VESSEL CAN GET US TO THE FLEET, ONCE WE'RE SPACE-BORNE?
ABSOLUTELY POSITIVE, SUPERMAN.
THEN DO WHATEVER YOU NEED TO, TO MAKE THIS BIRD SPACE-TIGHT...
...'CAUSE YOU'VE GOT YOURSELF A ONE-WAY TICKET INTO ORBIT...
...COURTESY OF THE SUPERMAN EXPRESS!!

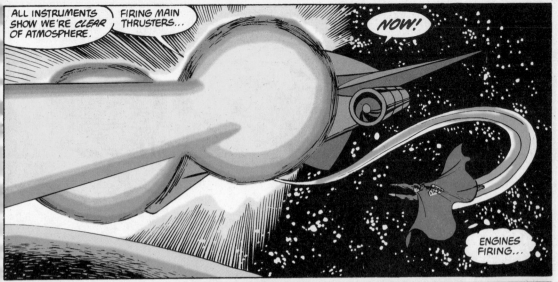

ALL INSTRUMENTS SHOW WE'RE *CLEAR* OF ATMOSPHERE.

FIRING MAIN THRUSTERS...

NOW!

ENGINES FIRING...

TIME FOR *YOURS TRULY* TO GET BACK ON BOARD.

I'M *FAST*-- BUT NOT FAST ENOUGH TO KEEP UP WITH A *STARSHIP!*

NOT AT *FULL THRUST,* ANYWAY.

AIRLOCK CYCLING COMPLETE, KATAR.

THE SHIP IS *SECURE.*

EXCELLENT! WE SHOULD ACHIEVE *LUNAR ORBIT* IN *TWELVE MINUTES!*

LUNAR ORBIT? SO YOUR INVASION FLEET IS *ON* OR *NEAR* THE *MOON?*

THAT MAKES *SENSE.* IT'S THE PERFECT *STAGING GROUND* FOR--

HM?

SAY... WE SEEM TO HAVE ONE *PASSENGER* I DIDN'T NOTICE BEFORE.

WHO'S *THIS* UNHAPPY *WANDERER?*

THAT IS *BYTH*...

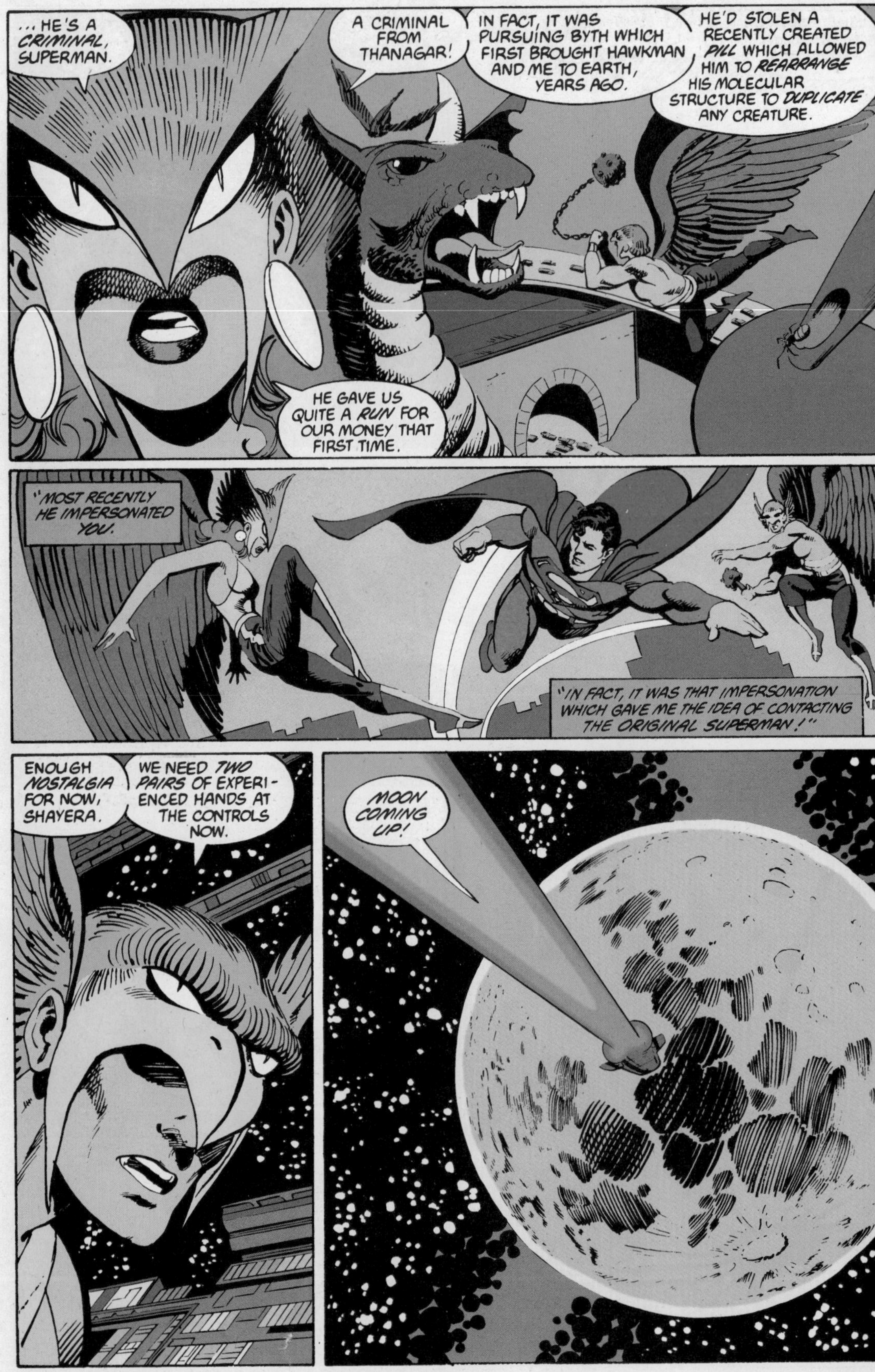

...HE'S A CRIMINAL, SUPERMAN.
A CRIMINAL FROM THANAGAR!
IN FACT, IT WAS PURSUING BYTH WHICH FIRST BROUGHT HAWKMAN AND ME TO EARTH, YEARS AGO.
HE'D STOLEN A RECENTLY CREATED PILL WHICH ALLOWED HIM TO REARRANGE HIS MOLECULAR STRUCTURE TO DUPLICATE ANY CREATURE.
HE GAVE US QUITE A RUN FOR OUR MONEY THAT FIRST TIME.
"MOST RECENTLY HE IMPERSONATED YOU.
"IN FACT, IT WAS THAT IMPERSONATION WHICH GAVE ME THE IDEA OF CONTACTING THE ORIGINAL SUPERMAN!"
ENOUGH NOSTALGIA FOR NOW, SHAYERA.
WE NEED TWO PAIRS OF EXPERI-ENCED HANDS AT THE CONTROLS NOW.
MOON COMING UP!

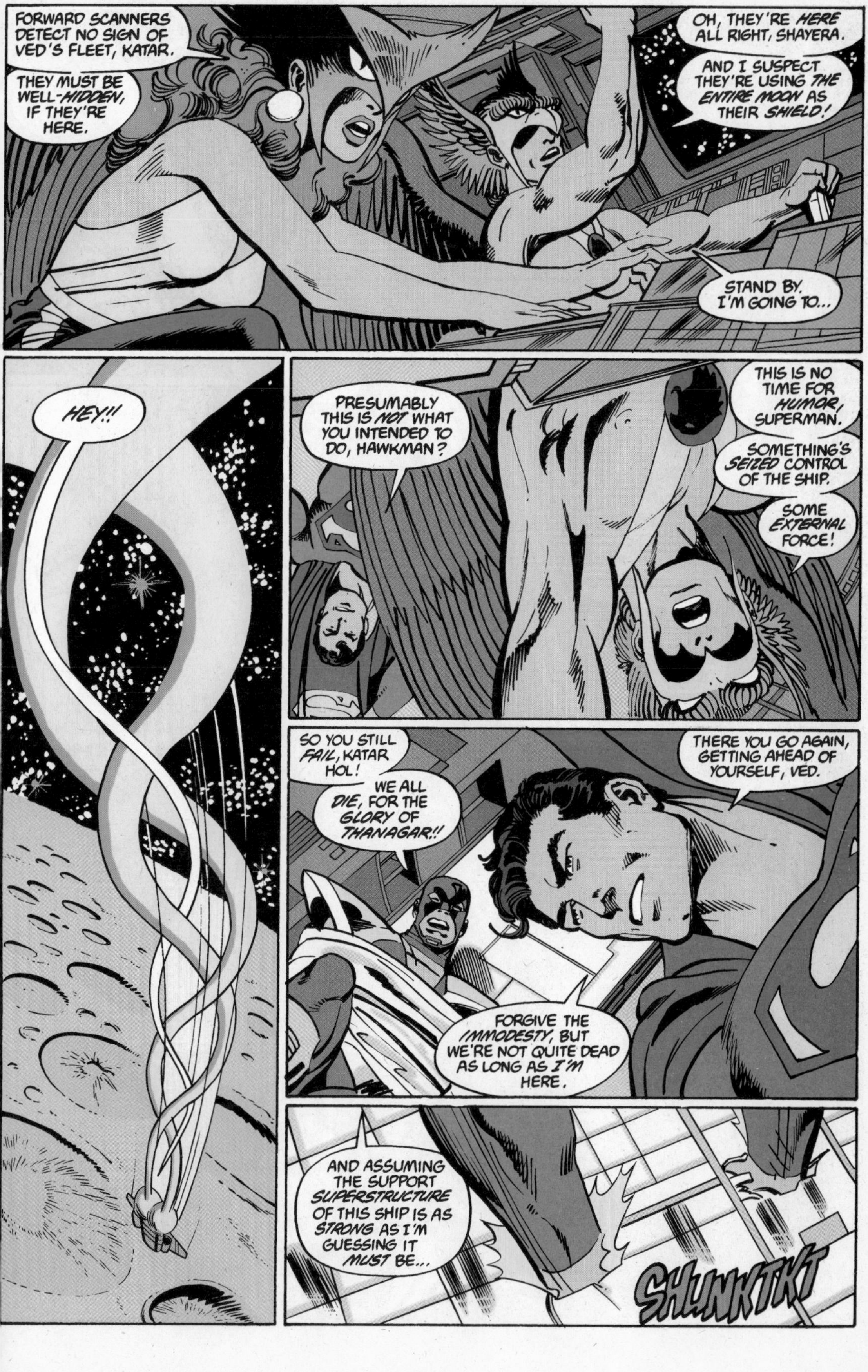
FORWARD SCANNERS DETECT NO SIGN OF VED'S FLEET, KATAR.
THEY MUST BE WELL-HIDDEN, IF THEY'RE HERE.
OH, THEY'RE HERE ALL RIGHT, SHAYERA.
AND I SUSPECT THEY'RE USING THE ENTIRE MOON AS THEIR SHIELD!
STAND BY. I'M GOING TO...
HEY!!
PRESUMABLY THIS IS NOT WHAT YOU INTENDED TO DO, HAWKMAN?
THIS IS NO TIME FOR HUMOR, SUPERMAN.
SOMETHING'S SEIZED CONTROL OF THE SHIP.
SOME EXTERNAL FORCE!
SO YOU STILL FAIL, KATAR HOL!
WE ALL DIE, FOR THE GLORY OF THANAGAR!!
THERE YOU GO AGAIN, GETTING AHEAD OF YOURSELF, VED.
FORGIVE THE IMMODESTY, BUT WE'RE NOT QUITE DEAD AS LONG AS I'M HERE.
AND ASSUMING THE SUPPORT SUPERSTRUCTURE OF THIS SHIP IS AS STRONG AS I'M GUESSING IT MUST BE...
SHUNKTKT

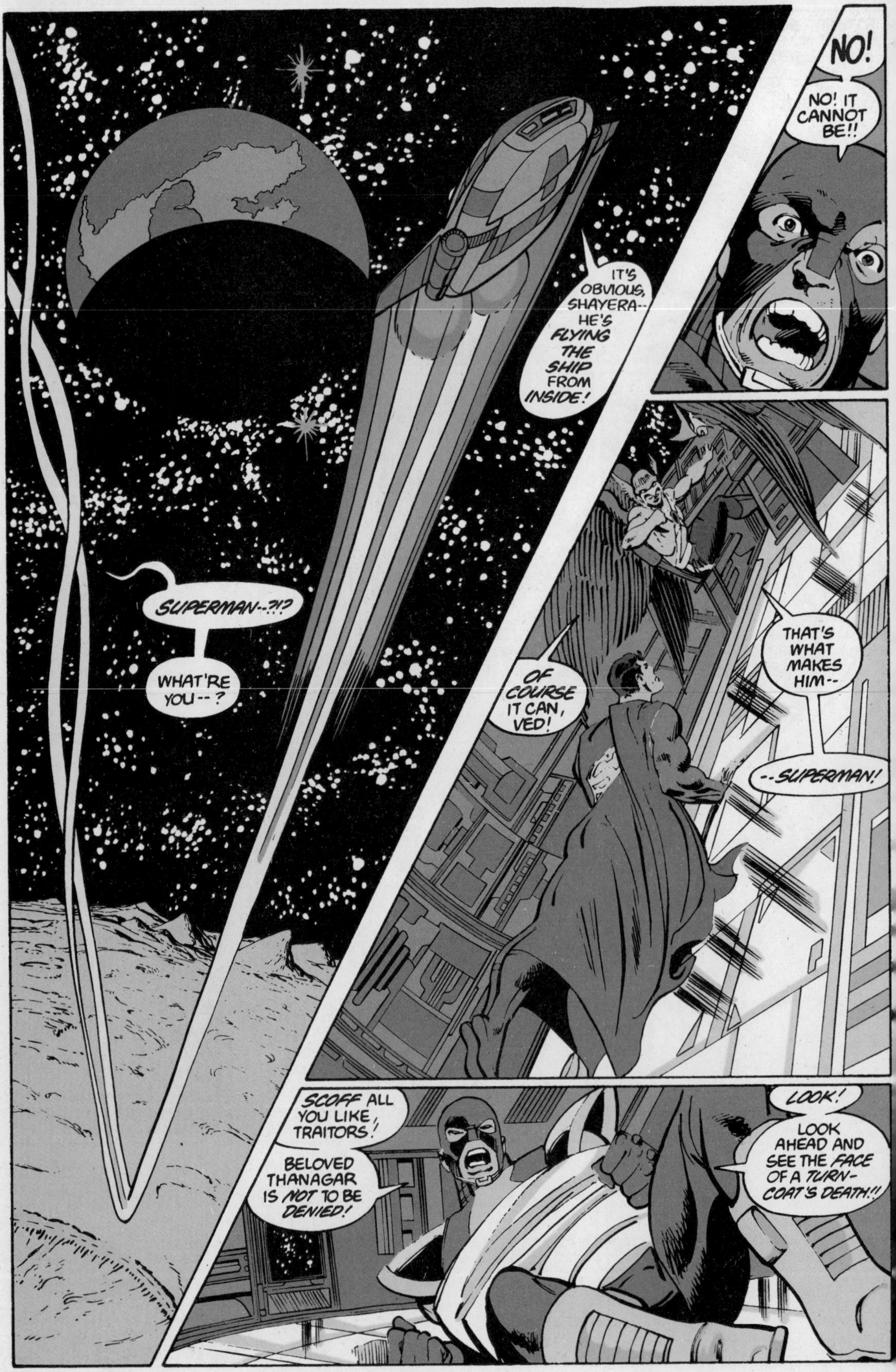
NO!
NO! IT CANNOT BE!!
IT'S OBVIOUS, SHAYERA-- HE'S FLYING THE SHIP FROM INSIDE!
SUPERMAN--?!?
WHAT'RE YOU--?
OF COURSE IT CAN, VED!
THAT'S WHAT MAKES HIM--
--SUPERMAN!
SCOFF ALL YOU LIKE, TRAITORS!
BELOVED THANAGAR IS NOT TO BE DENIED!
LOOK!
LOOK AHEAD AND SEE THE FACE OF A TURN-COAT'S DEATH!!

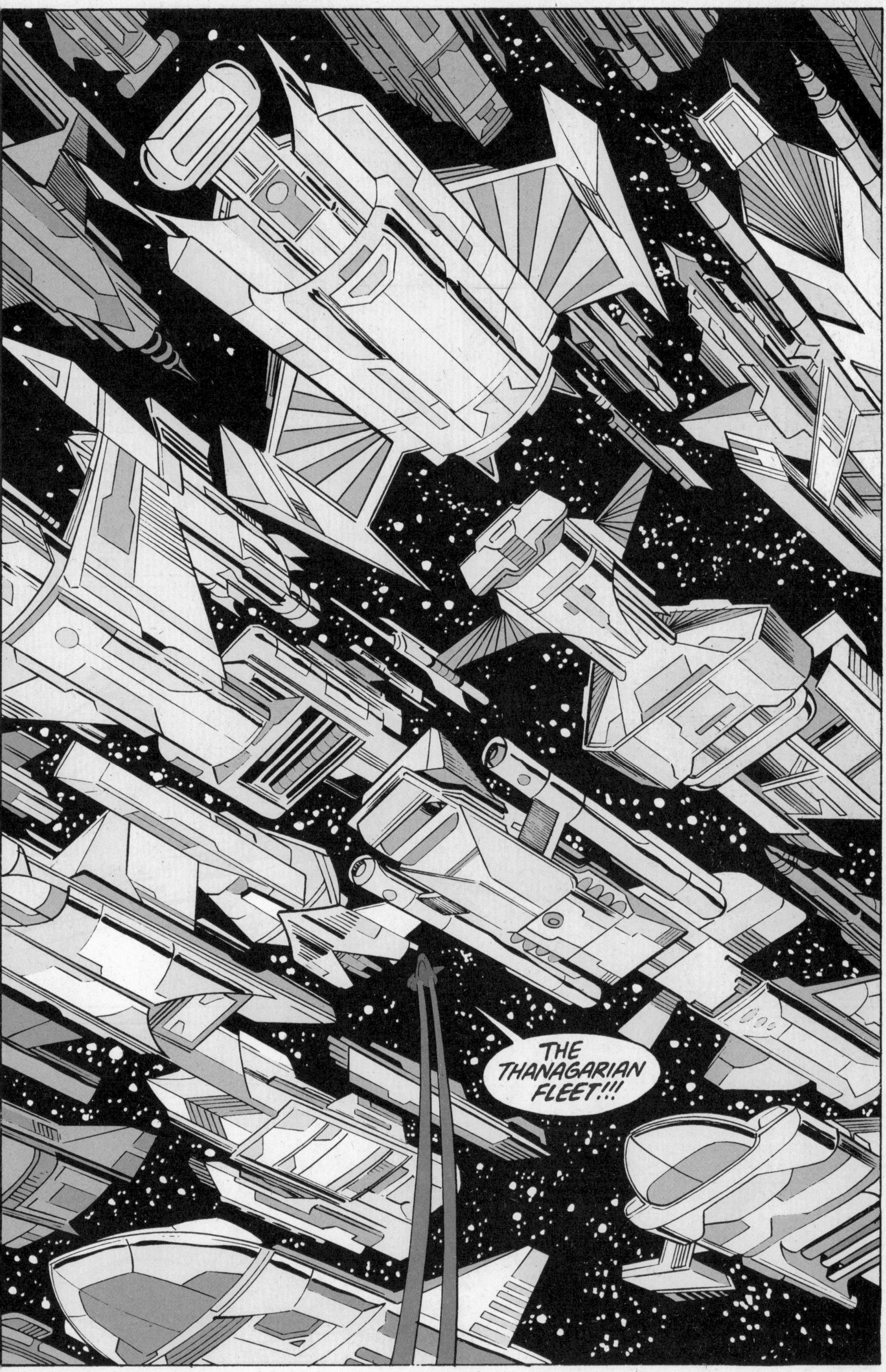
THE THANAGARIAN FLEET!!!

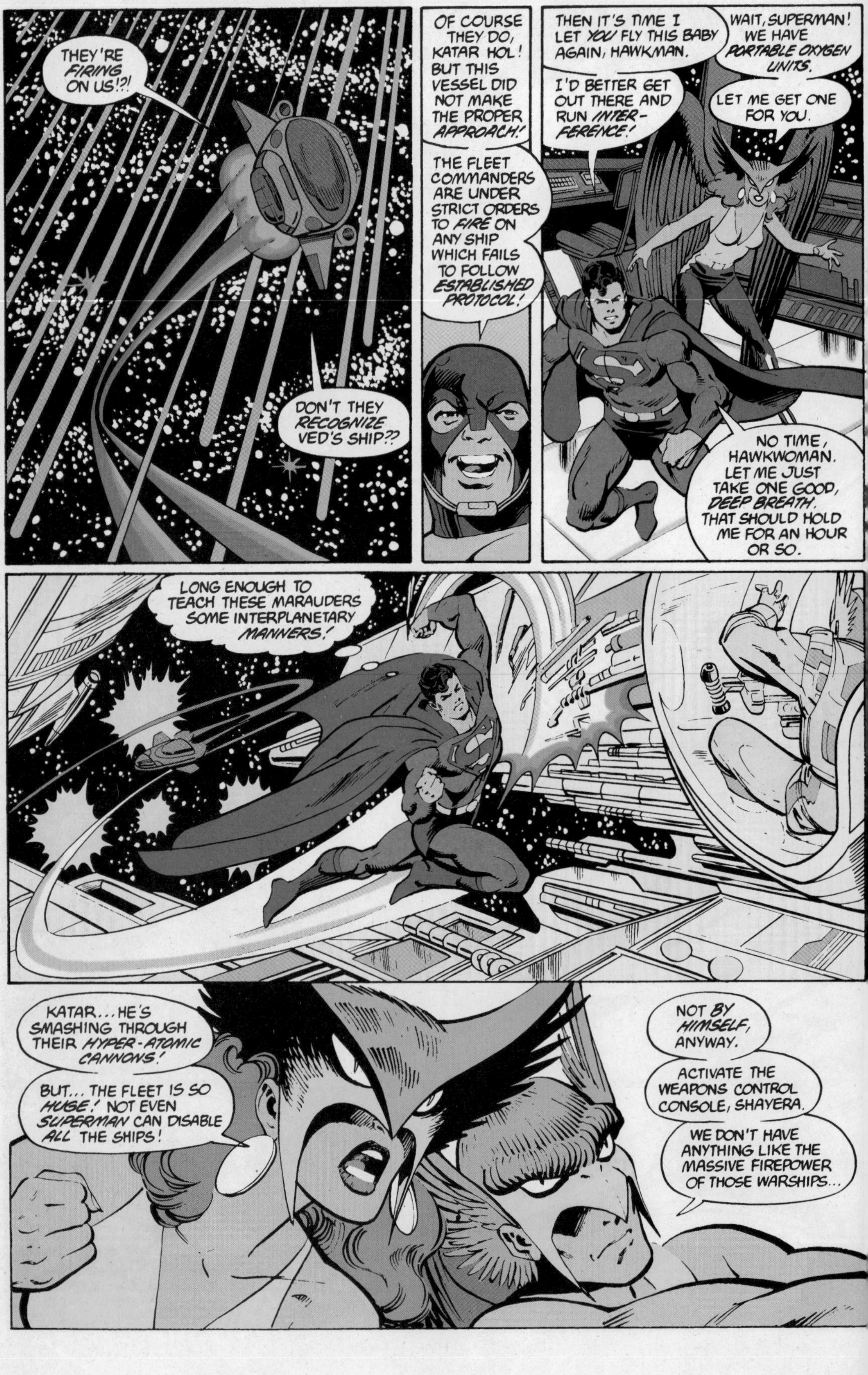
THEY'RE FIRING ON US!?!
DON'T THEY RECOGNIZE VED'S SHIP??
OF COURSE THEY DO, KATAR HOL! BUT THIS VESSEL DID NOT MAKE THE PROPER APPROACH!
THE FLEET COMMANDERS ARE UNDER STRICT ORDERS TO FIRE ON ANY SHIP WHICH FAILS TO FOLLOW ESTABLISHED PROTOCOL!
THEN IT'S TIME I LET YOU FLY THIS BABY AGAIN, HAWKMAN.
I'D BETTER GET OUT THERE AND RUN INTER-FERENCE!
WAIT, SUPERMAN! WE HAVE PORTABLE OXYGEN UNITS.
LET ME GET ONE FOR YOU.
NO TIME, HAWKWOMAN. LET ME JUST TAKE ONE GOOD, DEEP BREATH. THAT SHOULD HOLD ME FOR AN HOUR OR SO.
LONG ENOUGH TO TEACH THESE MARAUDERS SOME INTERPLANETARY MANNERS!
KATAR... HE'S SMASHING THROUGH THEIR HYPER-ATOMIC CANNONS!
BUT... THE FLEET IS SO HUGE! NOT EVEN SUPERMAN CAN DISABLE ALL THE SHIPS!
NOT BY HIMSELF, ANYWAY.
ACTIVATE THE WEAPONS CONTROL CONSOLE, SHAYERA.
WE DON'T HAVE ANYTHING LIKE THE MASSIVE FIREPOWER OF THOSE WARSHIPS...

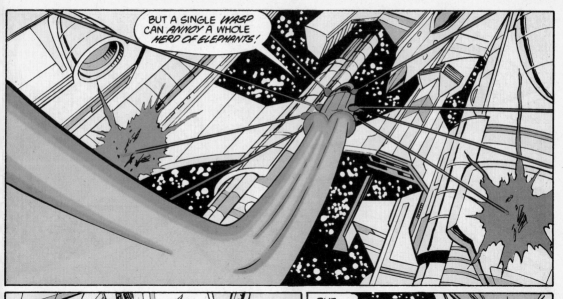

BUT A SINGLE *WASP* CAN *ANNOY* A WHOLE *HERD OF ELEPHANTS!*

HAWKMAN AND HAWKWOMAN ARE RUNNING A PRETTY GOOD *HARASSING MANEUVER!*

--THEY'RE DISTRACTING THE GUNMEN ON THESE BIG TUBS--

--WHICH AFFORDS *ME* A BETTER OPPORTUNITY TO *DESTROY* THEIR CANNONS!

BUT... FOR ALL THE *DAMAGE* WE'RE INFLICTING, IT'S STILL JUST A *DELAYING TACTIC.*

THIS MAY BE AN *INVASION FLEET,* BUT IT'S STILL MANNED BY INTELLIGENT *LIVING* BEINGS.

I'D PREFER TO AVOID WHOLESALE *SLAUGHTER* IF AT ALL POSSIBLE.

THERE MUST BE *ANOTHER WAY* TO PREVENT THE INVASION.!

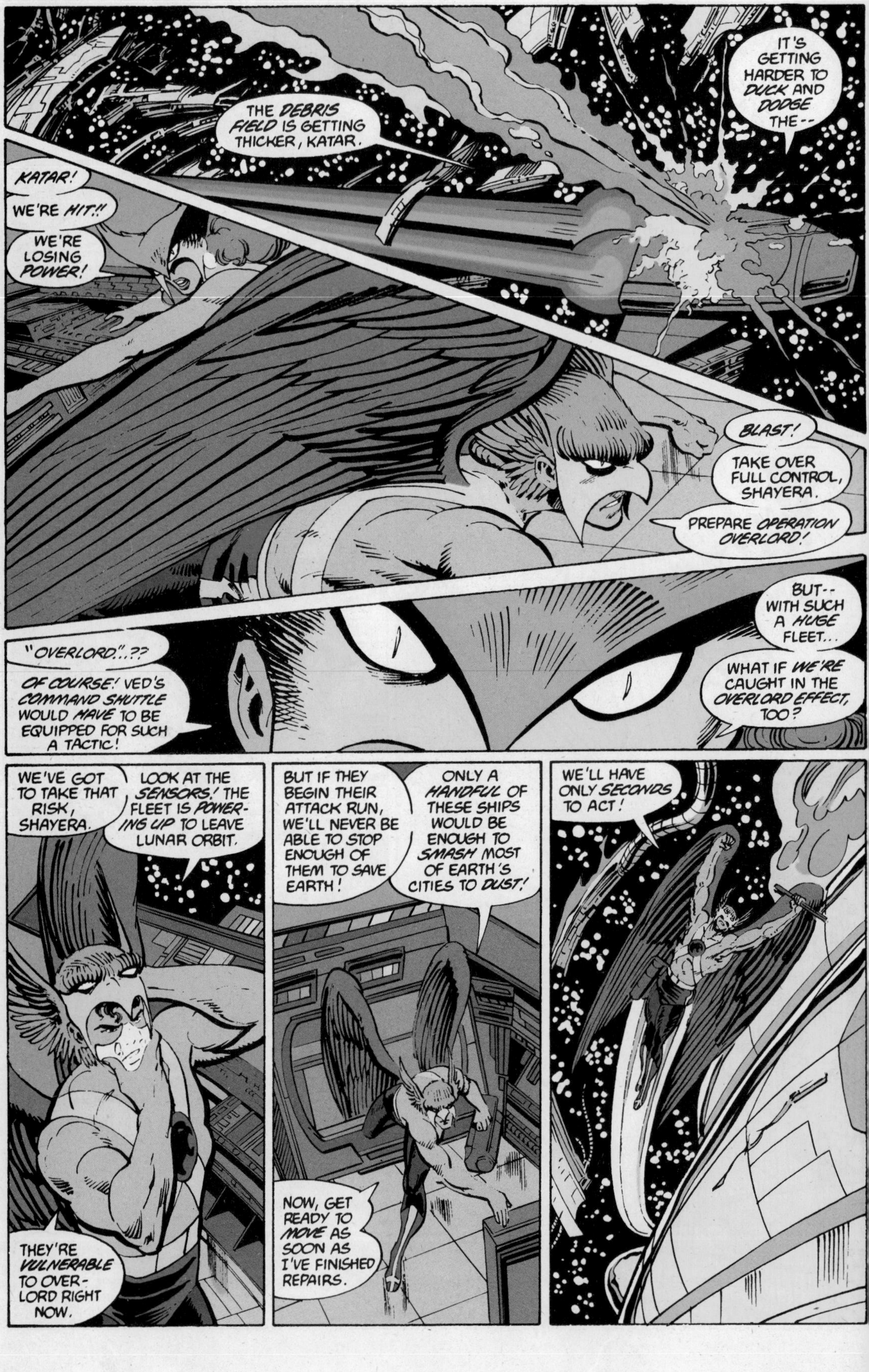
THE DEBRIS FIELD IS GETTING THICKER, KATAR.
IT'S GETTING HARDER TO DUCK AND DODGE THE--
KATAR!
WE'RE HIT!!
WE'RE LOSING POWER!
BLAST!
TAKE OVER FULL CONTROL, SHAYERA.
PREPARE OPERATION OVERLORD!
"OVERLORD"..??
OF COURSE! VED'S COMMAND SHUTTLE WOULD HAVE TO BE EQUIPPED FOR SUCH A TACTIC!
BUT-- WITH SUCH A HUGE FLEET...
WHAT IF WE'RE CAUGHT IN THE OVERLORD EFFECT, TOO?
WE'VE GOT TO TAKE THAT RISK, SHAYERA.
LOOK AT THE SENSORS! THE FLEET IS POWERING UP TO LEAVE LUNAR ORBIT.
THEY'RE VULNERABLE TO OVERLORD RIGHT NOW.
BUT IF THEY BEGIN THEIR ATTACK RUN, WE'LL NEVER BE ABLE TO STOP ENOUGH OF THEM TO SAVE EARTH!
ONLY A HANDFUL OF THESE SHIPS WOULD BE ENOUGH TO SMASH MOST OF EARTH'S CITIES TO DUST!
NOW, GET READY TO MOVE AS SOON AS I'VE FINISHED REPAIRS.
WE'LL HAVE ONLY SECONDS TO ACT!

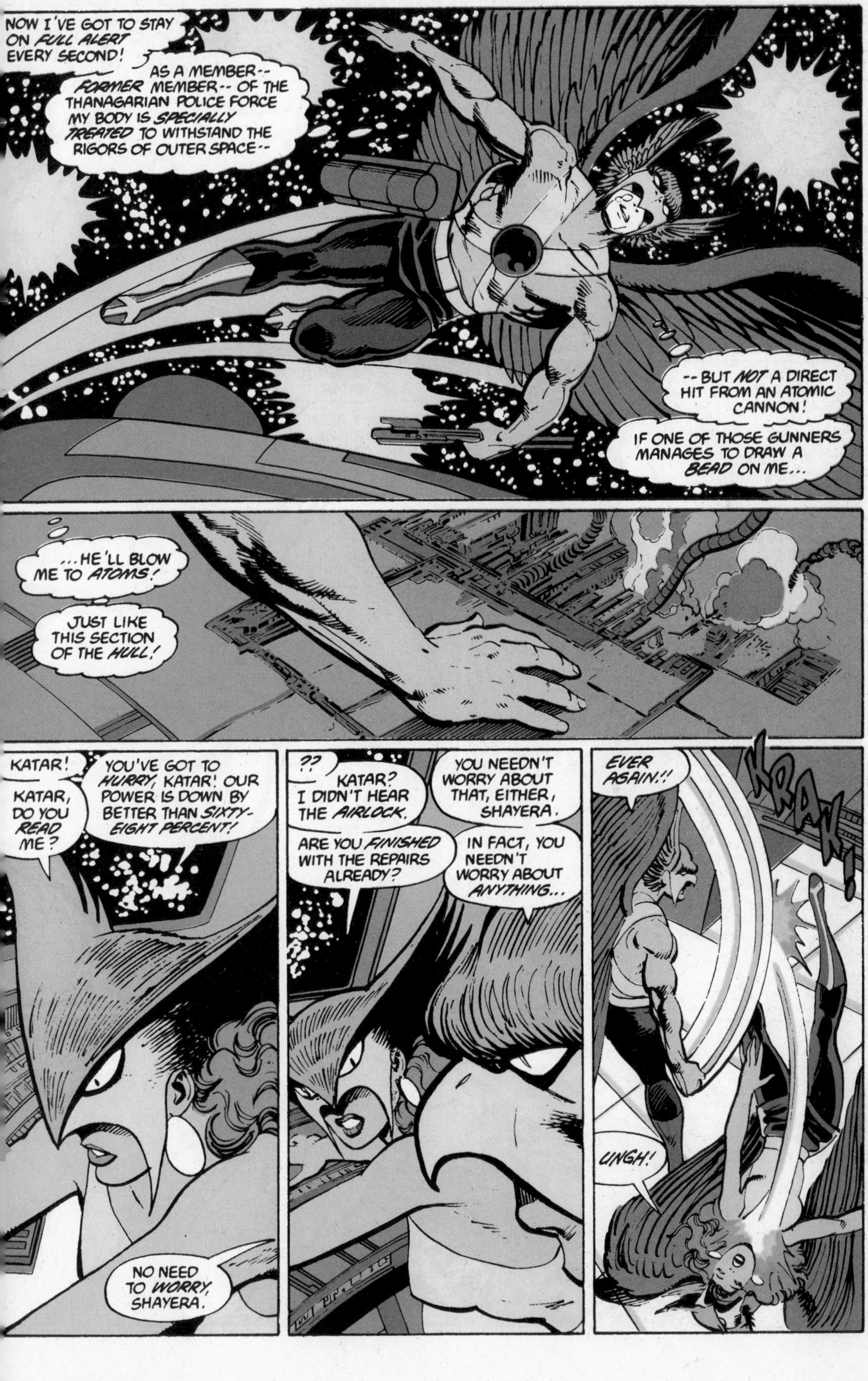
NOW I'VE GOT TO STAY ON FULL ALERT EVERY SECOND!
AS A MEMBER-- FORMER MEMBER-- OF THE THANAGARIAN POLICE FORCE MY BODY IS SPECIALLY TREATED TO WITHSTAND THE RIGORS OF OUTER SPACE--
--BUT NOT A DIRECT HIT FROM AN ATOMIC CANNON!
IF ONE OF THOSE GUNNERS MANAGES TO DRAW A BEAD ON ME...
...HE'LL BLOW ME TO ATOMS!
JUST LIKE THIS SECTION OF THE HULL!
KATAR!
KATAR, DO YOU READ ME?
YOU'VE GOT TO HURRY, KATAR! OUR POWER IS DOWN BY BETTER THAN SIXTY-EIGHT PERCENT!
NO NEED TO WORRY, SHAYERA.
?? KATAR? I DIDN'T HEAR THE AIRLOCK.
ARE YOU FINISHED WITH THE REPAIRS ALREADY?
YOU NEEDN'T WORRY ABOUT THAT, EITHER, SHAYERA.
IN FACT, YOU NEEDN'T WORRY ABOUT ANYTHING...
EVER AGAIN!!
KRAK!
UNGH!

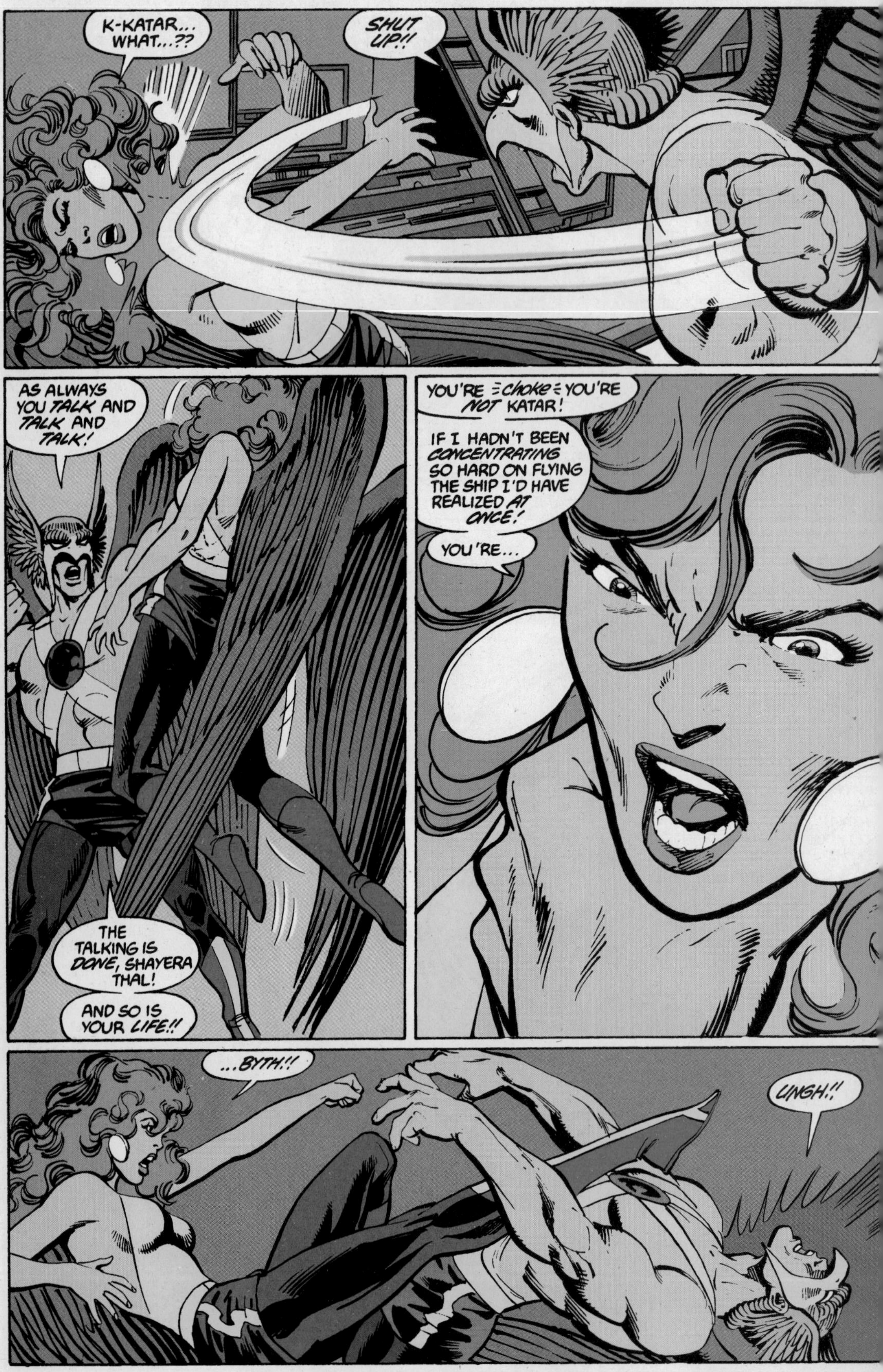
K-KATAR... WHAT...??
SHUT UP!!
AS ALWAYS YOU TALK AND TALK AND TALK!
THE TALKING IS DONE, SHAYERA THAL!
AND SO IS YOUR LIFE!!
YOU'RE =choke= YOU'RE NOT KATAR!
IF I HADN'T BEEN CONCENTRATING SO HARD ON FLYING THE SHIP I'D HAVE REALIZED AT ONCE!
YOU'RE...
...BYTH!!
UNGH!!

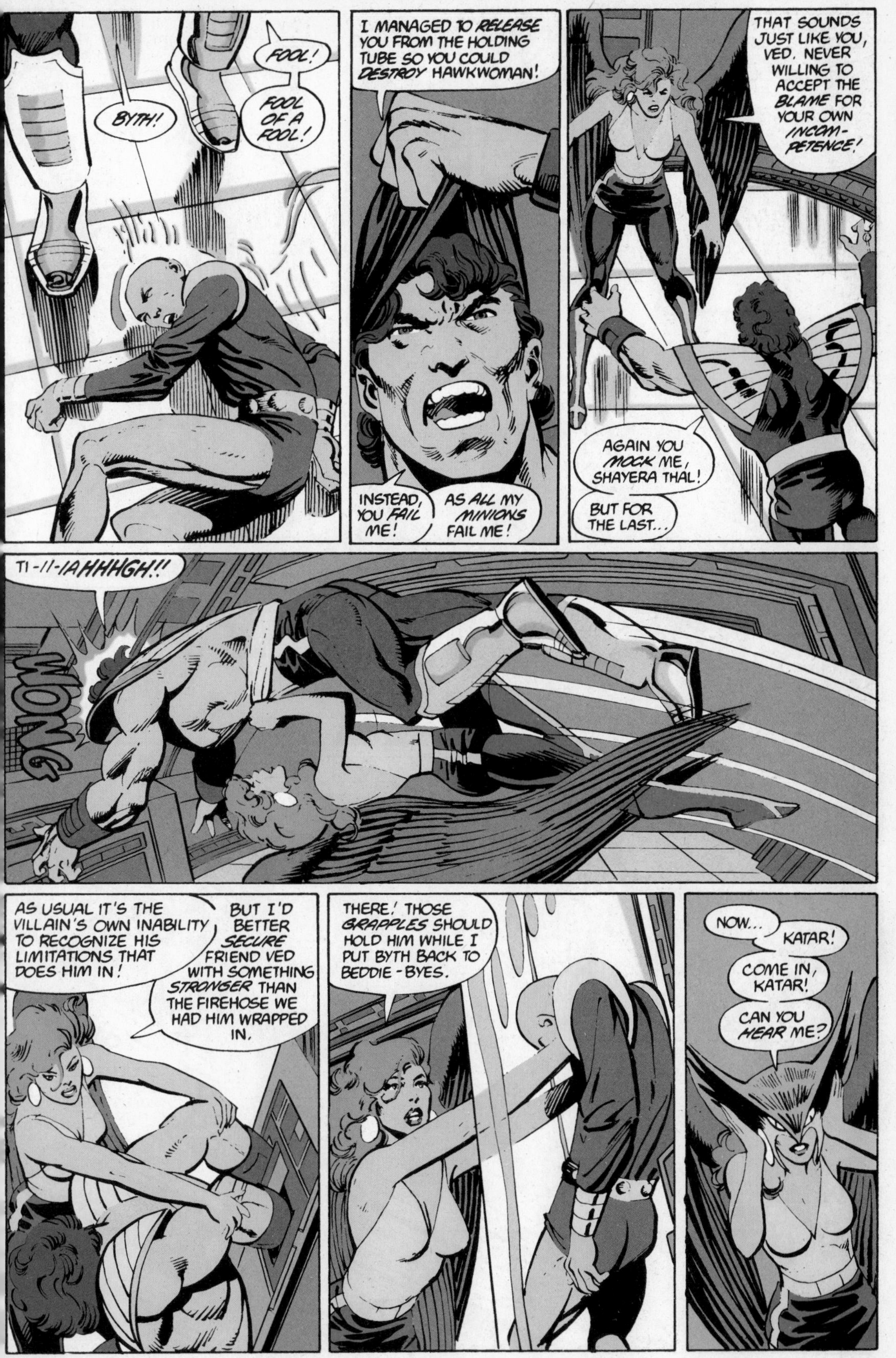
FOOL!
FOOL OF A FOOL!
BYTH!
I MANAGED TO RELEASE YOU FROM THE HOLDING TUBE SO YOU COULD DESTROY HAWKWOMAN!
INSTEAD, YOU FAIL ME!
AS ALL MY MINIONS FAIL ME!
THAT SOUNDS JUST LIKE YOU, VED. NEVER WILLING TO ACCEPT THE BLAME FOR YOUR OWN INCOM-PETENCE!
AGAIN YOU MOCK ME, SHAYERA THAL!
BUT FOR THE LAST...
TI-II-IAHHHGH!!
WONG
AS USUAL IT'S THE VILLAIN'S OWN INABILITY TO RECOGNIZE HIS LIMITATIONS THAT DOES HIM IN!
BUT I'D BETTER SECURE FRIEND VED WITH SOMETHING STRONGER THAN THE FIREHOSE WE HAD HIM WRAPPED IN.
THERE! THOSE GRAPPLES SHOULD HOLD HIM WHILE I PUT BYTH BACK TO BEDDIE-BYES.
NOW...
KATAR!
COME IN, KATAR!
CAN YOU HEAR ME?

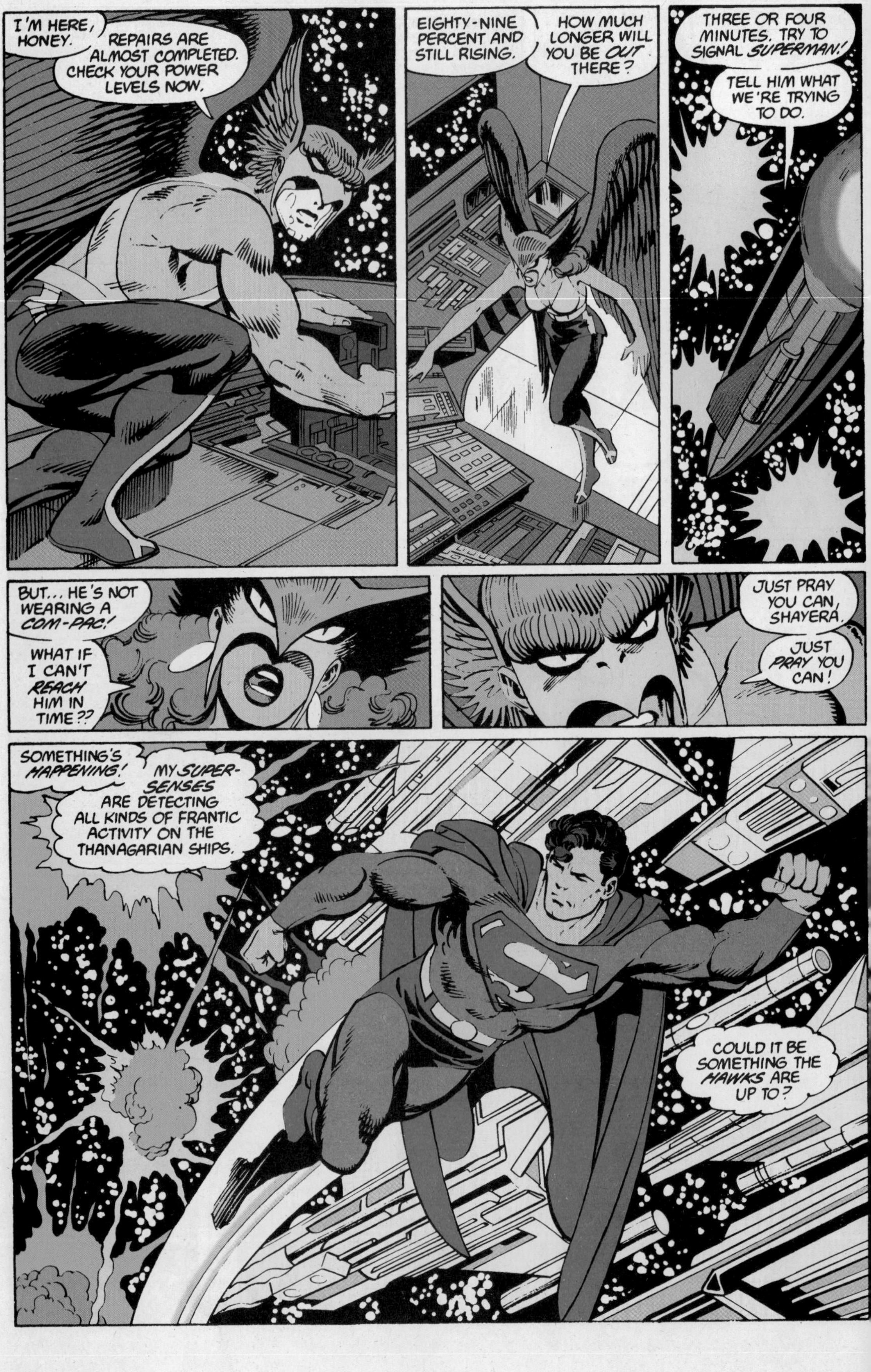

I'M HERE, HONEY.
REPAIRS ARE ALMOST COMPLETED. CHECK YOUR POWER LEVELS NOW.
EIGHTY-NINE PERCENT AND STILL RISING.
HOW MUCH LONGER WILL YOU BE OUT THERE?
THREE OR FOUR MINUTES. TRY TO SIGNAL SUPERMAN!
TELL HIM WHAT WE'RE TRYING TO DO.
BUT... HE'S NOT WEARING A COM-PAC!
WHAT IF I CAN'T REACH HIM IN TIME??
JUST PRAY YOU CAN, SHAYERA.
JUST PRAY YOU CAN!
SOMETHING'S HAPPENING!
MY SUPER-SENSES ARE DETECTING ALL KINDS OF FRANTIC ACTIVITY ON THE THANAGARIAN SHIPS.
COULD IT BE SOMETHING THE HAWKS ARE UP TO?

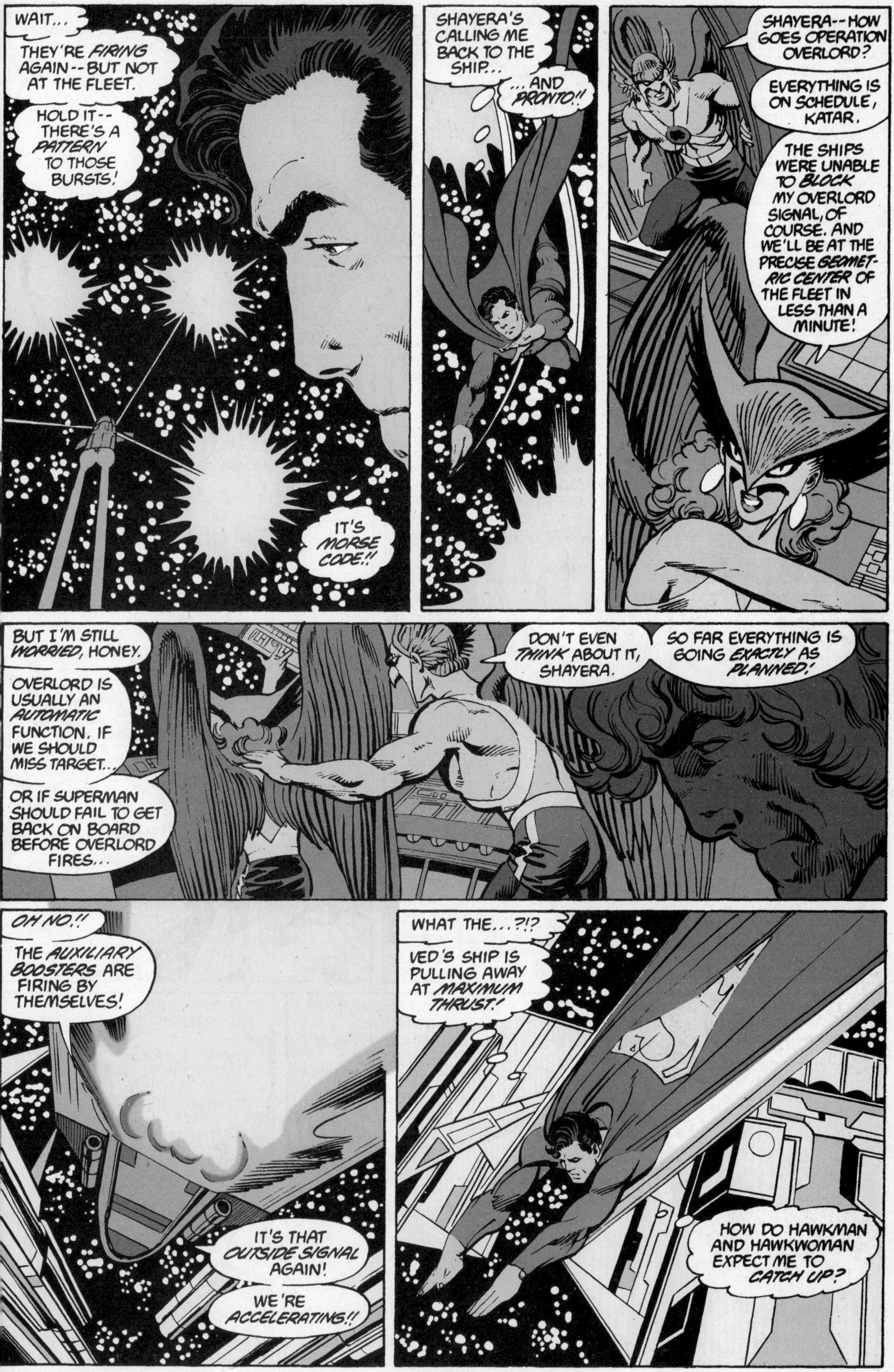
WAIT...
THEY'RE *FIRING* AGAIN--BUT NOT AT THE FLEET.
HOLD IT--THERE'S A *PATTERN* TO THOSE BURSTS!
IT'S *MORSE CODE!!*
SHAYERA'S CALLING ME BACK TO THE SHIP...
...AND *PRONTO!!*
SHAYERA--HOW GOES OPERATION OVERLORD?
EVERYTHING IS ON SCHEDULE, KATAR.
THE SHIPS WERE UNABLE TO *BLOCK* MY OVERLORD SIGNAL, OF COURSE. AND WE'LL BE AT THE PRECISE *GEOMETRIC CENTER* OF THE FLEET IN LESS THAN A MINUTE!
BUT I'M STILL *WORRIED*, HONEY.
OVERLORD IS USUALLY AN *AUTOMATIC* FUNCTION. IF WE SHOULD MISS TARGET...
OR IF SUPERMAN SHOULD FAIL TO GET BACK ON BOARD BEFORE OVERLORD FIRES...
DON'T EVEN *THINK* ABOUT IT, SHAYERA.
SO FAR EVERYTHING IS GOING *EXACTLY* AS *PLANNED!*
OH NO!!
THE *AUXILIARY BOOSTERS* ARE FIRING BY THEMSELVES!
IT'S THAT *OUTSIDE SIGNAL* AGAIN!
WE'RE *ACCELERATING!!*
WHAT THE...?!?
VED'S SHIP IS PULLING AWAY AT *MAXIMUM THRUST!*
HOW DO HAWKMAN AND HAWKWOMAN EXPECT ME TO *CATCH UP?*

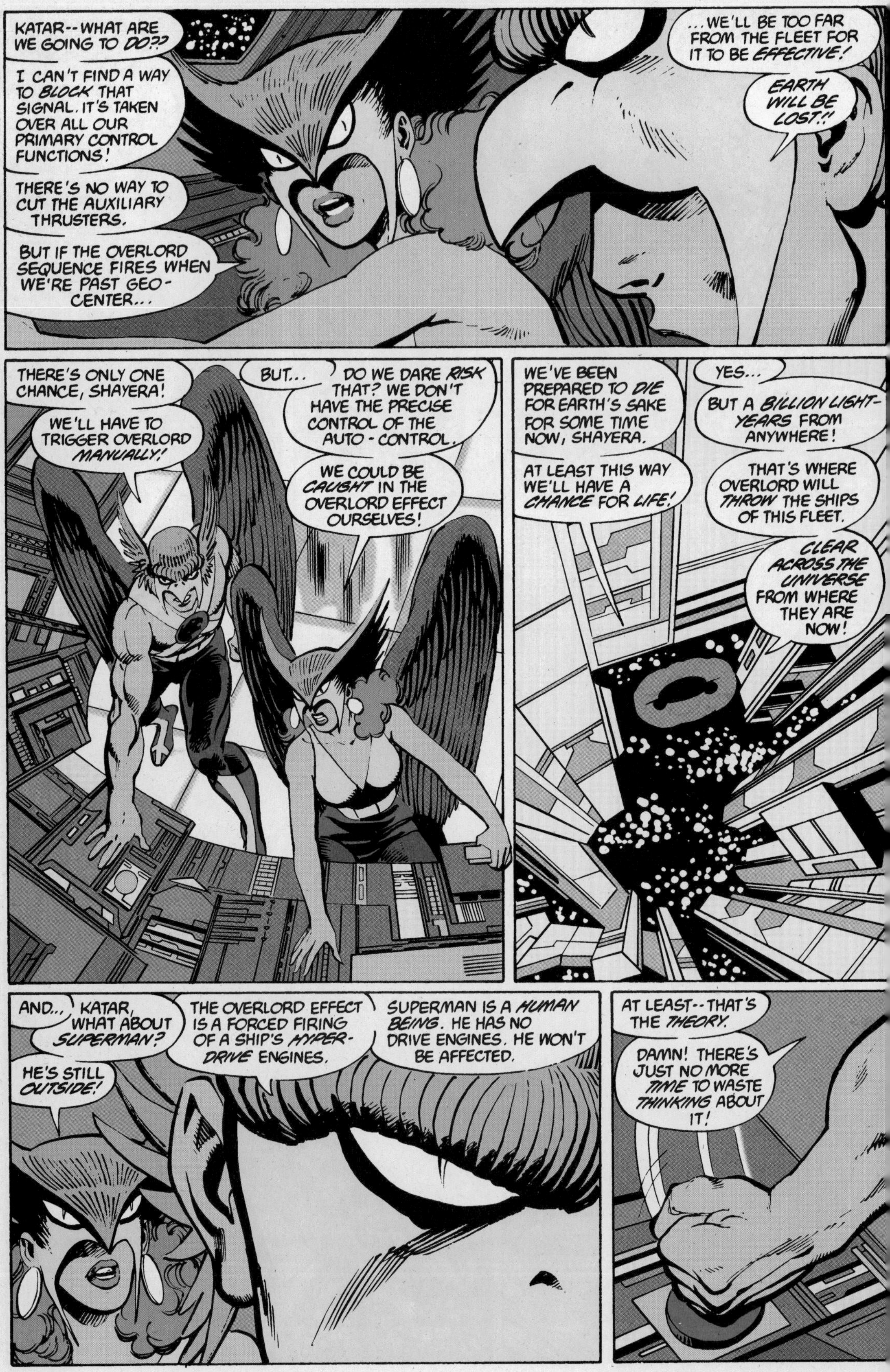
KATAR--WHAT ARE WE GOING TO DO??
I CAN'T FIND A WAY TO BLOCK THAT SIGNAL. IT'S TAKEN OVER ALL OUR PRIMARY CONTROL FUNCTIONS!
THERE'S NO WAY TO CUT THE AUXILIARY THRUSTERS.
BUT IF THE OVERLORD SEQUENCE FIRES WHEN WE'RE PAST GEO-CENTER...
...WE'LL BE TOO FAR FROM THE FLEET FOR IT TO BE EFFECTIVE!
EARTH WILL BE LOST!!
THERE'S ONLY ONE CHANCE, SHAYERA!
WE'LL HAVE TO TRIGGER OVERLORD MANUALLY!
BUT...
DO WE DARE RISK THAT? WE DON'T HAVE THE PRECISE CONTROL OF THE AUTO-CONTROL.
WE COULD BE CAUGHT IN THE OVERLORD EFFECT OURSELVES!
WE'VE BEEN PREPARED TO DIE FOR EARTH'S SAKE FOR SOME TIME NOW, SHAYERA.
AT LEAST THIS WAY WE'LL HAVE A CHANCE FOR LIFE!
YES...
BUT A BILLION LIGHT-YEARS FROM ANYWHERE!
THAT'S WHERE OVERLORD WILL THROW THE SHIPS OF THIS FLEET.
CLEAR ACROSS THE UNIVERSE FROM WHERE THEY ARE NOW!
AND... KATAR, WHAT ABOUT SUPERMAN?
HE'S STILL OUTSIDE!
THE OVERLORD EFFECT IS A FORCED FIRING OF A SHIP'S HYPER-DRIVE ENGINES.
SUPERMAN IS A HUMAN BEING. HE HAS NO DRIVE ENGINES. HE WON'T BE AFFECTED.
AT LEAST--THAT'S THE THEORY.
DAMN! THERE'S JUST NO MORE TIME TO WASTE THINKING ABOUT IT!

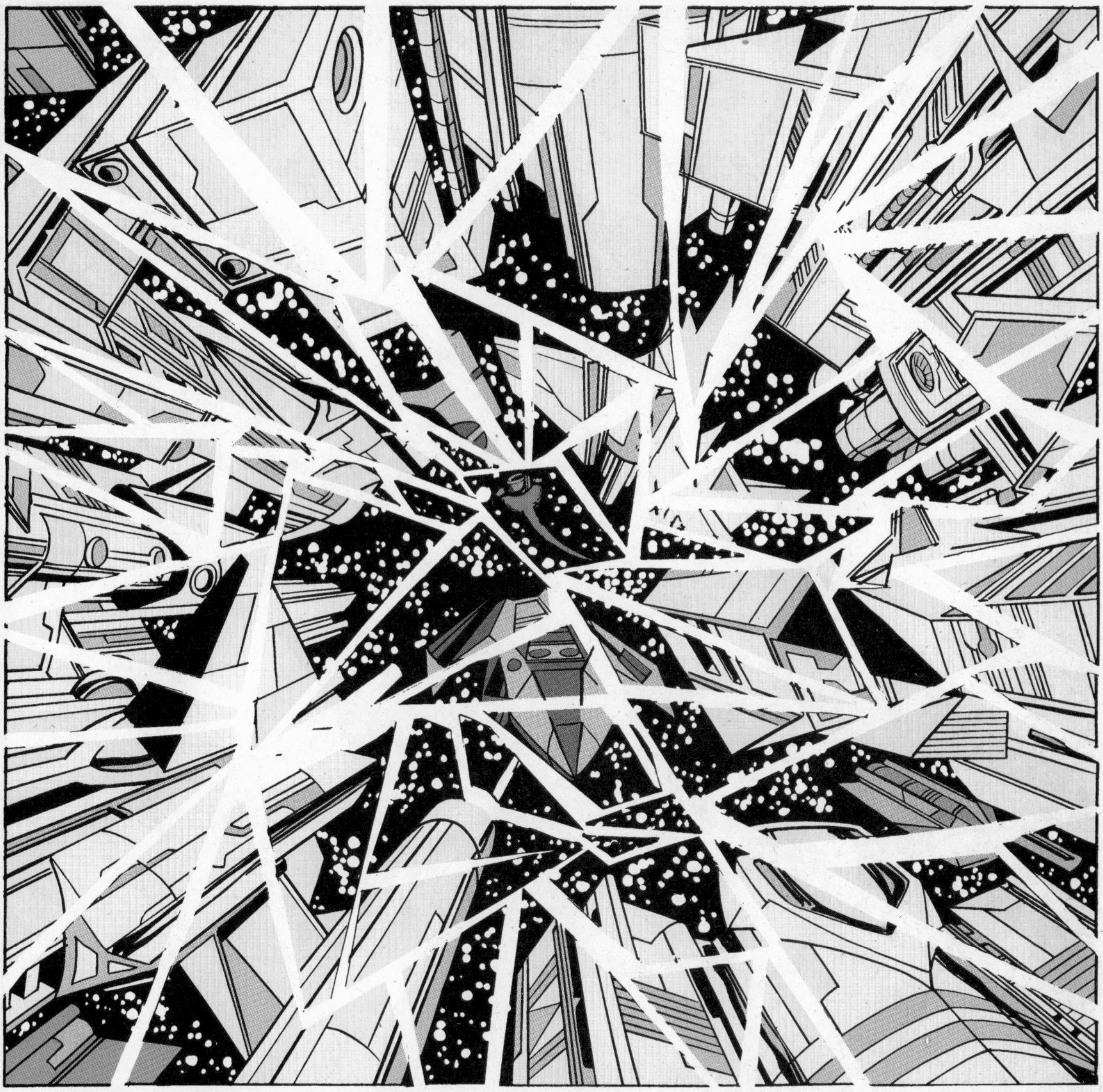

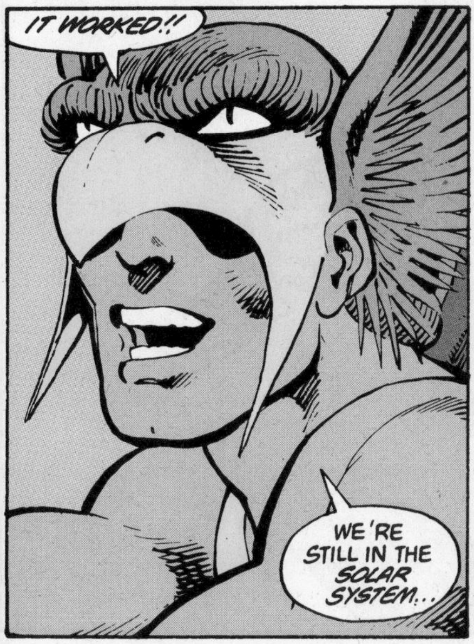
IT WORKED!!
WE'RE STILL IN THE SOLAR SYSTEM...

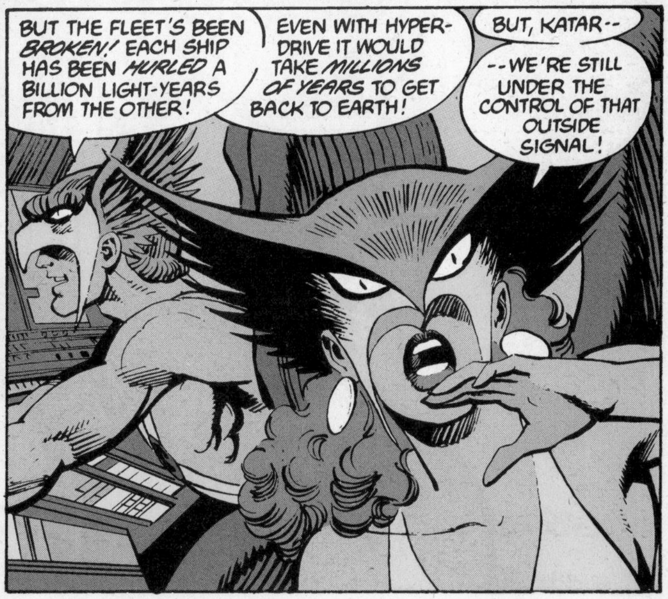
BUT THE FLEET'S BEEN BROKEN! EACH SHIP HAS BEEN HURLED A BILLION LIGHT-YEARS FROM THE OTHER!
EVEN WITH HYPER-DRIVE IT WOULD TAKE MILLIONS OF YEARS TO GET BACK TO EARTH!
BUT, KATAR--
--WE'RE STILL UNDER THE CONTROL OF THAT OUTSIDE SIGNAL!

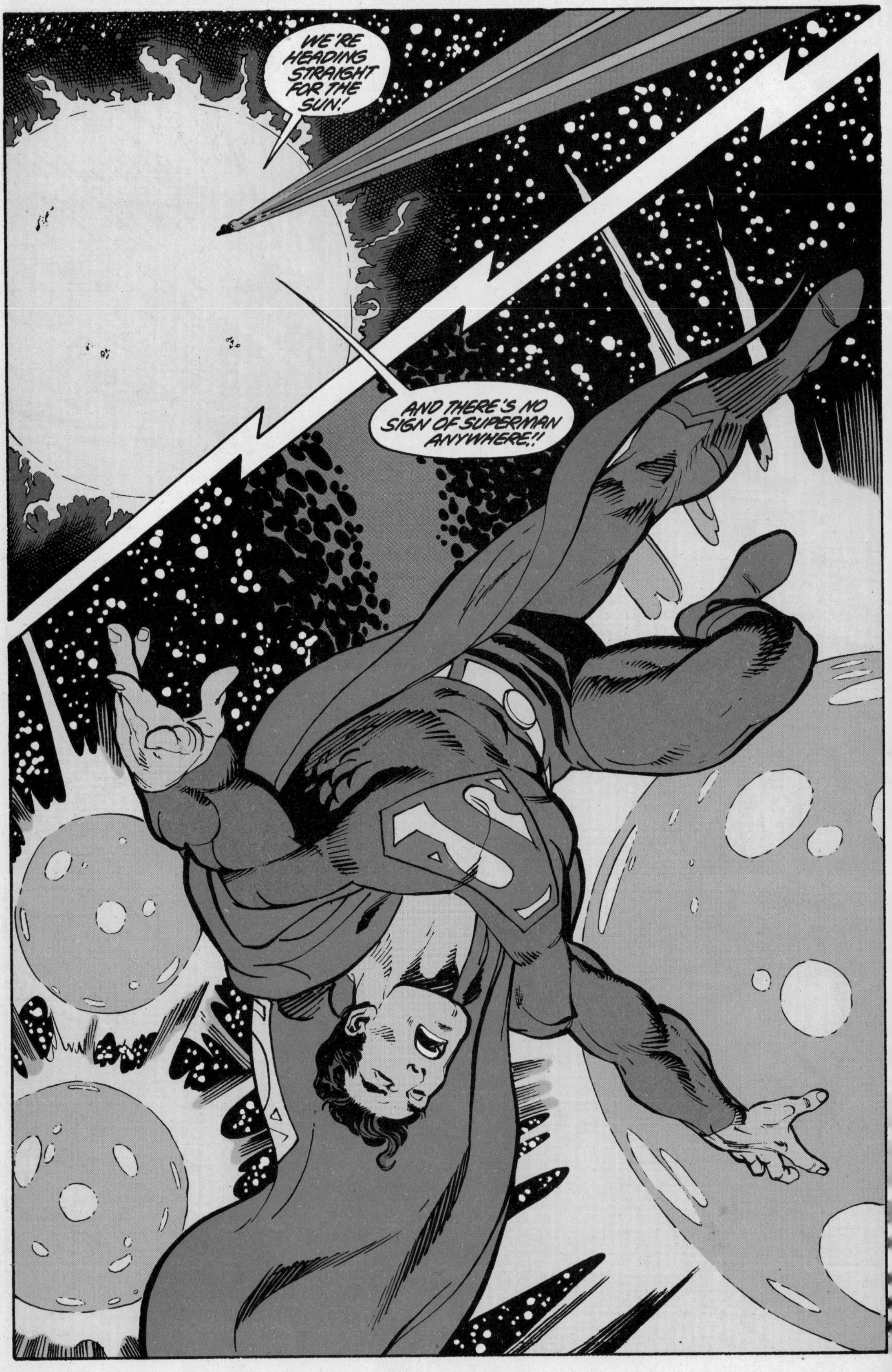
WE'RE HEADING STRAIGHT FOR THE SUN!
AND THERE'S NO SIGN OF SUPERMAN ANYWHERE!!

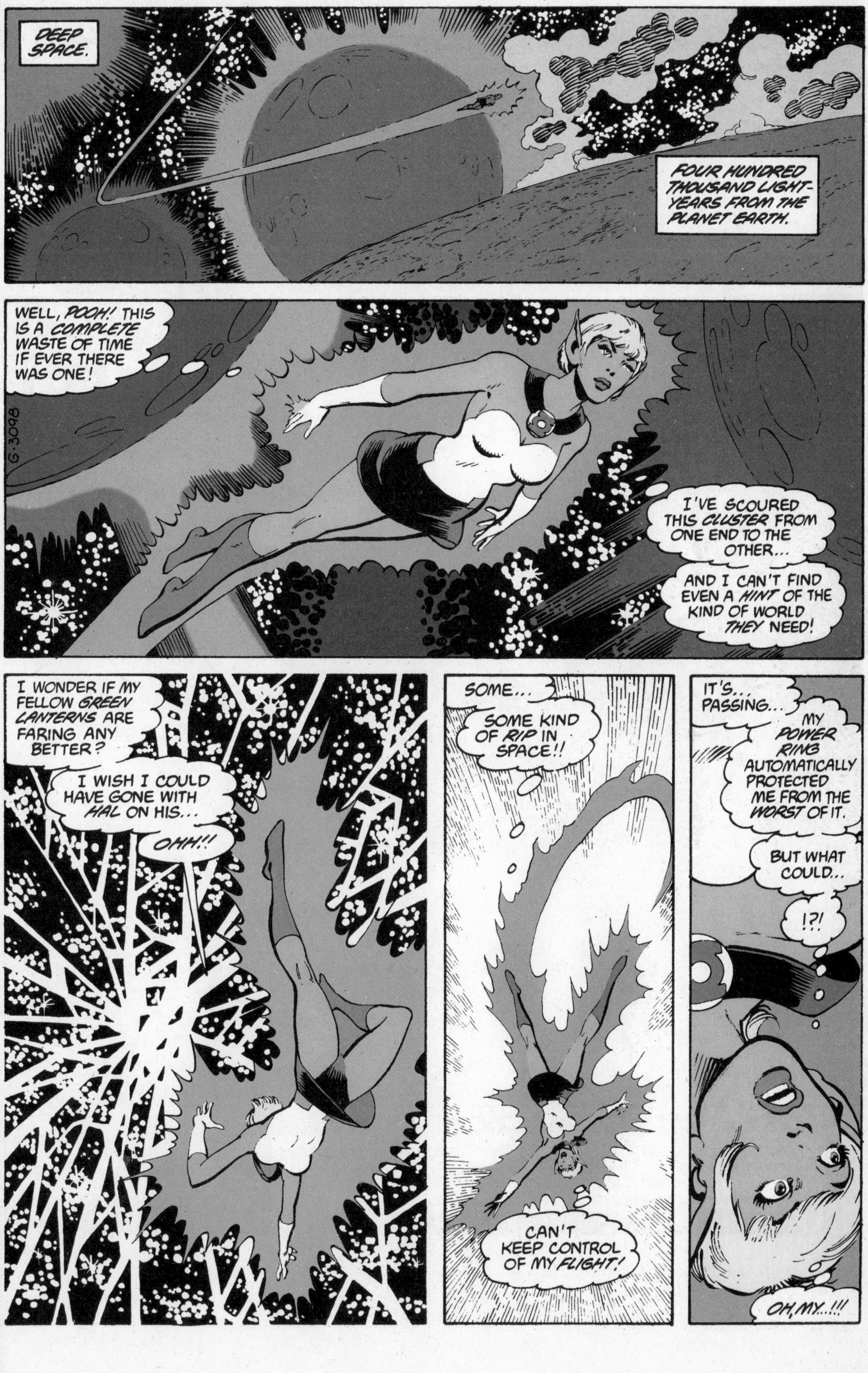
DEEP SPACE.
FOUR HUNDRED THOUSAND LIGHT-YEARS FROM THE PLANET EARTH.
WELL, POOH! THIS IS A COMPLETE WASTE OF TIME IF EVER THERE WAS ONE!
G-3098
I'VE SCOURED THIS CLUSTER FROM ONE END TO THE OTHER...
AND I CAN'T FIND EVEN A HINT OF THE KIND OF WORLD THEY NEED!
I WONDER IF MY FELLOW GREEN LANTERNS ARE FARING ANY BETTER?
I WISH I COULD HAVE GONE WITH HAL ON HIS...
OHH!!
SOME...
SOME KIND OF RIP IN SPACE!!
CAN'T KEEP CONTROL OF MY FLIGHT!
IT'S... PASSING...
MY POWER RING AUTOMATICALLY PROTECTED ME FROM THE WORST OF IT.
BUT WHAT COULD...
!?!
OH, MY...!!!

SUPERMAN and the GREEN LANTERN CORPS in...

GREEN ON GREEN

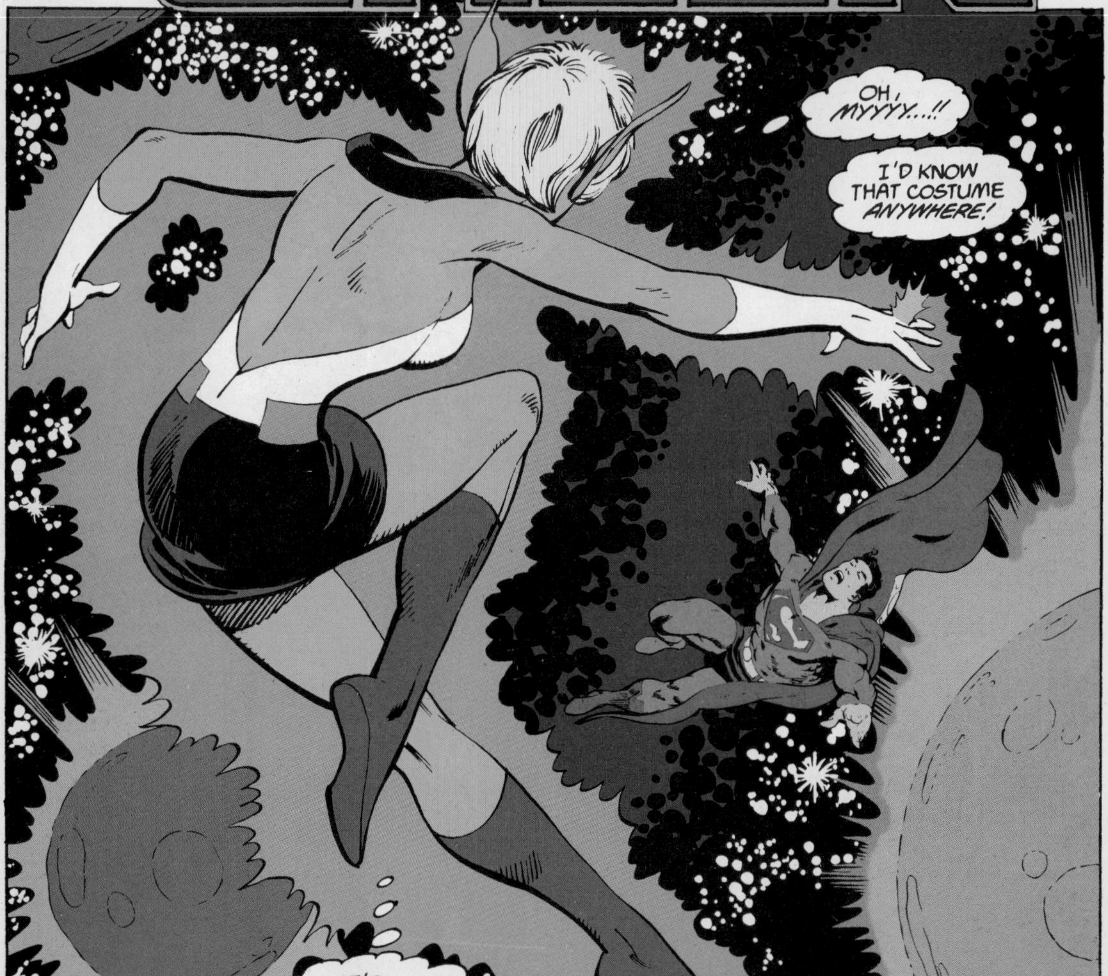
OH, MYYYY...!!
I'D KNOW THAT COSTUME ANYWHERE!
IT'S SUPERMAN!!
John Byrne . Dick Giordano . Tom Ziuko . John Costanza
words and pictures Embellisher colorist letterer
Michael Carlin & Andrew Helfer - editors
SUPERMAN CREATED BY JERRY SIEGEL AND JOE SHUSTER

HE'S ALIVE.

BUT, WHAT'S HE DOING WAY OUT HERE?

I DIDN'T THINK *SUPERMAN* COULD GET THIS FAR INTO SPACE UNDER HIS OWN POWER.

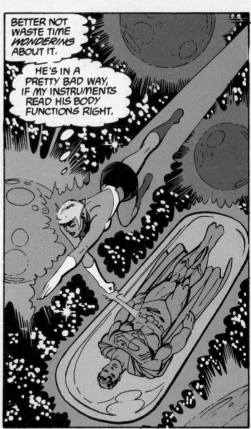

BETTER NOT WASTE TIME *WONDERING* ABOUT IT.

HE'S IN A PRETTY BAD WAY, IF MY INSTRUMENTS READ HIS BODY FUNCTIONS RIGHT.

GOT TO GET HIM BACK TO *BASE.*

KILOWOG WILL KNOW WHAT TO DO TO *SAVE* HIM!

SPACE AND TIME POLITELY BEND ASIDE...

...AND...

THERE'S OUR TEMPORARY SPACE CITADEL.

HMM... *GOOD!* INDICATIONS ARE EVERYONE ELSE IS BACK FROM THEIR PARTS OF THE *SEARCH.*

I WONDER IF ANYONE WAS MORE *SUCCESSFUL* THAN I WAS?

ARISIA!

OH MY STARS AND LITTLE FISHES! WHAT *HAVE* YOU GOT *THERE?*

SOMEONE IN NEED OF OUR HELP, *CH'P.* WHERE'S KILOWOG?

RIGHT HERE.

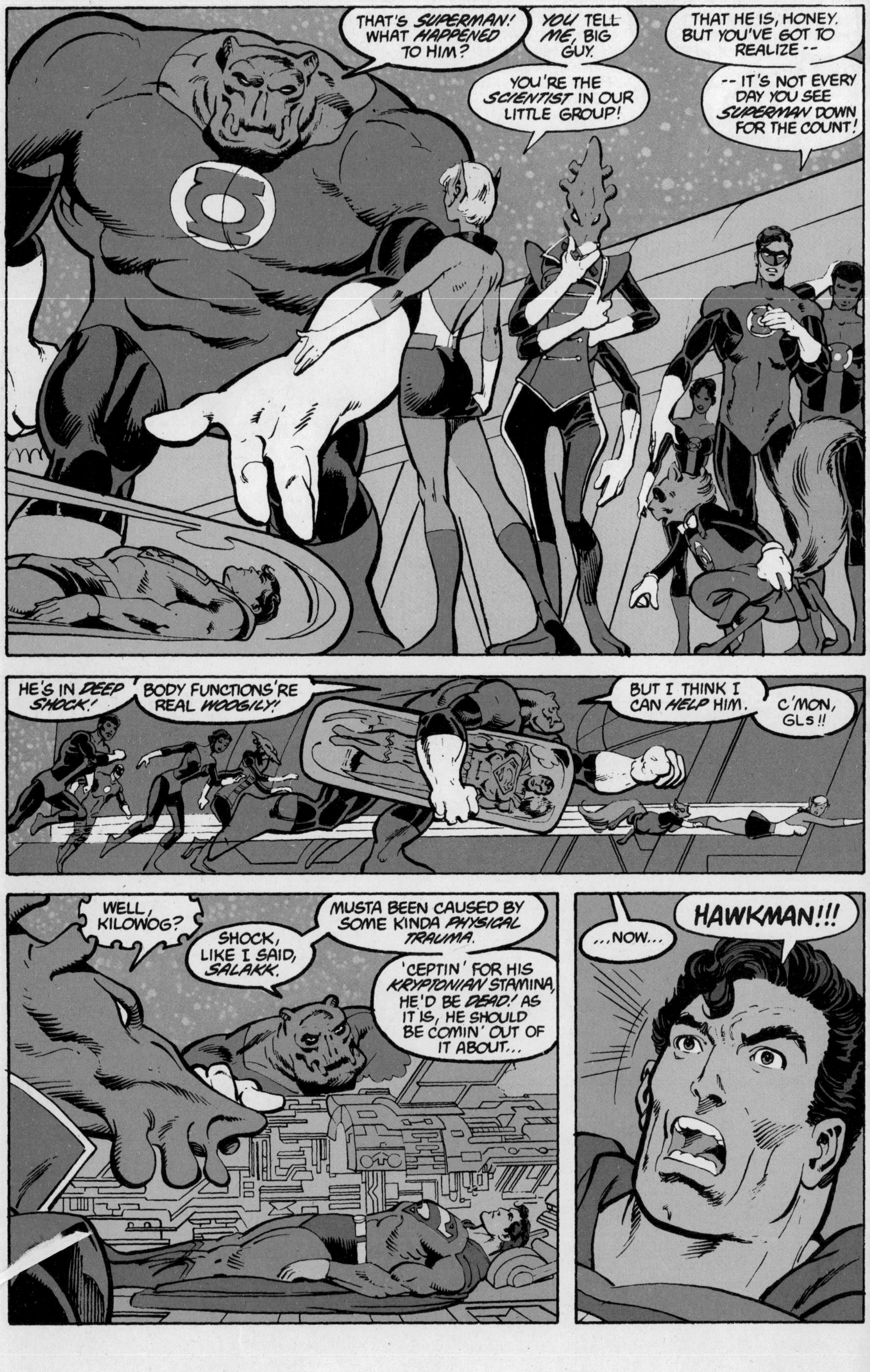

THAT'S SUPERMAN! WHAT HAPPENED TO HIM?
YOU TELL ME, BIG GUY.
YOU'RE THE SCIENTIST IN OUR LITTLE GROUP!
THAT HE IS, HONEY. BUT YOU'VE GOT TO REALIZE --
-- IT'S NOT EVERY DAY YOU SEE SUPERMAN DOWN FOR THE COUNT!
HE'S IN DEEP SHOCK!
BODY FUNCTIONS'RE REAL WOOGILY!
BUT I THINK I CAN HELP HIM.
C'MON, GLs!!
WELL, KILOWOG?
SHOCK, LIKE I SAID, SALAKK.
MUSTA BEEN CAUSED BY SOME KINDA PHYSICAL TRAUMA.
'CEPTIN' FOR HIS KRYPTONIAN STAMINA, HE'D BE DEAD! AS IT IS, HE SHOULD BE COMIN' OUT OF IT ABOUT...
...NOW...
HAWKMAN!!!

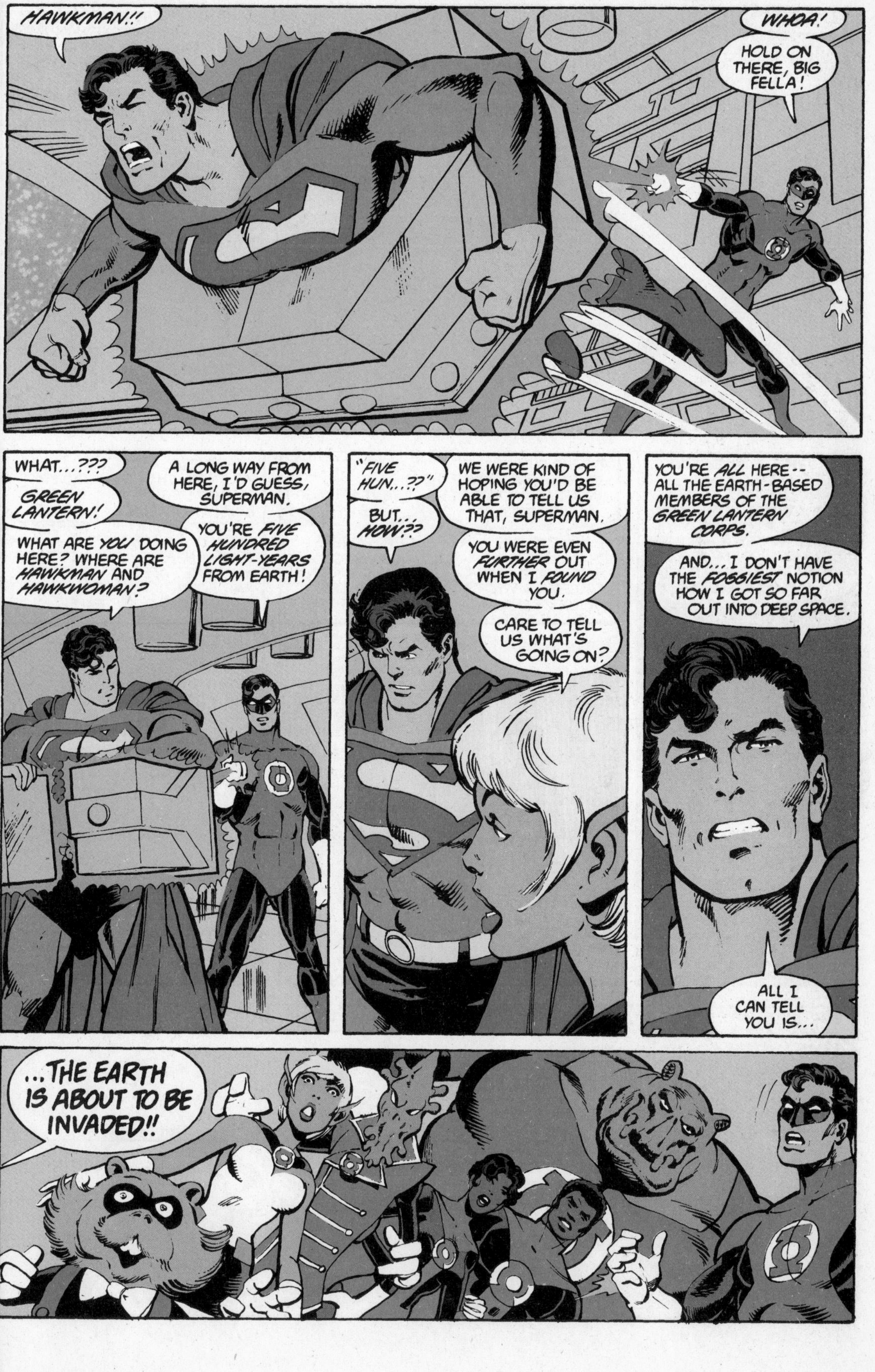
HAWKMAN!!
WHOA!
HOLD ON THERE, BIG FELLA!
WHAT...???
GREEN LANTERN!
WHAT ARE YOU DOING HERE? WHERE ARE HAWKMAN AND HAWKWOMAN?
A LONG WAY FROM HERE, I'D GUESS, SUPERMAN.
YOU'RE FIVE HUNDRED LIGHT-YEARS FROM EARTH!
"FIVE HUN...??"
BUT... HOW??
WE WERE KIND OF HOPING YOU'D BE ABLE TO TELL US THAT, SUPERMAN.
YOU WERE EVEN FURTHER OUT WHEN I FOUND YOU.
CARE TO TELL US WHAT'S GOING ON?
YOU'RE ALL HERE-- ALL THE EARTH-BASED MEMBERS OF THE GREEN LANTERN CORPS.
AND... I DON'T HAVE THE FOGGIEST NOTION HOW I GOT SO FAR OUT INTO DEEP SPACE.
ALL I CAN TELL YOU IS...
...THE EARTH IS ABOUT TO BE INVADED!!

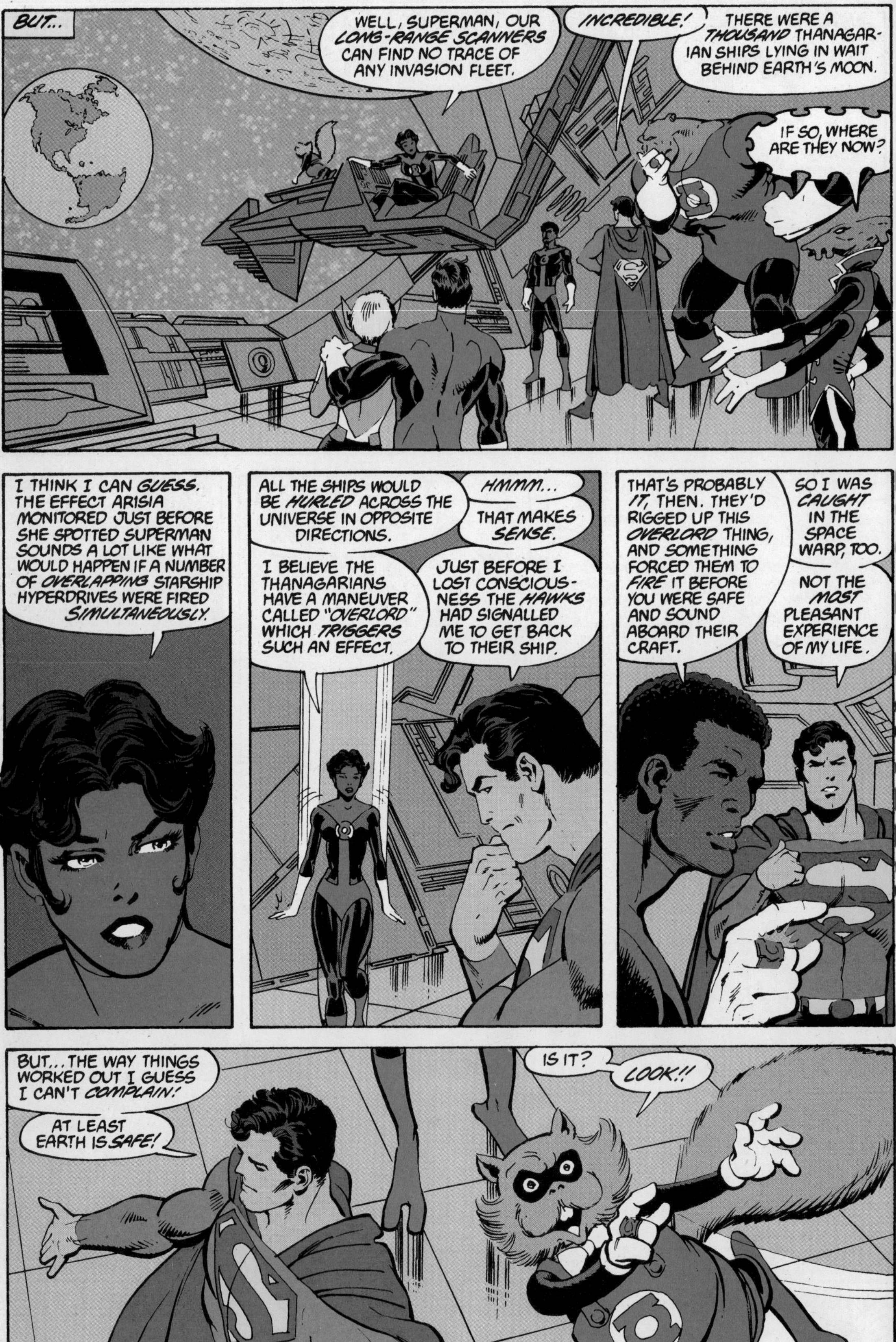
BUT...
WELL, SUPERMAN, OUR LONG-RANGE SCANNERS CAN FIND NO TRACE OF ANY INVASION FLEET.
INCREDIBLE!
THERE WERE A THOUSAND THANAGAR-IAN SHIPS LYING IN WAIT BEHIND EARTH'S MOON.
IF SO, WHERE ARE THEY NOW?
I THINK I CAN GUESS. THE EFFECT ARISIA MONITORED JUST BEFORE SHE SPOTTED SUPERMAN SOUNDS A LOT LIKE WHAT WOULD HAPPEN IF A NUMBER OF OVERLAPPING STARSHIP HYPERDRIVES WERE FIRED SIMULTANEOUSLY.
ALL THE SHIPS WOULD BE HURLED ACROSS THE UNIVERSE IN OPPOSITE DIRECTIONS.
HMMM...
THAT MAKES SENSE.
I BELIEVE THE THANAGARIANS HAVE A MANEUVER CALLED "OVERLORD" WHICH TRIGGERS SUCH AN EFFECT.
JUST BEFORE I LOST CONSCIOUS-NESS THE HAWKS HAD SIGNALLED ME TO GET BACK TO THEIR SHIP.
THAT'S PROBABLY IT, THEN. THEY'D RIGGED UP THIS OVERLORD THING, AND SOMETHING FORCED THEM TO FIRE IT BEFORE YOU WERE SAFE AND SOUND ABOARD THEIR CRAFT.
SO I WAS CAUGHT IN THE SPACE WARP, TOO.
NOT THE MOST PLEASANT EXPERIENCE OF MY LIFE.
BUT... THE WAY THINGS WORKED OUT I GUESS I CAN'T COMPLAIN!
AT LEAST EARTH IS SAFE!
IS IT?
LOOK!!

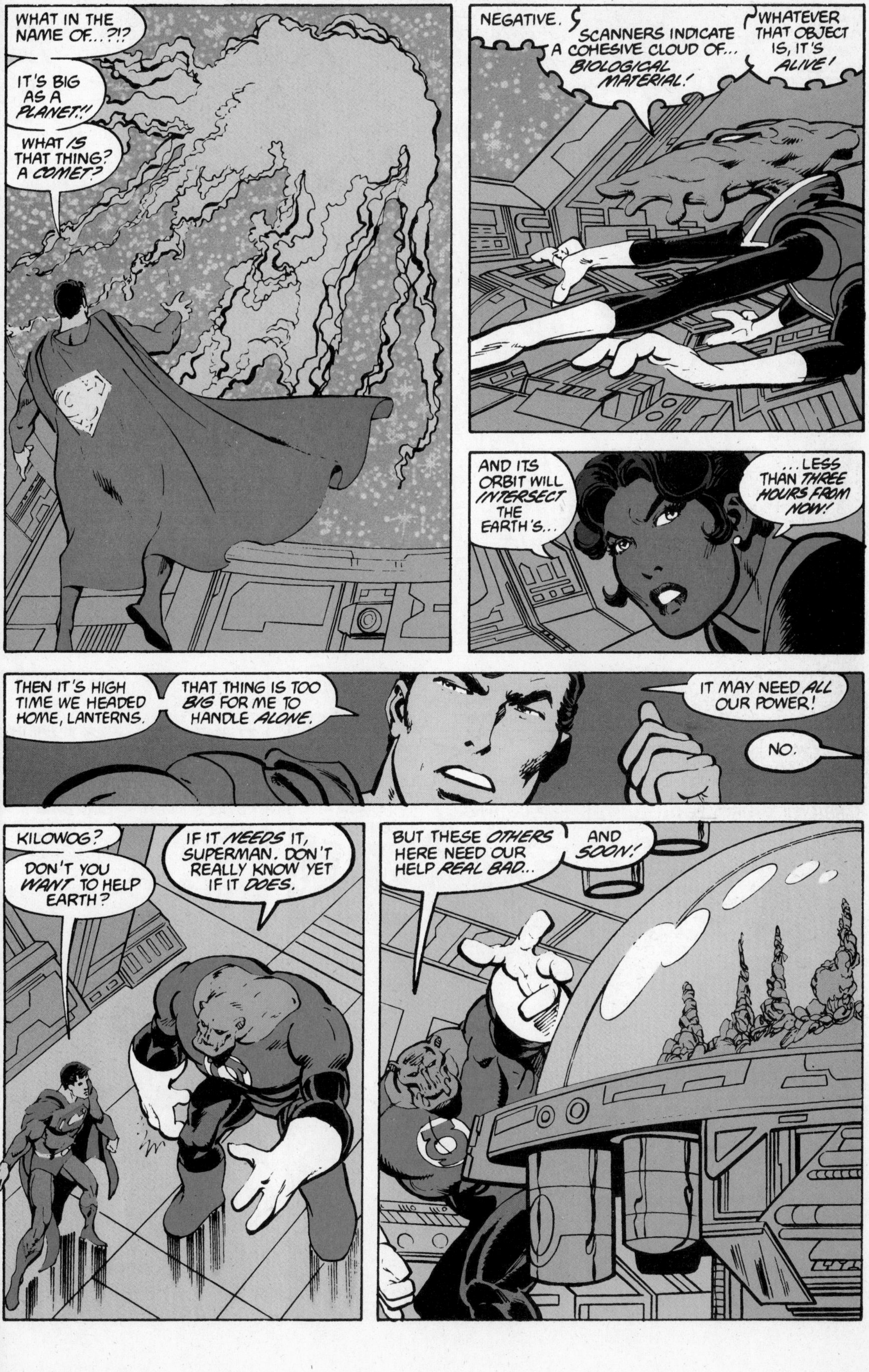

WHAT IN THE NAME OF...?!?
IT'S BIG AS A PLANET!!
WHAT IS THAT THING? A COMET?
NEGATIVE.
SCANNERS INDICATE A COHESIVE CLOUD OF... BIOLOGICAL MATERIAL!
WHATEVER THAT OBJECT IS, IT'S ALIVE!
AND ITS ORBIT WILL INTERSECT THE EARTH'S...
...LESS THAN THREE HOURS FROM NOW!
THEN IT'S HIGH TIME WE HEADED HOME, LANTERNS.
THAT THING IS TOO BIG FOR ME TO HANDLE ALONE.
IT MAY NEED ALL OUR POWER!
NO.
KILOWOG?
DON'T YOU WANT TO HELP EARTH?
IF IT NEEDS IT, SUPERMAN. DON'T REALLY KNOW YET IF IT DOES.
BUT THESE OTHERS HERE NEED OUR HELP REAL BAD...
AND SOON!

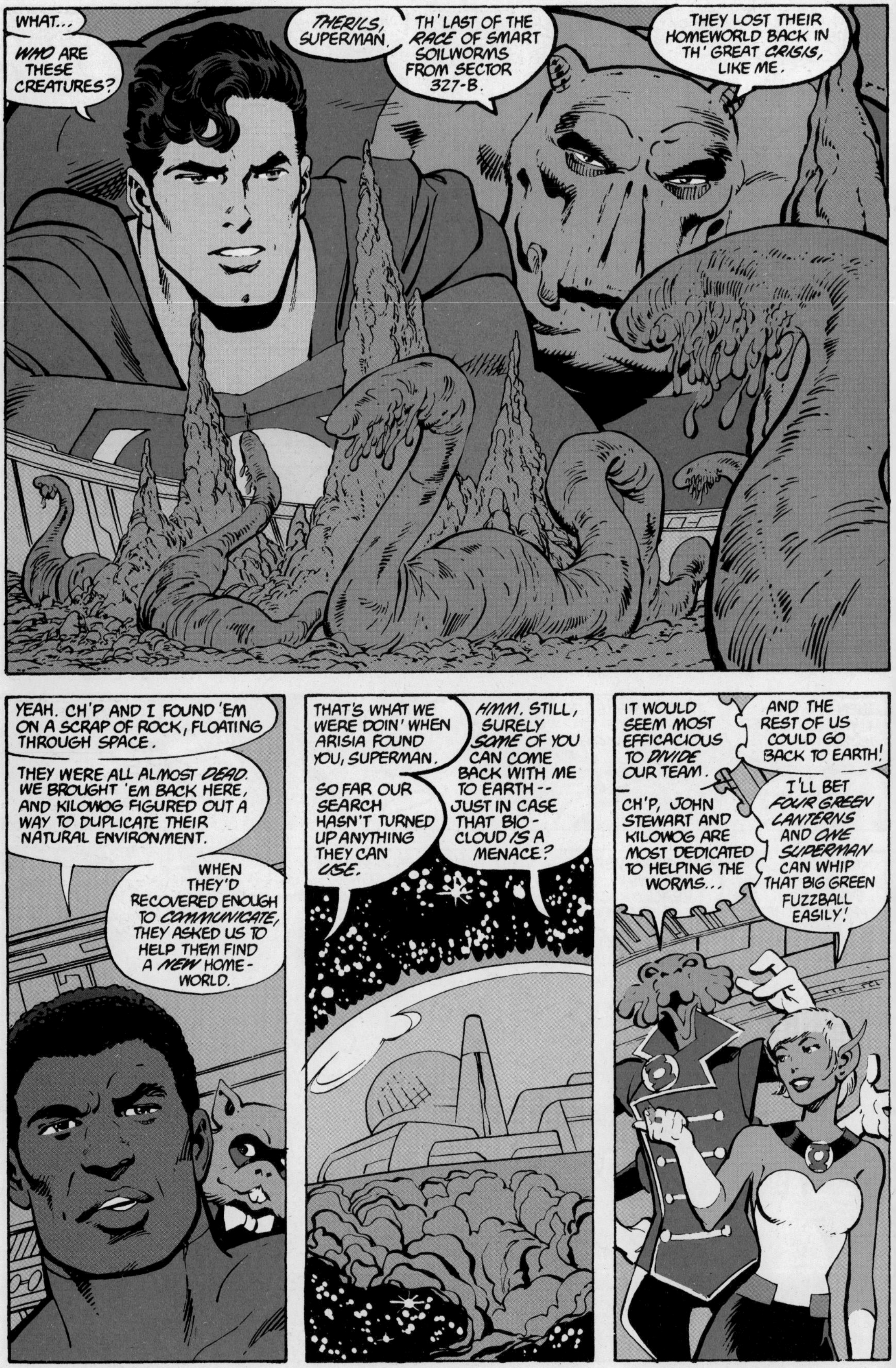

WHAT...
WHO ARE THESE CREATURES?
THERILS, SUPERMAN.
TH' LAST OF THE RACE OF SMART SOILWORMS FROM SECTOR 327-B.
THEY LOST THEIR HOMEWORLD BACK IN TH' GREAT CRISIS, LIKE ME.
YEAH. CH'P AND I FOUND 'EM ON A SCRAP OF ROCK, FLOATING THROUGH SPACE.
THEY WERE ALL ALMOST DEAD. WE BROUGHT 'EM BACK HERE, AND KILOWOG FIGURED OUT A WAY TO DUPLICATE THEIR NATURAL ENVIRONMENT.
WHEN THEY'D RECOVERED ENOUGH TO COMMUNICATE, THEY ASKED US TO HELP THEM FIND A NEW HOME-WORLD.
THAT'S WHAT WE WERE DOIN' WHEN ARISIA FOUND YOU, SUPERMAN.
SO FAR OUR SEARCH HASN'T TURNED UP ANYTHING THEY CAN USE.
HMM. STILL, SURELY SOME OF YOU CAN COME BACK WITH ME TO EARTH -- JUST IN CASE THAT BIO-CLOUD IS A MENACE?
IT WOULD SEEM MOST EFFICACIOUS TO DIVIDE OUR TEAM.
CH'P, JOHN STEWART AND KILOWOG ARE MOST DEDICATED TO HELPING THE WORMS...
AND THE REST OF US COULD GO BACK TO EARTH!
I'LL BET FOUR GREEN LANTERNS AND ONE SUPERMAN CAN WHIP THAT BIG GREEN FUZZBALL EASILY!

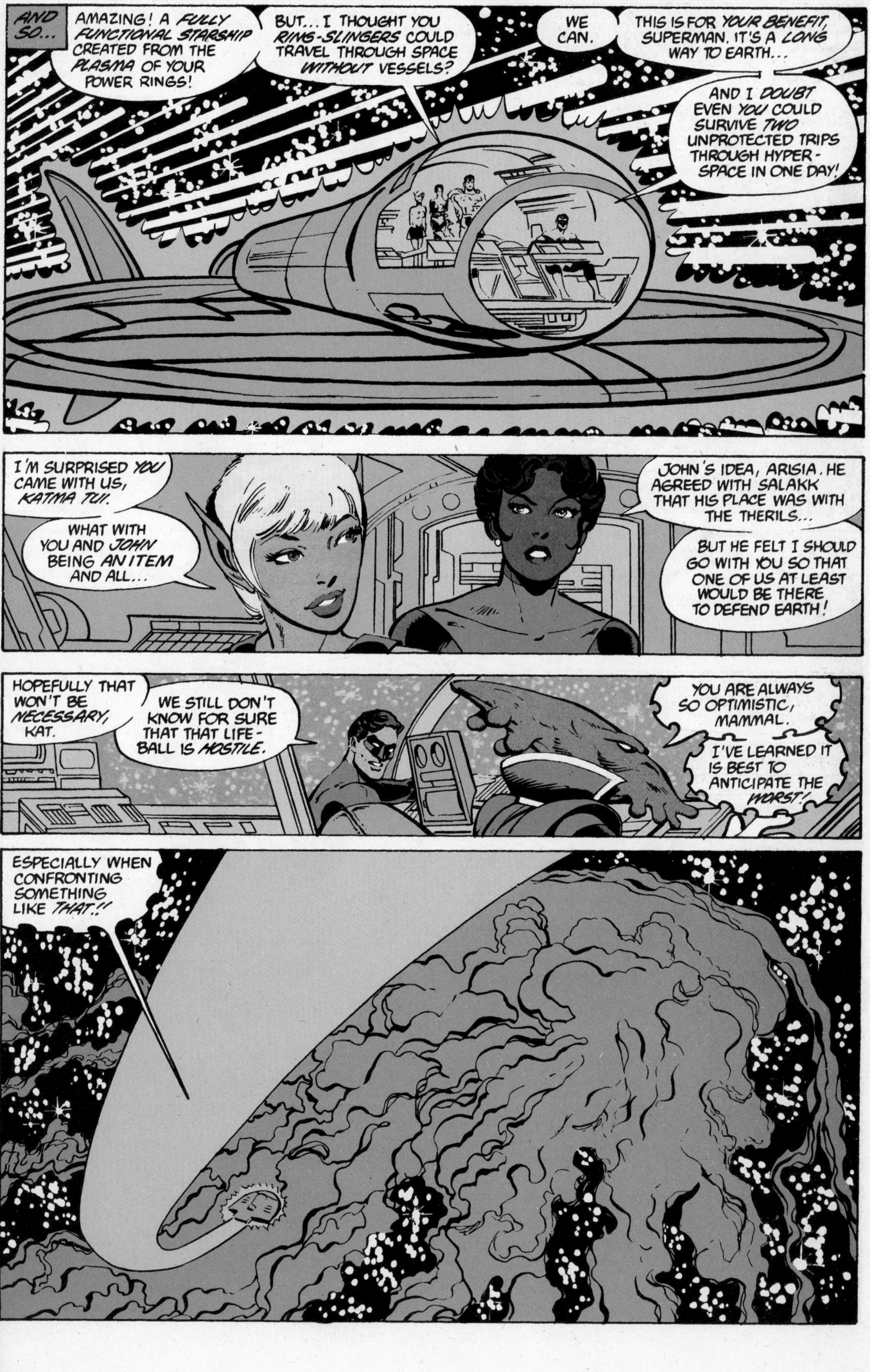
AND SO...
AMAZING! A FULLY FUNCTIONAL STARSHIP CREATED FROM THE PLASMA OF YOUR POWER RINGS!
BUT... I THOUGHT YOU RING-SLINGERS COULD TRAVEL THROUGH SPACE WITHOUT VESSELS?
WE CAN.
THIS IS FOR YOUR BENEFIT, SUPERMAN. IT'S A LONG WAY TO EARTH...
AND I DOUBT EVEN YOU COULD SURVIVE TWO UNPROTECTED TRIPS THROUGH HYPER-SPACE IN ONE DAY!
I'M SURPRISED YOU CAME WITH US, KATMA TUI.
WHAT WITH YOU AND JOHN BEING AN ITEM AND ALL...
JOHN'S IDEA, ARISIA. HE AGREED WITH SALAKK THAT HIS PLACE WAS WITH THE THERILS...
BUT HE FELT I SHOULD GO WITH YOU SO THAT ONE OF US AT LEAST WOULD BE THERE TO DEFEND EARTH!
HOPEFULLY THAT WON'T BE NECESSARY, KAT.
WE STILL DON'T KNOW FOR SURE THAT THAT LIFE-BALL IS HOSTILE.
YOU ARE ALWAYS SO OPTIMISTIC, MAMMAL.
I'VE LEARNED IT IS BEST TO ANTICIPATE THE WORST!
ESPECIALLY WHEN CONFRONTING SOMETHING LIKE THAT!!

IT'S *UN-BELIEVABLE!*

EACH OF THOSE... *TENDRILS* IS *THICKER* THAN THIS SHIP IS *WIDE...*

YET, THEY'RE *ALIVE!*

A *KIND* OF LIFE AT ANY RATE, SUPERMAN.

AT THIS CLOSER RANGE, MY SENSORS ARE COLLECTING MORE *DETAILED* INFORMATION.

AS *BIG* AS THIS OBJECT IS, IT DOES NOT APPEAR TO BE MUCH MORE *COMPLICATED* THAN SIMPLE *BACTERIA.*

ARE YOU SAYING... WAIT.

LOOK UP AHEAD! THERE'S SOMETHING *RISING* FROM THE THING'S ATMOSPHERE!

SCANNING.

AGAIN, THEY APPEAR TO BE SOME KIND OF GIGANTIC *MICROBES!*

MORE THAN JUST *MICROBES*, SALAKK!

DEFENSE ORGANISMS!

ANTIBODIES!!

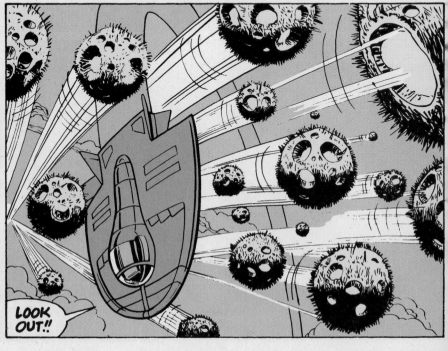

LOOK OUT!!

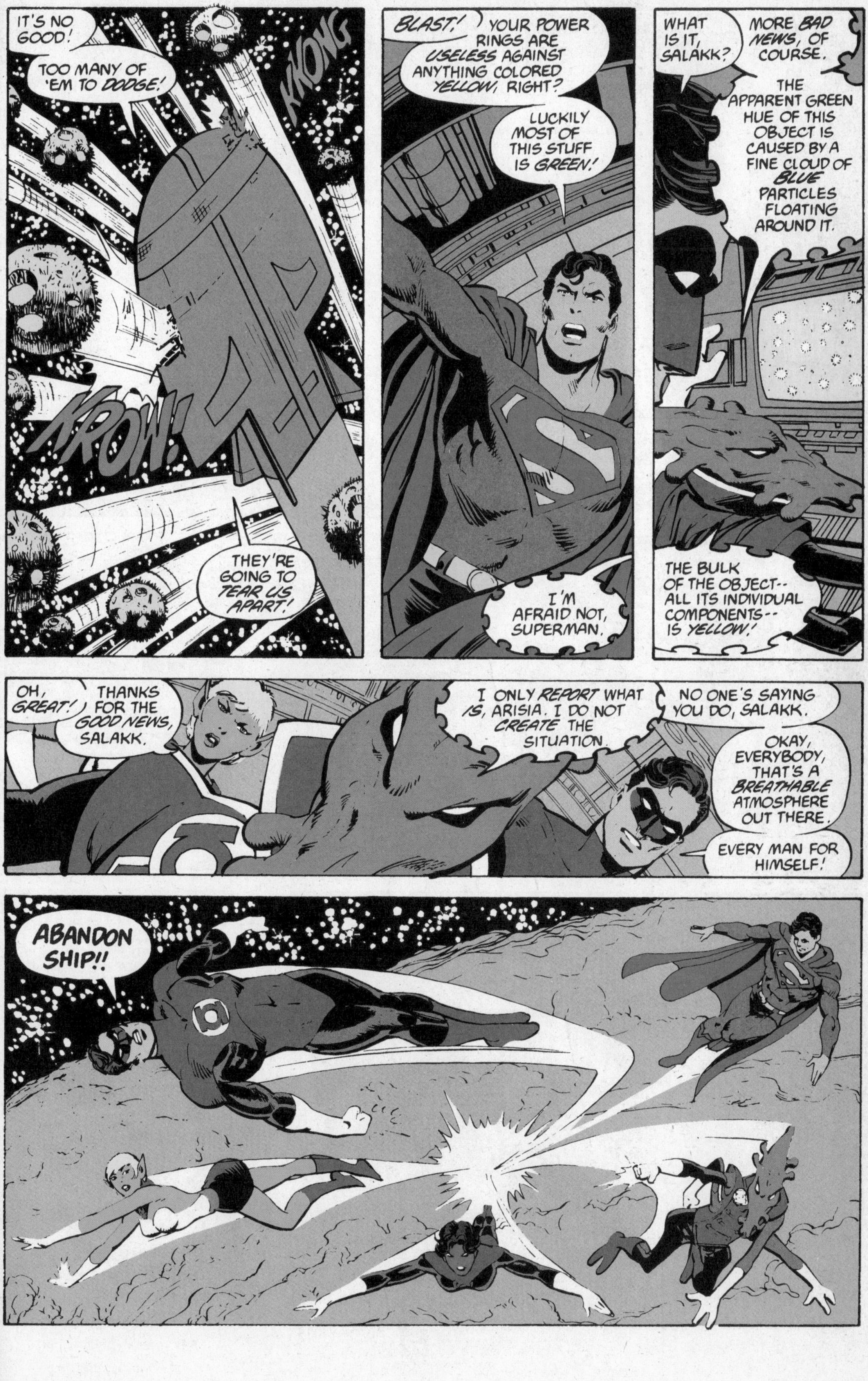
IT'S NO GOOD!
TOO MANY OF 'EM TO DODGE!
KKONG
KROW!
THEY'RE GOING TO TEAR US APART!
BLAST! YOUR POWER RINGS ARE USELESS AGAINST ANYTHING COLORED YELLOW, RIGHT?
LUCKILY MOST OF THIS STUFF IS GREEN!
I'M AFRAID NOT, SUPERMAN.
WHAT IS IT, SALAKK?
MORE BAD NEWS, OF COURSE.
THE APPARENT GREEN HUE OF THIS OBJECT IS CAUSED BY A FINE CLOUD OF BLUE PARTICLES FLOATING AROUND IT.
THE BULK OF THE OBJECT-- ALL ITS INDIVIDUAL COMPONENTS-- IS YELLOW!
OH, GREAT!
THANKS FOR THE GOOD NEWS, SALAKK.
I ONLY REPORT WHAT IS, ARISIA. I DO NOT CREATE THE SITUATION.
NO ONE'S SAYING YOU DO, SALAKK.
OKAY, EVERYBODY, THAT'S A BREATHABLE ATMOSPHERE OUT THERE.
EVERY MAN FOR HIMSELF!
ABANDON SHIP!!

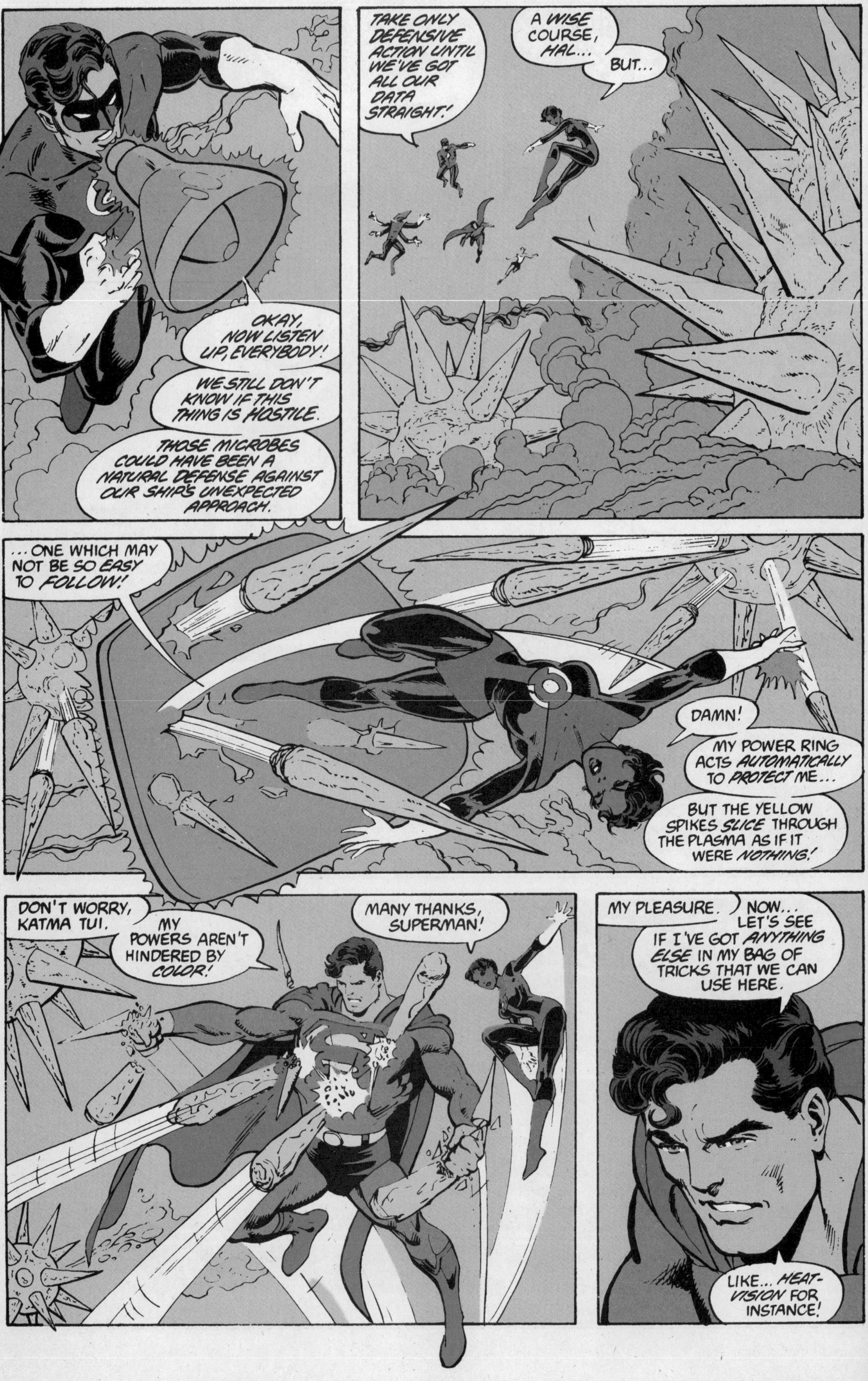
OKAY, NOW LISTEN UP, EVERYBODY!
WE STILL DON'T KNOW IF THIS THING IS HOSTILE.
THOSE MICROBES COULD HAVE BEEN A NATURAL DEFENSE AGAINST OUR SHIP'S UNEXPECTED APPROACH.
TAKE ONLY DEFENSIVE ACTION UNTIL WE'VE GOT ALL OUR DATA STRAIGHT!
A WISE COURSE, HAL...
BUT...
...ONE WHICH MAY NOT BE SO EASY TO FOLLOW!
DAMN!
MY POWER RING ACTS AUTOMATICALLY TO PROTECT ME...
BUT THE YELLOW SPIKES SLICE THROUGH THE PLASMA AS IF IT WERE NOTHING!
DON'T WORRY, KATMA TUI.
MY POWERS AREN'T HINDERED BY COLOR!
MANY THANKS, SUPERMAN!
MY PLEASURE.
NOW... LET'S SEE IF I'VE GOT ANYTHING ELSE IN MY BAG OF TRICKS THAT WE CAN USE HERE.
LIKE... HEAT-VISION FOR INSTANCE!

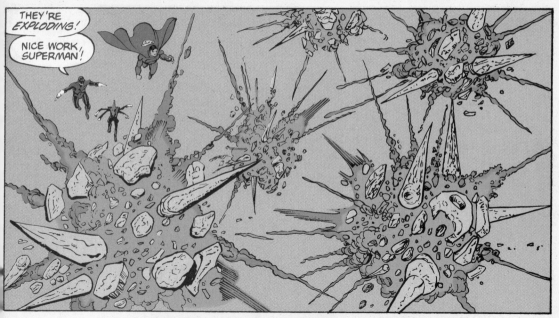

THEY'RE *EXPLODING!*

NICE WORK, SUPERMAN*!*

HMPH. TELEKINETIC AGITATION OF THEIR *MOLECULES?*

IMPRESSIVE ON A *SMALL SCALE...*

BUT I DOUBT IT WILL BE TERRIBLY EFFECTIVE AGAINST THE *WHOLE* OBJECT, SUPERMAN.

SALA-A-A-AKK!

DO YOU *HAVE TO* SEE THE *BLEAK SIDE* OF *EVERYTHING,* YOU BIG *GRUMP?*

I MERELY INDICATE THE *OBVI--*

ARISIA!!

OH-HHH!

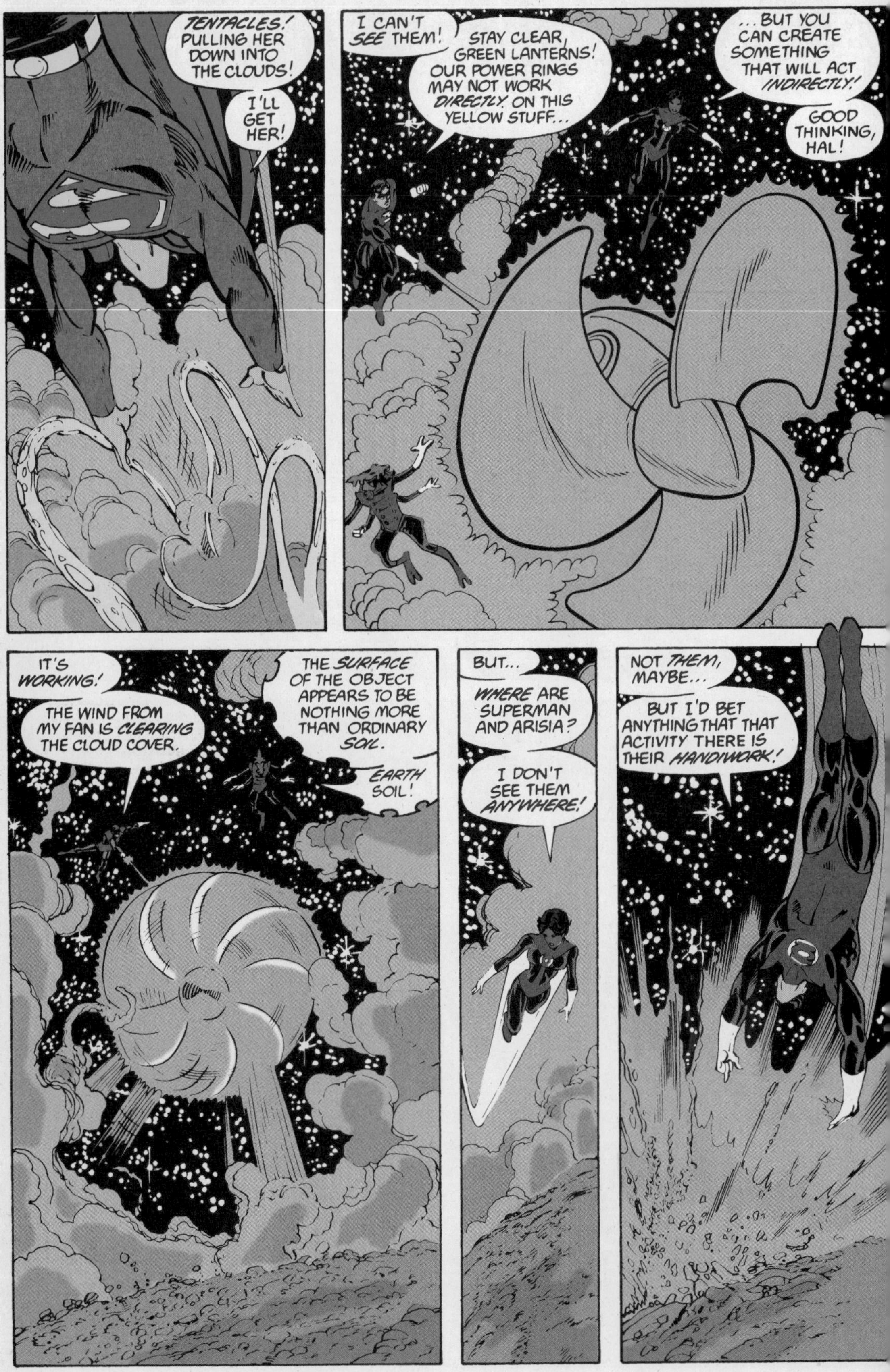

TENTACLES! PULLING HER DOWN INTO THE CLOUDS!
I'LL GET HER!
I CAN'T SEE THEM!
STAY CLEAR, GREEN LANTERNS! OUR POWER RINGS MAY NOT WORK DIRECTLY ON THIS YELLOW STUFF...
...BUT YOU CAN CREATE SOMETHING THAT WILL ACT INDIRECTLY!
GOOD THINKING, HAL!
IT'S WORKING!
THE WIND FROM MY FAN IS CLEARING THE CLOUD COVER.
THE SURFACE OF THE OBJECT APPEARS TO BE NOTHING MORE THAN ORDINARY SOIL.
EARTH SOIL!
BUT...
WHERE ARE SUPERMAN AND ARISIA?
I DON'T SEE THEM ANYWHERE!
NOT THEM, MAYBE...
BUT I'D BET ANYTHING THAT THAT ACTIVITY THERE IS THEIR HANDIWORK!

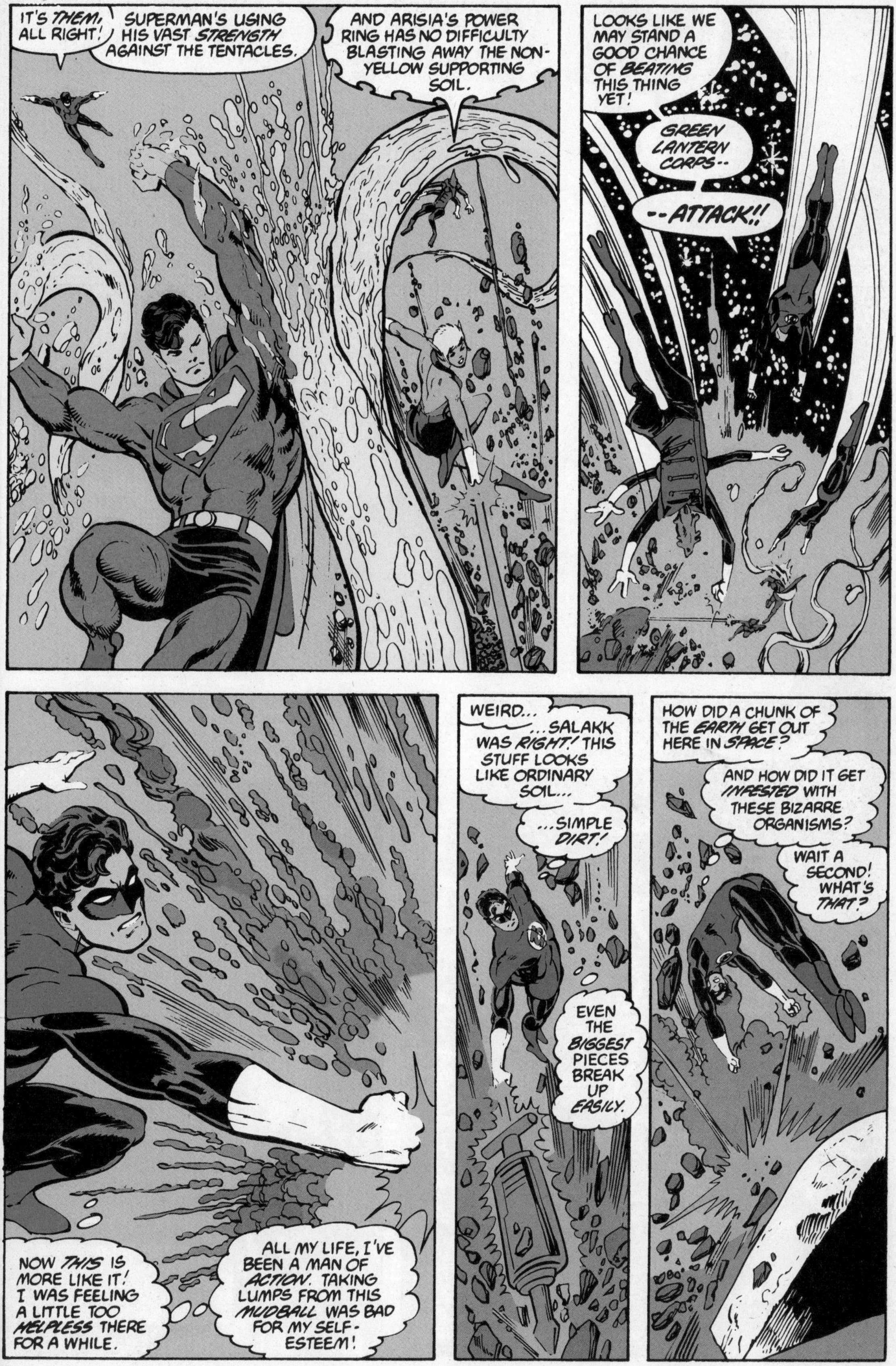
IT'S THEM, ALL RIGHT!
SUPERMAN'S USING HIS VAST STRENGTH AGAINST THE TENTACLES.
AND ARISIA'S POWER RING HAS NO DIFFICULTY BLASTING AWAY THE NON-YELLOW SUPPORTING SOIL.
LOOKS LIKE WE MAY STAND A GOOD CHANCE OF BEATING THIS THING YET!
GREEN LANTERN CORPS--
--ATTACK!!
NOW THIS IS MORE LIKE IT! I WAS FEELING A LITTLE TOO HELPLESS THERE FOR A WHILE.
ALL MY LIFE, I'VE BEEN A MAN OF ACTION. TAKING LUMPS FROM THIS MUDBALL WAS BAD FOR MY SELF-ESTEEM!
WEIRD...
...SALAKK WAS RIGHT! THIS STUFF LOOKS LIKE ORDINARY SOIL...
...SIMPLE DIRT!
EVEN THE BIGGEST PIECES BREAK UP EASILY.
HOW DID A CHUNK OF THE EARTH GET OUT HERE IN SPACE?
AND HOW DID IT GET INFESTED WITH THESE BIZARRE ORGANISMS?
WAIT A SECOND! WHAT'S THAT?

GREAT GUARDIANS!

IT'S A HUMAN GRAVE MARKER!

A TOMBSTONE!!

VINCKMAN ROMLEY 1915-1981

A... WHAT!?!

GOOD LORD!!

I KNOW WHAT THIS THING IS!!!

"SEVERAL WEEKS AGO I HELPED THE PHANTOM STRANGER BATTLE A MYSTICAL FORCE THAT HAD ANIMATED A PRISON GRAVEYARD.

"THE FORCE HAD DRAWN ON THE FESTERING EVIL OF THE EXECUTED CRIMINALS BURIED IN THAT UNHALLOWED PLOT.

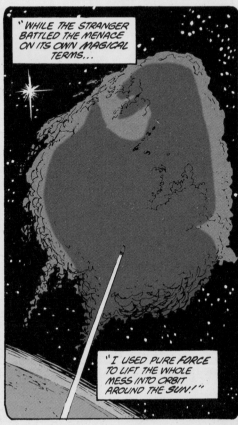

"WHILE THE STRANGER BATTLED THE MENACE ON ITS OWN MAGICAL TERMS...

"I USED PURE FORCE TO LIFT THE WHOLE MESS INTO ORBIT AROUND THE SUN!"

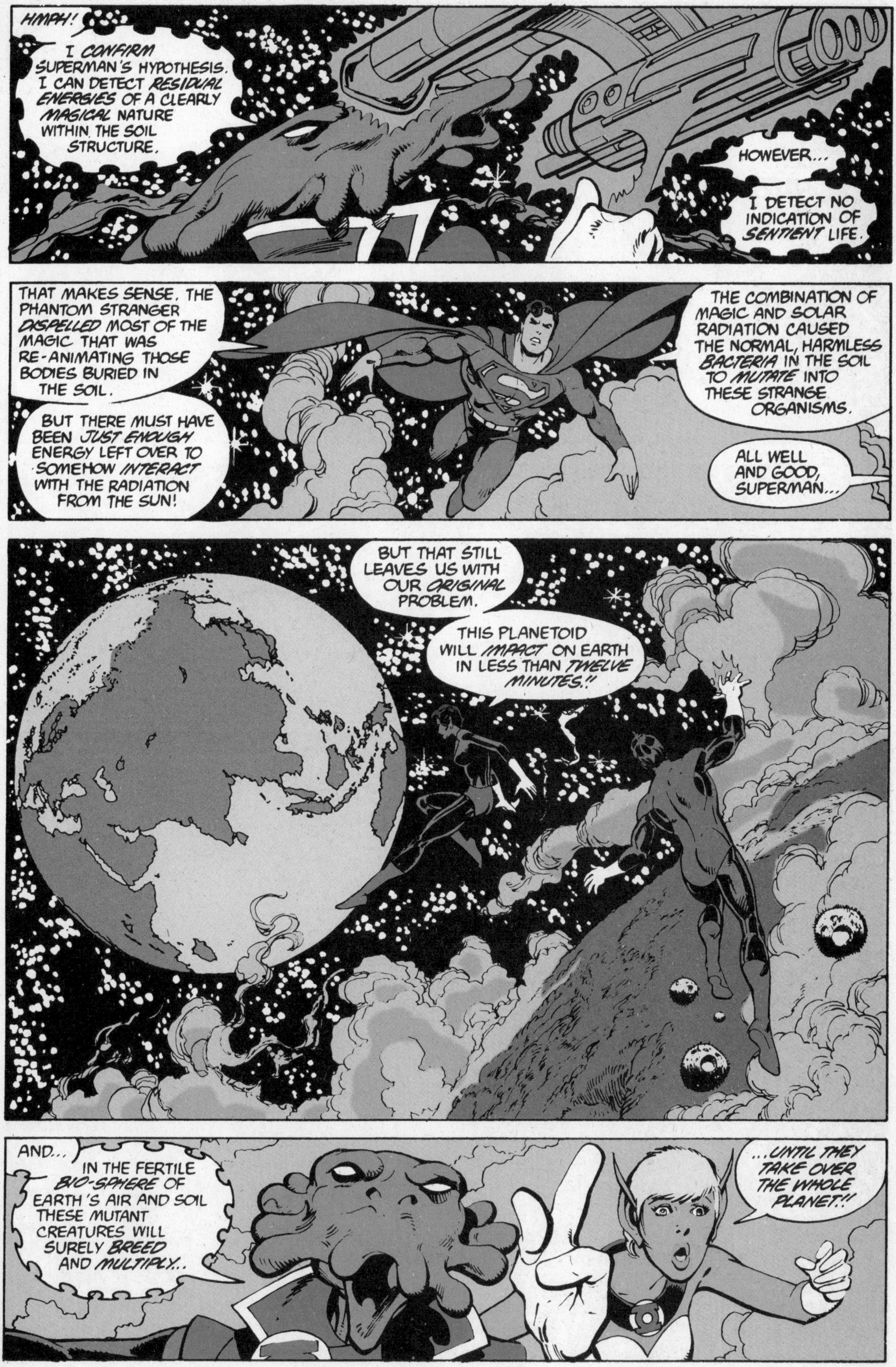
HMPH!
I CONFIRM SUPERMAN'S HYPOTHESIS. I CAN DETECT RESIDUAL ENERGIES OF A CLEARLY MAGICAL NATURE WITHIN THE SOIL STRUCTURE.
HOWEVER...
I DETECT NO INDICATION OF SENTIENT LIFE.
THAT MAKES SENSE. THE PHANTOM STRANGER DISPELLED MOST OF THE MAGIC THAT WAS RE-ANIMATING THOSE BODIES BURIED IN THE SOIL.
BUT THERE MUST HAVE BEEN JUST ENOUGH ENERGY LEFT OVER TO SOMEHOW INTERACT WITH THE RADIATION FROM THE SUN!
THE COMBINATION OF MAGIC AND SOLAR RADIATION CAUSED THE NORMAL, HARMLESS BACTERIA IN THE SOIL TO MUTATE INTO THESE STRANGE ORGANISMS.
ALL WELL AND GOOD, SUPERMAN...
BUT THAT STILL LEAVES US WITH OUR ORIGINAL PROBLEM.
THIS PLANETOID WILL IMPACT ON EARTH IN LESS THAN TWELVE MINUTES!!
AND...
IN THE FERTILE BIO-SPHERE OF EARTH'S AIR AND SOIL THESE MUTANT CREATURES WILL SURELY BREED AND MULTIPLY..
...UNTIL THEY TAKE OVER THE WHOLE PLANET!!

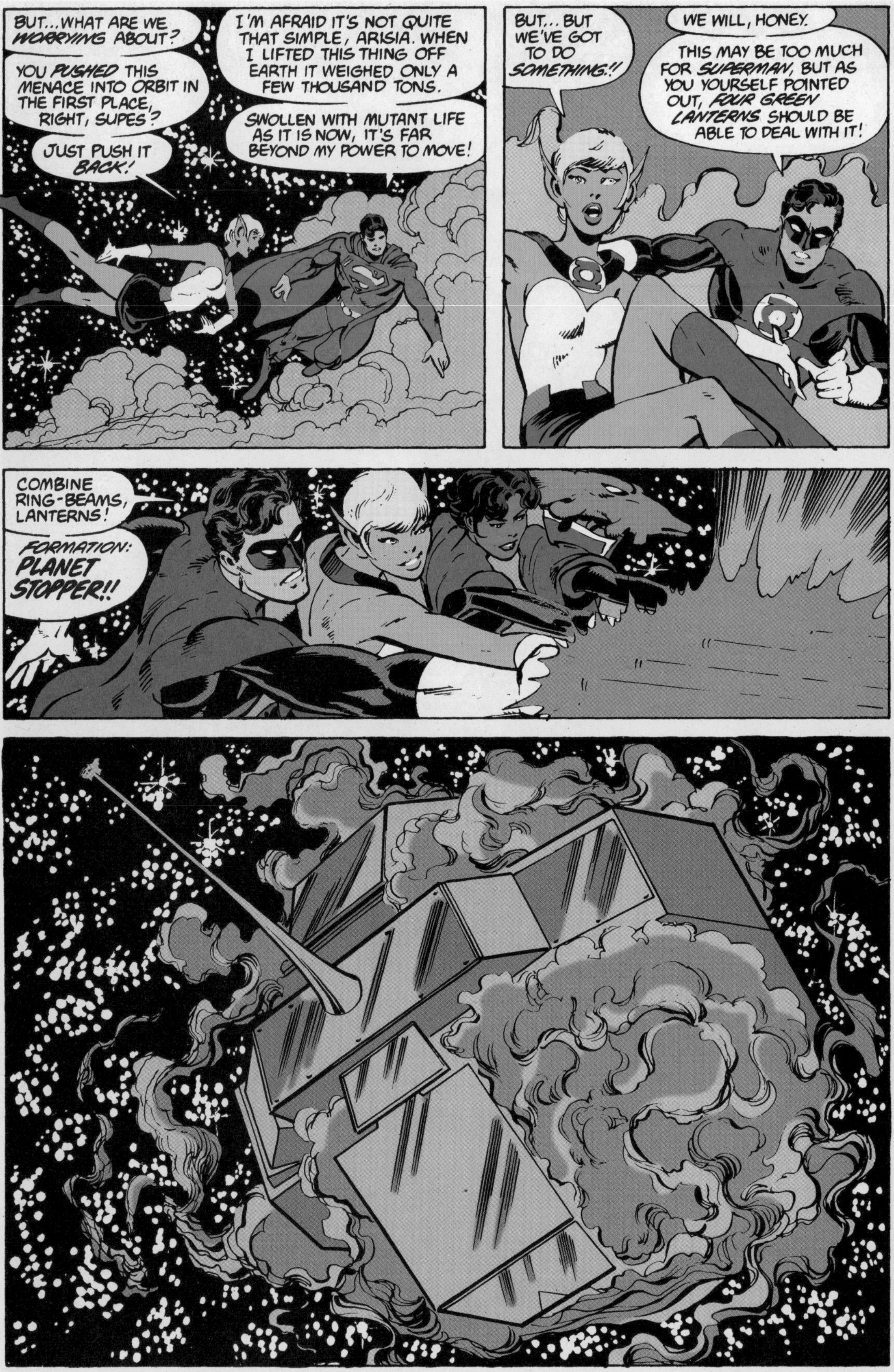
BUT...WHAT ARE WE *WORRYING* ABOUT?
YOU *PUSHED* THIS MENACE INTO ORBIT IN THE FIRST PLACE, RIGHT, SUPES?
JUST PUSH IT *BACK!*
I'M AFRAID IT'S NOT QUITE THAT SIMPLE, ARISIA. WHEN I LIFTED THIS THING OFF EARTH IT WEIGHED ONLY A FEW THOUSAND TONS.
SWOLLEN WITH MUTANT LIFE AS IT IS NOW, IT'S FAR BEYOND MY POWER TO MOVE!
BUT... BUT WE'VE GOT TO DO *SOMETHING!!*
WE WILL, HONEY.
THIS MAY BE TOO MUCH FOR *SUPERMAN*, BUT AS YOU YOURSELF POINTED OUT, *FOUR GREEN LANTERNS* SHOULD BE ABLE TO DEAL WITH IT!
COMBINE RING-BEAMS, LANTERNS!
FORMATION: **PLANET STOPPER!!**

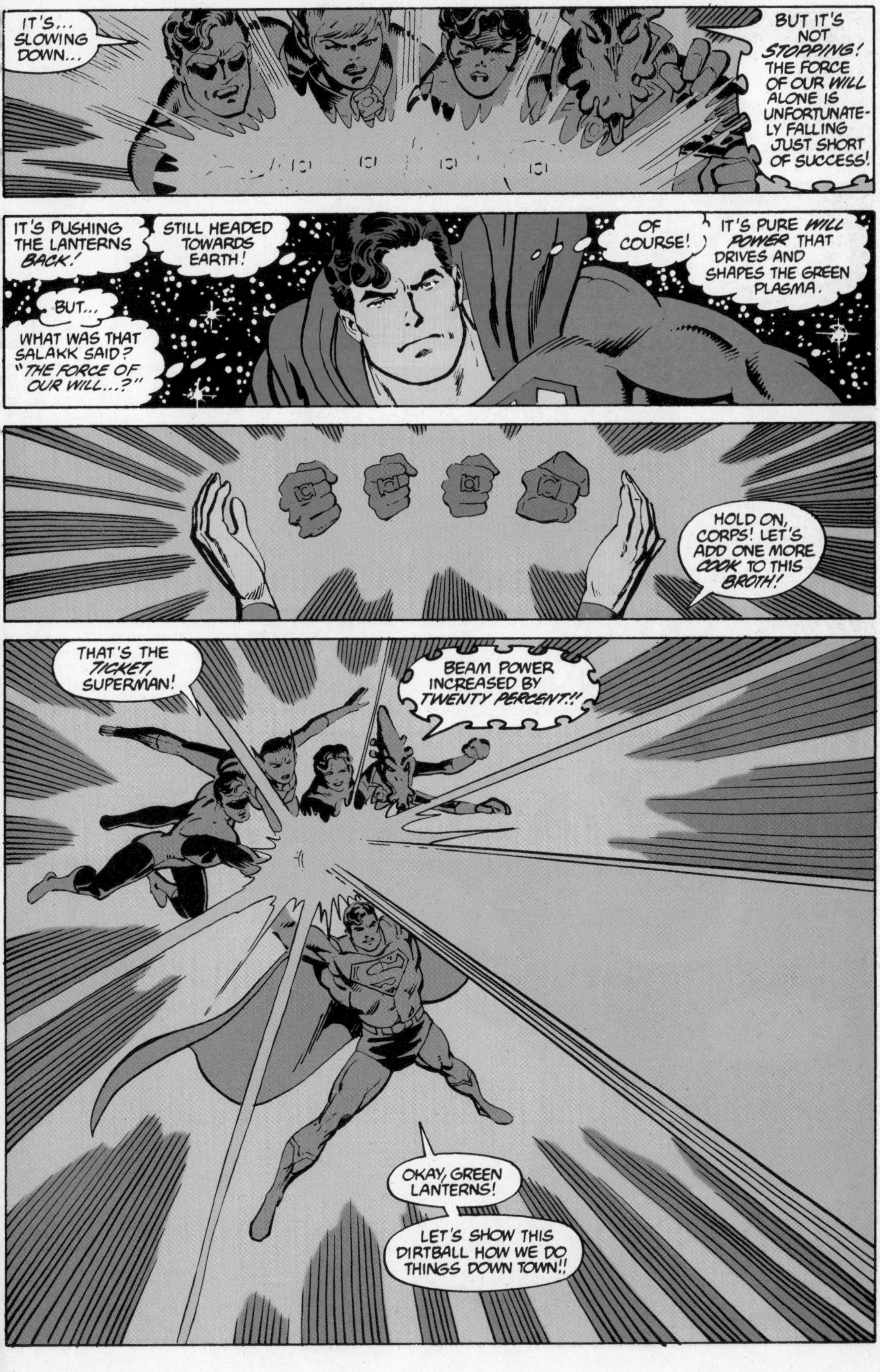
IT'S... SLOWING DOWN...
BUT IT'S NOT STOPPING! THE FORCE OF OUR WILL ALONE IS UNFORTUNATE-LY FALLING JUST SHORT OF SUCCESS!
IT'S PUSHING THE LANTERNS BACK!
STILL HEADED TOWARDS EARTH!
BUT...
WHAT WAS THAT SALAKK SAID? "THE FORCE OF OUR WILL...?"
OF COURSE!
IT'S PURE WILL POWER THAT DRIVES AND SHAPES THE GREEN PLASMA.
HOLD ON, CORPS! LET'S ADD ONE MORE COOK TO THIS BROTH!
THAT'S THE TICKET, SUPERMAN!
BEAM POWER INCREASED BY TWENTY PERCENT!!
OKAY, GREEN LANTERNS!
LET'S SHOW THIS DIRTBALL HOW WE DO THINGS DOWN TOWN!!

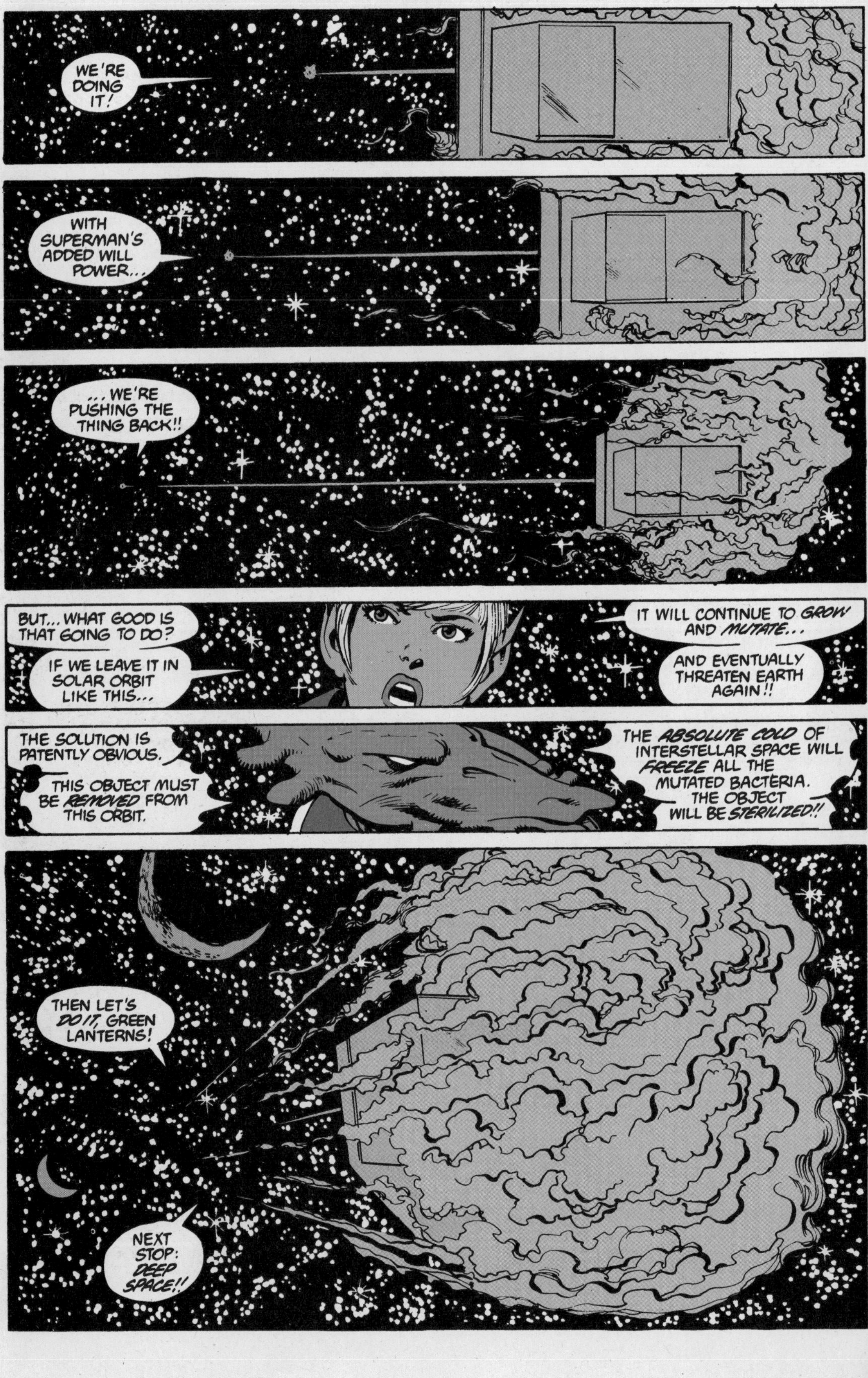
WE'RE DOING IT!
WITH SUPERMAN'S ADDED WILL POWER...
...WE'RE PUSHING THE THING BACK!!
BUT... WHAT GOOD IS THAT GOING TO DO?
IF WE LEAVE IT IN SOLAR ORBIT LIKE THIS...
IT WILL CONTINUE TO GROW AND MUTATE...
AND EVENTUALLY THREATEN EARTH AGAIN!!
THE SOLUTION IS PATENTLY OBVIOUS.
THIS OBJECT MUST BE REMOVED FROM THIS ORBIT.
THE ABSOLUTE COLD OF INTERSTELLAR SPACE WILL FREEZE ALL THE MUTATED BACTERIA. THE OBJECT WILL BE STERILIZED!!
THEN LET'S DO IT, GREEN LANTERNS!
NEXT STOP: DEEP SPACE!!

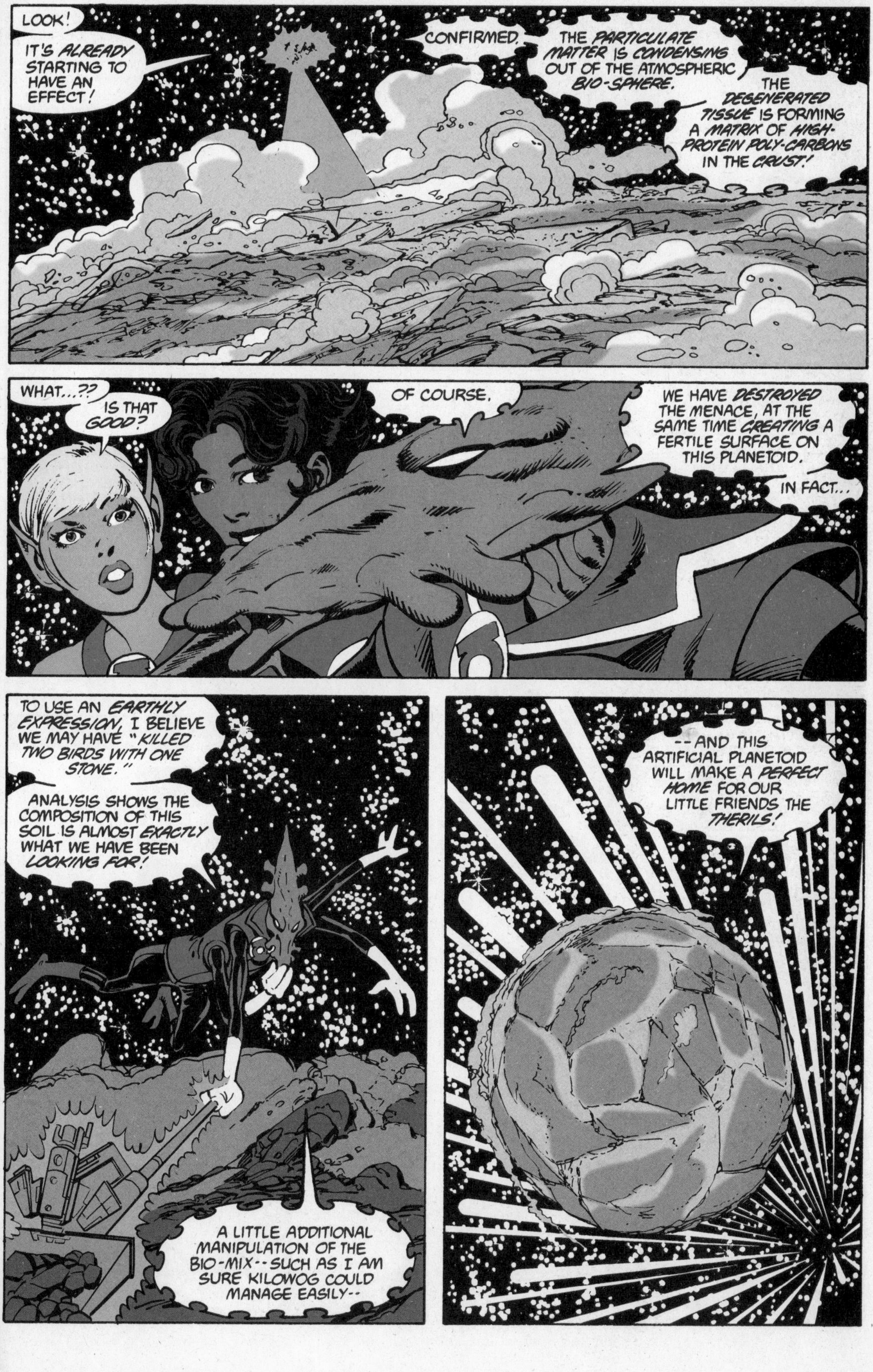
LOOK!
IT'S ALREADY STARTING TO HAVE AN EFFECT!
CONFIRMED.
THE PARTICULATE MATTER IS CONDENSING OUT OF THE ATMOSPHERIC BIO-SPHERE.
THE DEGENERATED TISSUE IS FORMING A MATRIX OF HIGH-PROTEIN POLY-CARBONS IN THE CRUST!
WHAT...??
IS THAT GOOD?
OF COURSE.
WE HAVE DESTROYED THE MENACE, AT THE SAME TIME CREATING A FERTILE SURFACE ON THIS PLANETOID.
IN FACT...
TO USE AN EARTHLY EXPRESSION, I BELIEVE WE MAY HAVE "KILLED TWO BIRDS WITH ONE STONE."
ANALYSIS SHOWS THE COMPOSITION OF THIS SOIL IS ALMOST EXACTLY WHAT WE HAVE BEEN LOOKING FOR!
A LITTLE ADDITIONAL MANIPULATION OF THE BIO-MIX--SUCH AS I AM SURE KILOWOG COULD MANAGE EASILY--
--AND THIS ARTIFICIAL PLANETOID WILL MAKE A PERFECT HOME FOR OUR LITTLE FRIENDS THE THERILS!

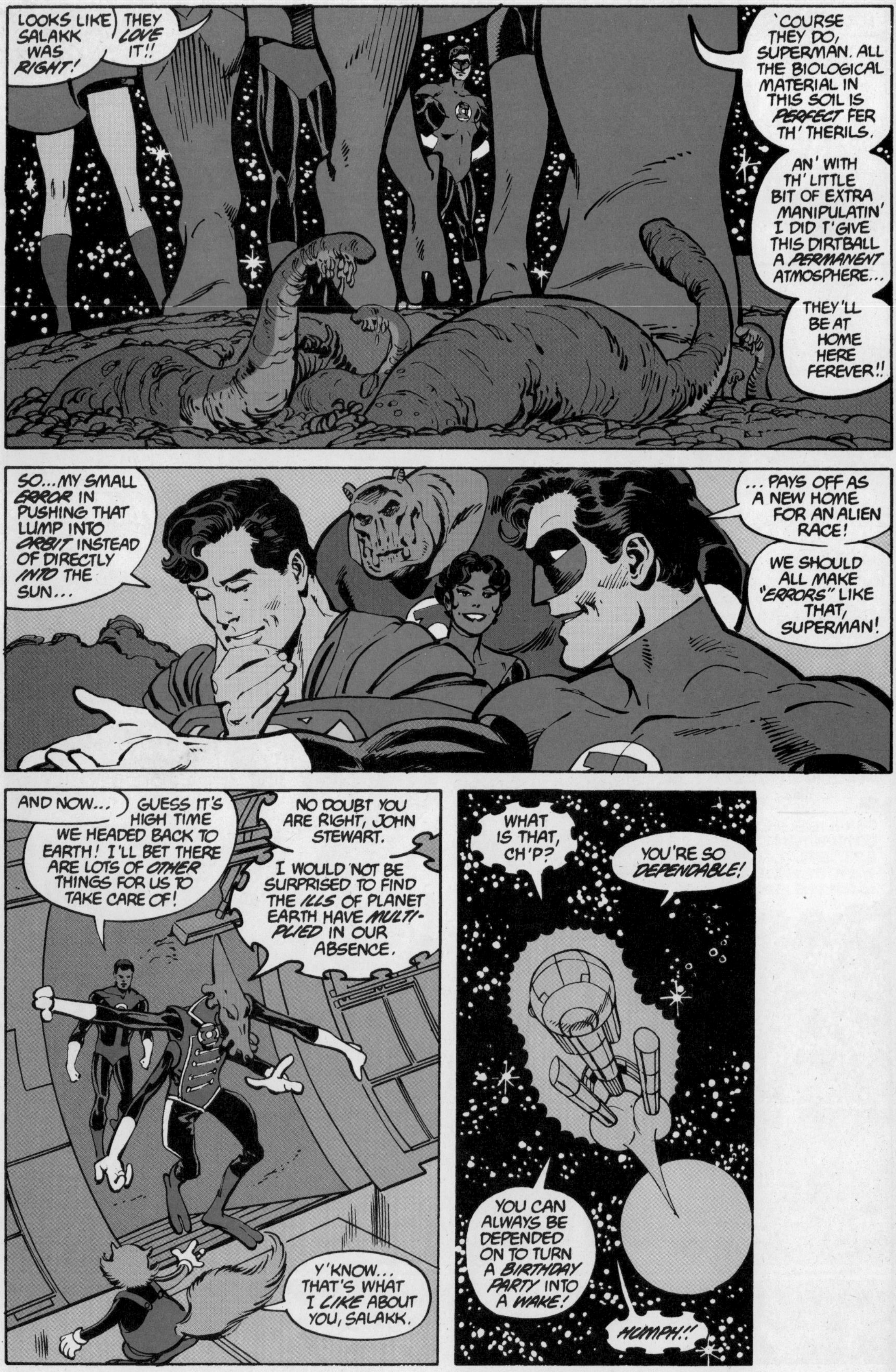

LOOKS LIKE SALAKK WAS RIGHT!
THEY LOVE IT!!
'COURSE THEY DO, SUPERMAN. ALL THE BIOLOGICAL MATERIAL IN THIS SOIL IS PERFECT FER TH' THERILS.
AN' WITH TH' LITTLE BIT OF EXTRA MANIPULATIN' I DID T'GIVE THIS DIRTBALL A PERMANENT ATMOSPHERE...
THEY'LL BE AT HOME HERE FEREVER!!
SO...MY SMALL ERROR IN PUSHING THAT LUMP INTO ORBIT INSTEAD OF DIRECTLY INTO THE SUN...
...PAYS OFF AS A NEW HOME FOR AN ALIEN RACE!
WE SHOULD ALL MAKE "ERRORS" LIKE THAT, SUPERMAN!
AND NOW...
GUESS IT'S HIGH TIME WE HEADED BACK TO EARTH! I'LL BET THERE ARE LOTS OF OTHER THINGS FOR US TO TAKE CARE OF!
NO DOUBT YOU ARE RIGHT, JOHN STEWART.
I WOULD NOT BE SURPRISED TO FIND THE ILLS OF PLANET EARTH HAVE MULTI-PLIED IN OUR ABSENCE.
Y'KNOW... THAT'S WHAT I LIKE ABOUT YOU, SALAKK.
WHAT IS THAT, CH'P?
YOU'RE SO DEPENDABLE!
YOU CAN ALWAYS BE DEPENDED ON TO TURN A BIRTHDAY PARTY INTO A WAKE!
HUMPH!!

C O V E R S

SUPERMAN
BLOODSPORT...
...HE PLAYS FOR KEEPS!

SUPERMAN
75¢
5
MAY 87
THE MUMMY STRIKES!
BY JOHN BYRNE & KARL KESEL

SUPERMAN
75¢
6
JUNE 87
DESTROY HIM!
DESTROY SUPERMAN!
BY JOHN BYRNE & KARL KESEL

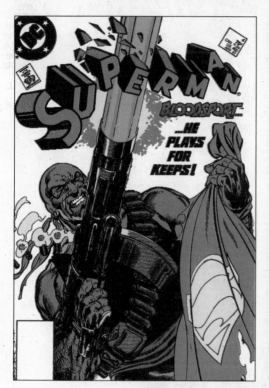

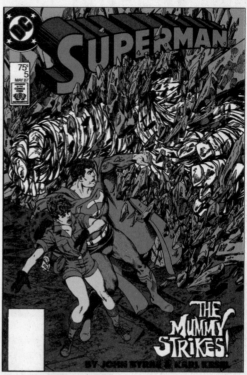

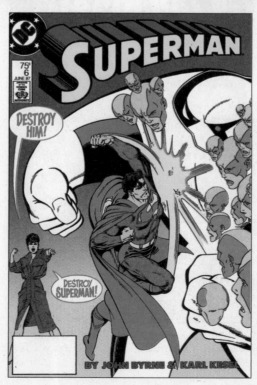

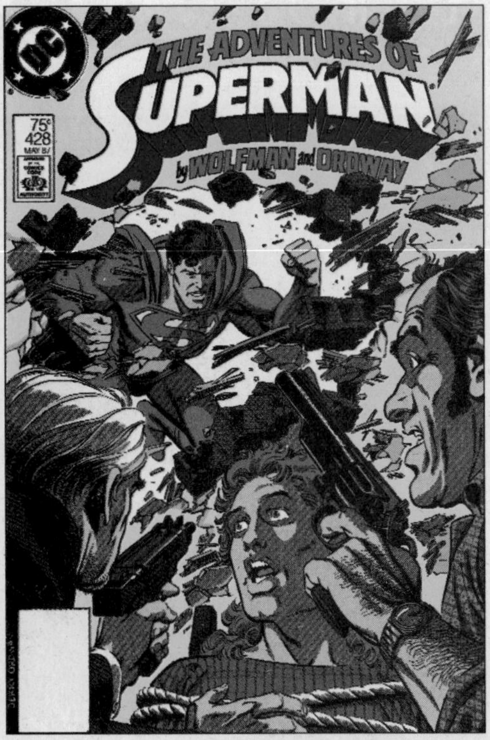
THE ADVENTURES OF
SUPERMAN
75¢
428
MAY 87
by WOLFMAN and ORDWAY

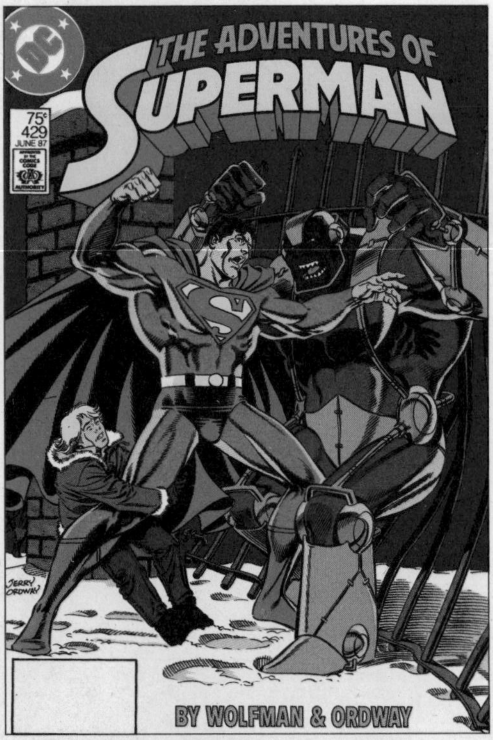
THE ADVENTURES OF
SUPERMAN
75¢
429
JUNE 87
JERRY ORDWAY
BY WOLFMAN & ORDWAY

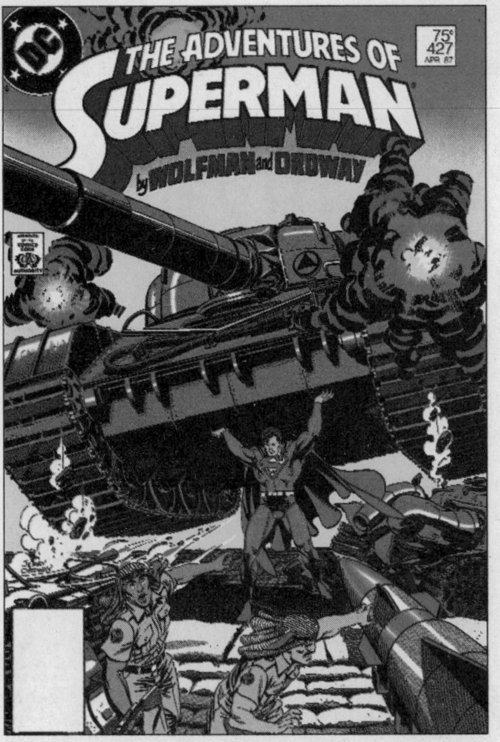
THE ADVENTURES OF
SUPERMAN
75¢
427
APR 87
by WOLFMAN and ORDWAY

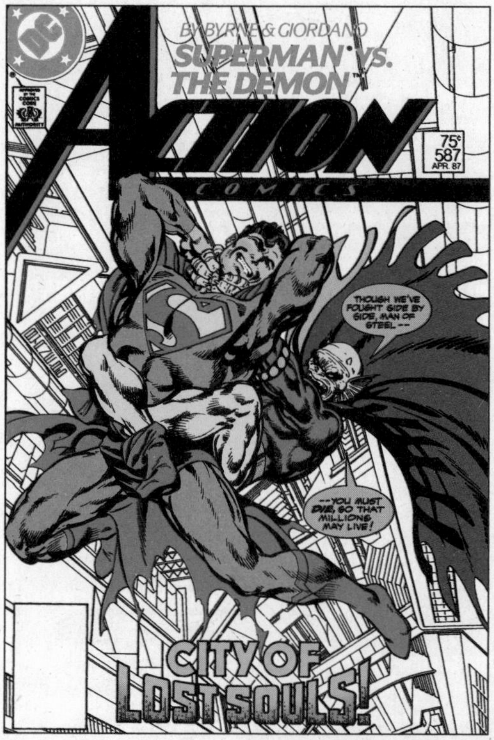
BY BYRNE & GIORDANO
SUPERMAN VS. THE DEMON
ACTION COMICS
75¢ 587 APR. 87
THOUGH WE'VE FOUGHT SIDE BY SIDE, MAN OF STEEL--
--YOU MUST DIE, SO THAT MILLIONS MAY LIVE!
CITY OF LOST SOULS!

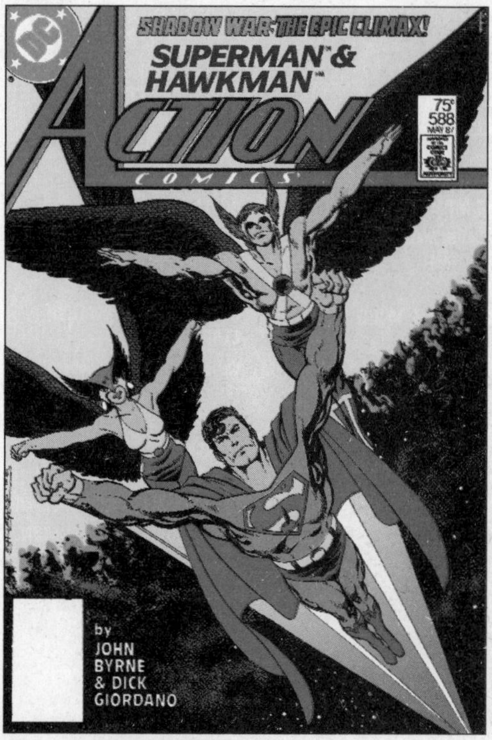
SHADOW WAR: THE EPIC CLIMAX!
SUPERMAN & HAWKMAN
ACTION COMICS
75¢ 588 MAY 87
by JOHN BYRNE & DICK GIORDANO

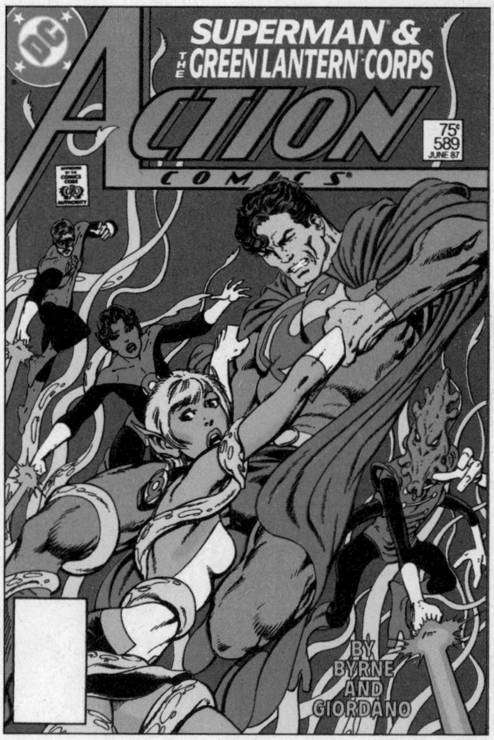
SUPERMAN & THE GREEN LANTERN CORPS
ACTION COMICS
75¢ 589 JUNE 87
BY BYRNE AND GIORDANO

S U P E R M A N
THE NEVER-ENDING BATTLE CONTINUES IN
THESE BOOKS FROM DC COMICS: